FUNDAMENTALS OF SWITCHING THEORY AND LOGIC DESIGN

Fundamentals of Switching Theory and Logic Design

A Hands on Approach

by

JAAKKO T. ASTOLA

Institute of Signal Processing,
Tampere University of Technology,
Tampere,
Finland

and

RADOMIR S. STANKOVIĆ

Dept. of Computer Science,
Faculty of Electronics,
Niš,
Serbia

Springer

A C.I.P. Catalogue record for this book is available from the Library of Congress.

ISBN-10 0-387-28593-8 (HB)
ISBN-13 978-0-378-28593-1 (HB)
ISBN-10 0-387-30311-1 (e-book)
ISBN-13 978-0-387-30311-6 (e-book)

Astola & Stankovic: Fundamentals of Switching Theory and Logic Design

First Indian Reprint 2008

ISBN 978-81-8128-804-2

This edition is manufactured in India for sale only in India, Pakistan, Bangladesh, Nepal and Sri Lanka and any other country as authorized by the publisher.

This edition is published by Springer (India) Private Limited,
A part of Springer Science+Business Media, Registered Office: 906-907,
Akash Deep Building, Barakhamba Road, New Delhi – 110 001, India.

Printed in India by Raj Press, New Delhi.

Contents

Preface

Information Science and Digital Technology form an immensely complex and wide subject that extends from social implications of technological development to deep mathematical foundations of the techniques that make this development possible. This puts very high demands on the education of computer science and engineering. To be an efficient engineer working either on basic research problems or immediate applications, one needs to have, in addition to social skills, a solid understanding of the foundations of information and computer technology. A difficult dilemma in designing courses or in education in general is to balance the level of abstraction with concrete case studies and practical examples.

In the education of mathematical methods, it is possible to start with abstract concepts and often quite quickly develop the general theory to such a level that a large number of techniques that are needed in practical applications emerge as "simple" special cases. However, in practice, this is seldom a good way to train an engineer or researcher because often the knowledge obtained in this way is fairly useless when one tries to solve concrete problems. The reason, in our understanding, is that without the drill of working with concrete examples, the human mind does not develop the "feeling" or intuitive understanding of the theory that is necessary for solving deeper problems where no recipe type solutions are available.

In this book, we have aimed at finding a good balance between the economy of top-down approach and the benefits of bottom-up approach. From our teaching experience, we know that the best balance varies from student to student and the construction of the book should allow a selection of ways to balance between abstraction and concrete examples.

Switching theory is a branch of applied mathematics providing mathematical foundations for logic design, which can be considered as the part

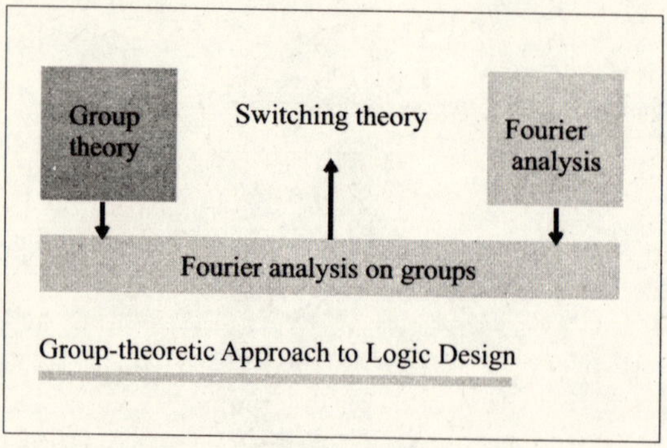

Figure 1. Switching theory and Fourier analysis.

of digital system design concerning realizations of systems whose inputs and outputs are described by logic functions. Thus, switching theory can be viewed as a part of Systems Theory and it is closely related to Signal Processing.

The basic concepts are first introduced in the classical way with Boolean expressions to provide the students with a concrete understanding of the basic ideas. The higher level of abstraction that is essential in the study of more advanced concepts is provided by using algebraic structures, such as groups and vector spaces, to present, in a unified way, the functional expressions of logic functions. Then, from spectral (Fourier-like) interpretation of polynomial, and graphic (decision diagrams) representations of logic functions, we go to a group-theoretic approach and to optimization problems in switching theory and logic design. Fig. 0.1 illustrates the relationships between the switching theory and Fourier analysis on groups. A large number of examples provides intuitive understanding of the interconnections between these viewpoints.

Consequently, this book discusses the fundamentals of switching theory and logic design from a slightly alternative point of view and also presents links between switching theory and related areas of signal processing and system theory. In addition, we have paid attention to cover the core topics as recommended in IEEE/ACM curricula for teaching and study in this area. Further, we provide several elective lectures discussing topics for further research work in this area.

JAAKKO T. ASTOLA, RADOMIR S. STANKOVIĆ

Acronyms

ACDD	Arithmetic transform decision diagram
ACDT	Arithmetic transform decision tree
BDD	Binary decision diagram
BDT	Binary decision tree
BMD	Binary moment diagram
BMT	Binary moment tree
*BMD	*Binary moment diagram
DD	Decision diagram
DT	Decision tree
DTL	Decision Type List
EVBDT	Edge-valued binary decision diagram
EVBDT	Edge-valued binary decision tree
ExtDTL	Extended Decision Type List
FFT	Fast Fourier transform
FDD	Functional decision diagram
FDT	Functional Decision tree
FEVBDD	Factored edge-valued binary decision diagram
FPGA	Field-programmable gate array
FPRM	Fixed-polarity Reed-Muller expression
KDD	Kronecker decision diagram
KDT	Kronecker decision tree
LUT	Look-up-table
MPGA	Mask programmable gate array
MTBDD	Multi-terminal binary decision diagram
MTBDT	Multi-terminal binary decision tree
PKDD	Pseudo-Kronecker decision diagram
PKDT	Pseudo Kronecker decision tree
PLA	Programmable logic array
PPRM	Positive-polarity Reed-Muller expression
POS	Product-of-Sum expression
RAM	Random-access memory
ROM	Read-only memory
SBDD	Shared binary decision diagrams
SOP	Sum-of-Product expression
STDT	Spectral transform decision tree
STDD	Spectral transform decision diagram
TVFG	Two-variable function generator
ULM	Universal logic module
WDD	Walsh decision diagram
WDT	Walsh decision tree

Chapter 1

SETS, RELATIONS, LOGIC FUNCTIONS

1. Sets

In mathematics, *set* is a basic notion defined as a collection of objects that we call *elements.* Typically these objects have similar properties. Set theory can be developed in an axiomatic way but, in this book, we use the intuitive notion of sets that is entirely sufficient for our purposes. Two sets are defined to be equal iff they have the same elements. A set is finite iff it has a finite number of elements.

We denote the fact that an element x belongs to a set X as $x \in X$. Consider two sets X and Y, if every element of X is also element of Y, then X is a *subset* of Y, and we denote this by $X \subseteq Y$. If at least a single element of X does not belong to Y, then X is a *proper subset* of Y, $X \subset Y$. Every set has itself as an *improper subset.* The empty set $\emptyset$, which is the set with no elements, is also a subset of any set.

DEFINITION 1.1 *(Operations over sets)*
The union X of a collection of sets $X_1, X_2, \ldots, X_n$ is the set $X = X_1 \cup X_2 \cup \ldots \cup X_n$ the elements of which are all the elements of $X_1, X_2, \cdots, X_n$.

The intersection of a collection of sets $X_1, X_2, \ldots, X_n$ is a set $X = X_1 \cap X_2 \cap \ldots \cap X_n$ consisting of the elements that belong to every set $X_1, X_1, \ldots, X_n$.

The power set $P(X)$ of a set X is the set of all subsets of X.

A tuple (x, y) of two elements arranged in a fixed order is a *pair.* In general, a tuple of n elements $(x_1, x_2, \ldots, x_n)$ is an n-tuple. Two n-tuples $(x_1, x_2, \ldots, x_n)$ and $(y_1, y_2, \ldots, y_n)$ are equal iff $x_i = y_i$ for all i.

DEFINITION 1.2 *(Direct product)*
The set of all pairs (x, y) *is the direct product, or the Cartesian product, of two sets* X *and* Y,

$$X \times Y = \{(x, y)|x \in X, y \in Y\}.$$

EXAMPLE 1.1 *For* $X = \{0, 1\}$ *and* $Y = \{0, 1, 2\}$,

$$X \times Y = \{(0,0), (0,1), (0,2), (1,0), (1,1), (1,2)\}.$$

Similarly, the direct product of the sets $X_1, \ldots, X_n$ is defined as

$$\times_{i=1}^{n} X_i = \{(x_1, \ldots, x_n)|\ x_i \in X_i, i = 1, \ldots, n\}$$

and if $X_i = X$ for all i we write $\times_{i=1}^{n} X_i = X^n$ Note that if any of the factor sets is empty, so is the direct product.

The identification of a set of the form X^n where $|X| = m$ with the set $\{0, 1, \ldots, m^n - 1\}$ is particularly simple as the correspondence can be written as

$$(x_1, \ldots, x_n) \leftrightarrow x_1 + x_2 m + x_3 m^2 + \ldots + x_n m^{n-1}.$$

2. Relations

DEFINITION 1.3 *(Relation)*
A subset R *of the direct product* $X \times Y$ *of two sets* X *and* Y *is a binary relation from* X *to* Y*, i.e., if* $R \subseteq X \times Y$, $x \in X$, $y \in Y$*, and* $(x, y) \in R$*, then* x *and* y *are in the relation* R*, or the relation* R *holds for* x *and* y.

A binary relation from X to X is a binary relation on X. An n-ary relation is a subset of the direct product of n sets $X_1 \times X_2 \times \cdots \times X_n$. If x is in relation R with y then y is in inverse relation R^{-1} with x.

DEFINITION 1.4 *(Inverse relation)*
If R *is a relation from* X *to* Y*, then the inverse relation of* R *is* $R^{-1} = \{(y, x)|(x, y) \in R\}$.

DEFINITION 1.5 *(Equivalence relation)*
Let R *be a binary relation on* X*. If*

1 $(x, y) \in R$ *for all* $x \in X$*, (reflexivity),*

2 $(x, y) \in R$ *implies* $(y, x) \in R$*, (symmetricity),*

3 $(x, y) \in R$ *and* $(y, z) \in R$*, imply* $(x, z) \in R$*, (transitivity),*

then, R *is called an* equivalence relation.

The set $\{x \in X | (x, y) \in R\}$ is called the equivalence class of X containing y. The equivalence classes form a partition of X, i.e., they are disjoint and their union is X. The elements of a partition P are called *blocks* of the partition P.

EXAMPLE 1.2 *(Partition)*
The set $\{1, 2, 3\}$ has five partitions $\{\{1\}, \{2\}, \{3\}\}$, $\{\{1, 2\}, \{3\}\}$, $\{\{1, 3\}, \{2\}\}$, $\{\{1\}, \{2, 3\}\}$, and $\{\{1, 2, 3\}\}$.

Notice that $\{\emptyset, \{1, 3\}, \{2\}\}$ is not a partition (of any set) since it contains the empty set. Similar, $\{\{1, 2\}, \{2, 3\}\}$ is not a partition (of any set), since the element 2 is contained in two distinct sets. Further, $\{\{1\}, \{2\}\}$ is not a partition of $\{1, 2, 3\}$, since none of the blocks contains 3, however, it is a partition of $\{1, 2\}$.

EXAMPLE 1.3 *Let $X = Z$ and define xRy if g divides $x - y$. It is easy to see that R is an equivalence relation. Clearly, the numbers $0, 1, \ldots, g - 1$ each define an equivalence class. For instance, 1 defines the equivalence class of integers having the reminder =1 when divided by g.*

EXAMPLE 1.4 *Let $X = R^2 = \{(x, y) | x, y \in R\}$ and let $(x, y)R(u, v)$ if $x - u = y - v$. It is easy to see that R is an equivalence relation. The equivalence classes are straight lines with slope = 1. Thus, each class has infinite number of elements, and there are an infinite number of classes.*

EXAMPLE 1.5 *Equivalence of sets, as considered above, is an equivalence relation.*

DEFINITION 1.6 *(Order relation)*
Let R be a binary relation on X. If

1 *$(x, x) \in R$ for all $x \in X$, (reflexivity),*

2 *$(x, y) \in R$ and $(y, x) \in R$ imply $x = y$, (anti-symmetricity),*

3 *$(x, y) \in R$ and $(y, z) \in R$ imply $(x, z) \in R$, (transitivity),*

then R is called an order relation or partial order relation. If R is a partial order relation and $(x, y) \in R$ or $(y, x) \in R$ for all $x, y \in X$, then R is the total order relation.

EXAMPLE 1.6 *Consider a set $\{\{0\}, \{1\}, \{0, 1\}\}$, and define a relation $X \subset Y$. Then, $\subset$ is a partial order relation, since there is no relation $\subset$ between $\{0\}$ and $\{1\}$.*

EXAMPLE 1.7 *Consider the set of integers Z. The relation $x \leq y$ meaning x is smaller or equal to y, is a total order relation.*

DEFINITION 1.7 *(Ordered set)*
A pair $\langle X, \leq_R \rangle$, where X is a set and $\leq_R$ an order relation on X is an ordered set. If $\leq_R$ is a partial or total order relation, the $\langle X, \leq_R \rangle$ is the partially or totally ordered set, respectively.

The partially and totally ordered sets are also called posets, and chains, respectively.

EXAMPLE 1.8 *Consider the power set $P(X)$ of a set X, i.e., $P(X)$ is a set of all proper subsets of X. Then, $\langle P(X), \leq \rangle$ is a partially ordered set.*

EXAMPLE 1.9 *The pair $\langle Z, \leq \rangle$, where Z is the set of integers and $x \leq y$ means x smaller or equal to y, is a totally ordered set or a chain.*

Any two elements of a chain are mutually comparable. In logic design, it is convenient to encode values applied to the inputs of circuits by elements of a chain, since it is convenient to have possibility to compare values applied at the inputs. Another interesting application of the notion of chain is related to the extensions of the notion of an algebra to multiple-valued functions, in the cases when the Boolean algebra, defined below, and the generalized Boolean algebra cannot be used [124].

DEFINITION 1.8 *Consider two sets X_1 and X_2 ordered with respect to the order relations $\leq_1$ and $\leq_2$, respectively. If there exists a bijective mapping ϕ between X_1 and X_2 such that $x \leq_1 y$ implies $\phi(x) \leq_2 \phi(y)$, then X_1 and X_2 are called isomorphic with respect to the order relations $\leq_1$ and $\leq_2$, respectively. The mapping ϕ is denoted as the isomorphism with respect to the order relation.*

3. Functions

DEFINITION 1.9 *(Function, or Mapping)*
Let f be a binary relation from a set X to a set Y. If for each element $x \in X$ there exists a unique element $y \in Y$ such than xfy, then f is a function from X to Y, i.e., $f : X \to Y$.

The set X is the domain of f. The element y in Y that corresponds to an element $x \in X$ is the value of the function f at x and we write $f(x) = y$. The set $f(X)$ of all function values in the domain of f is the range R of f and is a subset of Y. Thus, a function is a special type of relation and each function f defines a relation R_f by $(x, y) \in R_f$ iff $f(x) = y$.

Notice that f^{-1}, the inverse relation of R_f, in general, is not a function. However, it is usually called the inverse function of f and $f^{-1}(y)$ is a subset of X.

EXAMPLE 1.10 *Consider a function $f(x) = x^2$ from the set Z of integers to Z. The inverse relation is clearly not a function since, for example, there is no $x \in Z$ such that $3R_f^{-1}x$, i.e. $f(x) = 3$. The inverse function f^{-1} is not a function even from the range of f to Z because, for instance, $4R_f^{-1}2$ and $4R_f^{-1}(-2)$.*

This definition of functions through relations makes it sometimes possible to prove the existence of a function without being able to calculate its values explicitly for any element of the domain. Also, it allows to prove general properties of functions independently on their form. However, in many considerations, the following informal definition is sufficient.

DEFINITION 1.10 *A function is a rule that associates each element $x \in D$ to a unique element $y = f(x) \in R$, symbolically $f : D \to R$. The first set is called the domain, the second the range of f.*

DEFINITION 1.11 *Let f be a function form D to R, i.e., $f : D \to R$. The function f is called*

1 *injective (or one-to-one) if $x \neq y$ implies $f(x) \neq f(y)$.*

2 *surjective (or onto) if for each $y \in R$ there is $x \in D$ such that $f(x) = y$.*

3 *bijective if it is both injective and surjective.*

EXAMPLE 1.11 *The function $f : Z \to Z$ defined by $f(x) = x + 1$ is both injective and surjective and thus a bijection. The function $f : Z \to Z$ defined by $f(x) = x^3$ is injective, but not surjective. The function $f : Z \times Z \to Z$ defined by $f(x, y) = x + y$ is surjective but not injective.*

DEFINITION 1.12 *Let $f : D \to R$ be a function, S a binary relation on D and T a binary relation on R. If xSy implies $f(x)Tf(y)$, then f is a homomorphism with respect to S and T. If f is also a bijection, we say that f is an isomorphism with respect to S and T.*

EXAMPLE 1.12 *Let D be the set of complex numbers and R the set of real numbers. xSy if $x - y = 1 + j$, where j is the imaginary unit. If the relation T is defined by uTv if $u - v = 1$, then the function $f(x_1 + jx_2) = x_1$ is a homomorphism with respect to S and T.*

Two sets X and Y are equivalent if there exists a bijective mapping between them, i.e., to each element in X at most one element of Y can be assigned, and vice versa.

EXAMPLE 1.13 *The set of natural numbers is equivalent to the set of even numbers, since to the sequence* $1, 2, \ldots$ *we can assign the sequence* $2, 4, \ldots$.

If two sets X and Y are equivalent, we say that X and Y have the same *cardinal number* or X and Y are sets of the same *cardinality.* Thus, cardinality is the joint characteristics of all equivalent sets.

Sets equivalent to the set of natural numbers N are often meet in practice and are denoted as the *countable* sets, and their cardinality is denoted by the symbol $\aleph_0$. Sets equivalent to the set of real numbers have the cardinality of the *continuum*, which is denoted by c. For finite sets, the cardinality corresponds to the number of elements in the set and is denoted by $|X|$. Often, we identify a finite set X of cardinality k with the set of first k non-negative integers and write $X = \{0, \ldots, k-1\}$.

Notice that for the infinite sets, two sets may have the same cardinality although a set may be a proper subset of the other, as for instance in the above example.

In this book, we are concerned with functions on finite sets and look closer at different ways of expressing them.

DEFINITION 1.13 *A finite n-variable discrete function* $f(x_1, \ldots, x_n)$ *is defined as*

$$f : \times_{i=1}^{n} D_i \rightarrow R^q,$$

where D_i *and* R *are finite sets, and* $x_i \in D_i$.

DEFINITION 1.14 *A multi-output function* f *is a function where* $q > 1$. *Thus, it is a system of functions* $f = (f_0, \ldots, f_{q-1})$.

In some practical applications, a multi-output function can be replaced by an equivalent single output function f_z where the output is defined as a weighted sum of outputs $\sum_{j=0}^{q-1} f_j w^j$ where w is the weighting coefficient. It may be convenient to enumerate the outputs in reverse order, i.e., $f = (f_{q-1}, \ldots, f_0)$ to have the expression appear similar to radix w numbers.

EXAMPLE 1.14 *A digital circuit with n inputs and q outputs defines a switching (or Boolean) function* $f : \{0,1\}^n \rightarrow \{0,1\}^q$. *Consider the case where* $n = 3$ *and* $q = 1$. *The function can be given by listing its values* $f(x_1, x_2, x_3)$ *as* (x_1, x_2, x_3) *runs through the domain* $\{0,1\}^3$.

x_1, x_2, x_3	$f(x_1, x_2, x_3)$
000	$f(0,0,0)$
001	$f(0,0,1)$
010	$f(0,1,0)$
011	$f(0,1,1)$
100	$f(1,0,0)$
101	$f(1,0,1)$
110	$f(1,1,0)$
111	$f(1,1,1)$

If we use the correspondence $\{0,1\}^3 \leftrightarrow \{0,1,\ldots,7\}$ given by

$$(x_1, x_2, x_3) \leftrightarrow x_1 + 2x_2 + 4x_3,$$

the function f can be compactly represented by the vector

$$\mathbf{F} = [f(0), f(1), f(2), f(3), f(4), f(5), f(6), f(7)]^T,$$

where T denotes transpose.

EXAMPLE 1.15 *Consider a two-output function $f = (f_0, f_1) : \{0,1\}^3 \rightarrow \{0,1\}^2$, where f_0 is defined by $\mathbf{F}_0 = [1,0,1,1,0,1,1,1,]^T$ and f_1 by $\mathbf{F}_1 = [1,0,0,1,1,1,0,0]^T$. The function f can be represented as a single function $f' = 2f_1 + f_0$. Often, we view the domain and range as subsets of the set of integers $Z = \{\ldots,-2,-1,0,1,\ldots\}$ and write $f = f_Z : Z \rightarrow Z$ defined by $\mathbf{F}_Z = [3,0,2,3,1,3,2,2]^T$. Note that if the domain and range sets had originally some structure imposed on them, it is lost in the representation by subsets of integers.*

It is clear that a similar "coding" of the domain and range can be used for any finite sets.

EXAMPLE 1.16 *Consider a function $f : X_0 \times X_1 \rightarrow Y$ where $X_0 = \{0,1\}$ and $X_1 = \{0,1,2\}$ and $Y = \{0,1,2,3\}$. Writing $x = 3x_0 + x_1$, we get*

X_0	X_1	X	$f(x)$
0	0	0	$f(0)$
0	1	1	$f(1)$
0	2	2	$f(2)$
1	0	3	$f(3)$
1	1	4	$f(4)$
1	2	5	$f(5)$

In general, a function $f : \times_{i=0}^{n-1} X_i \rightarrow Y$, where $X_i = \{0,1,\ldots,m_i - 1\}$, and $m_0 \leq m_1 \leq \cdots \leq m_{n-1}$ can be represented using the coding

$$(x_0, x_1, \ldots, x_{n-1}) \leftrightarrow \sum_{i=0}^{n-1} x_i \prod_{j=i+1}^{n} m_j,$$

Table 1.1. Discrete functions.

$f : \times_{i=1}^{n}\{0,\ldots,m_i-1\} \to \{0,\ldots,\tau-1\}$	Integer
$f : \{0,\ldots,\tau-1\}^n \to \{0,\ldots,\tau-1\}$	Multiple-valued
$f : \{0,1\}^n \to \{0,1\}$	Switching, or Boolean
$f : \times_{i=1}^{n}\{0,\ldots,m_i-1\} \to \{0,1\}$	Pseudo-logic
$f : \{0,1\}^n \to \{0,\ldots,\tau-1\}$	Pseudo-logic
$f : \{0,1\}^n \to R$	Pseudo-Boolean
$f : \{GF(p)\}^n \to GF(p)$	Galois
$f : I^n \to I$, $I = [0,1]$	Fuzzy

Table 1.2. Binary-valued input functions.

	$x_1x_2x_3$	f
0.	000	$f(0)$
1.	001	$f(1)$
2.	010	$f(2)$
3.	011	$f(3)$
4.	100	$f(4)$
5.	101	$f(5)$
6.	110	$f(6)$
7.	111	$f(7)$

where $m_n = 1$.

The number of discrete functions is exponential in the cardinality of the domain. Consider discrete functions $f : X \to Y$. Each function is uniquely specified by a vector of its values the length of which is $|\mathbf{X}|$ as there are $|Y|$ choices for each component, the total number of functions is $|Y|^{|X|}$.

EXAMPLE 1.17 *The number of Boolean functions $f : \{0,1\}^n \to \{0,1\}$ is 2^{2^n}. Similarly, the number of ternary functions $f : \{0,1,2\}^n \to \{0,1,2\}$ is 3^{3^n}. For $n = 2$, there are 16 Boolean (two-valued) functions and 19683 ternary functions.*

Table 1.1 shows examples of different classes of discrete functions. In this book we mainly consider switching, multiple-valued, and integer functions.

Table 1.3. Binary-valued input two-output functions.

	x_1x_2	f
0.	00	$f_0(0)f_1(0)$
1.	01	$f_0(1)f_1(1)$
2.	10	$f_0(2)f_1(2)$
3.	11	$f_0(3)f_1(3)$

Table 1.4. Multiple-valued input functions.

	x_1x_2	f
0.	00	$f(0)$
1.	01	$f(1)$
2.	02	$f(2)$
3.	10	$f(3)$
4.	11	$f(4)$
5.	12	$f(5)$

In the above tables, the left part shows all possible *assignments* of values to the variables. Therefore, a discrete function is uniquely specified by the enumeration of its values for all the assignments.

4. Representations of Logic Functions

Discrete functions, having finite sets as domains, are conveniently defined by tables showing elements of the domain in the left part, and the corresponding function values in the right part. In the case of switching functions, these tables are the truth-tables, and function values are represented by truth-vectors. Table 1.2, Table 1.3, and Table 1.4 show tables that define functions with domains considered in Example 1.14, Example 1.15, and Example 1.16. The size of tables defining discrete functions is exponentially dependent on the number of variables. Therefore, this method, and equally the vector representations, the right part of tables, are unsuitable for functions of a large number of variables.

In tabular representations, all the function values are explicitly shown, without taking into account their possible relationships. The reduced representations can be derived by exploiting peculiar properties of switching functions. Various representations, both analytical and graphic representations, will be discussed in Chapters 3, 4, and 5. Here, we briefly introduce by simple examples some of the classical representations of switching functions.

Cubes

Since switching functions take two possible values 0 and 1, it is not necessary to show the complete truth-table or the truth-vector. It is sufficient to enumerate the points where a given function f takes either the value 0 or 1, and assume that in other points out of 2^n possible points

Table 1.5. 0- and 1-fields.

0-field	1-field
000	001
010	101
011	111
100	110

Table 1.6. Cubes for f in Example 1.18.

0-cubes	1-cubes
xx0	x01
01x	1x1

of the domain of definition f has the other value 1 or 0, respectively. In this way, f is given by the 0-field, or 1-field.

EXAMPLE 1.18 *(0- and 1-fields)*
With the above convention, a three-variables function f whose truth-vector is $F = [0,1,0,0,0,1,0,1]^T$ is completely specified by showing the corresponding either 0-field or 1-field given in Table 1.5. Usually, we select the field with smaller number of entries.

If in a function, the appearance of a certain combination of inputs is hardly expected, the function value for this combination of inputs need not be specified. Such function is a *incompletely specified function*, and the points where the value for f is not assigned, are called *don't cares*. In this case, since there are three possible values for f, 0, 1, and $-$ to denote don't cares, two of three fields should be shown to define f.

The 0- and 1-field can be written in reduced form by introducing a symbol x which can take either the value 0 or 1. In this way, n-variable switching function f is given by *cubes* which are sequences of the length n with elements 0, 1 and x.

EXAMPLE 1.19 *(Cubes) The 0-field and 1-field in Table 1.5 can be represented as set of cubes in Table 1.6. In these cubes, the symbol x can take either value 0 or 1.*

Table 1.7. 0-, 1-, and 2-fields.

0-field	1-field	2-field
00	01	10
11	02	12
20	21	22

Table 1.8. Cubes for f in Example 1.20.

0-cubes	1-cubes	2-cubes
y0	0x	1y
11	21	22

$y \in \{0,2\}$, $x \in \{1,2\}$

Extension of these ways to represent switching functions to other classes of discrete functions is straightforward.

EXAMPLE 1.20 *(Fields and cubes for multiple-valued functions)*
Table 1.7 and Table 1.8 show the specification of a two-variable ternary function f given by the truth=vector $\mathbf{F} = [0,1,1,2,0,2,0,1,2]^T$ *by arrays and cubes.*

Diagrams and Maps

Switching functions of small number of variables, up to five or six, are conveniently represented graphically by various diagrams or maps. Widely used examples are Veitch diagrams and Karnaugh maps [76]. It should be noted the data in these representations are ordered in different ways. In Veitch diagrams, the lexicographic order is used, and in Karnaugh maps the order of Gray code is used.

EXAMPLE 1.21 *(Veitch diagram)*
Fig. 1.1 shows a Veitch diagram for a four-variable switching function whose truth-vector is

$$\mathbf{F} = [0,0,0,1,0,0,0,0,0,0,0,1,0,0,0,1]^T.$$

EXAMPLE 1.22 *Fig. 1.2 shows a Karnaugh map for the function f in Example 1.21.*

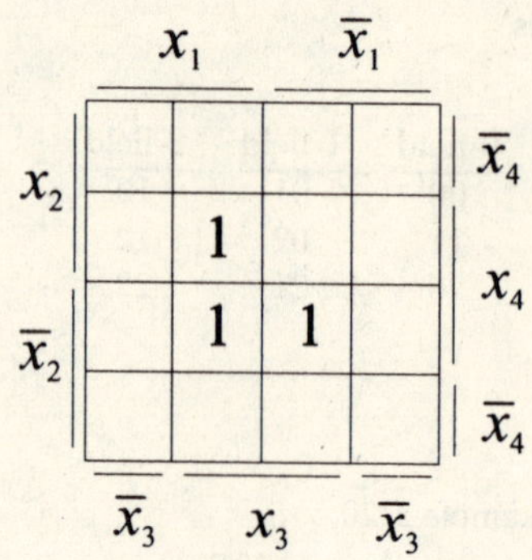

Figure 1.1. Veitch diagram for f in Example 1.21.

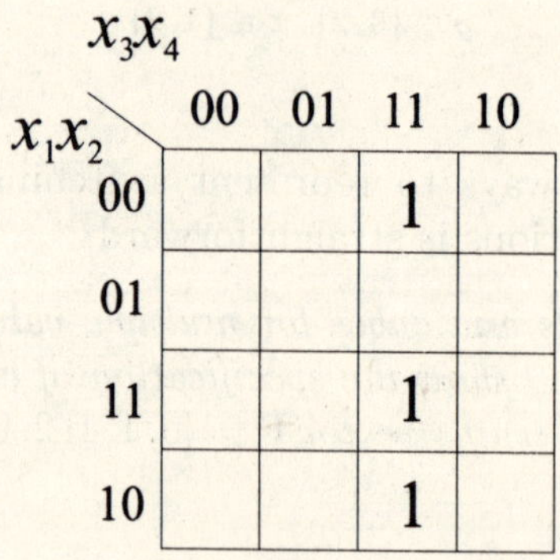

Figure 1.2. Karnaugh map for f in Example 1.21.

Hypercubes

For visual representation and analysis of switching functions and their properties, it may be convenient to use graphic representations as n-dimensional hypercubes, where n is the number of variables, and change of values for each variable is shown along an edge in the hypercube. The vertices colored in two different colours show the logic values 0 and 1 a function can take.

EXAMPLE 1.23 *Fig. 1.3 shows representation of a two-variable functions f_1 and a three-variable function f_2 by two-dimensional and three dimensional hypercubes. Truth vectors for these functions are* $\mathbf{F}_1 = [0,1,0,1]^T$ *and* $\mathbf{F}_2 = [0,1,1,0,1,0,1,0]^T$.

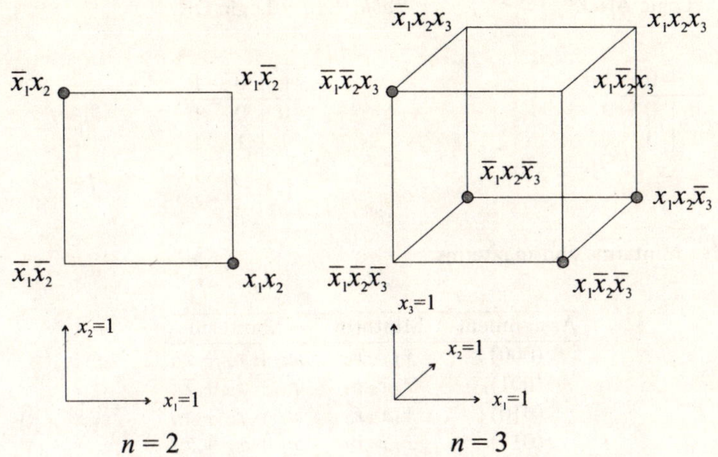

Figure 1.3. Hypercubes for function in Example 1.23.

4.1 SOP and POS expressions

Tabular representations of switching functions in Example 1.14 can be easily converted to their analytical representations, meaning that the function is presented as a formula written in terms of some basic expressions. In order to do this, some definitions should be introduced. Extensions and generalizations to other classes of discrete functions are possible and for some classes of discrete functions straightforward when the corresponding basic concepts provided and properly defined.

DEFINITION 1.15 *(Literals)*
A two-valued variable x_i may be written in terms of two literals, the positive literal x_i and the negative literal $\overline{x}_i$. The positive literal x_i is usually assigned to the logic value 1, and the negative literal $\overline{x}_i$ to the logic value 0.

A logical product of variables is defined in terms of the logic AND defined in Table 1.9 and denoted as multiplication. Similar, a logical sum is defined in terms of logic OR defined in Table 1.10 and denoted as sum.

A logical product of variables where each variable is represented by a single literal is a product term or a product. A product can be a single literal or may consists of literals for all the variables, in which case is denoted as a minterm. *Similarly, a logical sum of variables, where each variable is represented by a single literal is a* sum term. *A sum term can be a single literal or may consist of all n-literals in which case it is called a maxterm.*

Table 1.9. Logic AND.

$\cdot$	0	1
0	0	0
1	0	1

Table 1.10. Logic OR.

$+$	0	1
0	0	1
1	1	1

Table 1.11. Minterms and maxterms.

Assignment	Minterm	Maxterm
(000)	$\overline{x}_1\overline{x}_2\overline{x}_3$	$x_1 + x_2 + x_3$
(001)	$\overline{x}_1\overline{x}_2x_3$	$x_1 + x_2 + \overline{x}_3$
(010)	$\overline{x}_1x_2\overline{x}_3$	$x_1 + \overline{x}_2 + x_3$
(011)	$\overline{x}_1x_2x_3$	$x_1 + \overline{x}_2 + \overline{x}_3$
(100)	$x_1\overline{x}_2\overline{x}_3$	$\overline{x}_1 + x_2 + x_3$
(101)	$x_1\overline{x}_2x_3$	$\overline{x}_1 + x_2 + \overline{x}_3$
(110)	$x_1x_2\overline{x}_3$	$\overline{x}_1 + \overline{x}_2 + x_3$
(111)	$x_1x_2x_3$	$\overline{x}_1 + \overline{x}_2 + \overline{x}_3$

EXAMPLE 1.24 *The left part in Table 1.2 shows the assignments of values to variables in the function f whose truth-vector is shown in the right part of the table. Each assignment determines a minterm and a maxterm as specified in Table 1.11.*

Table 1.12. Function f for SOP and POS.

	x_1, x_2, x_3	f
0.	000	1
1.	001	0
2.	010	1
3.	011	1
4.	100	0
5.	101	1
6.	110	1
7.	111	1

DEFINITION 1.16 *A canonical sum-of-products expression (canonical SOP) is a logical sum of minterms, where all the minterms are different.*

A canonical product-of-sums (canonical POS) is a logical product of maxterms, where all the maxterms are different.

The canonical SOPs and POSs are also called as a canonical disjunctive form *or a minterm expression, and a canonical conjunctive form or a maxterm expression, since logic operations OR and AND are often called the disjunction and conjunction.*

DEFINITION 1.17 *An arbitrary logic function f can be represented by a canonical SOP defined as a logic sum of product terms where $f = 1$.*

Similar, an arbitrary logic function f can be represented by a canonical POS defined as a logical product of maxterms where $f = 0$.

In this definition, the term canonical means that this representation is unique for a given function f.

EXAMPLE 1.25 *For the function f in Table 1.12 the canonical SOP is*

$$f = \overline{x}_1\overline{x}_2\overline{x}_3 + \overline{x}_1 x_2\overline{x}_3 + \overline{x}_1 x_2 x_3 + x_1\overline{x}_2 x_3 + x_1 x_2\overline{x}_3 + x_1 x_2 x_3,$$

and the canonical POS is

$$f = (x_1 + x_2 + \overline{x}_3)(\overline{x}_1 + x_2 + x_3).$$

These canonical representations will be discussed also later in this book in the context of the Boolean algebra and its applications. In particular, notice that canonical POS for a function f is a logical product of maxterms which are obtained as logic complements of false minterms for f. Further, the canonical POS is obtained by applying the *De Morgan theorem* to the canonical SOP for the logic complement $\overline{f}$ of f.

SOPs and POSs are considered as two-level representations, since in circuit synthesis may be realized with networks of the same number of levels. For instance, in SOPs, the first level consists of AND circuits realizing the products, which are added in the sense of logic OR by the OR circuit in second level, assuming that circuits have the corresponding number of inputs. It is similar with networks derived from POSs, where the first level are OR circuits and the second level is an AND circuit.

EXAMPLE 1.26 *Fig. 1.4 shows logic networks realizing SOP and POS in Example 1.25. It should be noticed that in some cases the number of circuits and their inputs can be reduced by the manipulation with the SOP and POS representations.*

When circuits with the required number of inputs are unavailable, then they may be realized by subnetworks of circuits with fewer number of nodes. Fig. 1.5 shows two realizations of the OR circuit with six inputs.

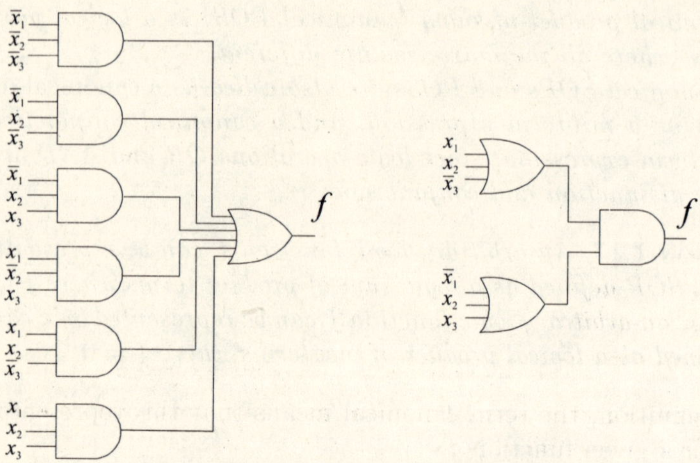

Figure 1.4. Networks from SOP and POS for f in Example 1.25.

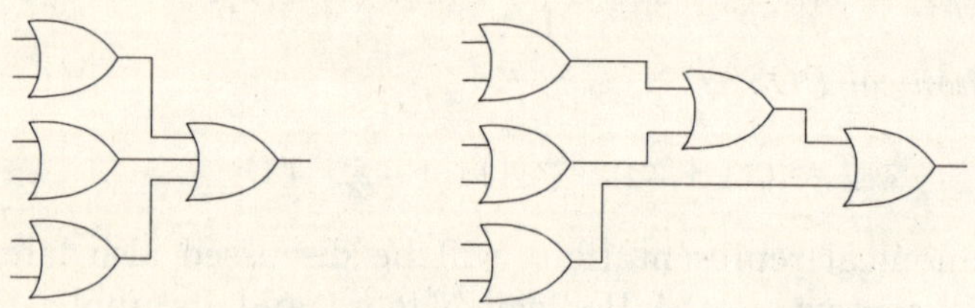

Figure 1.5. Realizations of six inputs OR circuit.

In this way, the *multi-level* logic networks are produced [155]. These networks may be also derived by the application of different minimization techniques to reduce the number of required circuits and their inputs. These techniques consist of the manipulations and transformations of SOPs and POSs as will be discussed later. Multi-level networks are conveniently described by the *factored expressions.*

4.2 Positional Cube Notation

The positional cube notation, also called bit-representations, is a binary encoding of implicants. A binary valued input can take symbols 0, 1 and $*$, which denotes the unspecified value, i.e., don't care. In positional cube notation, these symbols are encoded by two bits as follows

Ø	00
0	10
1	01
$*$	11

Table 1.13. Representation of f in Example 1.27.

x_1x_4	01	11	11	01
$\overline{x}_1x_3$	10	11	01	11
$x_2x_3\overline{x}_4$	11	01	01	10
$\overline{x}_1\overline{x}_3x_4$	10	11	10	01

where 10, 01, and 11 are the allowed symbols, and Ø means none of the allowed symbols. Thus, Ø means that a given input is void and should be deleted from the functional expression in terms of implicants.

Such notation simplifies manipulation with implicants, although increases the number of columns in the truth-table. In particular, the intersection of two implicants reduces in the positional cube notation to their bitwise product.

EXAMPLE 1.27 *Table 1.13 shows the positional cube notation for the function*

$$f = x_1x_4 + \overline{x}_1x_3 + x_2x_3\overline{x}_4 + \overline{x}_1\overline{x}_3x_4.$$

The intersection of cubes x_1x_4 and $\overline{x}_1x_3$ is 00, 11, 01, 01, *thus, it is void. Similarly, the intersection of $\overline{x}_1x_3$ and $x_2x_3\overline{x}_4$ is* 10, 01, 01, *and* 10, *thus, it is $\overline{x}_1x_2x_3\overline{x}_4$.*

EXAMPLE 1.28 *The multiple-output function $f = (f_1, f_2, f_3)$ where*

$$\begin{aligned} f_1 &= \overline{x}_1\overline{x}_2 + x_1x_2, \\ f_2 &= x_1x_2, \\ f_3 &= x_1\overline{x}_2 + \overline{x}_1x_2, \end{aligned}$$

can be represented by the position cube notation as in Table 1.14.

5. Factored Expressions

Factored expressions (FCE) can be characterized as expressions for switching functions, with application of logic complement restricted to switching variables, which means that complements cannot be performed over subexpressions in an expressions for a given function f. Therefore, the following definition of factored expressions can be stated.

Table 1.14. Representation of f in Example 1.28.

$\overline{x}_1\overline{x}_2$	10	10	100
$\overline{x}_1x_2$	10	01	001
$x_1\overline{x}_2$	01	10	001
x_1x_2	01	01	110

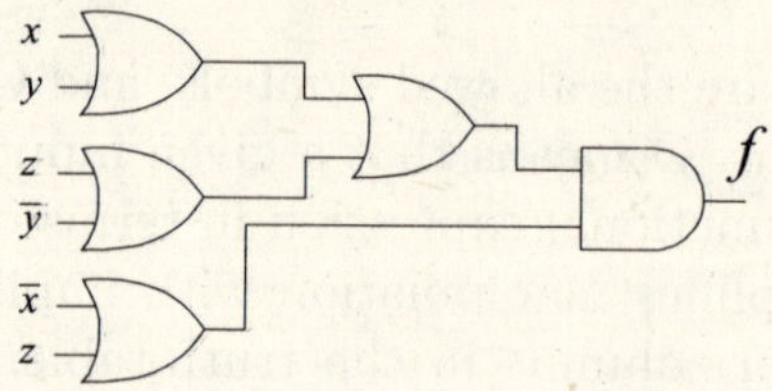

Figure 1.6. Multi-level network.

DEFINITION 1.18 *(Factored expressions)*

1 *A literal is a FCE.*

2 *Logic OR of FCEs is a FCE.*

3 *Logic AND of FCEs is a FCE.*

If in a given FCE for a function f, logic AND and logic OR are mutually replaced and positive literals for variables x_i are replaced by the negative literals and vice versa, then FCE for f is converted into a FCE for the logic complement $\overline{f}$ of f. Thus derived FCE for $\overline{f}$ has the same number of terms as FCE for f. For a given function f there are few factored expressions, and their useful feature is that FCSs describe fan-out free networks, which means that output of each circuit at a level is connected to the input of a single circuit at the next level in a multi-level network. In FCS, hierarchy among subexpressions, which define levels, is determined by brackets.

EXAMPLE 1.29 *Fig. 1.6 shows a multi-level network that realizes the function defined by the FCS*

$$f = ((x + y) + (z + \overline{y}))(\overline{x} + z).$$

6. Exercises and Problems

EXERCISE 1.1 *Consider the set A of all divisors of the number 100 and the binary relation ρ over A defined by $x\rho y$ if and only if x divides y. Show that this relation is a partial order relation in A.*

EXERCISE 1.2 *Consider the set A of all divisors of the number 8 and the binary relation ρ over A defined by $x\rho y$ if and only if x divides y. Show that this relation is a total order relation in A.*

EXERCISE 1.3 *Show that the following switching functions are equal to the constant function 1*

1 $(x_1 \wedge x_2) \to x_1$,

2 $(x_1 \wedge (x_1 \to x_2)) \to x_2$,

3 $(((x_1 \to x_2) \to x_1) \to x_1)$, - *Pierce law,*

4 $\overline{(x_1 \to x_2)} \vee (\overline{x}_2 \to \overline{x}_1)$,

5 $(x_1 \to x_2) \wedge (x_3 \to x_4) \to ((x_1 \vee x_3) \to (x_2 \vee x_4))$,

where $\wedge$ and $\vee$ are the logic AND and OR, and $\to$ denotes the implication defined by the Table 1.15.

Table 1.15. Implication.

$\to$	0	1
0	1	1
1	0	1

EXERCISE 1.4 *Show that the following switching functions are equal to the constant function 0*

1 $(x_1 \vee x_2)\overline{x}_1 \wedge \overline{x}_2$,

2 $\overline{(x_1 \to (\overline{x}_1 \to \overline{x}_2))}$,

3 $\overline{(x_1 \to x_2)} \wedge (x_1 \wedge \overline{x}_2)$,

4 $\overline{(x_1 \to (x_1 \vee x_2))}$.

EXERCISE 1.5 *Show that the following switching functions are equal*

$$\begin{aligned} f_1(x_1, x_2) &= \overline{(x_1 \vee x_2)} \vee \overline{(x_1 \downarrow x_2)}, \\ f_2(x_1, x_2) &= \overline{(\overline{x}_1 \rightarrow x_2)} \vee \overline{(x_1 \rightarrow \overline{x}_2)}, \\ f_3(x_1, x_2) &= \overline{(x_1 \vee x_2)} \vee (x_1 \wedge x_2), \end{aligned}$$

where $\downarrow$ *denotes the logic NAND.*

EXERCISE 1.6 *Determine the complete disjunctive normal form of the function* $f(x_1, x_2, x_3, x_4)$ *defined by the set of decimal indices where it takes the value* 1 *as* $f^{(1)} = \{0, 1, 4, 6, 7, 10, 15\}$. *Then, define the complete disjunctive normal form for the logic complement* $\overline{f}$ *of* f.

EXERCISE 1.7 *Determine the complete disjunctive and conjunctive forms of the function* $f(x_1, x_2, x_3, x_4)$ *defined as*

$$f(x_1, x_2, x_3, x_4) = x_1 + \overline{x}_2 x_3 + \overline{x}_1 x_3 x_4.$$

Represent this function as the Karnaugh map.

EXERCISE 1.8 *Show that switching functions*

$$\begin{aligned} f_1(x_1, x_2, x_3) &= x_1 x_2 + x_2 x_3 + \overline{x}_1 x_3, \\ f_2(x_1, x_2, x_3) &= x_1 x_2 + \overline{x}_1 x_3, \end{aligned}$$

have the same disjunctive normal form, i.e., they are equal functions. Prove the equivalence of these functions also by using the complete conjunctive normal form.

EXERCISE 1.9 *Determine the complete conjunctive normal form for the function* $g + h$, *if*

$$\begin{aligned} g(x_1, x_2, x_3) &= \overline{x}_1 \overline{x}_2 + \overline{x}_1 x_2 + \overline{x}_1 x_2 x_3, \\ h(x_1, x_2, x_3) &= \overline{x}_1 \overline{x}_2 \overline{x}_3 + \overline{x}_1 \overline{x}_2 x_3 + x_1 x_2. \end{aligned}$$

EXERCISE 1.10 *A switching function* $f(x_1, x_2, x_3)$ *has the value* 0 *at the binary triples where two or more bits have the value* 1, *and the value* 1 *at all other triplets. Represent this function at the Karnaugh map and determine the complete disjunctive and conjunctive forms.*

EXERCISE 1.11 *Determine the complements and show the positional cube notation for of the following switching functions*

$$\begin{aligned} f_1(x_1, x_2, x_3) &= x_1(x_2 \overline{x}_3 \vee \overline{x}_1 x_3, \\ f_2(x_1, x_2, x_3) &= x_1 \rightarrow x_2 x_3, \\ f_3(x_1, x_2, x_3) &= ((x_1 \downarrow x_2) + x_2 x_3))\overline{x}_3, \\ f_4(x_1, x_2, x_3) &= (x_1 \oplus x_2) \oplus x_3. \end{aligned}$$

Chapter 2

ALGEBRAIC STRUCTURES FOR LOGIC DESIGN

1. Algebraic Structure

By an *algebraic system* we mean a set that is equipped with operations, that is rules that produce new elements when operated on a number of elements (such as addition producing the sum of two elements) and a set of constants. It is useful to specify classes of systems by agreeing about sets of axioms so that all systems that satisfy certain axioms belong to that particular class. These classes are called algebraic structures and form abstractions of common features of the systems.

DEFINITION 2.1 *An algebraic structure is a triple* $\langle A, O, C \rangle$, *where*

1 A is a nonempty set, the underlying set,

2 O is the operation set,

3 C is the set of constants.

REMARK 2.1 *An* i-ary operation *on A is a function* $o : A^i \to A$. *Thus we can write* $O = \bigcup_{i=0}^{n} O_i$ *where* O_i *is the set of i-ary operations. Usually we consider binary operations such as addition and multiplication, etc. Sometimes the set of constants is not specified because any constant can be represented as a* $0-ary$ *operation* $c : A^0 = \{\emptyset\} \to A$.

Below we discuss algebraic structures that are useful in Switching Theory a Logic Design.

2. Finite Groups

Group is an example of algebraic structures with a single binary operation, where a binary operation on a set X is a function of the form

$f : X \times X \rightarrow X$. Binary operations are often written using infix notation such as $x + y$, $x \cdot y$, or by juxtaposition xy, rather than by functional notation of the form $f(x, y)$. Examples of operations are the addition and the multiplication of real and complex numbers as well as the composition of functions.

DEFINITION 2.2 *(Group)*
An algebraic structure $\langle G, \circ, 0\rangle$ *with the following properties is a group.*

1 *Associative law:* $(x \circ y) \circ z = x \circ (y \circ z)$, $x, y, z \in G$.

2 *There is identity: For all* $x \in G$, *the unique element 0 (identity) satisfies* $x \circ 0 = 0 \circ x = x$.

3 *Inverse element: For any* $x \in G$, *there exists an element* x^{-1} *such that* $x \circ x^{-1} = x^{-1} \circ x = 0$.

Usually we write just G instead $\langle G, \circ, 0\rangle$.

A group G is an *Abelian group* if $x \circ y = y \circ x$ for each $x, y \in G$, otherwise G is a *non-Abelian group.*

DEFINITION 2.3 *Let* $\langle G, \circ, 0\rangle$ *be a group and* $0 \in H \subseteq G$. *If* $\langle H, \circ, 0\rangle$ *is a group, it is called a subgroup of* G.

The following example illustrates some groups that will appear later in the text.

EXAMPLE 2.1 *The following structures are groups.*

$\mathbf{Z}_q = \langle\{0, 1, \ldots, q-1\}, \oplus_q\rangle$, *the group of integers modulo q. As special cases we have, for instance,* $\mathbf{Z}_2 = \langle\{0, 1\}, \oplus\rangle$, *the simplest nontrivial group and* $\mathbf{Z}_6 = \langle\{0, 1, 2, 3, 4, 5\}, \oplus\rangle$, *the additive group of integers modulo* 6.

Notice that addition modulo 2, symbolically $\oplus$, *is equivalent to the logic operation* EXOR *usually denoted in switching theory simply as* $\oplus$. *Likewise, multiplication modulo 2 is equivalent to logic* AND.

The symmetric group S_3 $\langle\{a, b, c, d, e, f\}, \circ\rangle$ *with the operation defined by the Table 2.1*

Notice that groups of the same order can have totally different structure. For instance, the symmetric group S_3 and $\mathbf{Z}_6$ have the same number of elements. This feature is often exploited in solving some tasks in Logic Design.

EXAMPLE 2.2 *(Groups of different structure)*
Consider the group of integers modulo 4, $\mathbf{Z}_4 = (\{0, 1, 2, 3\}, \oplus_4)$ *and the*

Table 2.1. Group operation $\circ$ of the symmetric group S_3.

$\circ$	1	a	b	c	d	e
1	1	a	b	c	d	e
a	a	b	1	e	c	d
b	b	1	a	d	e	c
c	c	d	e	1	a	b
d	d	e	c	b	1	a
e	e	c	d	a	b	1

group $B_2 = (\{(0,0),(0,1),(1,0),(1,1)\},\oplus)$, *where* $\oplus$ *is pairwise* EXOR. *In* $\mathbf{Z}_4$ *we have* $1 \oplus_4 1 = 2 \neq 0$, *but in* B_2, *it is* $(x,y) \oplus (x,y) = (0,0)$ *for any* $(x,y) \in B_2$.

As examples of infinite groups, notice that the set of integers Z under the usual addition is a group. The real numbers R form a group under addition and the nonzero real numbers form a group under multiplication.

DEFINITION 2.4 *Let* $\langle G_i, \oplus_i, 0_i \rangle$ *be a group of order* g_i, $i = 1, \ldots, n$. *Then,* $\langle \times_{i=1}^n G_i, \oplus, (0_1, \ldots, 0_n) \rangle$ *where* $\oplus$ *denotes componentwise addition is group, and it is called the direct product of* G_i, $i = 1, \ldots, n$. *It is clear that the order of* $G = \times_{i=1}^n G_i$ *is* $g = \Pi_{i=1}^n g_i$.

Let $\langle G, \oplus, 0 \rangle$ be a finite group and a an element of the group. As a, $a \oplus a$, $a \oplus a \oplus a, \ldots$ cannot all be different there is the smallest positive integer n such that $na = 0$. This number n is called the order of the element a and it always divides the order of the group.

If G is decomposable as a direct product of $\langle \mathcal{G}_i, \oplus_i, 0_i \rangle$, a function $f(x)$ on G can be considered alternatively as an n-variable function $f(x_1, \ldots x_n)$, $x_i \in G_i$.

EXAMPLE 2.3 *Let* $f : \times_{i=1}^n G_i \to R$ *be a function. We can alternatively view* f *as a single variable function* $f(\mathbf{x})$, $\mathbf{x} \in \times_{i=1}^n G_i$, *or an* n*-variable function* $f(x_1, \ldots, x_n)$, *where* $x_i \in G_i$.

In a decomposable group $\langle \mathcal{G}_i, \oplus_i, 0_i \rangle$, if $g_i = p$ for each i, we get a group C_p^n used as the domain for p-valued logic functions, and C_2^n, when $g_i = 2$ for each i, used as the domain for switching functions.

EXAMPLE 2.4 *The set* B^n *of binary* n*-tuples* $(x_1, \ldots, x_n)$, $x_i \in \{0, 1\}$ *has the structure of a group of order* 2^n *under the componentwise* EXOR.

The identity is the zero n-tuple $O = (0, \ldots, 0)$ and each element is its self-inverse. This group is called the finite dyadic group C_2^n.

The finite dyadic group is used as the domain of switching functions, since C_2 has two elements corresponding to two logic values, as it will be discussed later.

EXAMPLE 2.5 *For $n = 3$, a three-variable function $f(x_1, x_2, x_3)$, $x_i \in \{0, 1\}$, can be represented by the truth-vector*

$$\mathbf{F} = [f(000), f(001), f(010), f(011), f(100), f(101), f(110), f(111)]^T,$$

often written as

$$\mathbf{F} = [f_{000}, f_{001}, f_{010}, f_{011}, f_{100}, f_{101}, f_{110}, f_{111}]^T.$$

The set $B^3 = \{(x_1, x_2, x_3) | x_i \in B\}$ of binary triplets with no structure specified, can be considered as the underlying set of the dyadic group C_2^3, and the values for x_i are considered as logic values 0 and 1. If we perform the mapping $z = 4x_1 + 2x_2 + x_3$, where the values of x_i are considered as integer values 0 and 1, and the addition and multiplication are over the integers, we have one-to-one correspondence between B^3, the underlying set of C_2^3 and the cyclic group of order 8, $\mathbf{Z}_8 = (\{0, 1, 2, 3, 4, 5, 6, 7\}, \oplus_8)$. Therefore, f can be alternatively viewed as a function of two very different groups, C_2^3 and $\mathbf{Z}_8$, of the same order.

3. Finite Rings

A ring is a much richer structure than a group, and has two operations which are tied together by the distributivity law. The other operation besides the addition $\oplus$, is the multiplication $\cdot$ for elements in G. We get the structure of a ring if the multiplication is associative and distributivity holds.

DEFINITION 2.5 *(Ring)*
An algebraic structure $\langle R, \oplus, \cdot \rangle$ with two binary operations $\oplus$ and $\cdot$ is a ring if

1. *$\langle R, \oplus \rangle$ is an Abelian group,*
2. *$\langle R, \cdot \rangle$ is a semigroup, i.e., the multiplication is associative.*
3. *The distributivity law holds, i.e., $x(y \oplus z) = xy \oplus xz$, and $(x \oplus y)z = xz \oplus yz$ for each $x, y, z \in R$.*

EXAMPLE 2.6 *(Ring)*
$\langle B, \oplus, \cdot \rangle$, where $B = \{0, 1\}$, and $\oplus$, and $\cdot$ are EXOR *and logic* AND, *respectively, forms a ring, a Boolean ring.*

EXAMPLE 2.7 *(Ring)*
Consider $\langle \{0,1\}^n, \oplus, \cdot \rangle$, *where* $\oplus$ *and* $\cdot$ *are applied componentwise. It is clearly a commutative ring, i.e., multiplication is commutative. It is the Boolean ring of* 2^n *elements. The zero element is* $(0,0,\ldots,0)$ *and the multiplicative unity is* $(1,1,\ldots,1)$. *It is in some sense a very extreme structure. For instance, each element has additive order 2* $(a \oplus a = 0$ *for all* $a)$, *each element is idempotent* $(a \cdot a = a$ *for all* $a)$, *and no element except* $\mathbf{1} = (1,1,\ldots,1)$ *has a multiplicative inverse.*

EXAMPLE 2.8 *(Ring)*
Consider $\langle \{x + y\sqrt{2} | x, y \in Y\}, +, \cdot \rangle$, *i.e., real numbers of the form* $x + y\sqrt{2}$, *where* x *and* y *are integers. It is clearly a commutative ring with multiplicative identity and it is obtained from the ring of integers by adjoining* $\sqrt{2}$ *to it.*

EXAMPLE 2.9 *Consider the ring* $Z_2 = \langle \{0,1\}; \oplus, \cdot \rangle$ *and consider polynomials over* Z_2, *i.e., expressions of the form*

$$p(\xi) = p_0 + p_1\xi + \ldots + p_n\xi^n,$$

where $p_i \in Z_2$, $i = 0, 1, \ldots, n$. *These polynomials form a ring under the usual rules of manipulating polynomials and taking all coefficient operations in* Z_2, *for instance,*

$$\begin{aligned} (1+\xi^2) + (1+\xi+\xi^2) &= (1+1) + (0+1)\xi + (1+1)\xi^2 = \xi \\ (1+\xi^2)(1+\xi+\xi^2) &= 1+\xi+\xi^2+\xi^2+\xi^3+\xi^4 = 1+\xi+\xi^3+\xi^4. \end{aligned}$$

Consider the equation $x^2 + x + 1 = 0$ *in* Z_2. *Clearly, neither 0 or 1 satisfies the equation, and so, it has no root in* Z_2.

Assume that in some enlargement of Z_2, *it has a root* θ *say. Then, over* Z_2, *the elements* $0 = 0 + 0 \cdot \theta$, $1 = 1 + 0 \cdot \theta$, θ, *and* $1 + \theta$ *are different and we get their addition and multiplication rules from the rules for polynomials and always reducing higher order terms using the relation* $\theta^2 = \theta + 1$. *Thus, we have the structure* $\langle \{0, 1, \theta, 1+\theta\}, +, \cdot \rangle$ *with the addition and multiplication defined in Table 2.2 and Table 2.3.*

As we can associate $0 = (0,0)$, $1 = (2,0)$, $\theta = (0,1)$, $1 + \theta = (1,1)$, *we see that this ring has the same underlying set as the Boolean ring of* 2^2 *elements. The additive structure is actually the same in both, but the multiplicative structures are very different.*

4. Finite Fields

If the non-zero elements of a ring form an Abelian group with respect to multiplication, the resulting structure is called a field. It is the abstract structure that has the familiar properties of e.g., the real, or the complex numbers.

Table 2.2. Addition in the extension of Z_2.

$+$	0	1	θ	$1+\theta$
0	0	1	θ	$1+\theta$
1	1	0	$1+\theta$	θ
θ	θ	$1+\theta$	0	1
$1+\theta$	$1+\theta$	θ	1	0

Table 2.3. Multiplication in the extension of Z_2.

	0	1	θ	$1+\theta=\theta^2$
0	0	0	0	0
1	0	1	θ	$1+\theta$
θ	0	θ	$1+\theta$	1
$1+\theta$	0	$1+\theta$	1	θ

DEFINITION 2.6 *(Field)*
A ring $\langle R, \oplus, \cdot, 0\rangle$ is a field if $\langle R\backslash\{0\}, \cdot\rangle$ is an Abelian group. The identity element of this multiplicative group is denoted by 1.

EXAMPLE 2.10 *(Field)*

1 *The complex numbers with usual operations, i.e., $\langle C, +, \cdot, 0, 1\rangle$ is a field, the complex field C.*

2 *The real numbers with usual operations, i.e., $\langle R, +, \cdot, 0, 1\rangle$ is a field, the real-field R.*

3 *The integers modulo k, $\mathbf{Z}_k$ form a ring. The underlying set for this ring is $\{0, 1, \ldots, k-1\}$ and the operations are the usual addition and multiplication, but if the result is greater or equal to k, it is replaced by the remainder when divided by k. It is easy to check that these operations modulo k $(\text{mod}k)$ are well defined. Notice that this ring has the multiplicative identity 1. In general, not all non-zero elements have multiplicative inverse and, thus, it is not necessarily a field. For example, In $\mathbf{Z}_4 = \langle\{0, 1, 2, 3\}, \oplus, \cdot\rangle$, where $\oplus$ and $\cdot$ are taken modulo 4, there is no element x such that $2 \cdot x = 1$. However, if k is a prime number, then $\mathbf{Z}_k$ is a field.*

The fields with finitely many elements are *finite fields.* It can be shown that for any prime power p^n, there exists essentially a single finite field with p^n elements.

The finite fields can be constructed in the same way that the field of Example 2.9 was constructed.

EXAMPLE 2.11 *If* $p = 2$, *and* $n = 2$, *then* $\langle\{0, 1, \theta, 1+\theta\}, \oplus, \cdot\rangle$ *is a finite field if the addition* $\oplus$ *and multiplication* $\cdot$ *are defined as in Table 2.2 and Table 2.3, respectively. This can be checked directly, but, in general, follows from the construction. Note that the field* $GF(4)$ *is quite different to the ring* Z_4 *of integers modulo 4. The other possible definitions of operations over four elements that fulfill requirements of a field, can be obtained by renaming the elements.*

The fields with p^n elements are most frequently used in Switching Theory and Logic Design, since their elements may be encoded by p-valued n-tuples. Further, the case $p = 2$ corresponds to realizations with two-stable state elements. It should be noted, that also logic circuits with more than two states, in particular three and four stable states have been developed and realized [155].

However, for the prevalence of binary valued switching functions in practice, the most widely used field in Logic Design is the field of order 2, i.e. $Z_2 = \{0, 1\}$.

Fig. 2.1 shows relationships between discussed algebraic structures, groups, rings and fields, imposed on a set G by introducing the addition $\oplus$, the multiplication $\cdot$ and by requiring some relations among them.

5. Homomorphisms

A function from an algebraic structure to another such that it is compatible with both structures is called a homomorphism. Unless the function mapping is too trivial, this implies that the structures must be quite similar. Homomorphisms can be defined in a general way, but in the following we give definitions for groups sand rings. Note that this also covers fields that are rings with additional properties.

DEFINITION 2.7 *(Group homomorphism)*
Let $\langle A, \oplus\rangle$ *and* $\langle B, \oplus\rangle$ *be groups and* $f : A \rightarrow B$ *a function. If for all* $a, b \in A$

$$f(a \oplus b) = f(a) \oplus f(b),$$

then f *is a group homomorphism.*

EXAMPLE 2.12 *Let* $f : Z_3 \rightarrow Z_6$ *be defined by*

$$f(x) = 2x = x \oplus x,$$

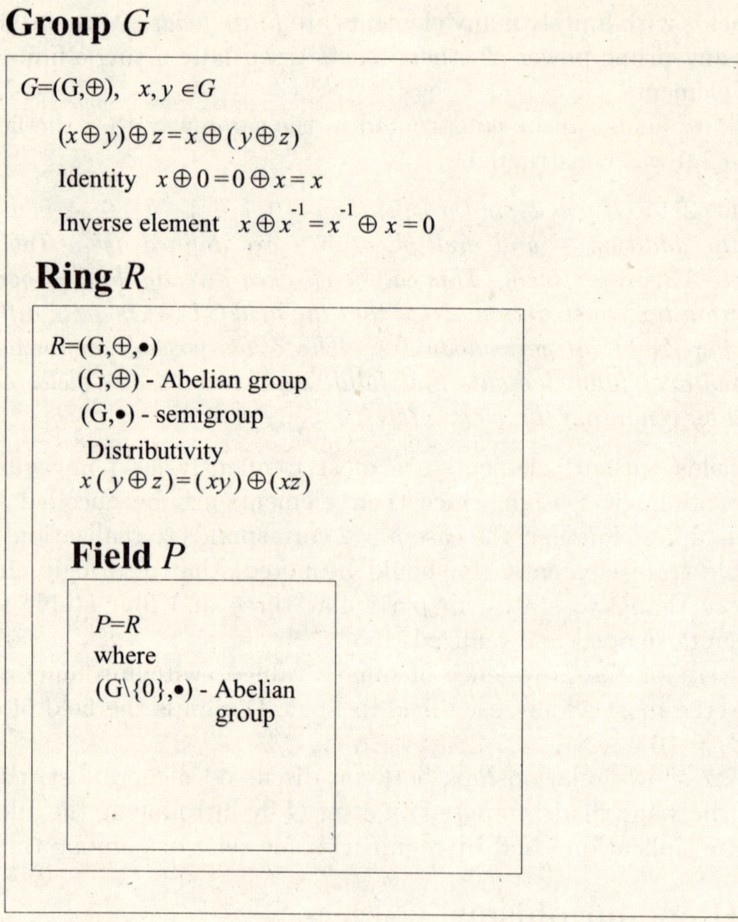

Figure 2.1. Relationships between algebraic structures.

is a homomorphism. As it is injective it means that Z_6 has the group Z_3 "inside" it.

EXAMPLE 2.13 *Let $f : \langle R, + \rangle \rightarrow \langle C^*, \cdot \rangle$ (the multiplicative group of nonzero complex numbers) be defined by*

$$f(x) = e^{jx} = \cos x + j \sin x.$$

Then f is a homomorphism. It is clearly not injective as $f(n \cdot 2\pi) = 1$ for all $n \in Z$.

EXAMPLE 2.14 *Let $f : \langle R, + \rangle \rightarrow \langle R_+, \cdot \rangle$ (the multiplicative group of positive real numbers) be defined by*

$$f(x) = e^x.$$

Then f is a bijective homomorphism, an isomorphism, which means that these groups have an identical structure.

DEFINITION 2.8 *(Ring homomorphism)*
Let $\langle A, \oplus, \cdot \rangle$ and $\langle B, \oplus, \cdot \rangle$ be rings and $f : A \to B$ a function. If for all $a, b \in A$,

$$f(a \oplus b) = f(a) \oplus f(b),$$

and

$$f(a \cdot b) = f(a) \cdot f(b),$$

then f is a ring homomorphism. If, in addition, f is bijective, it is called an isomorphism.

EXAMPLE 2.15 *Let $f : Z \to Z$ be defined by*

$$f(a) = g^a,$$

where g is a natural number. Then, f is an injective homomorphism.

Note that both $f(A)(\subseteq B)$ and $f^{-1}(B)(\subseteq A)$ are subrings. Thus, for instance $f^{-1}(0)$, the kernel of f is a subring of A.

EXAMPLE 2.16 *Let B be a ring with (multiplicative) unity 1. Define $f : Z \to B$ by $f(n) = n \cdot 1$. It is obvious that*

$$(n + m) \cdot 1 = n \cdot 1 + m \cdot 1,$$

and

$$(n \cdot m) \cdot 1 = (n \cdot 1)(m \cdot 1),$$

in B. Thus, f is a ring homomorphism.

The *characteristic* of a ring with unity is the smallest number k such that $k \cdot 1 = 0$. If such number does not exist, we say that the characteristic is zero. If a ring has characteristic, then f is clearly injective and B contains a subring isomorphic to Z.

EXAMPLE 2.17 *Let B be a ring with characteristic k. Consider again the homomorphism $f : Z \to B$ defined by $f(n) = n \cdot 1$. Obviously,*

$$f(Z) = \{f(0), f(1), \ldots, f(k-1)\},$$

and, thus, B contains a subring isomorphic to Z_k. If B is a field, then k must be prime, because if $k = r \cdot s$, where $r, s > 1$, then we would have $f(r)f(s) = f(r \cdot s) = k \cdot 1 = 0$ contradicting the fact that in a field the product of two nonzero elements cannot be zero.

The following section discusses some more algebraic concepts such as matrices.

6. Matrices

Let P be a field. Recall that a rectangular array

$$\mathbf{A} = \begin{bmatrix} a_{1,1} & \cdots & a_{1,n} \\ & & \vdots \\ a_{m,1} & \cdots & a_{m,n} \end{bmatrix}$$

where $a_{i,j} \in P$ is called a $(m \times n)$ *matrix* (over P). When the size of the matrix is evident from the context, we may write $\mathbf{A} = [a_{i,j}]$. The addition of matrices of the same size is defined componentwise, i.e., if $\mathbf{A} = [a_{i,j}]$, $\mathbf{B} = [b_{i,j}]$, then $\mathbf{A} + \mathbf{B} = [a_{i,j} + b_{i,j}]$. Similarly, we can define multiplication of $\mathbf{A}$ by an element $\lambda \in P$ by $\lambda\mathbf{A} = [\lambda a_{i,j}]$.

The multiplication of matrices is defined only when the number of columns in the first factor equals the number of rows in the second. Let $\mathbf{A} = [a_{i,j}]$ be a $(m \times k)$ matrix, and $\mathbf{B} = [b_{i,j}]$ a $(k \times n)$ matrix. Then, $\mathbf{AB}$ is the $(m \times n)$ matrix

$$\mathbf{AB} = \left[\sum_{l=1}^{k} a_{i,l} b_{l,j}\right].$$

It is straightforward to show that matrix product is associative whenever the sizes are such that the product is defined.

Consider the set of $(n \times n)$ square matrices over P. It clearly forms a ring where the zero element is the matrix $\mathbf{0} = [0_{i,j}]$, where $0_{i,j} = 0$ for all i, j. The matrix $\mathbf{I} = [\delta_{i,j}]$, where

$$\delta_{i,j} = \begin{cases} 1 & \text{if } i = j, \\ 0 & \text{if } i \neq j, \end{cases}$$

is the multiplicative identity. The matrix $\mathbf{I}$ is usually called the *identity matrix.*

The *transposed matrix* $\mathbf{M}^T$ of a matrix $\mathbf{M}$ is a matrix derived by interchanging rows and columns.

EXAMPLE 2.18 *If* $\mathbf{M} = \begin{bmatrix} m_{1,1} & m_{1,2} \\ m_{2,1} & m_{2,2} \end{bmatrix}$, *then* $\mathbf{M}^T = \begin{bmatrix} m_{1,1} & m_{2,1} \\ m_{1,2} & m_{2,2} \end{bmatrix}$.

A matrix $\mathbf{M}$ for which

$$\mathbf{MM}^T = \mathbf{M}^T\mathbf{M} = k\mathbf{I},$$

is an *orthogonal matrix* up to the constant k. If $k = 1$, we simply say $\mathbf{M}$ is orthogonal.

A matrix $\mathbf{M}^{-1}$ is the *inverse* of a matrix $\mathbf{M}$ if

$$\mathbf{M}\mathbf{M}^{-1} = \mathbf{M}^{-1}\mathbf{M} = \mathbf{I}.$$

If $\mathbf{M}$ is orthogonal up to the constant k, then $\mathbf{M}^{-1} = k^{-1}\mathbf{M}^T$. The matrix $\mathbf{M}$ is a *symmetric matrix* if $\mathbf{M} = \mathbf{M}^T$, and $\mathbf{M}$ is self-inverse if $\mathbf{M} = k\mathbf{M}^{-1}$. Thus, if $\mathbf{M}$ is orthogonal up to a constant k and symmetric, then $\mathbf{M}$ is *self-inverse* up to the constant k.

EXAMPLE 2.19 *The matrix* $\mathbf{W} = \begin{bmatrix} 1 & 1 \\ 1 & -1 \end{bmatrix}$ *is a symmetric matrix since* $\mathbf{W} = \mathbf{W}^T$. *It is orthogonal up to* 2^{-1}, *since* $2^{-1}\mathbf{W}\mathbf{W} = \mathbf{I}$. *Thus, it is self-inverse up to the constant* 2^{-1}.

It is easy to find matrices $\mathbf{A}$ and $\mathbf{B}$ satisfying $\mathbf{AB} \neq \mathbf{BA}$. Thus, the set of $(n \times n)$ matrices forms a (in general noncommutative) ring. The set of invertible matrices, i.e., those having a (unique) inverse form a group under multiplication.

EXAMPLE 2.20 *Consider the set of* (2×2) *matrices over* P *of the form* $\mathbf{A} = \begin{bmatrix} 1 & a \\ 0 & 1 \end{bmatrix}$. *Now,* $\begin{bmatrix} 1 & -a \\ 0 & 1 \end{bmatrix}\begin{bmatrix} 1 & a \\ 0 & 1 \end{bmatrix} = \begin{bmatrix} 1 & a \\ 0 & 1 \end{bmatrix}\begin{bmatrix} 1 & -a \\ 0 & 1 \end{bmatrix} = \begin{bmatrix} 1 & 0 \\ 0 & 1 \end{bmatrix} = \mathbf{I}$, *and, thus, each element has the inverse. From the identity*

$$\begin{bmatrix} 1 & a \\ 0 & 1 \end{bmatrix}\begin{bmatrix} 1 & b \\ 0 & 1 \end{bmatrix} = \begin{bmatrix} 1 & a+b \\ 0 & 1 \end{bmatrix},$$

we see that this multiplicative group has exactly the same structure as the additive group of P.

DEFINITION 2.9 *(Kronecker product)*
Let $\mathbf{A}$ *be a* $(m \times n)$ *matrix, and* $\mathbf{B}$ *a* $(p \times q)$ *matrix. The Kronecker product* $\mathbf{A} \otimes \mathbf{B}$ *of* $\mathbf{A}$ *and* $\mathbf{B}$ *is the* $(mp \times nq)$ *matrix*

$$\mathbf{A} \otimes \mathbf{B} = \begin{bmatrix} a_{11}\mathbf{B} & a_{12}\mathbf{B} & \cdots & a_{1n}\mathbf{B} \\ \vdots & \vdots & & \vdots \\ a_{m1\{}\mathbf{B} & a_{m2}\mathbf{B} & \cdots & a_{mn}\mathbf{B} \end{bmatrix}$$

The Kronecker product satisfies several properties. For instance, if the products $\mathbf{aC}$ and $\mathbf{BD}$ exists, then the product $(\mathbf{A} \otimes \mathbf{B})(\mathbf{C} \otimes \mathbf{D})$ exists and it is equal to $(\mathbf{AC}) \otimes (\mathbf{BD})$. Also, $(\mathbf{A} \otimes \mathbf{B})^T = \mathbf{A}^T \otimes \mathbf{B}^T$ and if $\mathbf{A}$ and $\mathbf{B}$ are invertible, then $(\mathbf{A} \otimes \mathbf{B})^{-1} = \mathbf{A}^{-1} \otimes \mathbf{B}^{-1}$.

Consider a (2×2) matrix $\mathbf{M} = \begin{bmatrix} a & b \\ c & d \end{bmatrix}$. If we write $\Delta = ad - bc$, it is easy to verify that if $\Delta \neq 0$, the inverse of $\mathbf{M}$ exists and $\mathbf{M}^{-1} = \Delta^{-1} \begin{bmatrix} d & -b \\ -c & a \end{bmatrix}$.

The quantity Δ is called the determinant of the matrix $\mathbf{M}$ and denoted by $\det(\mathbf{M})$. It can be recursively defined for square matrices of any size by

1 For a (1×1) matrix $\mathbf{A} = [a]$, $det(\mathbf{A}) = a$.

2 Let $\mathbf{A} = [a_{i,j}]$ be a $(n \times n)$ matrix and denote by $\mathbf{A}_{i,j}$ the $((n-1) \times (n-1))$ submatrix obtained by deleting the row i and the column j of $\mathbf{A}$.

Then, we have

$$det(\mathbf{A}) = \sum_{i=1}^{n} (-1)^{i+j} a_{i,j} \det(\mathbf{A}_{i,j}) = \sum_{j=1}^{n} (-1)^{i+j} a_{i,j} \det(\mathbf{A}_{i,j}),$$

where in the first case we say that the determinant has been expanded with respect to the column j, and in the second case with respect to the row i.

EXAMPLE 2.21 *Consider a* (3×3) *matrix* $\mathbf{A} = [a_{i,j}]$. *Then,*

$$\begin{aligned} det\left(\begin{bmatrix} a_{1,1} & a_{1,2} & a_{1,3} \\ a_{2,1} & a_{2,2} & a_{2,3} \\ a_{3,1} & a_{3,2} & a_{3,3} \end{bmatrix}\right) &= a_{1,1}\det\left(\begin{bmatrix} a_{2,2} & a_{2,3} \\ a_{3,2} & a_{3,3} \end{bmatrix}\right) \\ &\quad - a_{1,2}\det\left(\begin{bmatrix} a_{2,1} & a_{2,3} \\ a_{3,1} & a_{3,3} \end{bmatrix}\right) \\ &\quad + a_{1,3}\det\left(\begin{bmatrix} a_{2,1} & a_{2,2} \\ a_{3,1} & a_{3,2} \end{bmatrix}\right). \end{aligned}$$

An important property of the determinant is that a matrix $\mathbf{A}$ has the inverse iff $det(\mathbf{A}) \neq 0$.

EXAMPLE 2.22 *Consider the matrix (Vandermonde matrix)*

$$\mathbf{A} = \begin{bmatrix} x_1^0 & x_2^0 & \cdot & x_n^0 \\ x_1^1 & x_2^1 & \cdot & x_n^1 \\ & & \cdots & \\ x_1^{n-1} & x_2^{n-1} & \cdot & x_n^{n-1} \end{bmatrix},$$

over a field P. It can be shown (e.g. by induction) that

$$det(\mathbf{A}) = \prod_{i<j}(x_j - x_i),$$

and so $\mathbf{A}$ *is invertible if $x_i \neq x_j$ for $i \neq j$. We will use this matrix when we discuss Fourier transform methods.*

7. Vector spaces

DEFINITION 2.10 *Given an Abelian group G and a field P. The pair (G, P) is a linear vector space, in short, vector space, if the multiplication of elements of G with elements of P, i.e., the operation $P \times G \to G$ is defined such that the following properties hold.*

For each $x, y \in G$, and $\lambda, \mu \in P$,

1. $\lambda x \in G$,
2. $\lambda(x \oplus y) = \lambda x \oplus \lambda y$,
3. $(\lambda + \mu)x = \lambda x \oplus \mu x$,
4. $\lambda(\mu x) = (\lambda\mu)x$,
5. $1 \cdot x = x$, *where* 1 *is the identity element in* P.

In what follows, we will consider the vector spaces of functions defined on finite discrete groups.

DEFINITION 2.11 *Denote by $P(G)$ the set of all functions $f : G \to P$, where G is a finite group of order g, and P is a field. In this book P is usually the complex-field C, the real-field R, the field of rational numbers Q or a finite (Galois) field $GF(p^k)$. $P(G)$ is a vector space if*

1. *For $f, h \in P(G)$, addition of f and h, is defined by*

$$(f + h)(x) = f(x) + h(x),$$

2. *Multiplication of $f \in P(G)$ by an $\alpha \in P$ is defined as*

$$(\alpha f)(x) = \alpha f(x).$$

Since the elements of $P(G)$ are vectors of the dimension g, it follows that the multiplication by $\alpha \in P$ can be viewed as the componentwise multiplication with constant vectors in $P(G)$.

EXAMPLE 2.23 *Consider the set $GF(C_2^n)$ of functions whose domain is C_2^n and range $GF(2)$. These functions can be conveniently represented* *by binary vectors of the dimension* 2^n*. This set is a vector space over* $GF(2)$ *with the operations defined above.*

Similarly, the set $C(C_2^n)$ *of functions whose domain is* C_2^n *and range the complex field* C *forms a set of complex vector space of the dimension* 2^n*.*

Generalizations to functions on other finite Abelian groups into different fields are also interesting in practice.

Very often the Abelian group in the definition of the vector space V is a direct product (power) of C, $GF(2)$, or some cyclic group C_p. Thus, the elements of V are "vectors" of the length n, say

$$V = \{(x_1, x_2, \ldots, x_n) | x_i \in C, i = 1, \ldots, n\}.$$

Vectors $v_1, \ldots, v_k$ are called *linearly independent* if $\lambda_1 v_1 + \cdots + \lambda_k v_k = 0$ implies $\lambda_1 = \lambda_2 = \cdots = \lambda_k = 0$, otherwise they are called *linearly dependent* (over P).

A system of vectors $v_1, \ldots, v_n$ is called a *basis* of V if they are linearly independent and any $v \in V$ can be expressed as a *linear combination* of $v_1, \ldots, v_n$, i.e., in the form $v = \lambda_1 v_1 + \cdots \lambda_n v_n$. The number n is called the *dimension* of V and any basis has n elements. The scalars $\lambda_1, \ldots \lambda_n$ are called the *coordinates* of v in the basis $v_1, \ldots, v_n$.

Let V be a vector space over P and consider a linear transformation $L : V \rightarrow V$, i.e., a mapping satisfying

$$\begin{array}{ll} L(u+v) = L(u) + L(v) & \text{for all } u, v \in V, \\ L(\lambda v) = \lambda L(v) & \text{for all } v \in V, \lambda \in P. \end{array} \tag{2.1}$$

Assume that V has the dimension n and $v_1, \ldots, v_n$ is a basis of V. Take any vector $v \in V$. Because $v_1, \ldots, v_n$ is a basis, we know that

$$v = \lambda_1 v_1 + \lambda_2 v_2 + \cdots + \lambda_n v_n,$$

where $\lambda_1, \ldots, \lambda_n \in P$, and $(n \times 1)$ matrix $[\lambda_1, \ldots, \lambda_n]^T$ constitutes the coordinates of v, and we may write $v = [\lambda_1, \ldots, \lambda_n]^T$ in the basis $v_1, \ldots, v_n$.

Now, by (2.1), we can write

$$u = L(v) = \lambda_1 L(v_1) + \cdots + \lambda_n L(v_n). \tag{2.2}$$

Because $v_1, \ldots, v_n$ is a basis, we have the representation

$$\begin{aligned} L(v_1) &= a_{11} v_1 + \cdots + a_{n1} v_n, \\ &\vdots \\ L(v_n) &= a_{1n} v_1 + \cdots + \lambda_n v_n, \end{aligned} \tag{2.3}$$

and combining (2.2) and (2.3), we have

$$\begin{aligned} u &= \lambda_1(a_{11}v_1 + \cdots + a_{n1}v_n) + \cdots + \lambda_n(a_{1n}v_1 + \cdots + a_{nn}\lambda_n) \\ &= (a_{11}\lambda_1 + \ldots + a_{1n}\lambda_n)v_1 + \cdots + (a_{n1}\lambda_1 + \cdots + a_{nn}\lambda_n)v_n \\ &= \mu_1 v_1 + \cdots + \mu_n v_n. \end{aligned} \tag{2.4}$$

The meaning of (2.3) is that for any linear transformation there is a fixed matrix $\mathbf{A} = [a_{ij}]$ such that the coordinate matrix of the transformed vector is obtained by matrix multiplication from the coordinate matrix of the original vector.

In symbolic notation, let $v = [\lambda_1, \ldots, \lambda_n]^T$ in the basis $v_1, \ldots, v_n$. Then,

$$\begin{bmatrix} \mu_1 \\ \mu_2 \\ \vdots \\ \mu_n \end{bmatrix} = \begin{bmatrix} a_{11} & \cdots & a_{1n} \\ \vdots & \vdots & \vdots \\ a_{n1} & \cdots & a_{nn} \end{bmatrix} \begin{bmatrix} \lambda_1 \\ \lambda_2 \\ \vdots \\ \lambda_n \end{bmatrix}. \tag{2.5}$$

Formula (2.5) gives us the coordinate vector of a linearly transformed vector. Another important task is to compute the coordinate matrices of a fixed vector with respect to different bases.

Assume that we have two bases $A = \{a_1, \ldots, a_n\}$ and $B = \{b_1, \ldots, b_n\}$. Let $v \in V$ and denote by $[\lambda_1, \ldots, \lambda_n]^T$ and $[\mu_1, \ldots, \mu_n]^T$ the coordinate vectors of v in A and B, respectively. As each element of B can be expressed in the basis A, we can write

$$\begin{aligned} v &= \lambda_1 a_1 + \ldots + \lambda_n a_n = \mu_1 b_1 + \cdots \mu_n b_n \\ &= \mu_1(\alpha_{11}a_1 + \alpha_{21}a_2 + \cdots + \alpha_{n1}a_n) \\ &\quad + \cdots + \mu_n(\alpha_{1n}a_1 + \alpha_{2n}a_2 + \cdots + \alpha_{nn}a_1) \\ &= (\alpha_{11}\mu_1 + \cdots + \alpha_{1n}\mu_n)a_1 + \cdots + (\alpha_{n1}\mu_1 + \ldots + \alpha_{nn}\mu_n)a_n, \end{aligned}$$

or equivalently,

$$\begin{bmatrix} \lambda_1 \\ \lambda_2 \\ \vdots \\ \lambda_n \end{bmatrix} = \begin{bmatrix} \alpha_{11} & \alpha_{12} & \cdots & \alpha_{1n} \\ \alpha_{21} & \alpha_{22} & \cdots & \alpha_{2n} \\ \vdots & \vdots & \vdots & \vdots \\ \alpha_{n1} & \alpha_{n2} & \cdots & \alpha_{nn} \end{bmatrix} \begin{bmatrix} \mu_1 \\ \mu_2 \\ \vdots \\ \mu_n \end{bmatrix}.$$

Notice that when we go from B to A, the columns of the transformation matrix (change of the basis matrix) are the coordinates of $b_1, \ldots, b_n$ when expressed in the basis A.

An immediate and important fact is that if $\mathbf{M}$ is the matrix of change from B to A, then $\mathbf{M}^{-1}$ is the matrix of change from A to B.

EXAMPLE 2.24 *Consider the logic function $f(x_1, x_2)$ given by the truth-vector $\mathbf{F} = [1,1,1,0]^T$, i.e., logic NAND. We can view $[1,1,1,0]^T$ as an element of C^4, i.e., the complex vector space of the dimension 4. It has the natural basis E:*

$$\mathbf{e}_1 = [1,0,0,0]^T, \mathbf{e}_2 = [0,1,0,0]^T, \mathbf{e}_3 = [0,0,1,0]^T, \mathbf{e}_4 = [0,0,0,1]^T,$$

and thus $[0,1,1,0]^T$ is (also) the coordinate vector of f (hence the term natural basis). Let us represent $\mathbf{F}$ in another basis

$$B = \{(1,1,1,1), (0,1,0,1), (0,0,1,1), (0,0,0,1)\}.$$

The rule is to take the coordinate vectors of basis elements of the original basis expressed in the target basis as columns of the change matrix. By the remark above we can equivalently first find the change of the basis matrix from B to E, that is just

$$\mathbf{R} = \begin{bmatrix} 1 & 0 & 0 & 0 \\ 1 & 1 & 0 & 0 \\ 1 & 0 & 1 & 0 \\ 1 & 1 & 1 & 1 \end{bmatrix},$$

and we know that the matrix to perform the change from E to B is

$$\mathbf{S} = \mathbf{R}^{-1} = \begin{bmatrix} 1 & 0 & 0 & 0 \\ -1 & 1 & 0 & 0 \\ -1 & 0 & 1 & 0 \\ 1 & -1 & -1 & 1 \end{bmatrix}.$$

Thus, the coordinate vector of f in B is

$$\begin{bmatrix} 1 & 0 & 0 & 0 \\ -1 & 1 & 0 & 0 \\ -1 & 0 & 1 & 0 \\ 1 & -1 & -1 & 1 \end{bmatrix} \begin{bmatrix} 1 \\ 1 \\ 1 \\ 0 \end{bmatrix} = \begin{bmatrix} 1 \\ 0 \\ 0 \\ -1 \end{bmatrix}.$$

Notice that the coordinate functions of the natural basis are the truth-vectors of $\overline{x}_1\overline{x}_2$, $\overline{x}_1 x_2$, $x_1\overline{x}_2$, and $x_1 x_2$, respectively (the Shannon basis). Thus, $f(x_1, x_2) = 1 - x_1 x_2$ for $x_1, x_2 \in \{0,1\} \subseteq C$.

Now, when represented in the natural basis, f has three non-zero entries in the coordinate vectors, while when represented in the arithmetical basis, it has two non-zero entries. This is of great importance when we are dealing with functions of large number of variables.

We can repeat the above computation in the case that $\mathbf{F} = [1,1,1,0]^T$ is considered as an element of the vector space over $GF(2)$. Again, consider the basis

$$D = \{(1,0,0,0), (0,1,0,0), (0,0,1,0), (0,0,0,1)\}.$$

The matrix $\mathbf{R}$ *stays the same, just with different interpretation of values for the entries, but over* $GF(2)$ *the inverse is different*

$$\mathbf{S} = \mathbf{R}^{-1} = \begin{bmatrix} 1 & 0 & 0 & 0 \\ 1 & 1 & 0 & 0 \\ 1 & 0 & 1 & 0 \\ 1 & 1 & 1 & 1 \end{bmatrix},$$

and the coordinate vector of f *in* B *is*

$$\begin{bmatrix} 1 & 0 & 0 & 0 \\ 1 & 1 & 0 & 0 \\ 1 & 0 & 1 & 0 \\ 1 & 1 & 1 & 1 \end{bmatrix} \begin{bmatrix} 1 \\ 1 \\ 1 \\ 0 \end{bmatrix} = \begin{bmatrix} 1 \\ 0 \\ 0 \\ 1 \end{bmatrix}.$$

Thus, $f(x_1, x_2) = 1 \oplus x_1 x_2$ *for* $x_1, x_2 \in GF(2)$.

8. Algebra

DEFINITION 2.12 *A vector space* $\langle V, \oplus \rangle$ *over a field* P *becomes an algebra* $\langle V, \oplus, \cdot \rangle$ *if a multiplication* $\cdot$ *is defined* V *such that*

$$\begin{aligned} x(y \oplus z) &= xy \oplus xz, \\ (y \oplus z)x &= yx \oplus zx, \end{aligned}$$

for each $x, y, z \in V$, *and*

$$\alpha x \cdot \beta y = (\alpha\beta)(x \cdot y),$$

for each $x, y \in V$ *and* $\alpha, \beta \in P$.

Two examples of algebras that will be exploited in this book are the algebras of complex functions with multiplications defined either componentwise or by convolution and the Boolean algebra.

EXAMPLE 2.25 *The space* $C(C_2^n)$ *may be given the structure of a complex function algebra by introducing the pointwise product of functions through* $(f \cdot g)(x) = f(x) \cdot g(x)$, *for all* $f, g \in C(C_2^n)$, *for all* $x \in C_2^n$.

Boolean algebras form an important class of algebraic structures. They were introduced by G. Boole [14], and used by C.E. Shannon as a basis for analysis of relay and switching circuits [163]. It is interesting to note that Japanese scientist A. Nakashima in 1935 to 1938 used an algebra for circuit design, which, as he realized in August 1938, is identical to the Boolean algebra, see discussion in [155]. These investigations are reported in few publications by Nakashima and M. Hanzawa [125], [126], [127]. Similar considerations of mathematical foundations of synthesis of logic circuits were considered also by V.I. Shestakov [166] and A. Piech [133].

Because of their importance in Switching Theory and Logic Design, we will study Boolean algebras in more details.

9. Boolean Algebra

Boolean algebras are algebraic structures which unify the essential features that are common to logic operations AND, OR, NOT, and the set theoretic operations union, intersection, and complement.

DEFINITION 2.13 *(Two-element Boolean algebra)*
The structure $\langle B, \vee, \wedge, - \rangle$ *where* $B = \{0, 1\}$ *and the operations* $\vee$, $\wedge$, *and* $-$ *are the logic OR, AND; and the complement (negation) respectively, is the two-element Boolean algebra.*

Here, for clarity, we use $\wedge$ and $\vee$ to denote operations that correspond to logic AND and OR, respectively. Later, we often use $\cdot$ and $+$ instead of $\wedge$ and $\vee$.

Using the properties of the logic operations, we see that the two-element Boolean algebra satisfies

1 $a \wedge b = b \wedge a$, $a \vee b = b \vee a$, commutativity,

2 $(a \wedge b) \wedge c = a \wedge (b \wedge c)$, $(a \vee b) \vee c = a \vee (b \vee c)$, associativity,

3 $a \wedge (b \vee c) = (a \wedge b) \vee (a \wedge c)$, $a \vee (b \wedge c) = (a \vee b) \wedge (a \vee c)$, distributivity,

4 $a \wedge a = a$, $a \vee a =$, idempotence,

5 $\overline{\overline{a}} = a$, involution,

6 $\overline{(a \wedge b)} = \overline{a} \vee \overline{b}$, $\overline{(a \vee b)} = \overline{a} \wedge \overline{b}$, de Morgan's law,

7 $a \wedge \overline{a} = 0$, $a \vee \overline{a} = 1$, $a \wedge 1 = a$, $a \vee 0 = a$, $a \wedge 0 = 0$, $a \vee 1 = 1$, $\overline{1} = 0$, $\overline{0} = 1$.

Despite its seemingly trivial form, the two-element Boolean algebra forms the basis of circuit synthesis. A binary circuit with n inputs can be expressed as a function $f : B^n \rightarrow B$, where $B = \{0, 1\}$.

The *general Boolean algebra* is defined by

DEFINITION 2.14 *The algebraic system* $\langle B, \vee, \wedge, - \rangle$ *is a Boolean algebra iff it satisfies the following axioms*

1 *The operation* $\vee$ *is commutative and associative, i.e.,* $a \vee b = b \vee a$ *and* $a \vee (b \vee c) = (a \vee b) \vee c$, *for all* a, b *in* B,

2 *There is a special element "zero" denoted by "0" such that* $0 \vee a = a$ *for all* a *in* B. *The element* $\overline{0}$ *is denoted by* 1,

3 $\overline{\overline{a}} = a$ *for all* a *in* B,

4 $a \vee \overline{a} = 1$ *for all* a *in* B,

5 $a \vee (b \wedge c) = (a \vee b) \wedge (a \vee c)$, *where* $a \wedge b = \overline{(\overline{a} \vee \overline{b})}$.

From these axioms one can deriver all other properties, eg., those presented above for the two-element Boolean algebra.

EXAMPLE 2.26 *(Boolean algebra of subsets)*
The power set of any given set X, $P(X)$ *forms a Boolean algebra with respect the operations of union and intersection, with the empty set* $\emptyset$ *representing the "zero" element 0, and the set* X *itself as the element 1.*

This Boolean algebra is important, since any finite Boolean algebra is isomorphic to the Boolean algebra of all subsets of a finite set. It follows that the number of elements of every Boolean algebra is a power of two, from which originate the difficulties in extending the theory of binary-valued switching functions to multiple-valued logic functions. Consider two Boolean algebras $\langle X, \vee, \wedge, -, 0_X, 1_X \rangle$, and $\langle Y, \vee, \wedge, -, 0_Y, 1_Y \rangle$. A mapping $f : X \to Y$ such that

1 For arbitrary $r, s \in X$, $f(r \vee s) = f(r) \vee f(s)$, $f(r \cdot s) = f(r) \cdot f(s)$, and $f(\overline{r}) = \overline{f}(r)$,

2 $f(0_X) = 0_Y$, $f(1_X) = f(1_B)$,

is a homomorphism. A bijective homomorphism is an isomorphism.

EXAMPLE 2.27 *(Homomorphism)*
Consider the Boolean algebras of subsets of $A = \{a, b\}$ *and* $B = \{a, b, c\}$ *and define* $f : A \to B$ *by* $\emptyset \to \emptyset$, $\{a\} \to \{a, c\}$, $\{b\} \to \{b\}$, $\{a, b\} \to \{a, b, c\}$. *Then,* f *is a homomorphism.*

EXAMPLE 2.28 *(Isomorphism)*
Let A *be the Boolean algebra* $\langle \{0, 1\}^n, \vee, \wedge, - \rangle$ *where the operations are taken componentwise and* B *the Boolean algebra* $\langle P(\{1, 2, \ldots, n\}), \cup, \cap, \sim \rangle$. *It is clear that the structures are identical and an isomorphism is given by*

$$f : B \to A, \quad f(X) = (x_1, \ldots, x_n),$$

where $x_i = 1$ *iff* $i \in X$.

EXAMPLE 2.29 *(The Boolean algebra of logic functions)*
Consider a logic function $f : B = \{0,1\}^n \to \{0,1\}$. *We define the Boolean operations in the set* B *of logic functions in the natural way*

$$(f \vee g)(x) = f(x) \vee g(x), (f \wedge g)(x) = f(x) \wedge g(x), \overline{f}(x) = \overline{f(x)}.$$

As each function is represented by its truth-vector that is of the length 2^n *and the definition of the operations (oper) is equivalent to componentwise operations on the truth-vectors,* $\langle B, \vee, \wedge, - \rangle$ *is isomorphic to* $\langle \{0,1\}^{2^n}, \vee, \wedge, - \rangle$ *and* $\langle P(\{1, \ldots 2^n\}), \vee, \wedge, -\}\rangle$. *Thus, there are* 2^{2^n} *logic functions of* n *variables.*

In this book, the two-element Boolean algebra and the Boolean algebra of all switching functions of a given number of variables n will be mostly studied. When we speak about Boolean algebra in the sequel, we mean the two-element Boolean algebra, or the corresponding Boolean algebra of switching functions.

9.1 Boolean expressions

More complicated relations and functions on Boolean algebras can be defined by using Boolean expressions. We typically use them for defining switching functions on the two-element Boolean algebra.

DEFINITION 2.15 *(Boolean expression)*
Consider a Boolean algebra $\langle B, \vee, \wedge, -, 0, 1 \rangle$. *A Boolean expression is defined recursively as*

1 *A variable taking values in* B, *the Boolean variable, is a Boolean expression,*

2 *An expression obtained as a finite combination of variables with the operators* $\vee$, $\wedge$ *and* $-$ *where the order is indicated with parenthesis, is a Boolean expression.*

The de Morgan laws formulated above for two variables, hold for n variables

$$\begin{aligned} \overline{x_1 \cdot x_2 \cdot \ldots \cdot x_n} &= \overline{x}_1 \vee \overline{x}_2 \vee \ldots \vee \overline{x}_n, \\ \overline{x_1 \vee x_2 \vee \ldots \vee x_n} &= \overline{x}_1 \wedge \overline{x}_2 \wedge \cdots \wedge \overline{x}_n, \end{aligned}$$

and can be applied to Boolean expressions.

DEFINITION 2.16 *(Complement of a Boolean expression)*
Given a Boolean expression in n *variables* $F(x_1, x_2, \ldots, x_n)$. *The Boolean expression is obtained from* F *by*

1 Adding the parenthesis depending on the order of operations,

2 Interchanging $\vee$ with $\wedge$, x_i with $\overline{x}_i$, and 0 with 1,

is the complement Boolean expression $\overline{F}(x_1, x_2, \cdots, x_n)$.

Boolean expressions are used in describing *Boolean functions.*

DEFINITION 2.17 *(Boolean functions)*
A mapping $f : B^n \rightarrow B$, that can be expressed by a Boolean expression is a Boolean function.

It should be noticed that not all the mappings $f : B^n \rightarrow B$ are necessarily Boolean functions for Boolean algebras with more than two elements.

EXAMPLE 2.30 *Consider a Boolean algebra where $B = \{\emptyset, \{a\}, \{b\}, \{a, b\}\}$. Then, $f : B^2 \rightarrow B$ defined as $f(x_1, x_2) = \{a\}$ for all x_1, x_2 cannot be defined as a Boolean function.*

A fundamental feature of Boolean algebras is the Principle of Duality.

DEFINITION 2.18 *(Principle of Duality)*
In a Boolean algebra, if an equation E holds, then the equation obtained from E by interchanging $\vee$ with $\wedge$, and 0 with 1, also holds.

DEFINITION 2.19 *(Dual Boolean expression)*
For a Boolean expression F, the dual Boolean expression F^D is defined recursively as follows

1 $0^D = 1$.

2 $1^D = 0$.

3 If x_i is a Boolean variable, then $x_i^D = \overline{x}_i$, $i = 1, \ldots n$.

4 For Boolean expressions X and Y, if $X = \overline{Y}$, then $X^D = \overline{(Y^D)}$.

5 For Boolean expressions X, Y, Z, if
$X = Y \vee Z$, *then* $X^D = Y^D \wedge Z^D$,
$X = Y \wedge Z$, *then* $X^D = Y^D \vee Z^D$.

The application of the principle of duality in study of Boolean functions is due to he following property. If two Boolean expressions X and Y represent the same Boolean function f, which we denote as $X \equiv Y$, then $X^D \equiv Y^D$. Therefore, if manipulation with dual expressions is simpler than with the original expressions describing a Boolean function, the principle of duality may be used to reduce complexity of processing a function f.

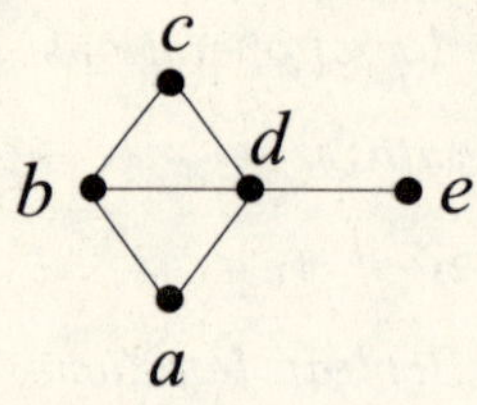

Figure 2.2. Graph.

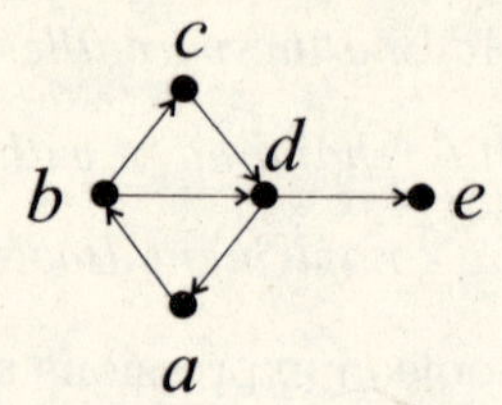

Figure 2.3. Directed graph.

10. Graphs

The concept of a *graph* is very useful in many applications. We have already informally used graphs for describing logic circuits and switching functions.

DEFINITION 2.20 *A graph $\mathcal{G}$ is a pair (V, E) where V is a set of so- called vertices (nodes) and E is a set of two-element subsets of V, so called edges.*

EXAMPLE 2.31 *(Graph)*
Let $V = \{a, b, c, d, e\}$ and $E = \{\{a, b\}, \{a, d\}, \{b, c\}\{b, d\}, \{c, d\}, \{d, e\}\}$. Then, $\mathcal{G}$ can be depicted as in Fig. 2.2.

Sometimes we want to extend the definition of graphs by allowing the edges to be directed. This is expressed formally so that E is a set of ordered pairs of elements of V so that, e.g., the edge (a, b) is directed from a to b. We call then $\mathcal{G}$ a *directed graph* or a *digraph*.

EXAMPLE 2.32 *Let V be as in the Example 2.31 and replace the edge set by the set of directed edges $E = \{(a, b), (d, a), (b, d), (b, c), (c, d), (d, e)\}$. This digraph can be depicted as in Fig. 2.3.*

DEFINITION 2.21 *(Terminology)*
Let (V, E) be a graph. We say that the vertices x and y are adjacent if $\{x, y\} \in E$, otherwise they are non-adjacent. A subgraph of (V, E) is a graph whose vertex and edge sets are subsets of those of (V, E). A walk in a graph is a sequence

$$(v_0, e_1, v_1, e_2, v_2, \ldots, e_n, v_n),$$

where $e_i = \{v_{i-1}, v_i\}$ for $i = 1, \ldots, n$. The length of the walk is the number of n of edges in the sequence.

A *path* is a walk whose vertices are distinct except possibly the first and the last and a *circuit* is a path whose first and the last vertices are equal.

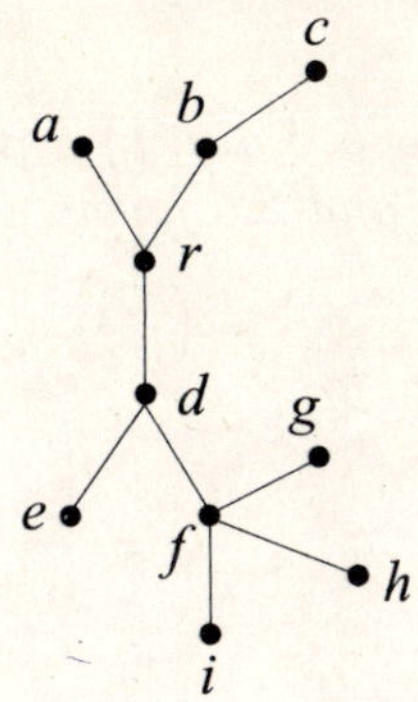

Figure 2.4. Tree.

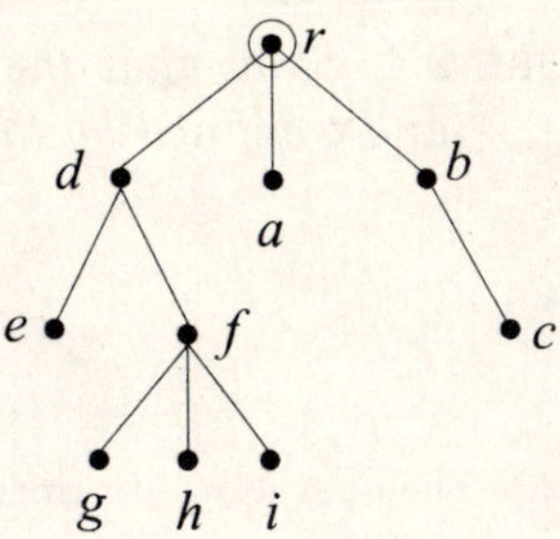

Figure 2.5. Rooted tree.

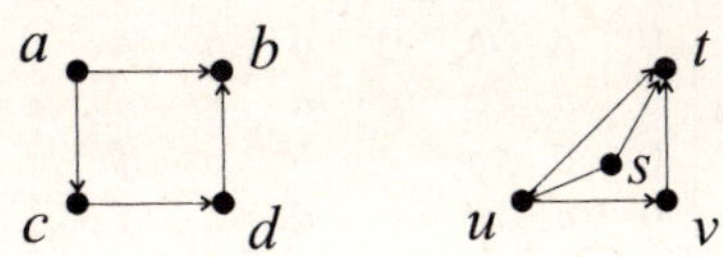

Figure 2.6. Isomorphic directed graphs.

We can define a relation ρ on V by $x\rho y$ iff there is a walk from x to y. It is easy to see that ρ is an equivalence relation and the equivalence classes are called the *(connected) components* of (V, E). A graph is *connected* if it has just one component. The *degree* of a vertex v in the graph (V, E) is the number of edges containing v.

Definition 2.22 *(Tree)*
A tree is a connected graph that contains no circuits. If there is a special vertex called the root, the tree is called a rooted tree. A vertex in a rooted tree is said to be at the level i if there is a path of the length i from the root to the vertex.

Example 2.33 *(Tree)*
Fig. 2.4 and Fig. 2.5 show a tree and a rooted tree, respectively.

Definition 2.23 *Two (directed) graphs $G = (V_{\mathcal{G}}, E_{\mathcal{G}})$, $H = (V_{\mathcal{H}}, E_{\mathcal{H}})$ are isomorphic if there exists a bijective mapping $\alpha : V_{\mathcal{G}} \rightarrow V_{\mathcal{H}}$ such that $(u, v) \in V_{\mathcal{G}}$ if and only if $(\alpha(u), \alpha(v)) \in E$.*

Example 2.34 *Two digraphs in Fig. 2.6 are clearly isomorphic.*

11. Exercises and Problems

EXERCISE 2.1 *Show that the set $B_8 = \{0, 1, a, b, c, d, e, f\}$ with operations $+$, $\cdot$, and $'$ defined by the Tables 2.4, 2.5 and 2.6 forms a Boolean algebra.*

Table 2.4. The operation $\cdot$ in Exercise 2.1.

$\cdot$	0	a	b	c	d	e	f	1
0	0	0	0	0	0	0	0	0
a	0	a	0	0	a	a	0	a
b	0	0	b	0	b	0	b	b
c	0	0	0	c	0	c	c	c
d	0	a	b	0	d	a	b	d
e	0	a	0	c	a	e	c	e
f	0	0	b	c	b	c	f	f
1	0	a	b	c	d	e	f	1

Table 2.5. The operation $+$ in Exercise 2.1.

$+$	0	a	b	c	d	e	f	1
0	a	a	b	c	d	e	f	1
a	a	a	d	e	d	e	1	1
b	b	d	b	f	d	1	f	1
c	c	e	f	c	1	e	f	1
d	d	d	d	1	d	1	1	1
e	e	e	1	e	1	e	1	1
f	f	1	f	f	1	1	f	1
1	1	1	1	1	1	1	1	1

Table 2.6. The operation $'$ in Exercise 2.1.

f	0	a	b	c	d	e	f	1
f'	1	f	e	d	c	b	a	0

EXERCISE 2.2 *Consider the set* $B = \{1, 2, 3, 7, 10, 14, 35, 70\}$ *with the operations* $+$ *as the greatest common divisor,* $\cdot$ *as the smallest common multiple, and* a' *as* 70 *divided by* a. *For instance,* $7+10 = 1$, $14+35 = 7$, $10 \cdot 14 = 70$, *and* $35' = 2$. *Show that* $\{B, +, \cdot, ', 1, 70\}$ *is a Boolean algebra.*

EXERCISE 2.3 *Denote by* $P(E)$ *the set of all subsets of a non-empty set* E, *i.e., the power set of* E. *The operations* $\cup$, $\cap$, $'$ *are the operations of the union, intersection, and complement in the set theory. Show that* $\{P(E), \cup, \cap, ', \emptyset, E\}$, *where* $\emptyset$ *is the empty set, forms a Boolean algebra.*

EXERCISE 2.4 *Let* x, y, *and* z *be elements of a Boolean algebra* B. *Prove the following relations*

1 $x + x = x$,

2 $x \cdot x = x$

3 $x + 1 = 1$,

4 $x \cdot 0 = 0$,

5 $x + xy = x$,

6 $x(x + y) = x$,

7 $x(x' + y) = xy$,

8 $x + x'y = x + y$,

9 $(x + y)(x' + z) = xz + x'y$.

EXERCISE 2.5 *Let* B *be a Boolean algebra and* $x, y \in B$. *Define* $x \leq y$ *if and only if* $x \wedge y = x$. *Show that* $\leq$ *is a partial order.*

EXERCISE 2.6 *Prove that in an arbitrary Boolean algebra, if* $x \leq y$, *then* $y' \leq x'$, *and if* $x' \leq y$, *then* $y \leq x$.

EXERCISE 2.7 *Determine assignments of* (x_1, x_2, x_3) *for which* $x_1 + x_2 = x_3$ *and* $x_1 \oplus x_2 x_3 = 1$.

EXERCISE 2.8 *Consider binary number* $(x_1 x_2 x_3)$ *and determine the truth-table of a function that has the value* 1 *if the number of* 1 *bits is even. Do the same for a function having the value* 1 *for an odd number of* 1*-bits.*

EXERCISE 2.9 *Consider two-bit binary numbers* $x = (x_1, x_0)$ *and* $y = (y_1, y_0)$. *Determine the truth-table for a function* $f(x_1, x_0, y_1, y_0)$ *having the value* 1 *when* $x < y$ *and* 0 *otherwise.*

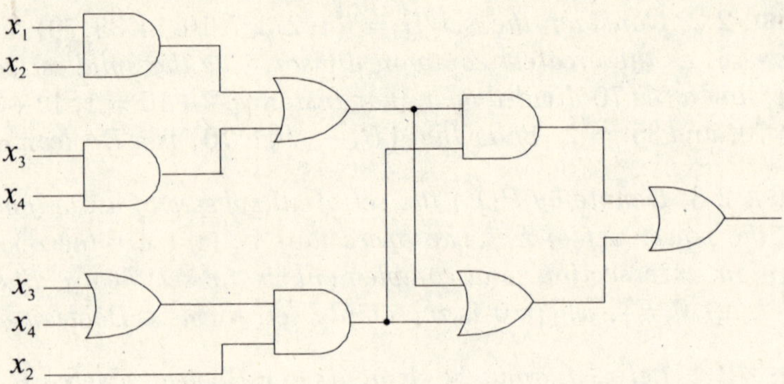

Figure 2.7. Logic network for the function f in Exercise 2.11.

EXERCISE 2.10 *Realize the function* $f(x_1, x_2, x_3, x_4) = x_1\overline{x}_2x_3 + x_1\overline{x}_2x_4 + x_2x_3x_4 + x_1x_2\overline{x}_3\overline{x}_4$ *by a network with three-input AND and OR elements. Assume that both variables and their complements are available as inputs.*

EXERCISE 2.11 *Analyze the logic network in Fig. 2.7 and simplify it by using properties of Boolean expressions. Determine the truth-table of the function realized by this network.*

Chapter 3

FUNCTIONAL EXPRESSIONS FOR SWITCHING FUNCTIONS

The complete Sum-Of-Product (SOPs) forms an analytical representation for switching functions when these functions are considered with the Boolean algebra as the underlying algebraic structure. The term analytical is used here in the sense of an expression or a formula written in terms of some elementary symbols, in this case minterms, to express a given switching function f. In this setting, SOPs can be viewed as analytical descriptions of truth-tables. Fig. 3.1 explains the relationship between the complete SOP and the truth-table for a two-variable function f. The assignments for variables are written in terms of literals, i.e., as minterms, which are then multiplied with function values. The minterms that get multiplied by 0 have no effect and are eliminated. The remaining 1-minterms are added to represent the given function f.

The following example discusses the same relationship from a slightly different point of view.

EXAMPLE 3.1 *Fig. 3.2 shows the truth-table for a function of* $n = 3$ *variables. The truth-vector of* f *is decomposed into a logic sum of subfunctions each of which can be represented by a single minterm. The addition of thus selected minterms produces the complete SOP for* f.

This example suggests that a complete SOP can be viewed as a series-like expressions where the basis functions are described by minterms and the coefficients are the function values. These functions are usually called the trivial basis in the space of binary-valued functions on the group C_2^n, $GF_2(C_2^n)$, which can be identified with the block-pulse functions. Fig. 3.3 shows the waveforms of the basis functions described by minterms.

In matrix notation, the minterms can be be generated through the Kronecker product of basic matrices $\mathbf{X}(1) = [\ \overline{x}_i \quad x_i\ ]$ for $i = 1, \ldots, n$.

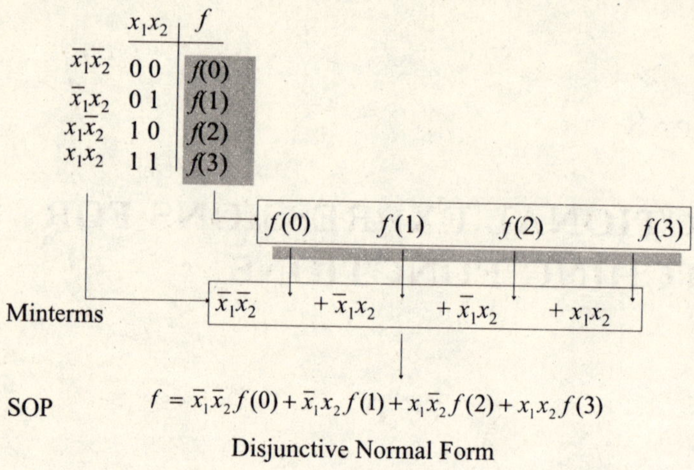

Figure 3.1. Truth-table and SOP for a two-variable function f.

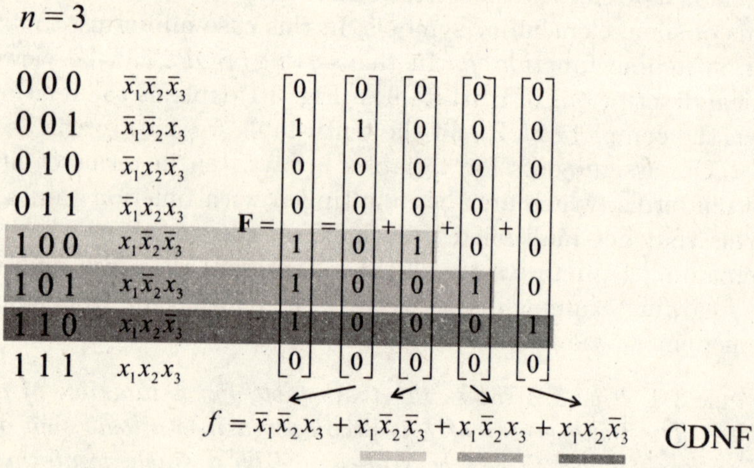

Figure 3.2. The decomposition of f in terms of minterms.

When written as columns of a $(2^n \times 2^n)$ matrix, the minterms produce the identity matrix, which explains why this basis is called the trivial basis, and that the coefficients in a series-like expansion in terms of this basis are equal to the function values. The identity matrix of size $(2^n \times 2^n)$ can be represented as the Kronecker product (or power) of the basic matrix $\mathbf{B}(1) = \begin{bmatrix} 1 & 0 \\ 0 & 1 \end{bmatrix}$.

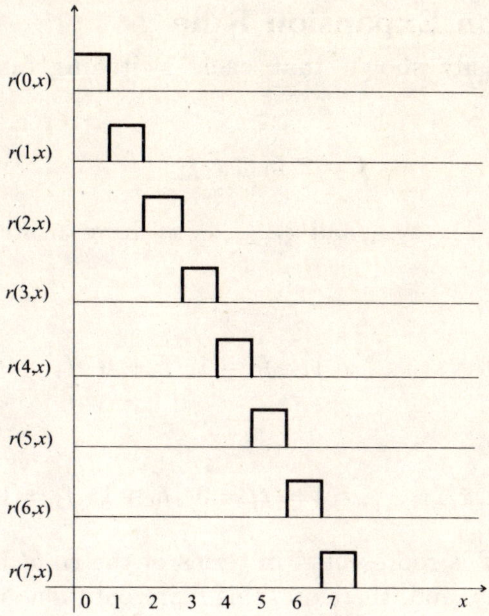

Figure 3.3. Waveforms of block-pulse functions.

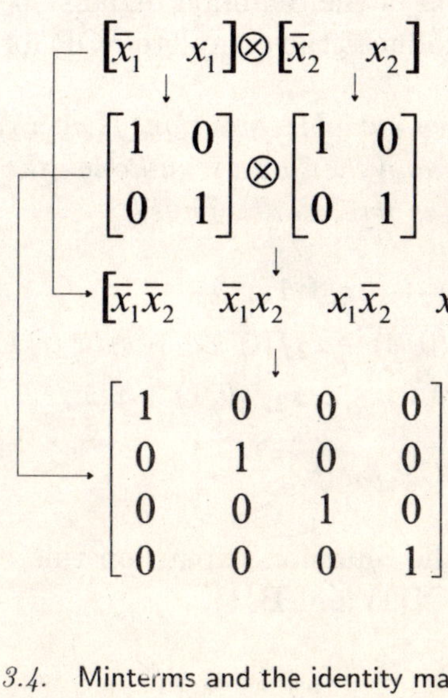

Figure 3.4. Minterms and the identity matrix for $n = 2$.

EXAMPLE 3.2 *Fig. 3.4 explains generation of the trivial basis for $n = 2$ and its Kronecker product structure.*

1. Shannon Expansion Rule

It can be easily shown that each switching function f can be represented as

$$f = \overline{x}_i f_0 \oplus x_i f_1. \tag{3.1}$$

Indeed, let $x_1, \ldots, x_{i-1}$ and $x_{i+1}, \ldots, x_n$ have arbitrary fixed values. Then,

$$f(x_1, \ldots, x_{i-1}, 0, x_{i+1}, \ldots, x_n) = f_0 = 1 \cdot f_0 \oplus 0 \cdot f_1 = \overline{0} \cdot f_0 \oplus 0 \cdot f_1,$$

and

$$f(x_1, \ldots, x_{i-1}, 1, x_{i+1}, \ldots, x_n) = f_1 = 0 \cdot f_0 \oplus 1 \cdot f_1 = \overline{1} \cdot f_0 \oplus 1 \cdot f_1.$$

In this way, f is represented in terms of the co-factors with respect to the variable x_i, and, therefore, this representation is an expansion or alternatively, decomposition of f. The rule (3.1) is usually called the *Shannon expansion* (decomposition) by referring to [163], although it has been used by J. Boole already in 1854 [14].

A recursive application of the Shannon expansion to all the variables in a given function f produces the complete SOP for f.

EXAMPLE 3.3 *For a two-variable function $f(x_1, x_2)$, we first perform the decomposition by x_1 and then by x_2, although the order in which the Shannon rule is applied is irrelevant. Thus,*

$$\begin{aligned} f(x_1, x_2) &= \overline{x}_1 f(0, x_2) \oplus x_1 f(1, x_2) \\ &= \overline{x}_1(\overline{x}_2 f(0,0) \oplus x_2 f(0,1)) \oplus x_1(\overline{x}_2 f(1,0) \oplus x_2 f(1,1)) \\ &= \overline{x}_1\overline{x}_2 f(0,0) \oplus \overline{x}_1 x_2 f(0,1) \oplus x_1\overline{x}_2 f(1,0) \oplus x_1 x_2 f(1,1), \end{aligned}$$

which is the complete SOP for f.

In matrix notation, the Shannon expansion rule can be expressed in terms of basic matrices $\mathbf{X}(1)$ and $\mathbf{B}(1)$,

$$f = \begin{bmatrix} \overline{x}_i & x_i \end{bmatrix} \begin{bmatrix} 1 & 0 \\ 0 & 1 \end{bmatrix} \begin{bmatrix} f_0 \\ f_1 \end{bmatrix},$$

which can be written as

$$f = \mathbf{X}(1)\mathbf{B}(1)\mathbf{F}.$$

Recursive application of the Shannon expansion to all the variables in f can be expressed using the Kronecker product. Thus, each n-variable switching function f can be represented as

$$f = \mathbf{X}(n)\mathbf{B}(n)\mathbf{F} = \left(\bigotimes_{i=1}^{n} \mathbf{X}(1)\right)\left(\bigotimes_{i=1}^{n} \mathbf{B}(1)\right)\mathbf{F},$$

which is the matrix notation for the complete SOP.

Example 3.4 *For $n = 2$,*

$$\begin{aligned} f &= \left(\left[\, \overline{x}_1 \;\; x_1 \,\right] \otimes \left[\, \overline{x}_2 \;\; x_2 \,\right]\right) \left(\begin{bmatrix} 1 & 0 \\ 0 & 1 \end{bmatrix} \otimes \begin{bmatrix} 1 & 0 \\ 0 & 1 \end{bmatrix}\right) \begin{bmatrix} f(0,0) \\ f(0,1) \\ f(1,0) \\ f(1,1) \end{bmatrix} \\ &= \left(\left[\, \overline{x}_1\overline{x}_2 \;\; \overline{x}_1 x_2 \;\; x_1\overline{x}_2 \;\; x_1 x_2 \,\right]\right) \begin{bmatrix} 1 & 0 & 0 & 0 \\ 0 & 1 & 0 & 0 \\ 0 & 0 & 1 & 0 \\ 0 & 0 & 0 & 1 \end{bmatrix} \begin{bmatrix} f(0,0) \\ f(0,1) \\ f(1,0) \\ f(1,1) \end{bmatrix} \\ &= \overline{x}_1\overline{x}_2 f(0,0) + \overline{x}_1 x_2 f(0,1) + x_1\overline{x}_2 f(1,0) + x_1 x_2 f(1,1). \end{aligned}$$

Notice that in the above expression, logic OR can be replaced by EXOR, since there are no common factors in the product terms. Thus, it is possible to write

$$f = \overline{x}_1\overline{x}_2 f(0,0) \oplus \overline{x}_1 x_2 f(0,1) \oplus x_1\overline{x}_2 f(1,0) \oplus x_1 x_2 f(1,1).$$

Matrix notation provides a convenient way for the transition from SOPs to other representations, as for example, the *polynomial expressions* for switching functions. In this approach, different choices of the basic matrices instead $\mathbf{B}(1)$, produce different expressions. We can also change the operations involved, for instance, instead of logic AND and OR, we may use AND and EXOR, which means that we change the algebraic structure from the Boolean algebra to the Boolean ring (or vectors space over $GF(2)$) to derive polynomial representations for switching functions.

2. Reed-Muller Expansion Rules

Recalling that in $GF(2)$, the logic complement $\overline{x}_i$ of a variable x_i can be viewed as the sum of x_i and the logic constant 1 in $GF(2)$, i.e., $\overline{x}_i = 1 \oplus x_i$, the Shannon expansion can be written as

$$\begin{aligned} f &= \overline{x}_i f_0 \oplus x_i f_1 \\ &= (1 \oplus x_i) f_0 \oplus x_i f_1 \\ &= 1 \cdot f_0 \oplus x_i f_0 \oplus x_i f_1 \\ &= 1 \cdot f_0 \oplus x_i (f_0 \oplus f_1). \end{aligned}$$

Thus derived expression

$$f = 1 \cdot f_0 \oplus x_i (f_0 \oplus f_1),$$

is called the *positive Davio (pD) expansion* (decomposition) rule. With this expansion we can represent a given function f in the form of a polynomial

$$f = c_0 \oplus c_i x_i,$$

where $c_0 = f_0$ and $c_1 = f_0 \oplus f_1$.

Recursive application of the pD-expansion to all the variables in a given function f produces the *Žegalkin polynomial* also called as the *Reed-Muller (RM) expression* for f, by referring to the work of Žegalkin in 1927 [206], and 1928 [207], and Reed [141] and Muller [119] in 1954. Since all the variables appear as positive literals, this expression is the *Positive Polarity Reed-Muller (PPRM) expression* for f.

EXAMPLE 3.5 *(PPRM)*
For $n = 2$,

$$\begin{aligned} f &= 1 \cdot f(0, x_2) \oplus x_1 (f(0, x_2) \oplus f(1, x_2)) \\ &= 1 \cdot (1 \cdot f(0,0) \oplus x_2 (f(0,0) \oplus f(0,1))) \\ &\quad \oplus x_1 (1 \cdot f(0,0) \oplus x_2 (f(0,0) \oplus f(0,1)) \\ &\quad \oplus 1 \cdot f(1,0) \oplus x_2 (f(1,0) \oplus f(1,1))) \\ &= 1 \cdot 1 f(0,0) \oplus x_2 (f(0,0) \oplus f(0,1)) \\ &\quad \oplus x_1 \cdot 1 \cdot (f(0,0) \oplus f(1,0)) \\ &\quad \oplus x_1 x_2 (f(0,0) \oplus f(0,1) \oplus f(1,0) \oplus f(1,1)) \\ &= c_0 \oplus c_1 x_2 \oplus c_2 x_1 \oplus c_3 x_1 x_2, \end{aligned}$$

where, obviously,

$$\begin{aligned} c_0 &= f_0, \\ c_1 &= f(0,0) \oplus f(0,1), \\ c_2 &= f(0,0) \oplus f(1,0), \\ c_3 &= f(0,0) \oplus f(0,1) \oplus f(1,0) \oplus f(1,1). \end{aligned}$$

These coefficients are the Reed-Muller (RM) coefficients.

Notice that the indices of c_i do not directly refer to the indices of variables in the corresponding monomials. However, when interpreted as binary numbers, there is correspondence and this will be used later when we discuss the matrix notation and the Hadamard ordering.

In matrix notation, the pD-expansion can be derived by starting from the Shannon expansion as follows

$$\begin{aligned} f &= \begin{bmatrix} \overline{x}_i & x_i \end{bmatrix} \begin{bmatrix} f_0 \\ f_1 \end{bmatrix} \\ &= \begin{bmatrix} \overline{x}_i & x_i \end{bmatrix} \begin{bmatrix} 1 & 0 \\ 1 & 1 \end{bmatrix} \begin{bmatrix} 1 & 0 \\ 1 & 1 \end{bmatrix} \begin{bmatrix} f_0 \\ f_1 \end{bmatrix} \\ &= \begin{bmatrix} \overline{x}_i \oplus x_i & x_i \end{bmatrix} \begin{bmatrix} 1 & 0 \\ 1 & 1 \end{bmatrix} \begin{bmatrix} f_0 \\ f_1 \end{bmatrix} \\ &= \begin{bmatrix} 1 & x_i \end{bmatrix} \begin{bmatrix} 1 & 0 \\ 1 & 1 \end{bmatrix} \begin{bmatrix} f_0 \\ f_1 \end{bmatrix}, \end{aligned}$$

or more compactly

$$f = \mathbf{X}_{rm}\mathbf{R}(1)\mathbf{F}, \tag{3.2}$$

where $\mathbf{X}_{rm} = \begin{bmatrix} 1 & x_i \end{bmatrix}$ and $\mathbf{R}(1) = \begin{bmatrix} 1 & 0 \\ 1 & 1 \end{bmatrix}$ is called the basic *Reed-Muller matrix.*

Extension to functions of an arbitrary number n of variables is done with the Kronecker product

$$f = \left(\bigotimes_{i=1}^{n} \mathbf{X}_{rm}(1) \right) \left(\bigotimes_{i=1}^{n} \mathbf{R}(1) \right) \mathbf{F}.$$

EXAMPLE 3.6 *For $n = 2$,*

$$\begin{aligned} f &= \left(\begin{bmatrix} 1 & x_1 \end{bmatrix} \otimes \begin{bmatrix} 1 & x_2 \end{bmatrix} \right) \left(\begin{bmatrix} 1 & 0 \\ 1 & 1 \end{bmatrix} \otimes \begin{bmatrix} 1 & 0 \\ 1 & 1 \end{bmatrix} \right) \begin{bmatrix} f(0,0) \\ f(0,1) \\ f(1,0) \\ f(1,1) \end{bmatrix} \\ &= \left(\begin{bmatrix} 1 & x_2 & x_1 & x_1x_2 \end{bmatrix} \right) \begin{bmatrix} 1 & 0 & 0 & 0 \\ 1 & 1 & 0 & 0 \\ 1 & 0 & 1 & 0 \\ 1 & 1 & 1 & 1 \end{bmatrix} \begin{bmatrix} f(0,0) \\ f(0,1) \\ f(1,0) \\ f(1,1) \end{bmatrix} \\ &= c_0 \oplus c_1x_2 \oplus c_2x_1 \oplus c_3x_1x_2. \end{aligned}$$

From linear algebra we know also that the change back is obtained just by the inverse matrix. Because over $GF(2)$,

$$\begin{bmatrix} 1 & 0 & 0 & 0 \\ 1 & 1 & 0 & 0 \\ 1 & 0 & 1 & 0 \\ 1 & 1 & 1 & 1 \end{bmatrix} \begin{bmatrix} 1 & 0 & 0 & 0 \\ 1 & 1 & 0 & 0 \\ 1 & 0 & 1 & 0 \\ 1 & 1 & 1 & 1 \end{bmatrix} = \begin{bmatrix} 1 & 0 & 0 & 0 \\ 0 & 1 & 0 & 0 \\ 0 & 0 & 1 & 0 \\ 0 & 0 & 0 & 1 \end{bmatrix},$$

the change of the basis matrix is self-inverse and we have

$$\begin{bmatrix} 1 \\ c_1 \\ c_2 \\ c_3 \end{bmatrix} = \begin{bmatrix} 1 & 0 & 0 & 0 \\ 1 & 1 & 0 & 0 \\ 1 & 0 & 1 & 0 \\ 1 & 1 & 1 & 1 \end{bmatrix} \begin{bmatrix} f_{00} \\ f_{01} \\ f_{10} \\ f_{11} \end{bmatrix}.$$

The matrix

$$R(n) = \bigotimes_{i=1}^{n} \mathbf{R}(1),$$

is called the Reed-Muller matrix and its columns are called the *Reed-Muller functions.* It is also called the *conjunctive matrix* and studied by Aizenberg et. al. [4], see also [2].

EXAMPLE 3.7 *Fig. 3.6 shows the Reed-Muller matrix for $n = 3$. Its columns, the Reed-Muller functions $rm(i, x)$, $i, x \in \{0, 1, \ldots, 7\}$, can be represented as elementary products of switching variables*

$$\begin{aligned} rm(0, x) &= 1 \\ rm(1, x) &= x_3 \\ rm(2, x) &= x_2 \\ rm(3, x) &= x_2x_3 \\ rm(4, x) &= x_1 \\ rm(5, x) &= x_1x_3 \\ rm(6, x) &= x_1x_2 \\ rm(7, x) &= x_1x_2x_3 \end{aligned}$$

Fig. 3.5 shows waveforms of Reed-Muller functions for $n = 3$.

This ordering of Reed-Muller functions is determined by the Kronecker product and is denoted as the Hadamard order [71].

The following recurrence relation is true for the Reed-Muller matrix

$$\mathbf{R}(n) = \begin{bmatrix} \mathbf{R}(n-1) & \mathbf{0}(n-1) \\ \mathbf{R}(n-1) & \mathbf{R}(n-1) \end{bmatrix}.$$

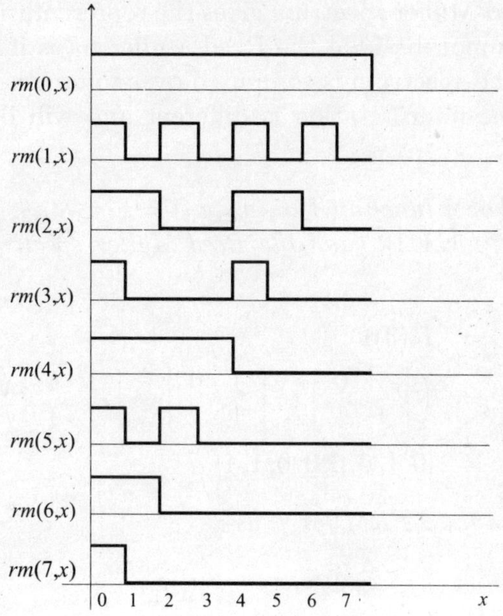

Figure 3.5. Waveforms of Reed-Muller functions for $n = 3$.

$$
\mathbf{R}(3) = \begin{bmatrix} 1 & 0 & 0 & 0 & 0 & 0 & 0 & 0 \\ 1 & 1 & 0 & 0 & 0 & 0 & 0 & 0 \\ 1 & 0 & 1 & 0 & 0 & 0 & 0 & 0 \\ 1 & 1 & 1 & 1 & 0 & 0 & 0 & 0 \\ 1 & 0 & 0 & 0 & 1 & 0 & 0 & 0 \\ 1 & 1 & 0 & 0 & 1 & 1 & 0 & 0 \\ 1 & 0 & 1 & 0 & 1 & 0 & 1 & 0 \\ 1 & 1 & 1 & 1 & 1 & 1 & 1 & 1 \end{bmatrix}.
$$

Figure 3.6. Reed-Muller matrix for $n = 3$.

with $\mathbf{R}(1)$ the basic Reed-Muller matrix and where $\mathbf{0}$ is the zero matrix, i.e., a matrix whose all elements are equal to 0.

DEFINITION 3.1 *(Reed-Muller spectrum)*
For a function f given by the truth-vector $\mathbf{F} = [f(0), \ldots, f(2^n-1)]^T$ the Reed-Muller spectrum is the vector $\mathbf{S}_f = [S_f(0), \ldots, S_f(2^n-1)]^T$ defined by

$$
\mathbf{S}_{f,rm} = \mathbf{R}(n)\mathbf{F}.
$$

Thus, the Reed-Muller spectrum gives the representation of a function given in the Shannon basis in the Reed-Muller basis if we are working over $GF(2)$. If the spectrum is computed over some other field, e.g., the real numbers, the interpretation is different and will be considered in detail later.

EXAMPLE 3.8 *For a function* $f(x_1, x_2, x_3) = x_1x_2 \vee x_3$, *the truth-vector is* $\mathbf{F} = [0,1,0,1,0,1,1,1]^T$ *and the Reed-Muller spectrum is calculated as*

$$\begin{aligned}\mathbf{S}_f &= \mathbf{R}(3)\mathbf{F} \\ &= \left(\begin{bmatrix} 1 & 0 \\ 1 & 1 \end{bmatrix} \otimes \begin{bmatrix} 1 & 0 \\ 1 & 1 \end{bmatrix} \otimes \begin{bmatrix} 1 & 0 \\ 1 & 1 \end{bmatrix}\right)\mathbf{F} \\ &= [0,1,0,0,0,0,1,1]^T,\end{aligned}$$

which determines the PPRM for f *as*

$$f = x_3 \oplus x_1x_2 \oplus x_1x_2x_3.$$

3. Fast Algorithms for Calculation of RM-expressions

By using the properties of the Kronecker product, it can be shown that a Kronecker product representable matrix can be represented as an ordinary matrix product of sparse matrices, each of which is again Kronecker product representable. This representation is usually called the Good-Thomas factorization theorem [52], [187]. In particular, for the Kronecker product of (2×2) matrices $\mathbf{Q}_i$,

$$\bigotimes_{i=1}^{n} \mathbf{Q}_i = \prod_{i=1}^{n} \left(\mathbf{I}_{2^{i-1}} \otimes \mathbf{Q}_i \otimes \mathbf{I}_{2^{k-i}}\right),$$

where $\mathbf{I}_r$ is an $(r \times r)$ identity matrix.

EXAMPLE 3.9 *For* $n = 2$,

$$\mathbf{R}(2) = \mathbf{R}(1) \otimes \mathbf{R}(1) = \mathbf{C}_1\mathbf{C}_2$$

where

$$\begin{aligned}\mathbf{C}_1 &= \mathbf{R}(1) \otimes \mathbf{I}(1) \\ &= \begin{bmatrix} 1 & 0 \\ 1 & 1 \end{bmatrix} \otimes \begin{bmatrix} 1 & 0 \\ 0 & 1 \end{bmatrix} = \begin{bmatrix} 1 & 0 & 0 & 0 \\ 0 & 1 & 0 & 0 \\ 1 & 0 & 1 & 0 \\ 0 & 1 & 0 & 1 \end{bmatrix},\end{aligned}$$

$$\begin{aligned}\mathbf{C}_2 &= \mathbf{I}(1)\otimes\mathbf{R}(1)\\ &= \begin{bmatrix}1&0\\0&1\end{bmatrix}\otimes\begin{bmatrix}1&0\\1&1\end{bmatrix}=\begin{bmatrix}1&0&0&0\\1&1&0&0\\0&0&1&0\\0&0&1&1\end{bmatrix}.\end{aligned}$$

We can directly verify

$$\begin{bmatrix}1&0&0&0\\0&1&0&0\\1&0&1&0\\0&1&0&1\end{bmatrix}\begin{bmatrix}1&0&0&0\\1&1&0&0\\0&0&1&0\\0&0&1&1\end{bmatrix}=\begin{bmatrix}1&0&0&0\\1&1&0&0\\1&0&1&0\\1&1&1&1\end{bmatrix}.$$

Each of the matrices $\mathbf{C}_1$ and $\mathbf{C}_2$ determines a step in the fast algorithm for calculation of the Reed-Muller coefficients. The non-zero elements in the i-th row of the matrix point out the values which should be added modulo 2 (EXOR) to calculate the i-th Reed-Muller coefficient. When in a row there is a single non-zero element the value pointed is forwarded to the output. From there, it is easy to determine a flow-graph of a fast algorithm to calculate the Reed-Muller spectrum with steps in the algorithm performed sequentially, meaning the input of a step is the output from the preceding step.

Fig. 3.7 shows the flow graph of the fast algorithm for calculation of the Reed-Muller coefficients.

4. Negative Davio Expression

By using the relation $x_i = 1 \oplus \overline{x}_i$ we can derive the *negative Davio (nD) expansion* from the Shannon expansion similarly to the case of the positive Davio expansion.

$$\begin{aligned} f &= \overline{x}_i f_0 \oplus x_i f_1\\ &= \overline{x}_i f_0 \oplus (1\oplus\overline{x}_i) f_1\\ &= \overline{x}_i f_0 \oplus 1\cdot f_1 \oplus \overline{x}_i f_1\\ &= 1\cdot f_1 \oplus \overline{x}_i f_0 \oplus \overline{x}_i f_1\\ &= 1\cdot f_1 \oplus \overline{x}_i (f_0\oplus f_1)\\ &= c_0 \oplus c_1\overline{x}_i.\end{aligned}$$

Recursive application of the nD-expansion results in the Reed-Muller polynomial where all the variables appear with negative literals, the negative polarity Reed-Muller expression (NPRM).

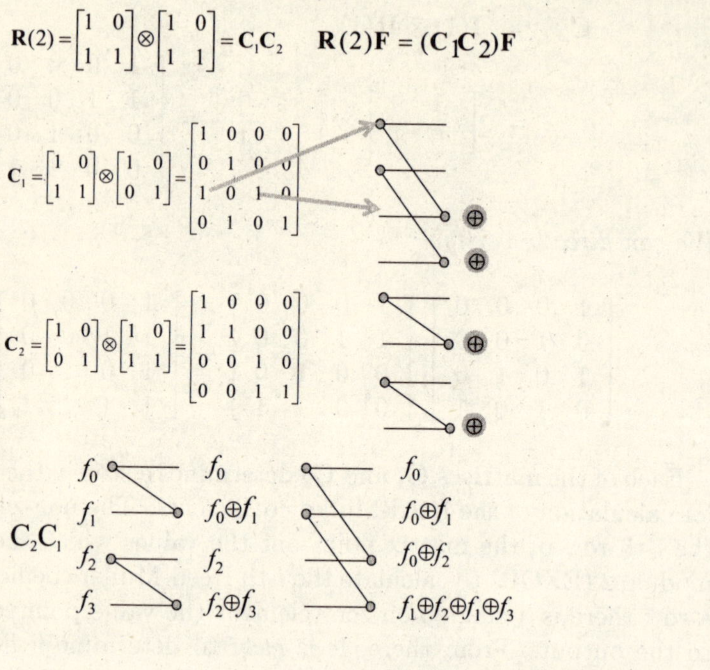

Figure 3.7. Fast Reed-Muller transform for $n = 2$.

In matrix notation, the nD-expansion can be represented as

$$f = \begin{bmatrix} 1 & \overline{x}_i \end{bmatrix} \begin{bmatrix} 0 & 1 \\ 1 & 1 \end{bmatrix} \begin{bmatrix} f_0 \\ f_1 \end{bmatrix}.$$

The matrix $\overline{\mathbf{R}}(1) = \begin{bmatrix} 0 & 1 \\ 1 & 1 \end{bmatrix}$ is the *basic negative Reed-Muller (nRM) matrix.* It should be noted that the negative literals for variables correspond to exchanging columns in the basic RM-matrix.

EXAMPLE 3.10 *For the function f in Example 3.8, the RM-expression with nD-expansion assigned to all the variables is determined as*

$$\begin{aligned} \mathbf{S}_f &= \overline{\mathbf{R}}(3)\mathbf{F} \\ &= \left(\begin{bmatrix} 0 & 1 \\ 1 & 1 \end{bmatrix} \otimes \begin{bmatrix} 0 & 1 \\ 1 & 1 \end{bmatrix} \otimes \begin{bmatrix} 0 & 1 \\ 1 & 1 \end{bmatrix} \right) \mathbf{F} \\ &= [1,0,0,1,0,1,0,1]^T, \end{aligned}$$

which gives the NPRM for f as

$$f = 1 \oplus \overline{x}_2\overline{x}_3 \oplus \overline{x}_1\overline{x}_3 \oplus \overline{x}_1\overline{x}_2\overline{x}_3.$$

Table 3.1. Fixed-polarity RM-expressions for $n = 2$.

Polarity	RM-expression
$(pD, pD) = (0,0)$	$f_{H=(0,0)} = c_{0(0,0)} \oplus c_{1(0,0)}x_2 \oplus c_{2(0,0)}x_1 \oplus c_{3(0,0)}x_1x_2$
$(pD, nD) = (0,1)$	$f_{H=(0,1)} = c_{0(0,1)} \oplus c_{1(0,1)}\overline{x}_2 \oplus c_{2(0,1)}x_1 \oplus c_{3(0,1)}x_1\overline{x}_2$
$(nD, pD) = (1,0)$	$f_{H=(1,0)} = c_{0(1,0)} \oplus c_{1(1,0)}x_2 \oplus c_{2(1,0)}\overline{x}_1 \oplus c_{3(1,0)}\overline{x}_1x_2$
$(nD, nD) = (1,1)$	$f_{H=(1,1)} = c_{0(1,1)} \oplus c_{1(1,1)}\overline{x}_2 \oplus c_{2(1,1)}\overline{x}_1 \oplus c_{3(1,1)}\overline{x}_1\overline{x}_2$

5. Fixed Polarity Reed-Muller Expressions

We can freely choose between the pD- and nD-expansions for a particular variable x_i in a given function f. In this way, we can produce 2^n different Reed-Muller expressions, where n is the number of variables. These expressions are called Fixed-polarity Reed-Muller (FPRM) expressions, since the polarity of the literal for each variable is fixed. The assignment of pD or nD-expansion rules to variables, i.e., the positive or negative literals in the elementary products in the Reed-Muller expression, is usually specified by the *polarity vector* $H = (h_1, \ldots, h_n)$, where the component $h_i \in \{0, 1\}$ specifies the polarity for the variable x_i. If $h_i = 0$, then the i-th variable is represented by the negative literal $\overline{x}_i$, and when $h_i = 0$, by the positive literal x_i.

For a given function f different FPRM expressions typically differ in the number in non-zero coefficients. A FPRM expression with the minimum number of non-zero coefficients is a minimum FPRM expression for f. It may happen that there are two or more FPRMs with the same number of non-zero coefficients. In this case, we select as the minimum FPRM the expressions in whose products there is a least number of variables.

In circuit synthesis from Reed-Muller expressions, reduction of the number of products reduces the number of circuits in the network, and the reduction of the number of literals in products implies reduction of the number of inputs of the circuits to realize the products.

EXAMPLE 3.11 *Table 3.1 shows the FPRM expressions for a two-variable function for different assignments of the positive and negative Davio rules. Table 3.2 shows the calculation of coefficients in these expressions and Table 3.3 specifies the matrices used in calculation of these coefficients.*

EXAMPLE 3.12 *Consider a function of two variables*

$$f = \overline{x}_1\overline{x}_2 \oplus x_1\overline{x}_2 \oplus x_1x_2 = \overline{x}_2 \vee x_1x_2.$$

Table 3.2. FPRM-coefficients.

$H = (0,0)$	$H = (01)$
$c_{0(0,0)} = f_0$	$c_{0(0,1)} = f_1$
$c_{1(0,0)} = f_0 \oplus f_1$	$c_{1(0,1)} = f_0 \oplus f_2$
$c_{2(0,0)} = f_0 \oplus f_2$	$c_{2(0,1)} = f_1 \oplus f_3$
$c_{3(0,0)} = f_0 \oplus f_1 \oplus f_2 \oplus f_3$	$c_{3(0,1)} = f_0 \oplus f_1 \oplus f_2 \oplus f_3$
$H = (1,0)$	$H = (11)$
$c_{0(1,0)} = f_2$	$c_{0(1,1)} = f_3$
$c_{1(1,0)} = f_2 \oplus f_3$	$c_{1(1,1)} = f_2 \oplus f_3$
$c_{2(1,0)} = f_0 \oplus f_2$	$c_{2(1,1)} = f_1 \oplus f_3$
$c_{3(1,0)} = f_0 \oplus f_1 \oplus f_2 \oplus f_3$	$c_{3(1,1)} = f_0 \oplus f_1 \oplus f_2 \oplus f_3$

The truth-vector for this function is $\mathbf{F} = [1,0,1,1]^T$. *Table 3.4 shows the Reed-Muller spectra for all possible polarities, the related FPRMs and the number of product terms.*

This example explains the rationale for studying of FPRM expressions. For some functions the number of products can be considerably reduced by choosing the best polarity. However, the problem is that there is no simple algorithm to select in advance the polarity for a particular function f. It can be shown that finding an optimal polarity is an NP-hard problem, [155]. Exact algorithms for the assignment of the decomposition rules to variables that produce the minimum FPRM, consist of the brute force search, which because of the large search space are restricted to the small number of variables. There are heuristic algorithms, for example, [32], [33], [152], that often find nearly optimal solutions, but there is no guarantee for the quality of the results achieved.

An approach, usually used in practice, is to find the coefficients in all the FPRM expressions for a given function f in an efficient way. To that order, it is convenient to consider the *FPRM polarity matrix* $\mathbf{FPRM}(n)$ defined as a $(2^n \times 2^n)$ matrix whose rows are coefficients in different FPRMs for f. Thus, the i-th column of the polarity matrix shows the i-th coefficient in all the FPRM for f. Since the logic complement of a variable x_i can be viewed as the EXOR addition with the logic 1, which can be considered as the shift on finite dyadic groups, it follows that the $\mathbf{FPRM}(n)$ expresses the structure of a convolution matrix on C_2^n.

Table 3.3. Matrices for FPRMs.

$H = (0,0)$

$$\mathbf{R}(1) \otimes \mathbf{R}(1) = \begin{bmatrix} 1 & 0 \\ 1 & 1 \end{bmatrix} \otimes \begin{bmatrix} 1 & 0 \\ 1 & 1 \end{bmatrix} = \begin{bmatrix} 1 & 0 & 0 & 0 \\ 1 & 1 & 0 & 0 \\ 1 & 0 & 1 & 0 \\ 1 & 1 & 1 & 1 \end{bmatrix}$$

$H = (0,1)$

$$\mathbf{R}(1) \otimes \overline{\mathbf{R}}(1) = \begin{bmatrix} 1 & 0 \\ 1 & 1 \end{bmatrix} \otimes \begin{bmatrix} 0 & 1 \\ 1 & 1 \end{bmatrix} = \begin{bmatrix} 0 & 1 & 0 & 0 \\ 1 & 1 & 0 & 0 \\ 0 & 1 & 0 & 1 \\ 1 & 1 & 1 & 1 \end{bmatrix}$$

$H = (1,0)$

$$\overline{\mathbf{R}}(1) \otimes \mathbf{R}(1) = \begin{bmatrix} 0 & 1 \\ 1 & 1 \end{bmatrix} \otimes \begin{bmatrix} 1 & 0 \\ 1 & 1 \end{bmatrix} = \begin{bmatrix} 0 & 0 & 1 & 0 \\ 0 & 0 & 1 & 1 \\ 1 & 0 & 1 & 0 \\ 1 & 1 & 1 & 1 \end{bmatrix}$$

$H = (1,1)$

$$\overline{\mathbf{R}}(1) \otimes \overline{\mathbf{R}}(1) = \begin{bmatrix} 0 & 1 \\ 1 & 1 \end{bmatrix} \otimes \begin{bmatrix} 0 & 1 \\ 1 & 1 \end{bmatrix} = \begin{bmatrix} 0 & 0 & 0 & 1 \\ 0 & 0 & 1 & 1 \\ 0 & 1 & 0 & 1 \\ 1 & 1 & 1 & 1 \end{bmatrix}$$

Table 3.4. Fixed-polarity Reed-Muller expressions.

S_f	FPRM	*# of products*
$\mathbf{S}_{f,(0,0)} = [1,1,0,1]^T$	$f = 1 \oplus x_2 \oplus x_1 x_2$	3
$\mathbf{S}_{f,(0,1)} = [0,1,1,1]^T$	$f = \overline{x}_2 \oplus x_1 \oplus x_1 \overline{x}_2$	3
$\mathbf{S}_{f,(1,0)} = [1,0,0,1]^T$	$f = 1 \oplus \overline{x}_1 x_2$	2
$\mathbf{S}_{f,(1,1)} = [1,0,1,1]^T$	$f = 1 \oplus \overline{x}_1 \oplus \overline{x}_1 \overline{x}_2$	3

Thus, if the convolution of two functions f and g on C_2^n, denoted as the *dyadic convolution*, is defined as

$$(f * g)(\tau) = \sum_{x=0}^{2^n-1} f(x)(x \oplus \tau),$$

where $\tau = 0, \ldots, 2^n - 1,$, then it can be shown that the columns of the polarity matrix can be calculated as the convolution with the corresponding rows of the Reed-Muller matrix $\mathbf{R}(n)$ [171].

EXAMPLE 3.13 *The FPRM polarity matrix for $n = 2$ is*

$$\mathbf{FPRM}(2) = \begin{bmatrix} c_{0(0,0)} & c_{1(0,0)} & c_{2(0,0)} & c_{3(0,0)} \\ c_{0(0,1)} & c_{1(0,1)} & c_{2(0,1)} & c_{3(0,1)} \\ c_{0(1,0)} & c_{1(1,0)} & c_{2(1,0)} & c_{3(1,0)} \\ c_{0(1,1)} & c_{1(1,1)} & c_{2(1,1)} & c_{3(1,1)} \end{bmatrix}.$$

The Reed-Muller matrix for $n = 2$ is

$$\mathbf{R}(2) = \begin{bmatrix} 1 & 0 & 0 & 0 \\ 1 & 1 & 0 & 0 \\ 1 & 0 & 1 & 0 \\ 1 & 1 & 1 & 1 \end{bmatrix}.$$

We denote the columns of these matrices $\mathbf{FPRM}(2)$ *and* $\mathbf{R}(2)$ *by* $\mathbf{c}_i$, *and* $\mathbf{r}_i$, $i = 0, 1, 2, 3$, *respectively. Then,*

$$\mathbf{c}_i = \mathbf{r}_i * \mathbf{F},$$

where $\mathbf{F}$ *is the truth-vector for a function* f *on* C_2^2.

6. Algebraic Structures for Reed-Muller Expressions

Fig. 3.8 specifies the algebraic structures that are used for the study of Reed-Muller expressions. We can use an algebra, that can be the classical two-element Boolean algebra, or the Gibbs algebra defined in [51]. In this case, the addition is considered as EXOR and the multiplication is defined as a convolution-like multiplication. Alternatively, RM- expressions can be studied in vectors spaces of function on finite dyadic groups into the field $GF(2)$.

Tables 3.5 and 3.6 illustrate the properties of the RM-expressions in the Boolean algebra and the Gibbs algebra, respectively. It should be

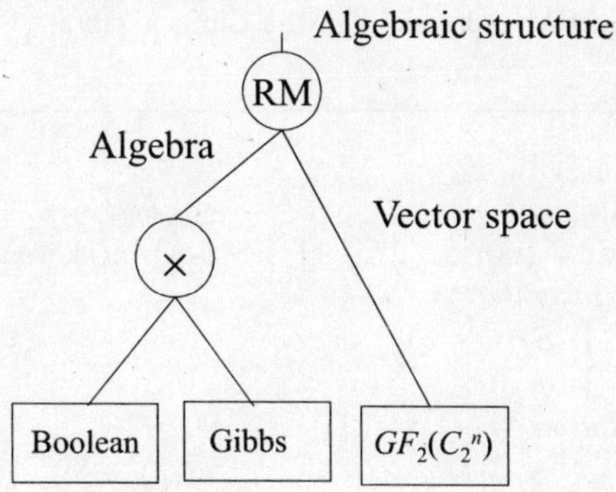

Figure 3.8. Algebraic structures for study of Reed-Muller expressions.

Table 3.5. Properties of RM-expressions in the Boolean algebra.

Function	Spectrum
$h(x) = f(x) \oplus g(x)$	$S_{h(w)} = S_f(w) \oplus S_g(w)$
$h(x) = f(x) \vee g(x)$	$S_{h(w)} = \oplus_{u \vee v} S_f(u) S_g(v)$
$h(x) = f(x) \wedge g(x)$	$S_{h(w)} = S_f(w) \oplus S_g(w) \oplus_{u \wedge v} S_f(w) S_g(w)$
Convolution theorem	
If $S_h(w) = S_f(w) \vee S_g(w)$	then $h(x) = \otimes_{y \vee z = x} f(y) g(z)$

noticed that in the case of the Boolean algebra, the relations in terms of the EXOR are simpler that in terms of logic OR, which suggests that the Boolean ring defined earlier for $R = \{0, 1\}$, is a more natural structure for spectral considerations of Reed-Muller expressions. In the Gibbs algebra, RM-expressions exhibit properties that are much more similar to the properties of the classical Fourier series, than in the case of the Boolean algebra. Notice that the convolution theorem in the Boolean algebra holds only in one direction. In the Gibbs algebra, the multiplication itself is defined as the convolution.

7. Interpretation of Reed-Muller Expressions

Fig. 3.9 explains that RM-expressions can be interpreted as polynomial expressions corresponding to the Taylor series in classical mathematical analysis, in which case the Reed-Muller coefficients can be

Table 3.6. Properties of RM-expressions in the Gibbs algebra.

Self-inverseness	
$S_{W^q}(w) - \delta(q,w)$	$S_{S_f}(w) = f$
$W(x) = 1, \forall x \in \{0m\ldots, 2^n - 1\}$	δ-Kronecker symbol
Translation formula	
$S_{W^q} f(w) = \begin{cases} S_f(w-q), & w > q, \\ 0, & w < q. \end{cases}$	
Parseval relation	
$\langle f, g\rangle = \sum_{w=0}^{2^n-1} S_f(w) S_g(w)$	$\langle f, g\rangle = \sum_{x=0}^{2^n-1} f(x)\overline{g}(x)$
$\overline{g}$ - the dyadic conjugate	$\overline{g} = \mathbf{R}^T g$
$\mathbf{R}$ - RM-transform matrix	
Convolution theorem	
$S_{f \cdot g}(w) = S_f(w) \cdot S(w)$	

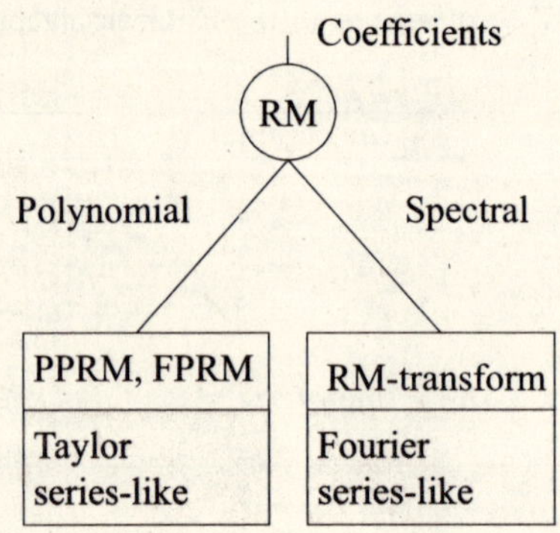

Figure 3.9. Interpretation of Reed-Muller expressions.

considered as the values of the Boolean differences, as will be discussed later.

Alternatively, RM-expressions can be considered as an analogue to Fourier series. Moreover, as it will be shown later, these expressions can be derived from the discrete Walsh series, which are the Fourier series on C_2^n.

8. Kronecker Expressions

Fixed-polarity Reed-Muller expressions (FPRMs) are generalizations of the Positive-polarity Reed-Muller expressions (PPRMs) and are derived by allowing to choose any of two possible decomposition rules for each variable in a function f. In this way 2^n possible expressions are determined for a given function f. A further generalization, called the *Kronecker expression*, is achieved by allowing to freely chose among the three decomposition rules, the Shannon (S), the positive Davio (pD), and the negative Davio (nD) rule for each variable. In this way, there are 3^n possible expansions for each function of n variables. The larger the number of possible expressions, the larger the possibility of finding an expressions with small numbers of non-zero coefficients.

Table 3.7 specifies the decomposition rules allowed in Kronecker expressions. Table 3.8 shows the basis functions in Kronecker expressions in symbolic and matrix notation.

Coefficients in these expressions can be calculated by using the Kronecker transform matrices defined as

$$\mathbf{K}(n) = \bigotimes_{i=1}^{n} \mathbf{K}_i(1),$$

where $\mathbf{K}_i(1)$ is any of the matrices for S, pD, and nD-expansion rule. Basis functions in Kronecker expressions are determined by columns of the inverse matrices $\mathbf{K}^{-1}(n)$ which are the Kronecker products of the inverse matrices for the basic matrices $\mathbf{K}_i(1)$ used in $\mathbf{K}(n)$. From Table 3.8, columns of $\mathbf{K}^{-1}(n)$ can be written in symbolic notation as

$$\mathbf{X}_k(n) = \bigotimes_{i=1}^{n} \mathbf{X}(1),$$

where the index k shows that this is the basis for a Kronecker expression which certainly depends on the choice of the basic matrices $\mathbf{K}_i(1)$.

Therefore, the Kronecker expressions are formally defined as

$$f = \mathbf{X}_k(n)\mathbf{K}(n)\mathbf{F}.$$

Since Kronecker expressions are defined in terms of Kronecker product representable matrices, where the basic matrices are the Reed-Muller matrices $\mathbf{R}(1)$, $\overline{\mathbf{R}}(1)$ and the identity matrix $\mathbf{I}(1)$, the coefficients in these expressions can be calculated by the same algorithms as the FPRMs, with steps corresponding to the Shannon nodes reduced to transferring output data from the previous step to input in the next step.

EXAMPLE 3.14 *Consider the assignment of decomposition rules to the variables of a three-variable function as*

$$\begin{aligned} x_1 \to \mathbf{K}_1(1) &= \mathbf{B}(1) \\ x_2 \to \mathbf{K}_2(1) &= \mathbf{R}(1) \\ x_3 \to \mathbf{K}_3(1) &= \overline{\mathbf{R}}(1) \end{aligned}$$

Table 3.7. Transform matrices in Kronecker expressions.

$\mathbf{B}(1) = \begin{bmatrix} 1 & 0 \\ 0 & 1 \end{bmatrix}$	$\mathbf{R}(1) = \begin{bmatrix} 1 & 0 \\ 1 & 1 \end{bmatrix}$	$\overline{\mathbf{R}}(1) = \begin{bmatrix} 0 & 1 \\ 1 & 1 \end{bmatrix}$

Table 3.8. Basis functions in Kronecker expressions.

$\begin{bmatrix} \overline{x}_i & x_i \end{bmatrix}$	$\begin{bmatrix} 1 & x_i \end{bmatrix}$	$\begin{bmatrix} 1 & \overline{x}_i \end{bmatrix}$
$\mathbf{B}^{-1}(1) = \begin{bmatrix} 1 & 0 \\ 0 & 1 \end{bmatrix}$	$\mathbf{R}^{-1}(1) = \begin{bmatrix} 1 & 0 \\ 1 & 1 \end{bmatrix}$	$\overline{\mathbf{R}}^{-1}(1) = \begin{bmatrix} 1 & 1 \\ 1 & 0 \end{bmatrix}$

This assignment determines the Kronecker transform matrix

$$\mathbf{K}(3) = \begin{bmatrix} 0 & 1 & 0 & 0 & 0 & 0 & 0 & 0 \\ 1 & 1 & 0 & 0 & 0 & 0 & 0 & 0 \\ 0 & 1 & 0 & 1 & 0 & 0 & 0 & 0 \\ 1 & 1 & 1 & 1 & 0 & 0 & 0 & 0 \\ 0 & 0 & 0 & 0 & 0 & 1 & 0 & 0 \\ 0 & 0 & 0 & 0 & 1 & 1 & 0 & 0 \\ 0 & 0 & 0 & 0 & 0 & 1 & 0 & 1 \\ 0 & 0 & 0 & 0 & 1 & 1 & 1 & 1 \end{bmatrix},$$

that should be used to determine the coefficients in the Kronecker expressions with respect to the set of basis functions represented by columns of the inverse matrix

$$\mathbf{K}^{-1}(3) = \begin{bmatrix} 1 & 1 & 0 & 0 & 0 & 0 & 0 & 0 \\ 1 & 0 & 0 & 0 & 0 & 0 & 0 & 0 \\ 1 & 1 & 1 & 1 & 0 & 0 & 0 & 0 \\ 1 & 0 & 1 & 0 & 0 & 0 & 0 & 0 \\ 0 & 0 & 0 & 0 & 1 & 1 & 0 & 0 \\ 0 & 0 & 0 & 0 & 1 & 0 & 0 & 0 \\ 0 & 0 & 0 & 0 & 1 & 1 & 1 & 1 \\ 0 & 0 & 0 & 0 & 1 & 0 & 1 & 0 \end{bmatrix},$$

thus, in symbolic notation in terms of switching variables, these basis functions are

$$\overline{x}_1 \quad \overline{x}_1\overline{x}_3 \quad \overline{x}_1x_2 \quad \overline{x}_1x_2\overline{x}_3 \quad x_1 \quad x_1\overline{x}_3 \quad x_1x_2 \quad x_1x_2\overline{x}_3.$$

8.1 Generalized bit-level expressions

In FPRM expressions above, the polarity of a variable is fixed throughout the expressions. Thus, each variable can appear as either positive or negative literal, but not both. Another restriction was imposed to the form of the product terms. We used the so-called *primary products*, and no products consisting of the same set of variables may appear.

The *generalized Reed-Muller expressions* (GRM) are derived by allowing to freely choose polarity for each variable in every product irrespective to the polarity of the same variable in other products. However, the restriction to primary products is preserved, i.e., no two products containing the same subset set of variables can appear.

EXAMPLE 3.15 *For $n = 3$, the GRM expressions is an expression of the form*

$$f = r_0 \oplus r_1 \,\widetilde{x}_3 \oplus r_2 \,\widetilde{x}_2 \oplus r_3 \,\widetilde{x}_2\widetilde{x}_3 \oplus r_4 \,\widetilde{x}_1 \oplus r_5 \,\widetilde{x}_1\widetilde{x}_3 \oplus r_6 \,\widetilde{x}_1\widetilde{x}_2 \oplus r_7 \,\widetilde{x}_1\widetilde{x}_2\widetilde{x}_3,$$

where $r_i \in \{0, 1\}$ and $\widetilde{x}_i$ denotes either $\overline{x}_i$ or x_i.

For example, the expression

$$f = \overline{x}_1\overline{x}_2 \oplus x_2\overline{x}_3 \oplus x_1x_3,$$

is a GRM expression, since no product have the same set of variables, and the variables x_1 and x_2 appears as both positive and negative literals, implying that it is not a FPRM.

For an n variable function, since each input can be 0,1 $\overline{x}_i$, or x_i, there are $n2^{n-1}$ possible combinations, and it follows that there are at most $2^{n2^{n-1}}$ GRM expressions.

The *EXOR sum-of-products expressions* (ESOPs) are the most general class of AND-EXOR expressions defined as an EXOR sum of arbitrary product terms, i.e., as the expressions of the form

$$f = \bigoplus_I \widetilde{x}_1\widetilde{x}_2 \cdots \widetilde{x}_n,$$

where the index set I is the set of all possible products, and $\widetilde{x}_i$ could be 1, $\overline{x}_i$ or x_i. It should be noticed that in ESOPs, each occurrence $\widetilde{x}_i$ can be chosen as 1, $\overline{x}_i$ or x_i independently of other choices for $\widetilde{x}_i$.

EXAMPLE 3.16 *For two-variable functions there are 9 ESOPs,*

$$\overline{x}\overline{y}, \overline{x}y, \overline{x}\cdot 1, x\overline{y}, xy, x\cdot 1, 1\cdot\overline{y}, 1\cdot y, 1.$$

EXAMPLE 3.17 *The expression $x_1x_2x_3 \oplus x_1x_2$ is a PPRM. The expression $x_1x_2\overline{x}_3 \oplus x_2\overline{x}_3$ is a FPRM, but not PPRM, since x_3 appear as the negative literal $\overline{x}_3$. The expression $x_1 \oplus x_2 \oplus \overline{x}_1x_2$ is a GRM but not FPRM, since it contains both x_1 and $\overline{x}_1$. The expression $x_1x_2\overline{x}_3 \oplus \overline{x}_1\overline{x}_2\overline{x}_3$ is an ESOP, since it contains products of the same form, i.e., containing variables from the same set.*

Increasing the freedom in choosing the form of product terms and in assigning polarities to the variables increases the number of possible expressions for a given function f, which improves possibilities to find a spares representation for f in the number of products count. However, the greater freedom makes it more difficult to determine all the possible expressions in order to find the best expression for the intended application.

There have been developed exact algorithms that are applicable to a relatively small number of variables, and heuristic algorithms for larger functions.

Table 3.9, the data in which are taken from in [153], clearly provides rationale for study of different expressions. It shows the number of functions representable by t product terms for different AND-EXOR expressions. For a comparison, the number of product terms in SOP, thus, AND-OR expressions, is also shown.

Some further generalizations of AND-EXOR expressions are derived by referring to the corresponding decisions diagrams and will be discussed in the corresponding chapters.

9. Word-Level Expressions

The expressions in previous sections are usually called *bit-level expressions*, since the coefficients are logic values 0 and 1. In the case of SOPs, these are function values, and in the other expressions, the coefficients are elements of the spectra that are obtained by the transform matrices representing the decomposition rules. Calculations are performed over the finite field of order 2, $GF(2)$.

The *word-level expressions* are generalizations of bit-level expressions. In word-level expressions the coefficients are viewed as elements of the field of rational numbers Q or more generally, complex numbers C. It is assumed, that logic values for variables and function values are interpreted as real or complex numbers 0 and 1.

Fig. 3.10 illustrates this extension of the theory of functional expressions for switching functions.

Table 3.9. Number of functions realizable by t product terms.

t	PPRM	FPRM	Kronecker	GRM	ESOP	SOP
0	1	1	1	1	1	1
1	10	81	81	81	81	81
2	120	836	2268	2212	2268	1804
3	560	3496	8424	20856	21774	13472
4	1820	8878	15174	37818	37530	28904
5	4368	17884	19260	4512	3888	17032
6	8008	20152	19440	56	24	3704
7	11440	11600	864	0	0	512
8	12870	2336	0	0	0	26
9	11440	240	0	0	0	0
10	8008	32	24	0	0	0
11	4368	0	0	0	0	0
12	1820	0	0	0	0	0
13	560	0	0	0	0	0
14	120	0	0	0	0	0
15	16	0	0	0	0	0
16	1	0	0	0	0	0
av.	8.00	5.50	4.73	3.68	3.66	4.13

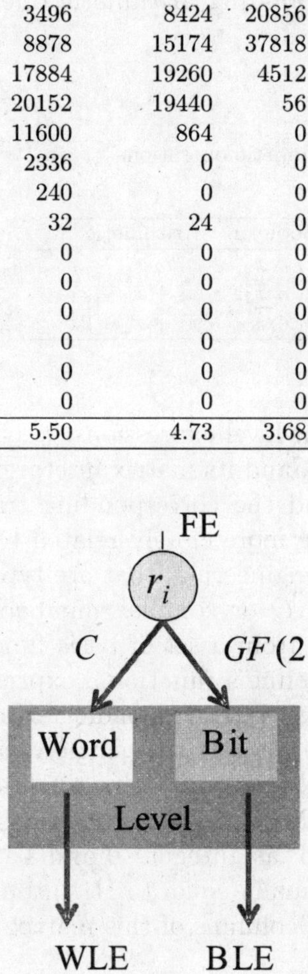

Figure 3.10. Bit-level and word-level expressions for switching functions.

9.1 Arithmetic expressions

Probably the simplest example of word-level expressions is the *Arithmetic expression* that can be viewed as the integer counterpart of a PPRM.

Arithmetic expressions (ARs) can be obtained by replacing the Boolean operation by the corresponding arithmetic operations as specified in Table 3.10.

Table 3.10. Boolean and arithmetic operations.

Boolean	Arithmetic
$x_1 \wedge x_2$	$x_1 x_2$
$x_1 \vee x_2$	$x_1 + x_2 - x_1 x_2$
$x_1 \oplus x_2$	$x_1 + x_2 - 2x_1 x_2$

When we considered bit-level expressions, we started from an expansion (decomposition) rule, and its matrix interpretation and derived the set of basic functions and the corresponding transform matrix. The word-level expressions are more closely related to other spectral transforms used in computer engineering, that are typically defined over the field of rational numbers Q or complex numbers C, and we take the opposite route. We start from a set of basis functions and the related transform matrix, and define a functional expression with word-level coefficients. Then, we derive the corresponding expansion (decomposition) rule as the transform with respect to a single variable.

To derive arithmetic expressions, we take the same set of basis functions as that used in PPRMs, specified by columns of $\mathbf{R}(n)$ and interpret the logic values 0 and 1 as integers 0 and 1. In this way, we get a matrix $\mathbf{A}(n)$ which is formally equal to $\mathbf{R}(n)$, but the entries are in C. In symbolic notation, the columns of this matrix are represented as

$$\mathbf{X}_a(n) = \bigotimes_{i=1}^{n} \mathbf{X}_a(1),$$

where $\mathbf{X}_a(1) = \begin{bmatrix} 1 & x_i \end{bmatrix}$, $x_i \in \{0,1\} \subset Z$. The matrix $\mathbf{A}^{-1}(n)$, inverse to $\mathbf{A}(n)$ over C, is then used to calculate the coefficients in ARs,

$$\mathbf{A}^{-1}(n) = \bigotimes_{i=1}^{n} \mathbf{A}^{-1}(1),$$

where $\mathbf{A}^{-1}(1) = \begin{bmatrix} 1 & 0 \\ -1 & 1 \end{bmatrix}$. This matrix $\mathbf{A}^{-1}(n)$ is called the *Arithmetic transform matrix* and $\mathbf{A}^{-1}(1)$ is the *basic arithmetic transform matrix.*

DEFINITION 3.2 *(Arithmetic expressions)*
For a function f defined by the truth-vector $\mathbf{F} = [f(0), \ldots, f(2^n - 1)]^T$, the arithmetic expression is defined as

$$f = \left(\bigotimes_{i=1}^{n} \mathbf{X}_a(1)\right)\left(\bigotimes_{i=1}^{n} \mathbf{A}^{-1}(1)\right)\mathbf{F}.$$

The arithmetic spectrum $\mathbf{S}_{a,f} = [S_{a,f}(0), \ldots, S_{a,f}(2^n - 1)]^T$ is defined as

$$\mathbf{S}_{a,f} = \mathbf{A}^{-1}(n)\mathbf{F}.$$

EXAMPLE 3.18 *The basis functions of ARs for $n = 2$ are specified by columns of the matrix*

$$\mathbf{A}(2) = \begin{bmatrix} 1 & 0 & 0 & 0 \\ 1 & 1 & 0 & 0 \\ 1 & 0 & 1 & 0 \\ 1 & 1 & 1 & 1 \end{bmatrix},$$

and the coefficients are calculated by using the matrix

$$\mathbf{A}^{-1}(2) = \begin{bmatrix} 1 & 0 & 0 & 0 \\ -1 & 1 & 0 & 0 \\ -1 & 0 & 1 & 0 \\ 1 & -1 & -1 & 1 \end{bmatrix},$$

For a function f given by the truth-vector $\mathbf{F} = [1, 0, 1, 1]^T$, the arithmetic expressions is

$$f = 1 - x_2 + x_1x_2,$$

since the arithmetic spectrum is

$$\mathbf{S}_{a,f} = \mathbf{A}^{-1}(2)\mathbf{F} = \begin{bmatrix} 1 & 0 & 0 & 0 \\ -1 & 1 & 0 & 0 \\ -1 & 0 & 1 & 0 \\ 1 & -1 & -1 & 1 \end{bmatrix}\begin{bmatrix} 1 \\ 0 \\ 1 \\ 1 \end{bmatrix} = \begin{bmatrix} 1 \\ -1 \\ 0 \\ 1 \end{bmatrix}.$$

The arithmetic expression for $n = 1$ is

$$f = \begin{bmatrix} 1 & x \end{bmatrix}\begin{bmatrix} 1 & 0 \\ -1 & 1 \end{bmatrix}\begin{bmatrix} f_0 \\ f_1 \end{bmatrix}.$$

This expression can be derived by starting form the Shannon expansion in the same way as the pD-expressions is obtained, if the logic complement of x is interpreted as $1-x$ over C.

$$\begin{aligned} f &= \begin{bmatrix} \overline{x}_i & x_i \end{bmatrix} \begin{bmatrix} f_0 \\ f_1 \end{bmatrix} \\ &= \begin{bmatrix} 1-x_i & x_i \end{bmatrix} \begin{bmatrix} 1 & 0 \\ 1 & 1 \end{bmatrix} \begin{bmatrix} 1 & 0 \\ -1 & 1 \end{bmatrix} \begin{bmatrix} f_0 \\ f_1 \end{bmatrix} \\ &= \begin{bmatrix} \overline{x}_i + x_i & x_i \end{bmatrix} \begin{bmatrix} 1 & 0 \\ -1 & 1 \end{bmatrix} \begin{bmatrix} f_0 \\ f_1 \end{bmatrix} \\ &= \begin{bmatrix} 1 & x_i \end{bmatrix} \begin{bmatrix} 1 & 0 \\ -1 & 1 \end{bmatrix} \begin{bmatrix} f_0 \\ f_1 \end{bmatrix}. \end{aligned}$$

When matrix operations performed, this expression can be written as

$$f = 1 \cdot f_0 + x(-f_0 + f_1). \tag{3.3}$$

This expansion is called the *arithmetic expansion (decomposition) rule.*

When applied to a particular variable x_i in an n-variable function $f(x_1, \ldots, x_{i-1}, x_i, x_{i+1}, \ldots x_n)$, this expression performs decomposition of f into cofactors with respect to x_i. Therefore, (3.3) written in terms of a variable x_i, defines the *arithmetic expansion* which is the integer counterpart of the Positive Davio expansion, since it has the same form, however, with arithmetic instead of Boolean operations.

Due to the Kronecker product structure, when applied to all the variables in an n-variable function f, the arithmetic expansion produces the arithmetic expressions for f, whose coefficients are the elements of the arithmetic spectrum in Hadamard ordering dictated by the Kronecker product. This completely corresponds to the recursive application of the pD-expansion to derive PPRMs. Therefore, the expansion (3.3) is the positive arithmetic (pAR) expansion. Recalling that the complement of a binary-valued variable taking values in $\{0, 1\} \subset Z$, can be defined as $\overline{x}_i = (1 - x_i)$, we may define the *negative arithmetic (nAR) expansion* as

$$f = 1 \cdot f_1 + \overline{x}_i(f_0 - f_1).$$

The *Fixed-Polarity Arithmetic Expressions (FPARs)* are defined by allowing to freely chose either the pAR or nAR-expansion for each variable in a given function f, in the same way as that is done in FPRMs [91], [101].

9.2 Calculation of Arithmetic Spectrum

Arithmetic expressions are defined with respect to the Reed-Muller functions, however, with different interpretation of their values. The arithmetic transform matrix has the same structure as the Reed-Muller matrix, therefore, calculation of the arithmetic spectrum can be performed by the same algorithm as the Reed-Muller spectrum with operations changed as specified in the transform matrix.

EXAMPLE 3.19 *For* $n = 2$,

$$\mathbf{A}^{-1}(2) = \mathbf{A}^{-1}(1) \otimes \mathbf{A}^{-1}(1) = \mathbf{C}_1\mathbf{C}_2$$

where

$$\begin{aligned} \mathbf{C}_1 &= \mathbf{A}^{-1}(1) \otimes \mathbf{I}(1) \\ &= \begin{bmatrix} 1 & 0 \\ -1 & 1 \end{bmatrix} \otimes \begin{bmatrix} 1 & 0 \\ 0 & 1 \end{bmatrix} = \begin{bmatrix} 1 & 0 & 0 & 0 \\ 0 & 1 & 0 & 0 \\ -1 & 0 & 1 & 0 \\ 0 & -1 & 0 & 1 \end{bmatrix}, \\ \mathbf{C}_2 &= \mathbf{I}(1) \otimes \mathbf{A}^{-1}(1) \\ &= \begin{bmatrix} 1 & 0 \\ 0 & 1 \end{bmatrix} \otimes \begin{bmatrix} 1 & 0 \\ -1 & 1 \end{bmatrix} = \begin{bmatrix} 1 & 0 & 0 & 0 \\ -1 & 1 & 0 & 0 \\ 0 & 0 & 1 & 0 \\ 0 & 0 & -1 & 1 \end{bmatrix}. \end{aligned}$$

We can directly verify

$$\begin{bmatrix} 1 & 0 & 0 & 0 \\ 0 & 1 & 0 & 0 \\ -1 & 0 & 1 & 0 \\ 0 & -1 & 0 & 1 \end{bmatrix} \begin{bmatrix} 1 & 0 & 0 & 0 \\ -1 & 1 & 0 & 0 \\ 0 & 0 & 1 & 0 \\ 0 & 0 & -1 & 1 \end{bmatrix} = \begin{bmatrix} 1 & 0 & 0 & 0 \\ -1 & 1 & 0 & 0 \\ -1 & 0 & 1 & 0 \\ 1 & -1 & -1 & 1 \end{bmatrix}.$$

Each of the matrices $\mathbf{C}_1$ *and* $\mathbf{C}_2$ *determines a step in the fast algorithm for calculation of the arithmetic coefficients. The non-zero elements in i-th row of the matrix point out the values which should be added to calculate the i-th arithmetic coefficient. When there is a single non-zero element, the values pointed are forwarded to the output. From there, it is easy to determine a flow-graph of a fast algorithm with steps performed sequentially, the input of a step is the output from the preceding step.*

Fig. 3.11 shows the flow graph of the fast algorithm for calculation of the arithmetic coefficients.

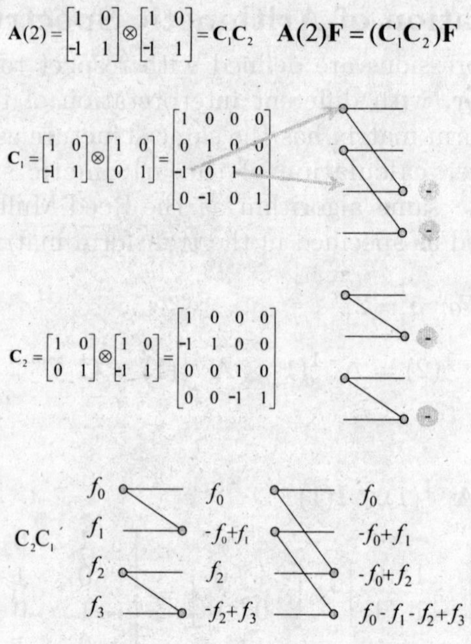

Figure 3.11. Fast arithmetic transform for $n = 2$.

9.3 Applications of ARs

An important application of arithmetic expressions is the representation of multi-output functions. In a representation of a multi-output function by bit-level expressions, each output should be represented by a separate polynomial. A considerable advantage of ARs is that it is possible to represent multiple-output functions by a single polynomial for the integer equivalent functions.

EXAMPLE 3.20 *[99]: Consider a system of functions*

$$(f_2(x_1, x_2, x_3), f_1(x_1, x_2, x_3), f_0(x_1, x_2, x_3)),$$

where

$$\begin{aligned} f_0(x_1, x_2, x_3) &= x_1\overline{x}_3 \oplus x_2, \\ f_1(x_1, x_2, x_3) &= x_2 \vee x_1\overline{x}_3, \\ f_2(x_1, x_2, x_3) &= x_1(x_2 \vee x_3). \end{aligned}$$

If we form the matrix $\mathbf{F}$ *whose columns are truth-vectors of* f_2, f_1, *and* f_0, *with their values interpreted as integers,*

$$\mathbf{F} = \begin{bmatrix} 0 & 0 & 0 \\ 0 & 0 & 0 \\ 0 & 1 & 1 \\ 0 & 1 & 1 \\ 0 & 1 & 1 \\ 1 & 0 & 0 \\ 1 & 1 & 0 \\ 1 & 1 & 1 \end{bmatrix} = [\mathbf{F}_2, \mathbf{F}_1, \mathbf{F}_0],$$

we have a compact representation for f_2, f_1, f_0. *Reading the rows of* $\mathbf{F}$ *as binary numbers, we obtain an integer valued representation for* f_2, f_1, f_0 *as* $f = 2^2 f_2 + 2f_1 + f_0$, *i.e.,*

$$\begin{bmatrix} 0 \\ 0 \\ 3 \\ 3 \\ 3 \\ 4 \\ 6 \\ 7 \end{bmatrix} = 2^2 \begin{bmatrix} 0 \\ 0 \\ 0 \\ 0 \\ 0 \\ 1 \\ 1 \\ 1 \end{bmatrix} + 2 \begin{bmatrix} 0 \\ 0 \\ 1 \\ 1 \\ 1 \\ 0 \\ 1 \\ 1 \end{bmatrix} + 1 \begin{bmatrix} 0 \\ 0 \\ 1 \\ 1 \\ 1 \\ 0 \\ 0 \\ 1 \end{bmatrix} = 4\mathbf{F}_2 + 2\mathbf{F}_1 + \mathbf{F}_0.$$

Now, the arithmetic spectrum of $\mathbf{F} = [0, 0, 3, 3, 3, 4, 6, 7]^T$ *is*

$$\mathbf{S}_f = \begin{bmatrix} 1 & 0 & 0 & 0 & 0 & 0 & 0 & 0 \\ -1 & 1 & 0 & 0 & 0 & 0 & 0 & 0 \\ -1 & 0 & 1 & 0 & 0 & 0 & 0 & 0 \\ 1 & -1 & -1 & 1 & 0 & 0 & 0 & 0 \\ -1 & 0 & 0 & 0 & 1 & 0 & 0 & 0 \\ 1 & -1 & 0 & 0 & -1 & 1 & 0 & 0 \\ 1 & 0 & -1 & 0 & -1 & 0 & 1 & 0 \\ -1 & 1 & 1 & -1 & 1 & -1 & -1 & 1 \end{bmatrix} \begin{bmatrix} 0 \\ 0 \\ 3 \\ 3 \\ 3 \\ 4 \\ 6 \\ 7 \end{bmatrix} = \begin{bmatrix} 0 \\ 0 \\ 3 \\ 0 \\ 3 \\ 1 \\ 0 \\ 0 \end{bmatrix} \begin{matrix} \leftrightarrow & 1 \\ \leftrightarrow & x_3 \\ \leftrightarrow & x_2 \\ \leftrightarrow & x_2x_3 \\ \leftrightarrow & x_1 \\ \leftrightarrow & x_1x_3 \\ \leftrightarrow & x_1x_2 \\ \leftrightarrow & x_1x_2x_3. \end{matrix}$$

Therefore, f is represented as the arithmetic polynomial

$$f(z) = 3x_2 + 3x_1 + x_1x_3.$$

From the linearity of the arithmetic transform, this polynomial can be generated as the sum of the arithmetic polynomials for f_1, f_2, f_3.

The arithmetic spectra for f_2, f_1, and f_0 are

$$\begin{aligned}\mathbf{A}_{f_2} &= [0,0,0,0,0,1,1,-1]^T,\\ \mathbf{A}_{f_1} &= [0,0,1,0,1,-1,-1,1]^T,\\ \mathbf{A}_{f_0} &= [0,0,1,0,1,-1,-2,2]^T,\end{aligned}$$

and, therefore,

$$\begin{bmatrix}0\\0\\3\\0\\3\\1\\0\\0\end{bmatrix} = 2^2\begin{bmatrix}0\\0\\0\\0\\0\\1\\1\\-1\end{bmatrix} + 2\begin{bmatrix}0\\0\\1\\0\\1\\-1\\-1\\1\end{bmatrix} + 1\begin{bmatrix}0\\0\\1\\0\\1\\-1\\-2\\2\end{bmatrix} = 4\mathbf{A}_{f_2} + 2\mathbf{A}_{f_1} + \mathbf{A}_{f_0}.$$

The corresponding arithmetic polynomials for f_2, f_1, and f_0 are

$$\begin{aligned}A_{f_2} &= x_1x_3 + x_1x_2 - x_1x_2x_3,\\ A_{f_1} &= x_2 + x_1 - x_1x_3 - x_1x_2 + x_1x_2x_3,\\ A_{f_0} &= x_2 + x_1 - x_1x_3 - 2x_1x_2 + 2x_1x_2x_3.\end{aligned}$$

Notice that since an integer $z = 2^2z_2 + 2z_1 + z_0$ can be represented in different ways for different assignments of integers to z_2, z_1, and z_0, it is not possible to deduce the arithmetic expressions of f_0, f_1, and f_2 from the arithmetic expressions of $2^2f_2 + 2f_1 + f_0$ directly. For instance, in the above example, the value 0 for the coefficients $S_{a,f}(0)$, $S_{a,f}(1)$ and $S_{a,f}(3)$ is written as $0 = (0,0,0)$, while for the coefficients $s_{a,f}(6)$ and $S_{a,f}(7)$ as $0 = (1,-1,-2)$ and $0 = (-1,1,2)$, respectively.

Arithmetic expressions are useful in design of arithmetic circuits [84], [85], [86], [87]. They were recommended by Aiken and his group [186], with which Komamiya worked for some time [179].

Arithmetic polynomials have proved useful also in testing of logical circuits [45], [63], [64], [91], [123], [136], and their efficiency in parallel calculations has been reported [88], [102], [103]. Further applications of ARs are considered in [99], [100], [101]. A brief review of arithmetic expressions is given in [44].

As another important example of word-level expressions, in the following section, we consider the Walsh expressions.

10. Walsh Expressions

Walsh expressions for discrete functions are defined in terms of *discrete Walsh functions*, that are the discrete version of Walsh functions introduced in 1923 by Joseph Leonard Walsh [199]. They were originally used for solving problems of uniform convergence in approximation of real-variable functions on the interval $[0,1)$. The discrete Walsh functions can be considered as sampled versions of Walsh functions, provided that the values at the points of discontinuity are handled properly [12], [181], [191]. Alternatively, discrete Walsh functions can be viewed as an independently defined set of discrete functions whose waveforms have shapes similar to those of Walsh functions [191]. In this approach, the matrix notation offers a simple way to define the discrete Walsh functions.

DEFINITION 3.3 *(Walsh functions)*
The discrete Walsh functions of order n*, denoted as* $wal(w,x)$*,* $x,k \in \{0,1,\ldots,2^n\}$*, are defined as columns of the* $(2^n \times 2^n)$ Walsh matrix

$$\mathbf{W}(n) = \bigotimes_{i=1}^{n} \mathbf{W}(1),$$

where the basic Walsh matrix $\mathbf{W}(1) = \begin{bmatrix} 1 & 1 \\ 1 & -1 \end{bmatrix}$.

EXAMPLE 3.21 *(Walsh functions)*
For $n=3$ *the Walsh matrix is*

$$\begin{aligned}
\mathbf{W}(3) &= \begin{bmatrix} 1 & 1 \\ 1 & -1 \end{bmatrix} \otimes \begin{bmatrix} 1 & 1 \\ 1 & -1 \end{bmatrix} \otimes \begin{bmatrix} 1 & 1 \\ 1 & -1 \end{bmatrix} \\
&= \begin{bmatrix}
1 & 1 & 1 & 1 & 1 & 1 & 1 & 1 \\
1 & -1 & 1 & -1 & 1 & -1 & 1 & -1 \\
1 & 1 & -1 & -1 & 1 & 1 & -1 & -1 \\
1 & -1 & -1 & 1 & 1 & -1 & -1 & 1 \\
1 & 1 & 1 & 1 & -1 & -1 & -1 & -1 \\
1 & -1 & 1 & -1 & -1 & 1 & -1 & 1 \\
1 & 1 & -1 & -1 & -1 & -1 & 1 & 1 \\
1 & -1 & -1 & 1 & -1 & 1 & 1 & -1
\end{bmatrix}.
\end{aligned}$$

Fig. 3.12 shows waveforms of the discrete Walsh functions for $n=3$.

From the Kronecker product structure, we obtain the following recurrence relation for the Walsh matrix

$$\mathbf{W}(n) = \begin{bmatrix} \mathbf{W}(n-1) & \mathbf{W}(n-1) \\ \mathbf{W}(n-1) & -\mathbf{W}(n-1) \end{bmatrix}.$$

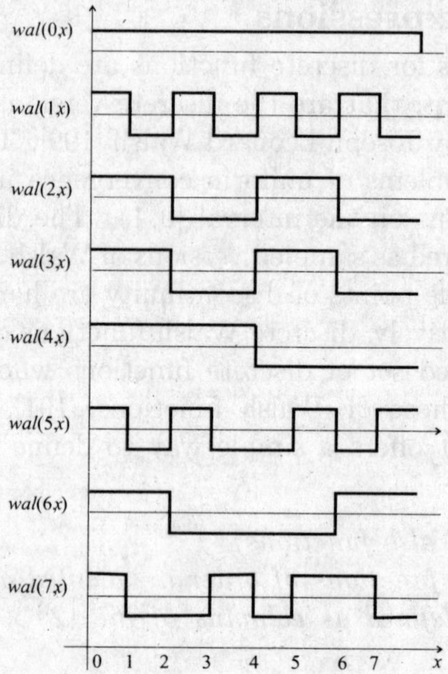

Figure 3.12. Waveforms of Walsh functions for $n = 3$.

Walsh functions with the indices $w = 2^i$, $i = 1, \ldots, n-1$ can be viewed as discrete Rademacher functions [135]. They are also called the basic Walsh functions, since other Walsh functions can be generated as the componentwise product of these basic Walsh (Rademacher) functions.

EXAMPLE 3.22 *In Example 3.21, basic Walsh functions are represented by columns* 0, 1, 2, 4. *The Walsh function in the column 3 is the componentwise product of the Walsh functions in columns 1 and 2. Similarly, the column 5 is the product of columns 1 and 2. The column 6 can be generated as the product of columns 1 and 3. The column 7 is the product of three basic Walsh functions, i.e.,* $wal(7, x) = wal(1, x) \cdot wal(2, x) \cdot wal(3, x)$.

The statement is true also for rows of the Walsh matrix, since it a symmetric matrix. Therefore, $\mathbf{W}(n) = \mathbf{W}^T(n)$ Moreover, since $\mathbf{W}(n)\mathbf{W}^T(n) = 2^{-n}\mathbf{I}(n)$, the Walsh matrix is an orthogonal matrix up to the constant 2^{-n}. It follows that being real-valued, symmetric, and orthogonal, the Walsh matrix is self-inverse matrix up to the constant 2^{-n}.

DEFINITION 3.4 *(Walsh spectrum)*
For a function f represented by the vector $\mathbf{F} = [f(0), \ldots, f(2^n - 1)]^T$,

the Walsh spectrum, in matrix notation, $\mathbf{S}_f = [S_f(0), \ldots, S_f(2^n-1)]^T$ *is defined as*

$$\mathbf{S}_f = \mathbf{W}(n)\mathbf{F}, \tag{3.4}$$

and the inverse transform is

$$\mathbf{F} = 2^{-n}\mathbf{W}(n)\mathbf{S}_f. \tag{3.5}$$

When the Walsh transform is applied to switching functions, it is implicitly assumed that logic values 0 and 1 are considered as integers 0 and 1.

EXAMPLE 3.23 *For a function* f *of three variables given by the vector* $\mathbf{F}=[1,0,1,1,0,0,1,1]^T$, *the Walsh spectrum is* $\mathbf{S}_f=[5,1,-3,1,1,1,1,1]^T$

The Kronecker product structure of the Walsh matrix, permits derivation of an FFT-like fast calculation algorithm for the Walsh transform (FWT) [2]. The method is identical to that used in the Reed-Muller and the arithmetic transform discussed above. The Good-Thomas factorization is used and the difference in the algorithms is in the weighting coefficients assigned to the edges in the flow-graph. The weighting coefficients actually determine operations that will be performed. In the case of Walsh transform these are operations of addition and subtraction, since all the elements in the Walsh matrix are either 1 or -1, thus, there are no multiplications, which means the weighting coefficients are also 1 and -1 and stand for addition and subtraction respectively. Since, unlike the Reed-Muller and the arithmetic transform, in the Walsh transform matrix there are no zero entries, there are no missing edges in the graph, and the basic operation is the complete butterfly as in the case of the Cooley-Tukey algorithm for the discrete Fourier transform (DFT) [29].

We will explain derivation of this algorithm by the example of the Cooley-Tukey algorithm [29] for the Walsh transform for $n=2$.

EXAMPLE 3.24 *For* $n=2$,

$$\mathbf{W}(2) = \mathbf{W}(1)\otimes\mathbf{W}(1) = \mathbf{C}_1\mathbf{C}_2$$

where

$$\begin{aligned}\mathbf{C}_1 &= \mathbf{W}(1)\otimes\mathbf{I}(1)\\ &= \begin{bmatrix}1 & 1\\ 1 & -1\end{bmatrix}\otimes\begin{bmatrix}1 & 0\\ 0 & 1\end{bmatrix} = \begin{bmatrix}1 & 0 & 1 & 0\\ 0 & 1 & 0 & 1\\ 1 & 0 & -1 & 0\\ 0 & 1 & 0 & -1\end{bmatrix},\end{aligned}$$

$$\mathbf{C}_2 = \mathbf{I}(1) \otimes \mathbf{W}(1)$$
$$= \begin{bmatrix} 1 & 0 \\ 0 & 1 \end{bmatrix} \otimes \begin{bmatrix} 1 & 1 \\ 1 & -1 \end{bmatrix} = \begin{bmatrix} 1 & 1 & 0 & 0 \\ 1 & -1 & 0 & 0 \\ 0 & 0 & 1 & 1 \\ 0 & 0 & 1 & -1 \end{bmatrix}.$$

We can directly verify

$$\begin{bmatrix} 1 & 0 & 1 & 0 \\ 0 & 1 & 0 & 1 \\ 1 & 0 & 1 & 0 \\ 0 & 1 & 0 & 1 \end{bmatrix} \begin{bmatrix} 1 & 1 & 0 & 0 \\ 1 & -1 & 0 & 0 \\ 0 & 0 & 1 & 1 \\ 0 & 0 & 1 & -1 \end{bmatrix} = \begin{bmatrix} 1 & 1 & 1 & 1 \\ 1 & -1 & 1 & -1 \\ 1 & 1 & -1 & -1 \\ 1 & -1 & -1 & 1 \end{bmatrix}.$$

Each of the matrices $\mathbf{C}_1$ *and* $\mathbf{C}_2$ *determines a step in the fast algorithm for calculation of the Walsh coefficients. The non-zero elements in the i-th row of the matrix point out the values which should be added to calculate the i-th Walsh coefficient. When there is a single non-zero element, the values pointed are forwarded to the output. From there, it is easy to determine a flow-graph of a fast algorithm with steps performed sequentially, the input of a step is the output from the preceding step.*

Fig. 3.13 shows the flow graph of the fast algorithm for calculation of the Walsh coefficients.

11. Walsh Functions and Switching Variables

Rademacher functions can be identified with trivial switching functions $f(x_1, \ldots, x_n) = x_i$ in $(0,1) \to (1,-1)$ encoding, i.e., $wal(2^i, x) = rad(i, x) = x_i$, $x_i \in \{1, -1\}$. In the usual 0,1 encoding, $wal(2^i, x) = rad(i, x) = 1 - 2x_i$.

EXAMPLE 3.25 *Table 3.11 shows vectors of trivial switching functions and Rademacher functions.*

12. Walsh Series

Columns of the basic Walsh matrix $\mathbf{W}(1) = \begin{bmatrix} 1 & 1 \\ 1 & -1 \end{bmatrix}$ can be expressed in terms of switching variables as $\begin{bmatrix} 1 & 1 - 2x_i \end{bmatrix}$. Since the Walsh matrix is self-inverse up to the constant 2^{-n},

$$f = \frac{1}{2} \begin{bmatrix} 1 & 1 - 2x_i \end{bmatrix} \begin{bmatrix} 1 & 1 \\ 1 & -1 \end{bmatrix} \begin{bmatrix} f_0 \\ f_1 \end{bmatrix}.$$

When the matrix calculations are performed,

$$f = \frac{1}{2}(1 \cdot (f_0 + f_1) + (1 - 2x_i)(f_0 - f_1)).$$

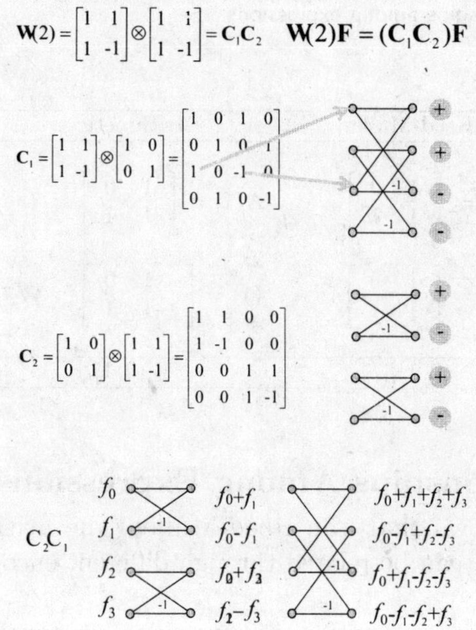

Figure 3.13. Fast Walsh transform for $n = 2$.

Table 3.11. Switching variables and Rademacher functions.

Switching variable	Rademacher function
$\mathbf{0} = [00000000]^T$	$\mathbf{rad}(0, x) = [11111111]^T$
$\mathbf{x}_1 = [00001111]^T$	$\mathbf{rad}(1, x) = [1111 - 1 - 1 - 1 - 1]^T$
$\mathbf{x}_2 = [00110011]^T$	$\mathbf{rad}(2, x) = [11 - 1 - 111 - 1 - 1]^T$
$\mathbf{x}_3 = [01010101]^T$	$\mathbf{rad}(3, x) = [1 - 11 - 11 - 11 - 1]^T$

This expression is called the *Walsh expansion (decomposition) rule* with respect to the variable x_i. Recursive application of this rule to all the variables can be expressed through the Kronecker product

EXAMPLE 3.26 *For* $n = 3$,

$$
\begin{aligned}
f &= \frac{1}{8}(\begin{bmatrix} 1 & 1-2x_1 \end{bmatrix} \otimes \begin{bmatrix} 1 & 1-2x_2 \end{bmatrix} \otimes \begin{bmatrix} 1 & 1-2x_3 \end{bmatrix}) \\
&\quad \left(\begin{bmatrix} 1 & 1 \\ 1 & -1 \end{bmatrix} \otimes \begin{bmatrix} 1 & 1 \\ 1 & -1 \end{bmatrix} \otimes \begin{bmatrix} 1 & 1 \\ 1 & -1 \end{bmatrix} \right) \mathbf{F}.
\end{aligned}
$$

Table 3.12. Relationships among expressions.

	Reed-Muller	Arithmetic	Walsh
Basis	$\mathbf{R}(1) = \begin{bmatrix} 1 & 0 \\ 1 & 1 \end{bmatrix}$	$\mathbf{A}(1) = \begin{bmatrix} 1 & 0 \\ 1 & 1 \end{bmatrix}$	$\mathbf{W}(1) = \begin{bmatrix} 1 & 1 \\ 1 & -1 \end{bmatrix}$
Transform	$\mathbf{R}^{-1}(1) = \begin{bmatrix} 1 & 0 \\ 1 & 1 \end{bmatrix}$	$\mathbf{A}^{-1}(1) = \begin{bmatrix} 1 & 0 \\ -1 & 1 \end{bmatrix}$	$\mathbf{W}^{-1}(1) = \frac{1}{2}\begin{bmatrix} 1 & 1 \\ 1 & -1 \end{bmatrix}$
Encoding	$(0,1)_{GF(2)}$	$(0,1)_Q$	$(0,1)_Q$

13. Relationships Among Expressions

Table 3.12 shows that the Reed-Muller, the arithmetic, and the Walsh expressions can be related through different encoding of switching variables.

In study of different functional expressions, we consider different representations for a given function f, which allows to select a representation the best suited for an intended particular application, with suitability judged with respect to different criteria. Whatever the representations, the complete information about f should be preserved, but may be distributed in different ways over the coefficients in the representations. We start from a given function and determine a different form representation for the same function f. It follows, that all the operations we perform to determine a representation, finally reduce to the identical mapping, however, written in different ways for different expressions. This consideration is the simplest explained through the matrix notation. In particular, if a function f is given by the vector of function values $\mathbf{F}$, we can multiply it by the identity matrix $\mathbf{I}$ provided that the corresponding dimensions agree. The identity matrix can be written as the product of two mutually inverse matrices, $\mathbf{I} = \mathbf{Q}\mathbf{Q}^{-1}$. The product of $\mathbf{Q}^{-1}$ and $\mathbf{F}$ defines the spectrum $\mathbf{S}_f$ for f with respect to the basis determined by the columns of the matrix $\mathbf{Q}$. This consideration can be summarized as

$$f := \mathbf{F} = \mathbf{IF} = \mathbf{Q}\mathbf{Q}^{-1}\mathbf{F} = \mathbf{Q}\mathbf{S}_f,$$

where $\mathbf{S}_f = \mathbf{Q}^{-1}\mathbf{F}$.

When the basis functions, (the columns of $\mathbf{Q}$) can be represented in terms of the variables of f, polynomial-like expressions result. We get polynomial expressions when the basis functions are expressed through products of variables and their powers, under suitably defined multiplication. This is the case for the Reed-Muller, arithmetic, and Walsh expressions.

Notice that if the columns of $\mathbf{Q} = \mathbf{W}(n)$ are written in terms of the discrete Walsh functions $wal(w, x)$, we get the orthogonal Walsh (Fourier) series. Thus, any function on C_2^n can be expressed as

$$f(x) = 2^{-n} \sum_{w=0}^{2^n-1} S_f(w) wal(w, x), \tag{3.6}$$

where $x = (x_1, \ldots, x_n)$ and the Walsh coefficients are defined as

$$S_f(w) = \sum_{x=0}^{2^n-1} f(x) wal(w, x). \tag{3.7}$$

The relations (3.7) and (3.6) define the direct and inverse Walsh transform pair, written in matrix notation in (3.4) and (3.5).

Notice that in both Walsh and arithmetic expressions we do not impose any restriction to the range of functions represented. Thus, they can be applied to integer valued or, more generally, complex-valued functions on C_2^n.

When applied to switching functions, Walsh and arithmetic expressions can be related to the Reed-Muller expressions, as will be explained by the following example.

EXAMPLE 3.27 *(Relationships among expressions)*
For $n = 2$, a function f on C_2^2 given by the vector of function values $\mathbf{F} = [f(0), f(1), f(2), f(3)]^T$ can be expressed as

$$\begin{aligned} f &= \frac{1}{4}(wal(0,x)S_f(0) + wal(1,x)S_f(1) & (3.8) \\ &\quad + wal(2,x)S_f(2) + wal(3,x)S_f(3)), & (3.9) \end{aligned}$$

where the Walsh coefficients are determined as specified by (3.7) as

$$\begin{aligned} S_f(0) &= f(0) + f(1) + f(2) + f(3), \\ S_f(1) &= f(0) - f(1) + f(2) - f(3), \\ S_f(2) &= f(0) + f(1) - f(2) - f(3), \\ S_f(0) &= f(0) - f(1) - f(2) + f(3). \end{aligned}$$

Since Walsh functions in Hadamard ordering can be expressed in terms of switching variables in integer encoding as

$$
\begin{aligned}
wal(0,x) &= 1, \\
wal(1,x) &= 1-2x_2, \\
wal(2,x) &= 1-2x_1, \\
wal(3,x) &= (1-2x_1)(1-2x_2),
\end{aligned}
$$

the Walsh series (3.8) can be written as

$$
\begin{aligned}
f &= \frac{1}{4}(1\cdot(f_0+f_1+f_2+f_3) \\
&\quad +(1-2x_2)(f_0-f_1+f_2-f_3) \\
&\quad +(1-2x_1)(f_0+f_1-f_2-f_3) \\
&\quad +(1-2x_1)(1-2x_2)(f_0-f_1-f_2+f_3)),
\end{aligned}
$$

that, after calculations and simplification performed, results in

$$
f = f_0 + x_2(-f_0+f_1) + x_1(-f_0+f_2) + x_1x_2(f_0-f_1-f_2+f_3),
$$

which is the arithmetic expression for f.

If in arithmetic expressions the operations of addition and subtraction are replaced by modulo 2 operations, i.e., EXOR, the Reed-Muller expressions are obtained. It is assumed that in this transition to modulo 2 operations, the integer values 0 and 1 for variables and function values are replaced by logic values 0 and 1.

In representation of switching functions by Walsh series, some advantages may be achieved by using $(0,1) \rightarrow (1,-1)$ encoding, which makes the functions more compatible to the transform [71]. In this coding, the Walsh spectral coefficients are even numbers in the range -2^n to 2^n, and their sum is 2^n. Further, there are restrictions to the combinations of even integers within this range which may appear in the Walsh spectra of switching functions. For instance, for $n = 3$, Walsh spectral coefficients may take values from three distinct sets $\{0,8\}$, $\{0,4,-4\}$, $\{2,-2,6\}$. However, not all the combinations within these distinct sets are allowed. For example, the vector $\frac{1}{8}[-2,-2,2,2,-6,-2,2,-2]^T$, does not correspond to any switching function as the Walsh spectrum.

There are some other spectral transforms that appears efficient in applications in switching theory and logic design, and among them the Haar transform appears particularly interesting, especially due to their computational simplicity, and basis functions that can be expressed in terms of switching variables, as the other considered transforms [69], [70], [71], [77], [176], [177].

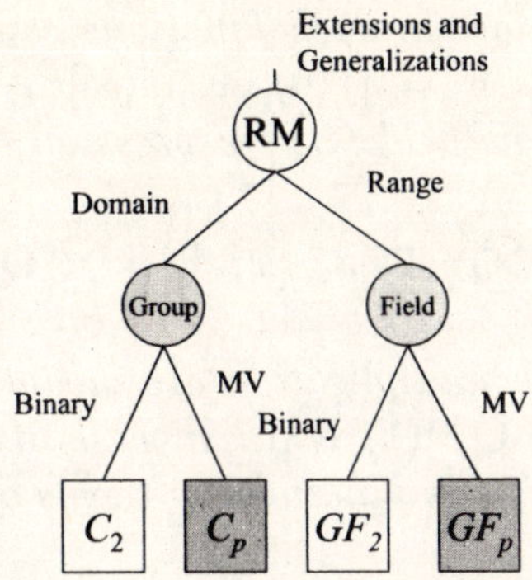

Figure 3.14. Extensions and generalizations of functional expressions.

14. Generalizations to Multiple-Valued Functions

Bit-level expressions for switching functions were extended into word-level expressions by changing the range of functions considered. In generalizations to multiple-valued (MV) functions, we change the domain of functions from the group C_2^n into C_p^n. For the range, the finite field of order p, or some other suitable algebraic structure can be used. In this way, we can consider bit-level expressions for MV functions, however, with multiple-valued bits. As in the binary case, extensions can be done by assuming the field of complex numbers for the range.

Fig. 3.14 shows basic directions in extensions and generalizations of functional expressions to MV functions.

For illustration, we will present an example of Galois field (GF) expressions for p-valued functions, where p-prime or a power of a prime number $f : \{0, 1, 2, \ldots, p-1\}^n \to \{0, 1, 2, \ldots, p-1\}$. We denoted by $GF(C_P^n)$ the space of such functions. In matrix notation, such functions can be defined by vectors of function values $\mathbf{F} = [f(0), \ldots, f(p^n - 1)]^T$.

DEFINITION 3.5 *(GF-expressions)*
Each function $f \in GF(C_p^n)$ can be represented as

$$f(x_1, \ldots, x_n) = \left(\bigotimes_{i=1}^{n} \begin{bmatrix} 1 & x_i & x_i^2 & \cdots & x_i^{p-1} \end{bmatrix} \right) \left(\bigotimes_{i=1}^{n} \mathbf{Q}^{-1}(1) \right) \mathbf{F},$$

where calculations are in $GF(p)$, and $\mathbf{Q}^{-1}(1)$ is a matrix inverse over $GF(p)$ of a matrix $\mathbf{Q}(1)$ whose columns are described by powers x_i^r, $r = 0, 1, \ldots, p-1$.

EXAMPLE 3.28 *(GF-expressions)*
Consider three-valued functions of $n = 2$ variables $f : \{0, 1, 2\}^2 \to$

$\{0,1,2\}$. In matrix notation, such functions can be represented by vectors of function values $\mathbf{F} = [f(0),\ldots,f(8)]^T$. Each function can be represented by the Galois field (GF) expression defined as

$$f(x_1,x_2) = \left(\bigotimes_{i=1}^{2}\begin{bmatrix} 1 & x_i & x_i^2 \end{bmatrix}\right)\left(\bigotimes_{i=1}^{2}\mathbf{Q}^{-1}(1)\right)\mathbf{F},$$

where the addition and multiplication are modulo 3 operations, and the basic transform matrix $\mathbf{Q}^{-1}(1)$ is the inverse of the matrix $\mathbf{Q}(1)$ whose columns determine the basis functions in terms of which GF-expressions are defined,

$$\mathbf{Q}(1) = \begin{bmatrix} 1 & 0 & 0 \\ 1 & 1 & 1 \\ 1 & 2 & 1 \end{bmatrix}.$$

Therefore,

$$\mathbf{Q}^{-1}(1) = \begin{bmatrix} 1 & 0 & 0 \\ 0 & 2 & 1 \\ 2 & 2 & 2 \end{bmatrix}.$$

Thus,

$$\begin{aligned} f(x_1,x_2) &= (\begin{bmatrix} 1 & x_1 & x_1^2 \end{bmatrix} \otimes_3 \begin{bmatrix} 1 & x_2 & x_2^2 \end{bmatrix}) \\ &\quad \left(\begin{bmatrix} 1 & 0 & 0 \\ 0 & 2 & 1 \\ 2 & 2 & 2 \end{bmatrix} \otimes_3 \begin{bmatrix} 1 & 0 & 0 \\ 0 & 2 & 1 \\ 2 & 2 & 2 \end{bmatrix}\right)\mathbf{F}. \end{aligned}$$

The corresponding transform matrix is

$$\begin{aligned} \mathbf{Q}^{-1}(2) &= \mathbf{Q}^{-1}(1) \otimes_3 \mathbf{Q}^{-1}(1) \\ &= \begin{bmatrix} 1 & 0 & 0 & 0 & 0 & 0 & 0 & 0 & 0 \\ 0 & 2 & 1 & 0 & 0 & 0 & 0 & 0 & 0 \\ 2 & 2 & 2 & 0 & 0 & 0 & 0 & 0 & 0 \\ 0 & 0 & 0 & 2 & 0 & 0 & 1 & 0 & 0 \\ 0 & 0 & 0 & 0 & 1 & 2 & 0 & 2 & 1 \\ 0 & 0 & 0 & 1 & 1 & 1 & 2 & 2 & 2 \\ 2 & 0 & 0 & 2 & 0 & 0 & 2 & 0 & 0 \\ 0 & 1 & 2 & 0 & 1 & 2 & 0 & 1 & 2 \\ 1 & 1 & 1 & 1 & 1 & 1 & 1 & 1 & 1 \end{bmatrix}. \end{aligned}$$

For a function f given by $\mathbf{F} = [2,0,1,1,1,0,0,0,2]^T$, coefficients in the GF-expression are given by $\mathbf{S}_f = [2,1,0,2,0,0,0,1,1]^T$. Thus,

$$f(x_1,x_2) = 2 \oplus x_2 \oplus 2x_1 \oplus x_1^2 x_2 \oplus x_1^2 x_2^2,$$

where addition and multiplication are modulo 3.

15. Exercises and Problems

EXERCISE 3.1 *Determine the basis functions in terms of which Sum-of-products expressions are defined for functions of $n = 3$ variables. Show their waveforms and discuss relationships with minterms. Explain relationships to the Shannon expansion rule.*

EXERCISE 3.2 *Write the Sum-of-products expression for the truth-table of a 2-bit comparator (f_1, f_2, f_3). Notice that a two-bit comparator compares two two-bit numbers $N_1 = (x_1x_2)$ and $N_2 = (x_3x_4)$ and produces the outputs $f_1 = 1$ when $N_1 = N_2$, $f_2 = 1$ when $N_1 < N_2$, and $f_3 = 1$ when $N_1 > N_2$.*

EXERCISE 3.3 *Consider the function $f(x_1, x_2, x_3)$ given by the set of decimals indices corresponding to the 1-minterms $\{2, 4, 7\}$. Write the Sum-of-products and Product-of-sums expressions for f. Notice that the list of decimal indices corresponding to 1-maxterms consists of numbers which do not appear in the list of decimal indices for 1-minterms.*

EXERCISE 3.4 *Derive the Positive-polarity Reed-Muller expression for functions of $n = 3$ variables by the recursive application of the positive Davio expansion rule. Determine the basis functions in terms of which these PPRM-expansions are defined, determine their waveforms, and write the Reed-Muller matrix.*

EXERCISE 3.5 *Determine the flow-graph of the FFT-like algorithm for calculation of PPRM-expressions for functions of $n = 3$ variables.*

EXERCISE 3.6 *Determine the PPRM-expressions for the functions*

$$\begin{aligned} f(x_1, x_2, x_3) &= x_1\overline{x}_2 + x_1x_3 + \overline{x}_1x_3, \\ f(x_1, x_2, x_3) &= (x_1 + x_2x_3)(x_1x_2 + \overline{x}_1x_3), \\ f(x_1, x_2, x_3) &= x_1 + x_2 + \overline{x}_1\overline{x}_2 + \overline{x}_2\overline{x}_3 + \overline{x}_1\overline{x}_3. \end{aligned}$$

EXERCISE 3.7 *Determine PPRM-expression for the function $f(x_1, x_2, x_3)$ which takes the value 0 for the assignments of input variables where two or more variables are 1, and the value 1 otherwise.*

EXERCISE 3.8 *How many Fixed-polarity Reed-Muller expressions there are for functions of $n = 3$ variables? Determine all them for the function given by the SOP-expression*

$$f(x_1, x_2, x_3) = \overline{x}_1x_2 + x_1x_3 + x_2\overline{x}_3 + x_1x_2x_3,$$

and compare their complexities in terms of the number of non-zero coefficients.

Table 3.13. Multi-output function in Exercise 3.14.

n	$x_1x_2x_3$	f_0	f_1
0.	000	1	1
1.	001	0	1
2.	010	0	1
3.	011	1	0
4.	100	1	0
5.	101	1	1
6.	110	0	0
7.	111	1	1

EXERCISE 3.9 *Compare the number of non-zero coefficients in the FPRM-expressions for the function f in Exercise 3.6.*

EXERCISE 3.10 *Calculate the FPRM-expression for the polarity $H =$ (110) for the function given by the truth vector $\mathbf{F} = [1,0,0,1,1,0,1,1]^T$ by exploiting the relationships between the Reed-Muller expressions and dyadic convolution.*

EXERCISE 3.11 *For the function in Exercise 3.10 determine the Kronecker expressions for the following assignments of the Shannon, positive Davio, and negative Davio expansion rules to the variables x_1, x_2, and x_3, respectively*

1.	*S, pD, nD,*	*3.*	*pD, S, S,*
2.	*S, nD, pD,*	*4.*	*nD, S, pD.*

Write the corresponding matrix relations and draw the flow-graphs of the related FFT-like algorithms.

EXERCISE 3.12 *Discuss differences and relationships between bit-level and word-level expressions and their applications.*

EXERCISE 3.13 *For functions in Exercise 3.8, determine the fixed polarity arithmetic expressions, and show that the FPRM-expressions can be derived from them by recalculating the coefficients modulo 2 and replacing the operations of the addition and subtraction by EXOR.*

EXERCISE 3.14 *Table 3.13 shows a multi-output function $f = (f_0, f_1)$. Determine the arithmetic and Walsh expressions for this function by converting it into the integer-valued function $f_z = 2f_1 + f_0$.*

Chapter 4

DECISION DIAGRAMS FOR REPRESENTATION OF SWITCHING FUNCTIONS

The way of representing a switching function is often related to the intended applications and determines the complexity of the implementation of related algorithms. Therefore, given a function f and determined the task, selecting a suitable representation for f is an important task. In this chapter, we will discuss decision diagrams for representation of discrete functions.

1. Decision Diagrams

Decision diagrams are data structures that are used for efficient representation of discrete functions such as switching functions or multiple-valued logic functions. There are several ways to define *decision diagrams* and we adopt the classical approach [19].

We will first consider an example to illustrate the idea of decision diagrams and then define them rigorously.

EXAMPLE 4.1 *Consider the logic function* $f(x_{12}, x_2, x_3) = x_1x_2 \vee x_3$. *We can represent all the possible combinations of values that the variables can have in a tree (decision tree) form (Fig. 4.1) and for each combination the value of the function is in a rectangular box. For instance, the combination* $x_1 = 0$, $x_2 = 1$, $x_3 = 0$, $f(0,1,0) = 0$ *is shown as the "thick" path.*

It is obvious that we can go directly to $\boxed{1}$, *from the right node* (x_2) *with value* $x_2 = 1$ *because* x_3 *has no effect anymore. Also, we can eliminate the left node for* x_2 *because both choices* $x_2 = 0$ $x_2 = 1$ *lead to the identical solution. In this way, we get a simpler representation for* f, *which is no more a tree, but a directed graph (Fig. 4.2). This is a much more compact representation than the full decision tree. It is also*

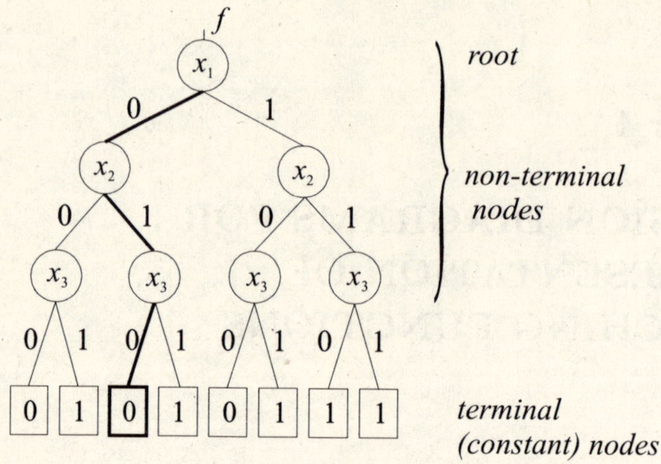

Figure 4.1. Decision tree for f in Example 4.1.

clear that this representation is minimal. Indeed, as there are no fictive variables, each must show at least once as a non-terminal node with two outgoing edges. Also, both terminal nodes are needed.

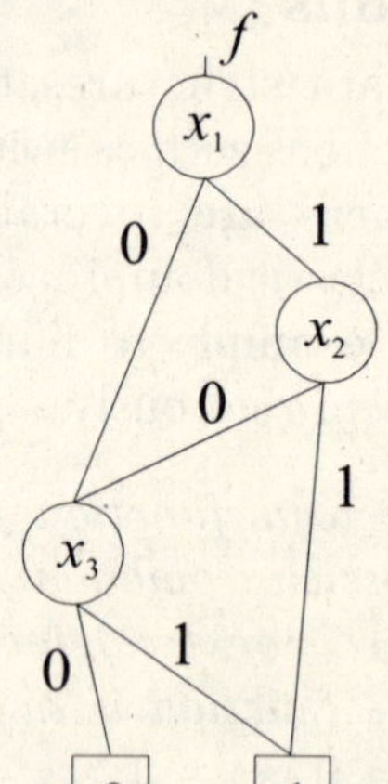

Figure 4.2. Decision diagram for f in Example 4.1.

We could equivalently first have the choices for x_3, *then for* x_1, *and finally for* x_2. *This would lead to the decision diagram in Fig. 4.3. If we choose the order* x_1, x_3, x_2, *we necessarily have two nodes for* x_3 *and this leads to a more complex diagram (Fig. 4.4).*

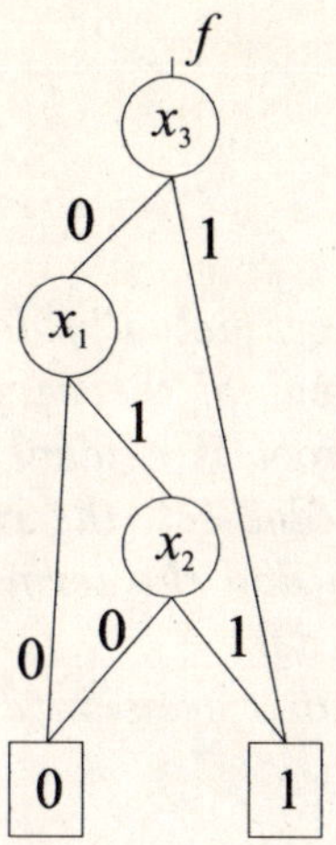

Figure 4.3. Decision diagram for f in Example 4.1 with order of variables x_3, x_2, x_1.

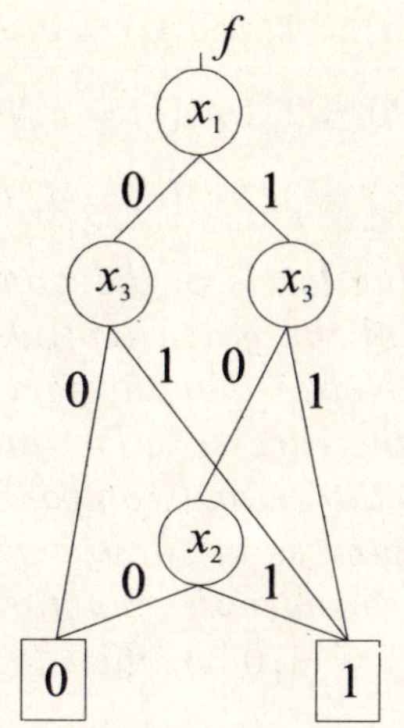

Figure 4.4. Decision diagrams for f in Example 4.1 with order of variables $x_1x_3x_2$.

DEFINITION 4.1 *An (ordered) binary decision diagram is a rooted directed graph with the vertex set V with two types of vertices. A non-terminal vertex has a label index*$(v) \in \{1, 2, \ldots, n\}$ *and two children low*(v) *and high*$(v) \in V$. *A terminal vertex has a label value*$(v) \in \{0, 1\}$. *Further, for any non-terminal vertex v, if low*(v) *(high*(v)*) is non-terminal, then* $index(low(v)) > index(v)$, $(index(high(v)) > index(v))$.

The function f represented by the decision diagram is defined as follows in a recursive manner.

Let $(x_1, \ldots, x_n) \in \{0, 1\}^n$ *and* $v \in V$. *The value of* $f(x_1, \ldots, x_n)$ *at* v, $f_v(x_1, \ldots, x_n)$ *is*

1 . $f_v(x_1, \ldots, x_n) = value(v)$ *if v is a terminal vertex,*

2 . $f_v(x_1, \ldots, x_n) = \overline{x}_{index(v)} f_{low(v)}(x_1, \ldots, x_n) + x_{index(v)} f_{high(v)}(x_1, \ldots, x_n)$ *and* $f(x_1, \ldots, x_n) = f_{root}(x_1, \ldots, x_n)$.

EXAMPLE 4.2 *Consider the following decision diagram.*

Vertex set (or node set) is $V = \{a, b, c, d, e\}$.

Edge set $E = \{(a, b), (a, c), (b, c), (b, e), (c, d), (c, e)\}$.

Non-terminal vertices are a, b, and c.

Terminal vertices are d and e.

The terminal vertices have labels $value(d) = 0$, $value(e) = 1$, *and the non-terminal vertices have the labels*

1 $index(a) = 1$, $low(a) = c$, $high(a) = b$,

2 $index(b) = 2$, $low(b) = c$, $high(b) = e$,

3 $index(c) = 3$, $low(c) = d$, $high(c) = e$.

Thus, the labels of the non-terminal vertices actually determine the structure of the graph and also the assignment of the variables to the vertices. Notice that the fact that a is the root is evident from either labels or the edge set. For instance, in the edge set, the root does not appear as the second component of any edge and the terminal vertices do not appear as the first component of any edge.

Let us consider the function f defined by this decision diagram. Let $(x_1, x_2, x_3) = (1, 0, 1)$, *then*

$$\begin{aligned} f(1,0,1) &= f_a(1,0,1) = \overline{1} \cdot f_c(1,0,1,) + 1 \cdot f_b(1,0,1) \\ &= 1 \cdot (\overline{0} \cdot f_c(1,0,1) + 0 \cdot f_e(1,0,1)) \\ &= 1 \cdot (1 \cdot (\overline{1} \cdot f_d(1,0,1) + 1 \cdot f_e(1,0,1))) \\ &= f_e(1,0,1) = value(e) = 1. \end{aligned}$$

We can also work backwards filling values of the function at each vertex

$$\begin{aligned} f_e(1,0,1) &= 1, \\ f_d(1,0,1) &= 0, \\ f_c(1,0,1) &= 0 \cdot f_d(1,0,1) + 1 \cdot f_e(1,0,1) = 1, \\ f_b(1,0,1) &= 1 \cdot f_c(1,0,1) + 0 \cdot f_e(1,0,1) = 1, \\ f_a(1,0,1) &= 0 \cdot f_c(1,0,1) + 1 \cdot f_b(1,0,1) = 1, \\ f(1,0,1) &= f_a(1,0,1) = 1. \end{aligned}$$

Of course, as the diagram is the same as in Fig. 4.2 in Example 4.1, all this is obvious just by a glance at the diagram.

For large functions and serious manipulation we need to represent the function/diagram in a computer.

A key property of ordered binary decision diagrams is that each switching function has a unique representation as a reduced BDD, where redundant nodes and edges have been removed. Thus, *Ordered Binary Decision Diagrams* form a canonic representation of switching functions. (A more rigorous discussion of reduction will be given later in this chapter).

Recall the Shannon expansion of a switching function

$$f = \overline{x}_i f_0 \oplus x_1 f_1,$$

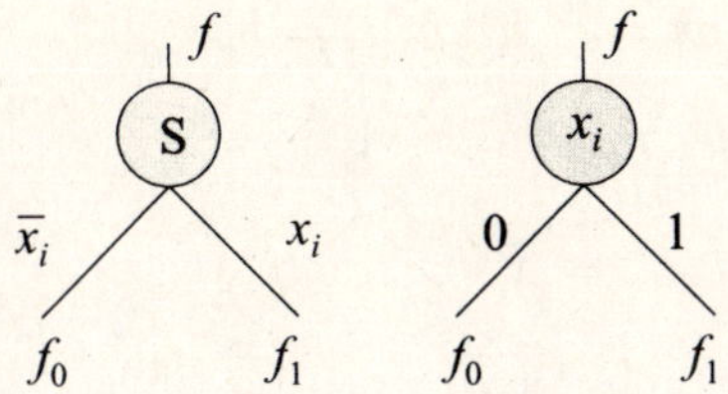

Figure 4.5. **Shannon node.**

where f_0 and f_1 are *cofactors* of f with respect to x_i. Fig. 4.5 shows graphic representation of the Shannon expansion which is called the Shannon (S) node. The outgoing edges can be alternatively labeled by $\overline{x}_i$ and x_i instead of 0 and 1, respectively. In this case, the node is denoted by the variable x_i that is called the decision variable assigned to the node.

Recursive application of the Shannon expression to all the variables in a given function f finally results in the complete disjunctive normal form. In the case of graphic representations, recursive application of the Shannon expansion can be represented by attaching non-terminal nodes to the outgoing edges of a node to represent cofactors pointed by the edges of the considered node. It is clear that the process of Example 4.1 and the way how function values are defined by a decision diagram correspond exactly to the Shannon expansion.

We read values that f takes at the 2^n possible assignments of logic values 0 and 1 to the binary variables $x_1, \ldots x_n$, by descending paths from the root node to the corresponding constant nodes [23].

EXAMPLE 4.3 *For functions of two variables $f(x_1, x_2)$ the application of the Shannon expansion with respect to x_1 produces*

$$f = \overline{x}_1 f_0 \oplus x_1 f_1.$$

The application of the same expansion with respect to x_2 yields the complete disjunctive normal form

$$\begin{aligned} f &= \overline{x}_2(\overline{x}_1 f_0 \oplus x_1 f_1) \oplus x_2(\overline{x}_1 f_0 \oplus x_1 f_1) \\ &= \overline{x}_2\overline{x}_1 f_{00} \oplus \overline{x}_2 x_1 f_{10} \oplus x_2\overline{x}_1 f_{01} \oplus x_1 x_2 f_{11}. \end{aligned}$$

Fig. 4.6 shows the graphic representation of this recursive application of the Shannon expansion to f, which is called the Binary decision tree, (BDT), for f [19].

The correspondence between the truth-table and the complete disjunctive normal form for a given function f is straightforward. The

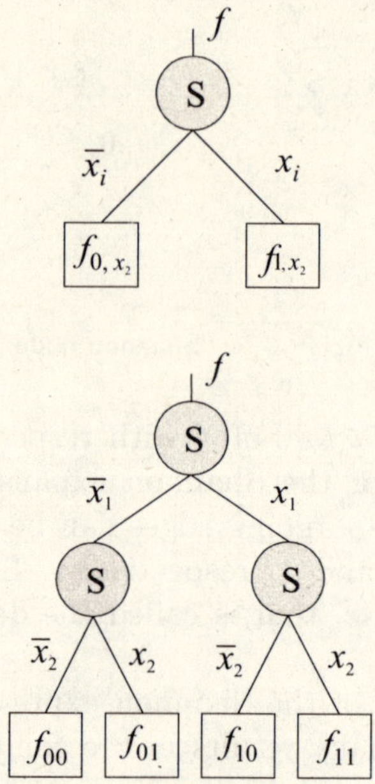

Figure 4.6. Binary decision tree for $n = 2$.

complete disjunctive normal form is an analytical description of the truth-table. Since a BDT is graphic representation of the complete disjunctive normal form, there is a direct correspondence between the truth-table and the BDT for f. Fig. 4.7 shows this correspondence for functions for $n = 3$ variables.

Notice that in the complete disjunctive normal form, the coefficients of the minterms are function values. In a BDT, each path from the root node corresponds to a minterm, which can be generated by multiplying labels at the edges in the path considered. Therefore, in a BDT, values of constant nodes are values of f at the corresponding minterms. Non-terminal nodes to which the same variable is assigned form a level in the BDT. Thus, the number of levels is equal to the number of variables. It follows that there is a direct correspondence between the truth-table for a given function f and the binary decision tree for f.

For this reason, we say that f is assigned to the BDT by the identity mapping which corresponds to the Shannon decomposition rule. However, we can as well use some other decomposition rule, but then the coefficients of the functional expressions are not function values, but something else. In fact, the constant nodes will be the spectral coefficients that correspond to the transform that is defined by the particular

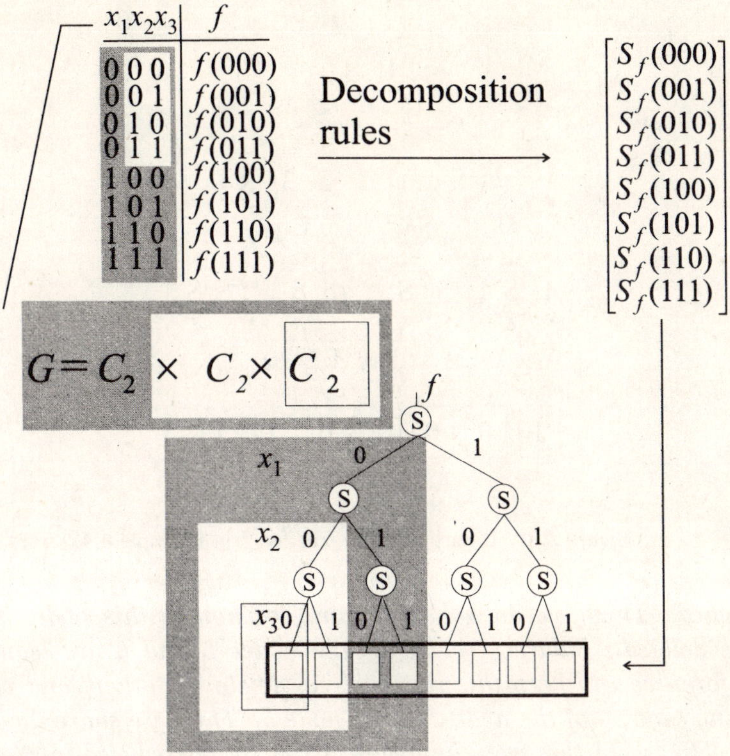

Figure 4.7. The correspondence between the truth-table and the BDT for $n = 3$.

decomposition rule applied. This will lead to spectral interpretation and a uniform treatment of decision diagrams and will be discussed below. Different decomposition rules produce different decision diagrams and e.g., in [175] there has been enumerated 48 essentially different types of decision diagrams.

EXAMPLE 4.4 *Fig. 4.8 shows the BDT for a function f for $n = 3$ given by the truth-vector $\mathbf{F} = [1, 0, 0, 1, 0, 1, 1, 1]^T$. For clarity the nodes are labelled by $1, \ldots, 7$. The paths from the root node to the constant nodes with the value 1, determine the minterms in the complete disjunctive normal form for f as*

$$f = \overline{x}_1\overline{x}_2\overline{x}_3 \oplus \overline{x}_1 x_2 x_3 \oplus x_1\overline{x}_2 x_3 \oplus x_1 x_2\overline{x}_3 \oplus x_1 x_2 x_3.$$

Conversely, this BDT represents f in the complete disjunctive normal form.

Notice that both outgoing edges of the node 7 points to the value 1. Therefore, whatever outgoing edge is selected, $\overline{x}_3$ or x_3 the same value

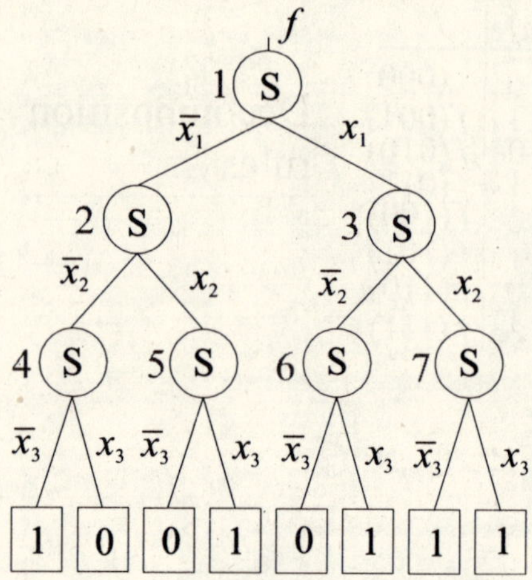

Figure 4.8. Binary decision tree for f in Example 4.4.

is reached. Thus, we do not make any decision in this node. Thus, it can be deleted. Subtrees rooted in the nodes 5 and 6 are isomorphic. Therefore, we can keep the first subtree, delete the other, and point the outgoing edge $\overline{x}_2$ of the node 3 to the node 5. Thus, we share the isomorphic subtrees. In this way, binary decision tree is reduced into a Binary decision diagram *(BDD) in Fig. 4.9. This BDD represents f in the form of a SOP*

$$f = \overline{x}_1\overline{x}_2\overline{x}_3 \oplus x_1x_2 \oplus \overline{x}_1x_2x_3 \oplus x_1\overline{x}_2x_3,$$

derived by using the property $x_1x_2\overline{x}_3 \oplus x_1x_2x_3 = x_1x_2$, *since* $\overline{x}_3 \oplus x_3 =$ 1. *Each product term corresponds to a path from the root node to the constant node with the value* 1.

The reduction of the number of nodes in a BDT described in the above example can be formalized as the *Binary decision diagrams reduction rules* (*BDD-reduction rules*) shown in Fig. 4.10. The reduction rules can be defined as follows.

DEFINITION 4.2 *(BDD reduction rules)*
In a Binary decision diagram,

1 *If two sub-graphs represent the same functions, delete one, and connect the edge to the remaining sub- graph.*

2 *If both edges of a node point to the same sub-graph, delete that node, and directly connect its edge to the sub-graph.*

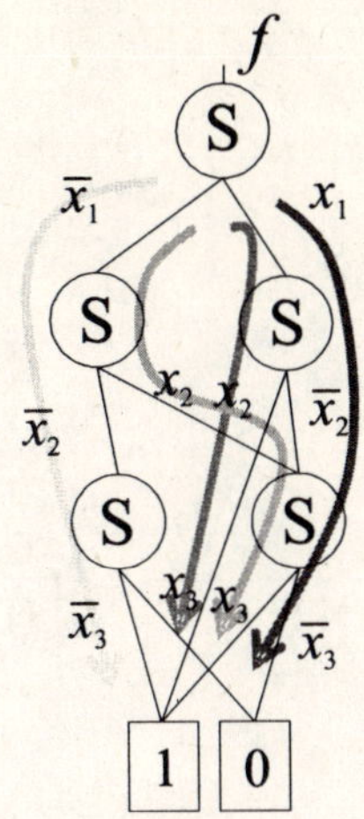

Figure 4.9. Binary decision diagram for f in Example 4.4.

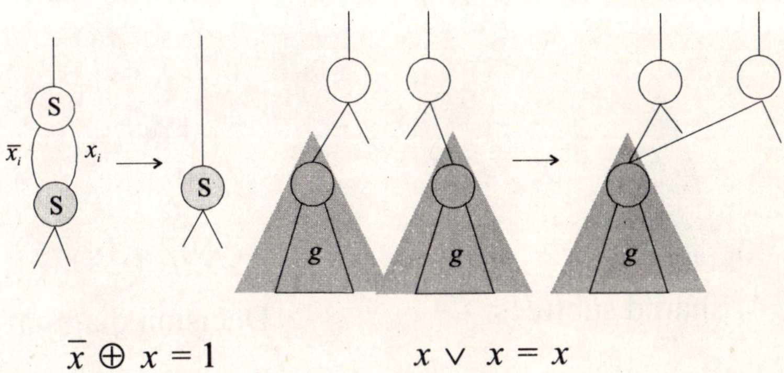

Figure 4.10. BDD-reduction rules.

EXAMPLE 4.5 *Fig. 4.11 shows reduction of a BDT for a function f given by the truth-vector* $\mathbf{F} = [0, 0, 0, 1, 1, 1, 0, 1]^T$ *into the BDD for* f.

2. Decision Diagrams over Groups

It is often useful to consider decision diagrams that have a more general structure, e.g., instead of branching into two directions, a node may have more children. Also, the values of the constant nodes can be arbitrary instead of binary or logic values 0 and 1.

Let G be a direct product of finite groups $G_1, \ldots, G_n$, where the order of G_i, $|G_i| = g_i$, $i = 1, \ldots, n$. Thus, G is also a finite group. Consider a

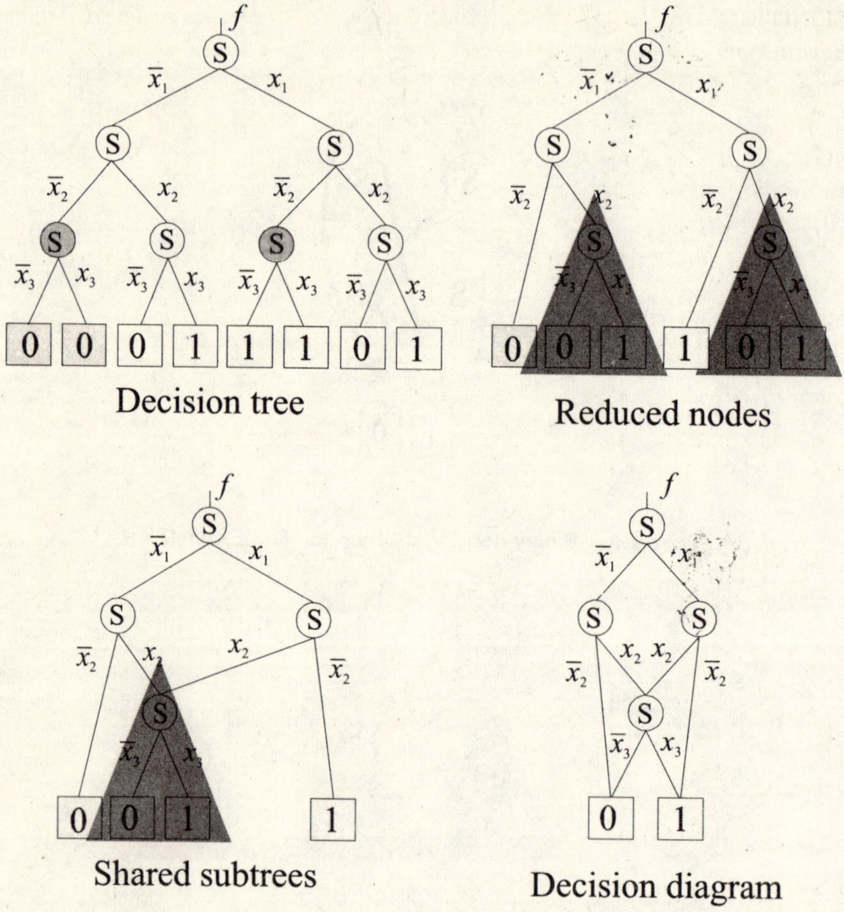

Figure 4.11. Reduction of the BDT into the BDD for f in Example 4.5.

function $f : G \to P$, where P is a field. Because

$$G = G_1 \times G_2 \times \cdots \times G_n,$$

we can write $f(x) = f(x_1, \ldots x_n)$, where $x_i \in G_i$. For each $i = 1, \ldots, n$, define (δ function) $\delta : G_i \to P$ by

$$\delta(x) = \begin{cases} 1 & \text{if } x = 0, \text{ the zero of } G_i, \\ 0 & \text{otherwise.} \end{cases}$$

To simplify the notation, we denote each function just by δ and the domain specifies which function is in question. We can define the more general concept of decision diagram in an analogous way.

DEFINITION 4.3 *Let G, P, f, and δ be as above. An ordered decision diagram over G is a rooted directed graph with two types of nodes. A non-terminal node has a label $index(v)$, and $g_{index(v)}$ children, $child(j,v)$, $j = 1,\ldots,g_{index(v)}$. Each edge $(v, child(j,v))$ has a distinct label $element(j,v) \in G_{index(v)}$. A terminal node has a label $value(v) \in P$. Further, for any non-terminal node v, if $child(i,v)$ is non-terminal, then $index(child(i,v)) > index(v)$.*

Again, the function f is represented by the decision diagram in a recursive manner as follows.

Let $(x_1,\ldots,x_n) \in G$ and $v \in V$. The value of f at v, $f_v(x_1,\ldots,x_n)$ is

1 If v is a terminal node, $f_v(x_1,\ldots,x_n) = value(v)$

2 If v is a non-terminal node,

$$f_v(x_1,\ldots,x_n) = \sum_{j=1}^{g_{index(v)}} \delta(x_{index(v)} - element(j,v)) f_{child(j,v)}(x_1,\ldots,x_n),$$

and $f(x_1,\ldots,x_n) = f_{root}(x_1,\ldots,x_n)$.

REMARK 4.1 *The recursion 2. is an exact generalization of the binary case, but because the variables take values in the domain groups G_i, the concept (label) $element(j,v)$ provides the correspondence between the elements of g_i and the outgoing edges of a node having the index i.*

REMARK 4.2 *In a decision diagram over a group $G = G_1 \times G_2 \times \cdots \times G_n$, the nodes on the level i (root being the level 1) correspond to the factor G_i in the sense that the elements of g_i correspond to the outgoing edges (decisions) of the nodes on the level i.*

EXAMPLE 4.6 *A three-variable switching function f is usually viewed as a function defined on C_2^3, in which case can be represented by the BDT as in Fig. 4.8. However,the same function can be viewed as a function defined on the groups $G = C_2 \times C_4$ and $G = C_4 \times C_2$. Fig. 4.12 shows the corresponding decision diagrams for f. It is obvious that change of the domain group for f results in diagrams of different structure.*

3. Construction of Decision Diagrams

A discrete function f can be specified in different ways, and there are procedures to construct a decision diagram for f by starting from almost any specification of f. We will illustrate this approach by the following example.

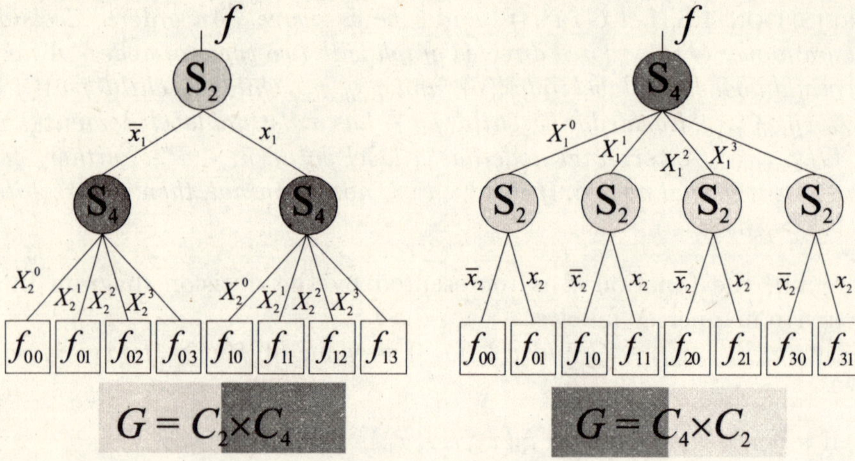

Figure 4.12. Binary decision trees of different structure.

EXAMPLE 4.7 *Consider BDD representation of a function f given by the disjunctive form*

$$f = x_1x_2 \vee x_3.$$

Let us first construct BDDs for the variables x_1 and x_2 and then perform logic AND over these diagrams. Thus, in the resulting diagram if $x_2 = 0$ the outgoing edge of the root node points to the logic values 0, which follows from the definition of logic AND. If $x_2 = 1$, we check what is the value for x_1. Then, we construct a BDD for x_3 and perform logic OR with the previously constructed BDD for x_1x_2. From definition of logic OR, if $x_3 = 1$, the outgoing edge pints to the logic 1, otherwise, it depends on x_1 and x_2. Fig. 4.13 illustrates construction of the BDD for f.

In general, consider the functions f and g and $h = f \odot g$ where $\odot$ is a binary operation such as AND or OR. The construction of the BDD for h is again done recursively. Let x be one of the variables. It is easy to see that

$$f \odot g = x(f_1 \odot g_1) \oplus \overline{x}(f_0 \odot g_0),$$

where f_1, f_0, g_1, and g_0 are the cofactors of f and g with respect to the variable x.

EXAMPLE 4.8 *Consider the function $f(x,y,z) = xy \vee xz \vee yz$. We can write*

$$f(x,y,z) = x(y \vee z) \vee \overline{x}(yz) = xf_1 \vee \overline{x}f_0.$$

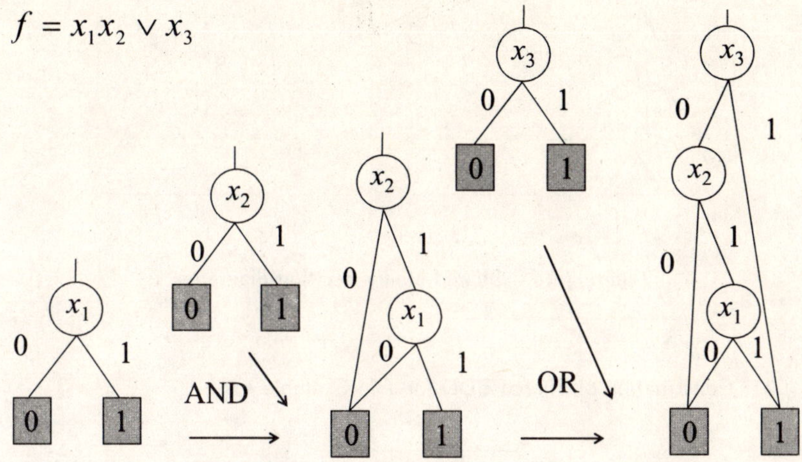

Figure 4.13. Construction of the BDD for f in Example 4.7.

Fig. 4.14 shows construction of the BDDs for the cofactors f_1 and f_0 and finally the BDD for f.

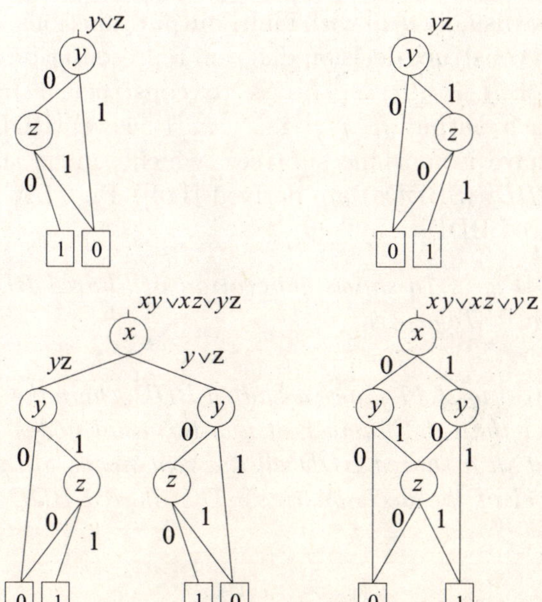

Figure 4.14. Construction of the BDD for f in Example 4.8.

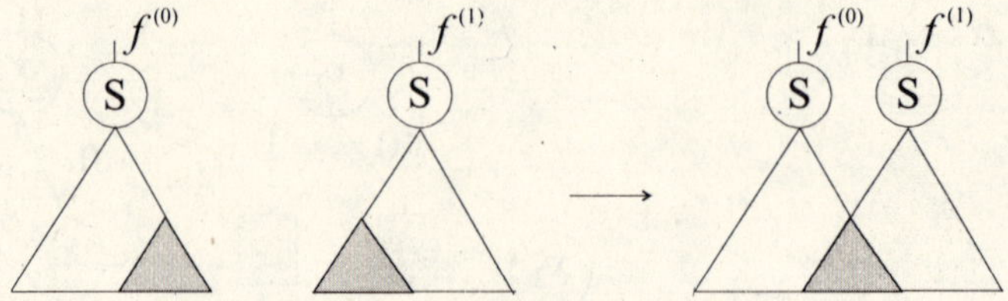

Figure 4.15. Shared binary decision diagrams.

Table 4.1. Construction of Shared BDD for f in Example 4.9.

	x_1x_2	f_0	f_1
0.	00	0	0
1.	01	0	1
2.	10	1	0
3.	11	1	0

4. Shared Decision Diagrams

In practice we usually deal with multi-output functions, and a straightforward way to construct decision diagram representation for a multiple-output function $f = (f_1, \ldots, f_k)$ is to construct a binary decision diagram for each output f_i, $i = 1, \ldots, k$. However, BDDs for different outputs may have isomorphic subtrees, which can be shared. In this way, *Shared BDDs* (SBDDs) are derived [114]. Fig. 4.15 illustrates the concept of shared BDDs.

EXAMPLE 4.9 *Fig. 4.16 shows generation of Shared BDDs for a two-output function in Table 4.1.*

EXAMPLE 4.10 *Fig. 4.17 shows a Shared BDD where the number of root nodes is greater than the number of non-terminal nodes. This example also shows that in a shared BDD all the root nodes are not necessarily at the first level of the decision tree. The Shared BDD represents the functions*

$$\begin{aligned} f_1 &= \overline{x}_1 x_2, \\ f_2 &= x_1 \oplus x_2, \\ f_3 &= \overline{x}_2, \\ f_4 &= x_1 \vee \overline{x}_2. \end{aligned}$$

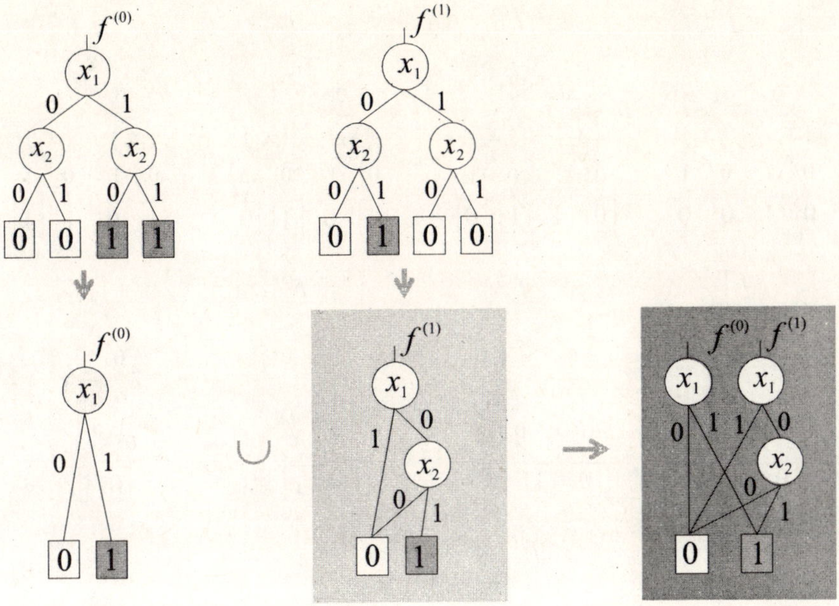

Figure 4.16. Construction of Shared BDD for f in Example 4.9.

5. Multi-terminal binary decision diagrams

BDDs and Shared BDDs are used to represent functions taking logic values. *Multi-terminal binary decision diagrams* (MTBDDs) [27] have been introduced to represent integer valued functions on C_2^n. Generalizations to functions defined on other finite groups is straightforward. For instance, a multiple-output function $f = (f_0, \ldots, f_k)$ can be represented by an integer-valued function f_z determined by summing the outputs f_i multiplied by 2^i. Then, f_z can be represented by a MTBDD instead of SBDD.

EXAMPLE 4.11 *Table 4.2 and Fig. 4.18 show a function* $f = (f_0, f_1)$, *and its representation by a Multi-terminal binary decision tree (MTBDT), reduced into the corresponding diagram (MTBDD), and a SBDD.*

6. Functional Decision Diagrams

Both BDDs and MTBDDs are decision diagrams defined with respect to the Shannon expansion rule. The difference is in the values of constant nodes and the interpretation of the values for variables in the functions represented. We can interpret BDDs and MTBDDs as decision diagrams defined with respect to the Shannon expansion over the finite field of

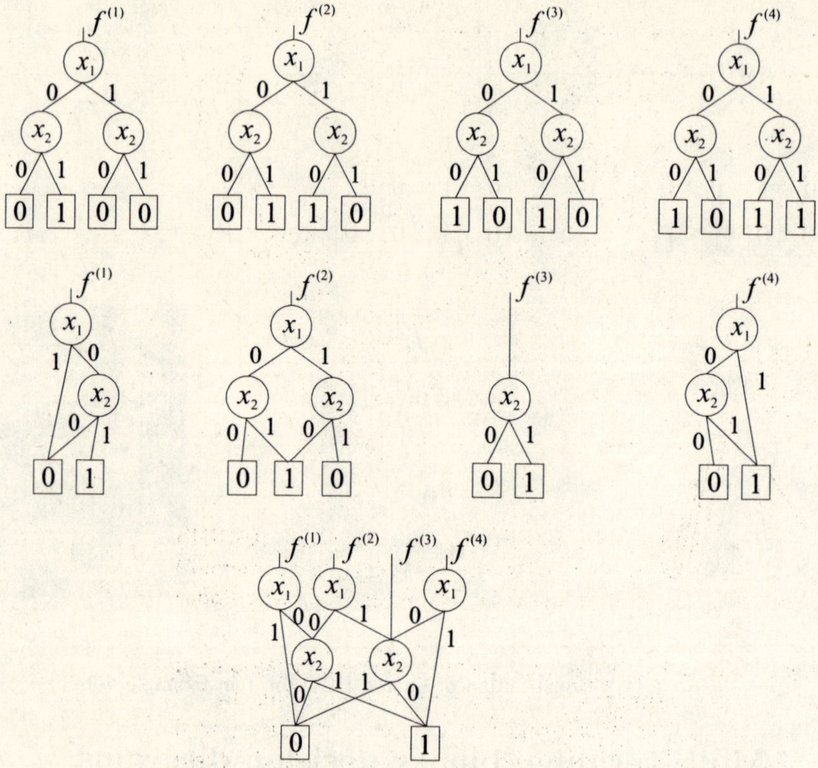

Figure 4.17. Shared BDD for functions f_1, f_2, f_3, and f_4 in Example 4.10.

Table 4.2. Representation of f in Example 4.11.

x_1, x_2	f_0	f_1	f_z
00	0	0	0
01	0	1	1
10	1	0	2
11	1	0	2

order 2 or the field of rational numbers as

$$f = \overline{x}_i f_0 \oplus x_1 f_1,$$

or

$$f = \overline{x}_i f_0 + x_i f_1,$$

where $\overline{x}_i = 1 \oplus x_i$ and $\overline{x}_i = 1 - x_i$, respectively.

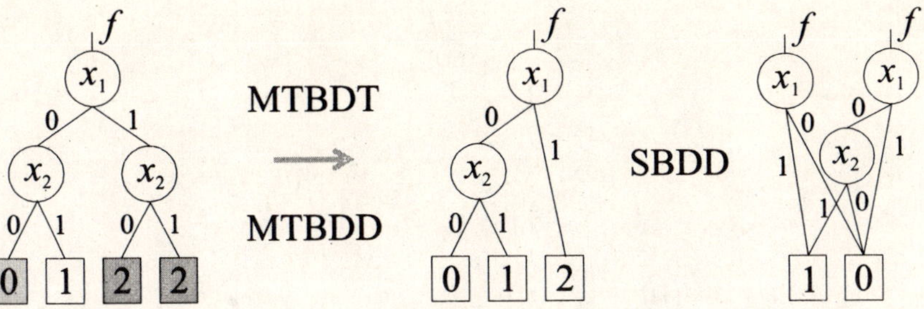

Figure 4.18. MTBDT, MTBDD, and SBDD in Example 4.11.

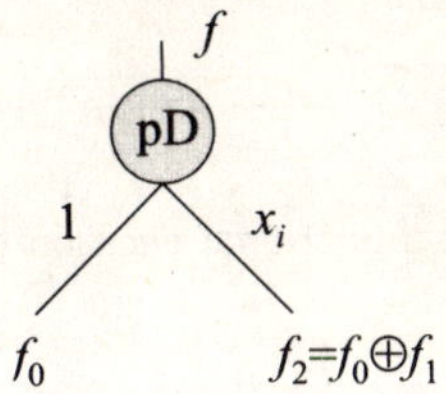

Figure 4.19. Positive Davio node.

For some functions, BDDs and MTBDDs have a large number of non-terminal nodes. However, with respect to some other decomposition rule, the number of nodes may be smaller and for that reason, decision diagrams defined with respect to various decomposition rules have been defined. In [175], 48 essentially different decision diagrams have been enumerated. We will introduce here the *Functional decision diagrams* (FDDs) which are the first extension of the notion of BDDs in this respect and have been introduced in [80]. FDDs are defined in terms of the positive Davio (pD) expansion $f = 1 \cdot f_0 \oplus x_i(f_0 \oplus f_1)$ whose graphic representation is the positive Davio (pD) node shown in Fig. 4.19. A FDT is defined as a decision tree which represents a given function f in terms of a Positive-polarity Reed-Muller (PPRM) expression. Thus, a FDT is a graphic representation of the recursive application of the pD-expansion to f and the values of constant nodes in a FDT are the Reed-Muller coefficients for f. In this way a FDT represents f in the form of the PPRM-expression. In contrast to a BDD, edges in a FDT are labeled by 1 and x_i, as follows from the pD-expansion rule, since 1 and x_i are assigned to f_0 and $f_2 = f_0 \oplus f_1$ to which the outgoing edges of a node point.

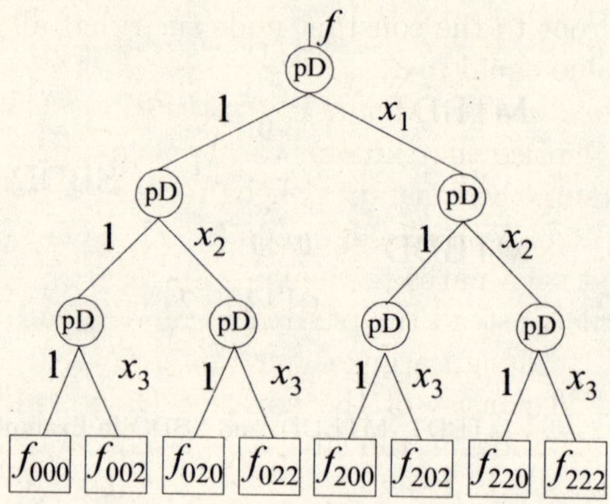

Figure 4.20. Functional decision tree for $n = 3$.

EXAMPLE 4.12 *Consider a switching function $f(x_1, x_2, x_3)$. It can be decomposed by the positive Davio expansion with respect to x_1 as*

$$f = 1 \cdot f_0 \oplus x_1(f_0 \oplus f_1) = 1 \cdot f_0 \oplus x_1 f_2.$$

Application of pD-expansion to cofactors f_0 and f_1 produces

$$\begin{aligned} f_0 &= 1 \cdot f_{00} \oplus x_2 f_{02}, \\ f_1 &= 1 \cdot f_{20} \oplus x_2 f_{22}, \end{aligned}$$

which results in positive polarity Reed-Muller expression for f

$$\begin{aligned} f &= 1 \cdot (1 \cdot f_{00} \oplus x_2 f_{02}) \oplus x_2(1 \cdot f_{20} \oplus f_{22}) \\ &= 1 \cdot f_{00} \oplus x_2 f_{02} \oplus x_1 f_{20} \oplus x_1 x_2 f_{22}. \end{aligned}$$

Fig. 4.20 shows a graphic representation of this functional expression which is called the Functional decision tree (FDT) for f.

Consider the functional decision tree for $f(x_1,x_2,x_3)$ shown in Fig. 4.20. The constant nodes are coefficients of the Positive-polarity Reed-Muller expression, i.e., the values of the Reed-Muller spectrum of $f(x_1, x_2, x_3)$. Thus, the FDT is the BDT of the Reed-Muller spectrum. Since the matrix of the Reed-Muller transform is self-inverse over $GF(2)$, the same relation holds also in the opposite direction, i.e., the BDT of f is the FDT for the Reed-Muller spectrum of f.

Notice that in FDT for fixed values of the variables $x_1, x_2, \ldots, x_n$, to find the value of the function one just sums the constant nodes that have a path from the root to the constant node such that all edges along the path have the value equal to 1.

A *functional decision diagram* (FDD) is obtained from a FDT by the reduction rules. Notice that, in this case, to compute the value of the function we just sum the constant nodes that have a path from the root to the constant node with all edges equal to 1, each as many times as there are different such paths to the node.

It is obvious that instead the pD-expansion, the negative-Davio rules can be also used to assign a given function f to a decision tree. This decision tree would consist of the negative Davio (nD) nodes, which differs from the pD-nodes in the label at the right outgoing edge, which is $\overline{x}_i$ instead of x_i.

EXAMPLE 4.13 *Consider the function* $f(x_1, x_2, x_3) = x_1x_2 \vee x_3$. *We can transfer it to Positive-polarity Reed-Muller form by the relation* $a \vee b = a \oplus b \oplus ab$ *giving*

$$f(x_1, x_2, x_3) = x_3 \oplus x_1x_2 \oplus x_1x_2x_3,$$

resulting in the FDD in Fig. 4.21.

We can write the Negative-polarity Reed-Muller form by using the relations $a = (1 \oplus \overline{a})$, $a \vee b = a \oplus b \oplus ab$, *giving*

$$\begin{aligned} f(x_1, x_2, x_3) &= (1 \oplus \overline{x}_1)(1 \oplus \overline{x}_2) \oplus (1 \oplus \overline{x}_3) \\ &\quad \oplus (1 \oplus \overline{x}_1)(1 \oplus \overline{x}_2)(1 \oplus \overline{x}_3) \\ &= 1 \oplus \overline{x}_2\overline{x}_3 \oplus \overline{x}_1\overline{x}_3 \oplus \overline{x}_1\overline{x}_2\overline{x}_3, \end{aligned}$$

resulting in the FDD in Fig. 4.22.

This example shows that choice of different decomposition rules produces FDDs with different number of nodes.

Depending on the properties of the function represented, a Functional decision tree reduces to a Functional decision diagram in the same way as a BDT reduces to a BDD. However, because of the expansion rules, and the properties of related Boolean expressions, some additional reduction rules for the positive Davio expansion have been defined in [112]. These rules utilize the fact that when the outgoing edge of a pD-node points to the value 0, this node can be deleted since the 0-value does not contribute to the PPRM-expression. As in the BDD reduction rules, isomorphic subtrees can be shared also in FDDs. These rules are called the *zero-suppressed BDD* (*ZBDD reduction rules*). They can be defined as follows.

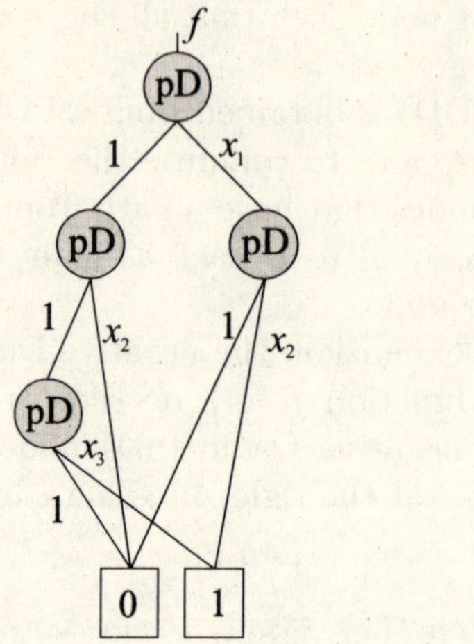

Figure 4.21. Positive-polarity FDD for f in Example 4.13.

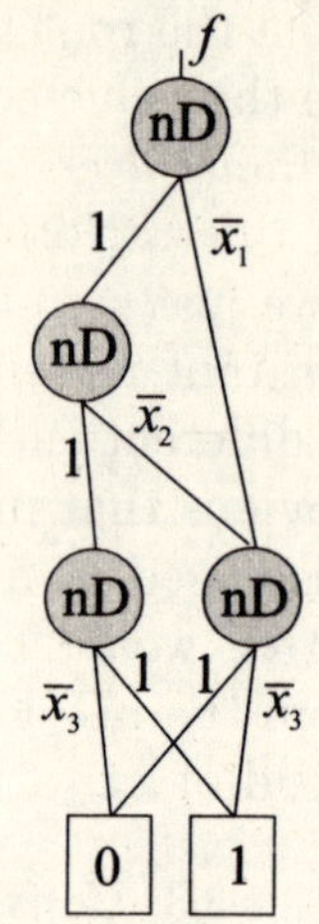

Figure 4.22. Negative-polarity FDD for f in Example 4.13.

DEFINITION 4.4 *(ZBDD-reduction rules)*
In a decision diagrams having Davio nodes

1 *Eliminate all the nodes whose one-edge points to the zero-terminal node, then connect the edge to the other subgraph directly.*

2 *Share all equivalent subgraphs.*

Fig. 4.23 shows BDD (*a*) and (*b*) and ZBDD reduction rules (*b*) and (*c*).

EXAMPLE 4.14 *Fig . 4.24 shows a FDT reduced by the BDD and ZBDD reduction rules. Both decision diagrams represent f in the form of the expression* $f = x_3 \oplus x_1x_3 \oplus x_1x_2$, *as can be determined by multiplying labels at the edges in all the paths from the root node to the constant nodes showing the value* 1.

7. Kronecker decision diagrams

The main idea in Functional decision diagrams is to exploit fact that for some functions the Reed-Muller spectrum gives more compact decision diagrams in the number of non-terminal nodes than the original function itself. The same idea can be further extended by defining *Kronecker decision diagrams* (KDDs) where a different decomposition rule, the Shannon, positive Davio or negative Davio rule, can be assigned to each variable in the function represented. Thus, a Kronecker decision

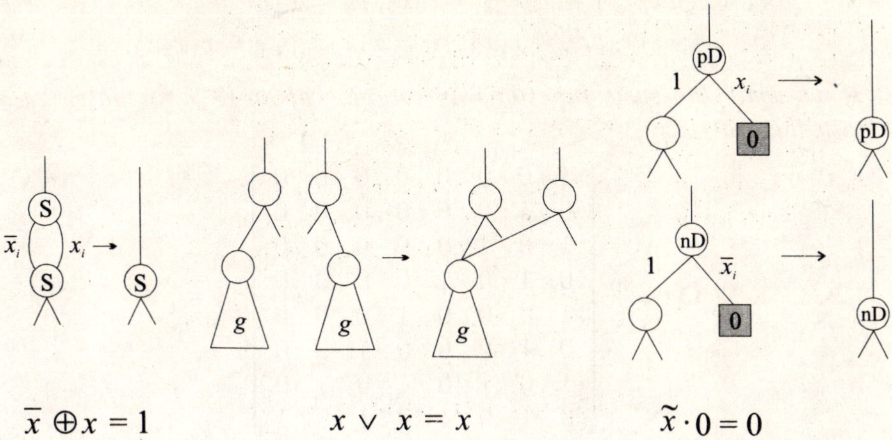

Figure 4.23. BDD and ZBDD reduction rules.

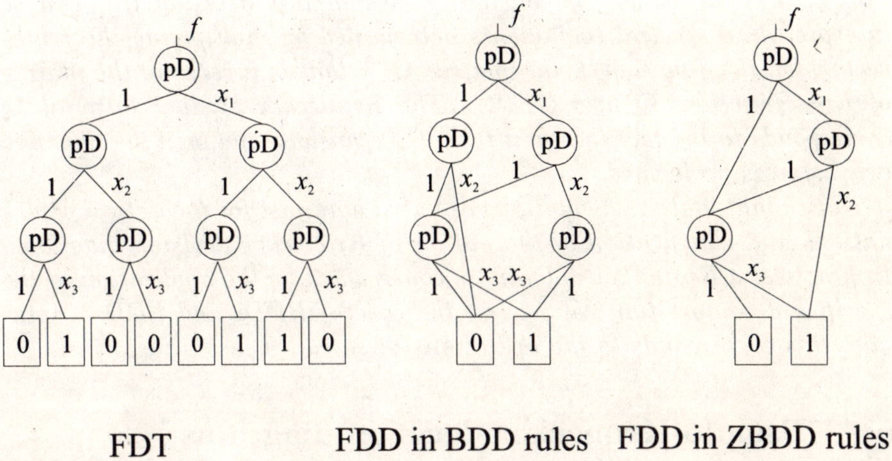

Figure 4.24. FBDT, and FDDs derived by BDD and ZBDD reduction rules for f in Example 4.14.

diagrams is completely specified by a *Decision Type List* (DTL) enumerating decomposition rules per levels in the diagram.

EXAMPLE 4.15 *Fig. 4.25 shows a Kronecker decision diagram for* $n = 3$ *defined by the DTL = (pD,pD,S). This decision diagram can be viewed as graphic representation of a functional expression in terms of basis functions.*

$$\begin{aligned}\varphi_0 &= \overline{x}_3, \varphi_1 = x_3, \varphi_2 = x_2\overline{x}_3, \varphi_3 = x_2x_3, \\ \varphi_4 &= x_1\overline{x}_3, \varphi_5 = x_1x_3, \varphi_6 = x_1x_2\overline{x}_3, \varphi_7 = x_1x_2x_3.\end{aligned}$$

If we write the basis functions as columns of an (8×8) *matrix, we obtain the matrix*

$$\mathbf{Q} = \begin{bmatrix} 1 & 0 & 0 & 0 & 0 & 0 & 0 & 0 \\ 0 & 1 & 0 & 0 & 0 & 0 & 0 & 0 \\ 1 & 0 & 1 & 0 & 0 & 0 & 0 & 0 \\ 0 & 1 & 0 & 1 & 0 & 0 & 0 & 0 \\ 1 & 0 & 0 & 0 & 1 & 0 & 0 & 0 \\ 0 & 1 & 0 & 0 & 0 & 1 & 0 & 0 \\ 1 & 0 & 1 & 0 & 1 & 0 & 1 & 0 \\ 0 & 1 & 0 & 1 & 0 & 1 & 0 & 1 \end{bmatrix} = \begin{bmatrix} 1 & 0 \\ 1 & 1 \end{bmatrix} \otimes \begin{bmatrix} 1 & 0 \\ 1 & 1 \end{bmatrix} \otimes \begin{bmatrix} 1 & 0 \\ 0 & 1 \end{bmatrix}.$$

On the other hand, the function is represented by the decision tree in Fig. 4.25. The values of constant nodes in this decision tree can be interpreted as spectral coefficients determined by multiplying the truth-vector for the function f *the matrix* $\mathbf{Q}^{-1}$ *that is inverse of the matrix of basis functions* $\mathbf{Q}$ *over* $GF(2)$*. The Kronecker product form of* $\mathbf{Q}$ *corresponds to the fact that first two pD-expansions and then the Shannon expansion is performed.*

Notice that matrix calculations are used here just for theoretical explanations and clarification of the notion of Kronecker decision diagrams. In practice, a Kronecker diagram is constructed by the application of the specified decomposition rules as in the case of BDDs and FDDs. Actually, this corresponds to the operations of so-called fast transforms.

8. Pseudo-Kronecker decision diagrams

A further extension of the decision diagrams is achieved by allowing to freely chose a decomposition rule from the set of nodes $\{S, pD, nD\}$ for each node in the decision diagram irrespective of the other nodes at the same level in the diagram. Such decision diagrams are called *Pseudo-Kronecker decision diagrams* (PKDDs) [158]. They are completely defined by specifying the assignment of decomposition rules to the nodes, which can be conveniently performed by establishing an *Extended Decision Type List* (ExtDTL) whose rows show assignment of decomposition rules to the nodes per levels. Notice that while compact representations are obtained, all regularity is lost.

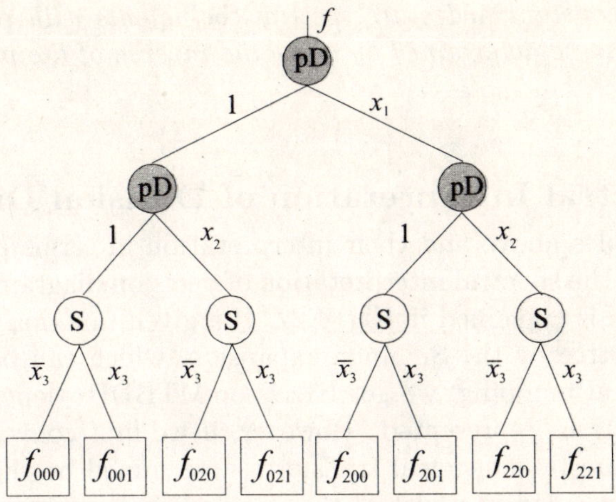

Figure 4.25. Kronecker decision diagram for the function f in Example 4.15.

EXAMPLE 4.16 *Fig. 4.26 shows a Pseudo-Kronecker decision tree for a function given by the truth-vector* $\mathbf{F} = [0,1,1,0,1,1,0,1]^T$, *and its reduction into the corresponding decision diagram by using both BDD and zero-suppressed BDD reduction rules, depending on the meaning of nodes. This diagram is specified by the ExtDTL*

Level	Decomposition rule			
1	S			
2	pD	nD		
3	S	pD	nD	S

In this Pseduo-Kronecker decision diagram, paths from the root node to the constant nodes determine basis functions

$$\begin{aligned}
\varphi_0 &= \overline{x}_1\overline{x}_3, \varphi_1 = \overline{x}_1 x_3, \varphi_2 = \overline{x}_1 x_2, \varphi_3 = \overline{x}_1 x_2 x_3, \\
\varphi_4 &= x_1, \varphi_5 = x_1\overline{x}_3, \varphi_6 = x_1\overline{x}_2\overline{x}_3, \varphi_7 = x_1\overline{x}_2 x_3.
\end{aligned}$$

In matrix notation, these basis functions are given by the (8×8) *matrix*

$$\mathbf{Q} = \begin{bmatrix}
1 & 0 & 0 & 0 & 0 & 0 & 0 & 0 \\
0 & 1 & 0 & 0 & 0 & 0 & 0 & 0 \\
1 & 0 & 1 & 0 & 0 & 0 & 0 & 0 \\
0 & 1 & 1 & 1 & 0 & 0 & 0 & 0 \\
0 & 0 & 0 & 0 & 1 & 1 & 1 & 0 \\
0 & 0 & 0 & 0 & 1 & 0 & 0 & 1 \\
0 & 0 & 0 & 0 & 1 & 1 & 0 & 0 \\
0 & 0 & 0 & 0 & 1 & 0 & 0 & 0
\end{bmatrix}.$$

Values of constant nodes are spectral coefficients with respect to this basis, thus, can be determined by using the inverse of the matrix $\mathbf{Q}$ *over* $GF(2)$.

9. Spectral Interpretation of Decision Diagrams

The examples above and their interpretation in terms of basis functions yield to the spectral interpretation of decision diagrams [175]. This interpretation is explained in Fig. 4.27. If a given function f is assigned to a decision tree by the Shannon expansion, which can be interpreted as the identical mapping, we get BDDs or MTBDDs depending on the range of functions represented. However, if we first convert a function into a spectrum by a spectral transform determined by the decomposition rules performed in nodes of the decision tree, and then assign the spectrum S_f by the identical mapping to the decision tree, we get a *Spectral transform decision tree* (STDT). In STDTs, the values of constant nodes are the spectral coefficients, and the labels at the edges are determined by the decomposition rules such that they give the inverse transform to determine function values from the spectral coefficients. Therefore, from a STDT, if we follow labels at the edges by starting from constant nodes, we read f by calculation the inverse expansion of the function. However, if we formally replace labels at the edges by these used in Shannon nodes, we can read the spectrum of f from a STDT. This would be the spectrum of f with respect to the transform used in definition of the STDT. However, the same approach can be used in the opposite direction to calculate spectral transforms over BDTs and MTBDTs. Since constant nodes in these decision diagrams show function values for f, we can compute the spectrum S_f by performing at each node calculations determined by the basic transform matrix in a Kronecker product representable spectral transform. In BDDs and MTBDDs, this means replacement of labels at the edges by the ones that are used in the corresponding spectral transform decomposition rules and then reading the spectrum by traversing paths in the diagram starting from constant nodes.

9.1 Spectral transform decision diagrams

In this section, we will discuss two examples of spectral transform decision diagrams where values of constant nodes are in the field of rational numbers. Also, the operations are done over the rationals, e.g., $\overline{x} = 1 - x$, etc. Such decision diagrams are called the word-level decision diagrams, unlike bit-level decision diagrams where constant nodes have logic values 0 and 1.

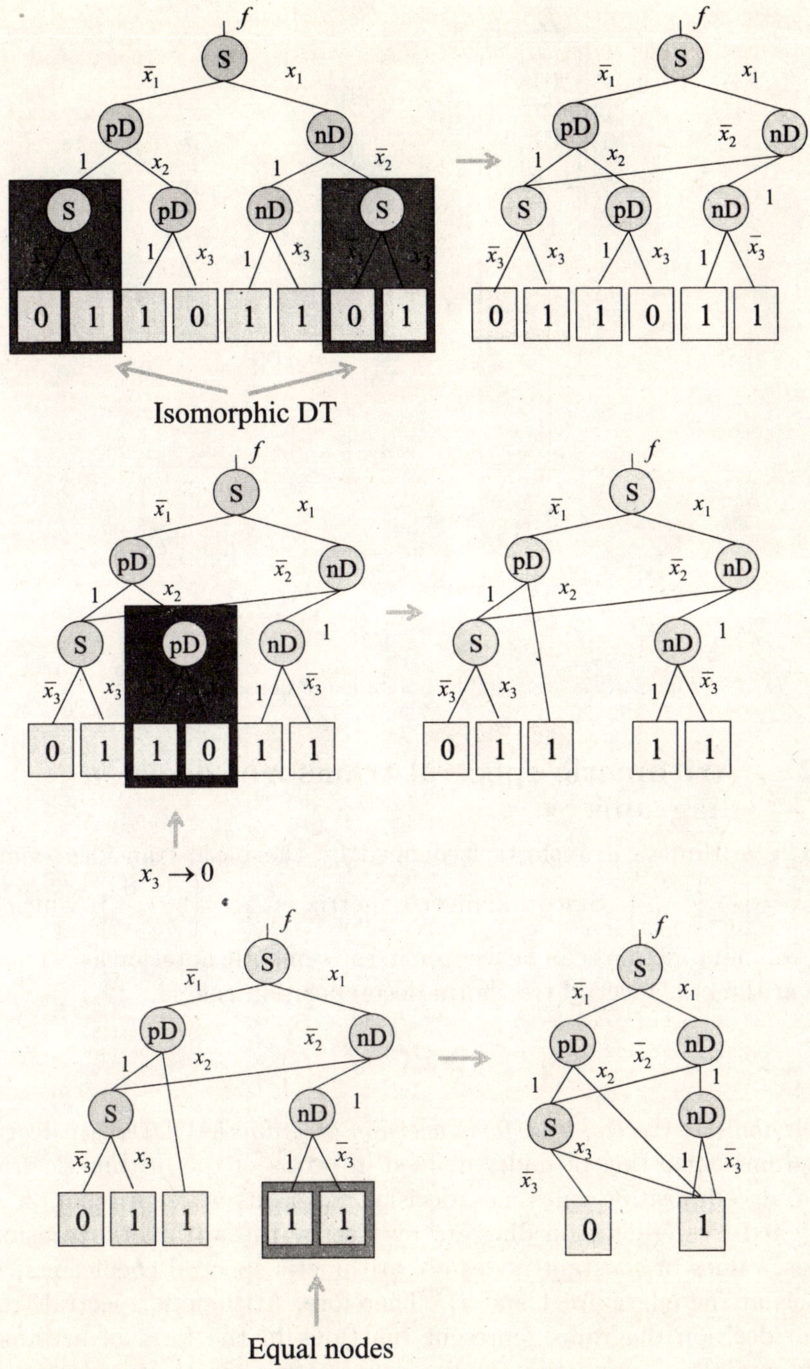

Figure 4.26. Pesudo-Kronecker decision tree and its reduction into the corresponding diagram for the function f in Example 4.16.

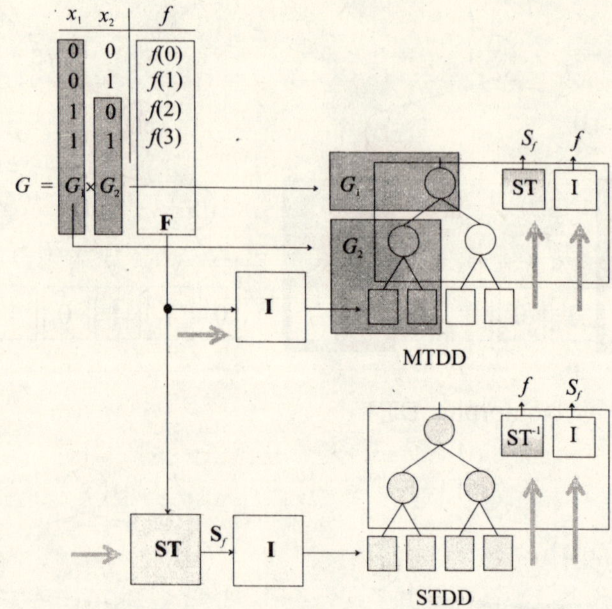

Figure 4.27. Spectral interpretation of decision diagrams.

9.2 Arithmetic spectral transform decision diagrams

The arithmetic transform is defined by the basic transform matrix $\mathbf{A}^{-1} = \begin{bmatrix} 1 & 0 \\ -1 & 1 \end{bmatrix}$. Since the inverse matrix is $\mathbf{A} = \begin{bmatrix} 1 & 0 \\ 1 & 1 \end{bmatrix}$, which using column functions can be written in the symbolic notation as $\begin{bmatrix} 1 & x_i \end{bmatrix}$, the arithmetic spectral transform decomposition rule is

$$f = 1 \cdot f_0 + x_i(-f_0 + f_1).$$

Arithmetic spectral transform decision diagrams (ACDDs) are decision diagrams consisting of nodes defined in terms of the arithmetic transform decomposition rules, i.e., decision diagrams where a function f is assigned to the decision diagram by tree by the arithmetic transform. Thus, values of constant nodes are arithmetic spectral coefficients, and labels at the edges are 1 and x_i. Therefore, Arithmetic spectral transform decision diagrams represent functions in the form of arithmetic polynomials. Notice that in literature there are at least four other decision diagrams that exploit arithmetic transform coefficients to assign a function to a decision tree [173], [175]. These are *Edge-valued binary*

Table 4.3. Function $f = (f_0, f_1)$ in Example 4.17.

	x_0, y_0	f_0	f_1
0.	00	0	0
1.	01	0	1
2.	10	0	1
3.	11	1	0

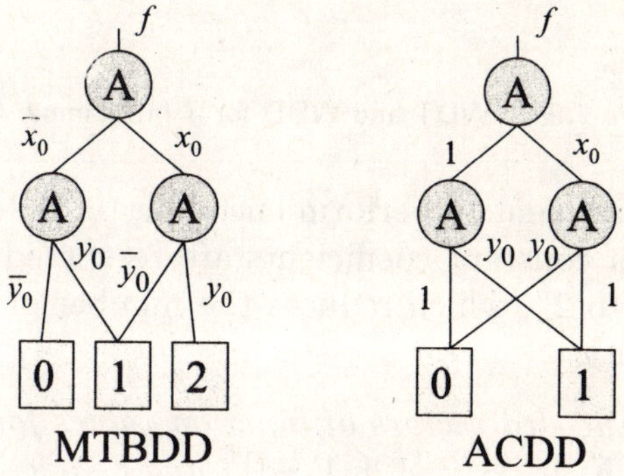

Figure 4.28. MTBDD and ACDD for f in Example 4.17.

decision diagrams (EVBDDs) [93], [92], *Factored EVBDDs* [198], *Binary moment diagrams* (BMDs), and their edge-valued version $*$BMD [20], [25].

EXAMPLE 4.17 *Table 4.3 shows a function $f(x_0, y_0) = (f_0, f_1)$ specifying the half-bit adder. Thus, $f_0(x_0, y_0) = x_0 \oplus y_0$, and $f_1(x_0, y_0) = x_0 y_0$. This function f can be converted into the equivalent integer-valued function $f_z = 2f_1 + f_0$ given by the vector $\mathbf{F}_z = [0, 1, 1, 2]^T$. The arithmetic spectrum of f_z is $\mathbf{A}_z = [0, 1, 1, 0]^T$.*

Fig. 4.28 shows MTBDD and ACDD defined by using $\mathbf{F}_z$ and $\mathbf{A}_f$ as vectors of constant nodes, respectively.

9.3 Walsh decision diagrams

Walsh decision diagrams (WDDs) are defined in terms of the Walsh expansion rule $f = -\frac{1}{2}(f_0 + f_1) + (1 - 2x_i)(f_0 - f_1)$ derived from the basic Walsh matrix $\mathbf{W}(1) = \begin{bmatrix} 1 & 1 \\ 1 & -1 \end{bmatrix}$ in the same way as above for the Arithmetic transform. If WDDs are used to represent binary valued

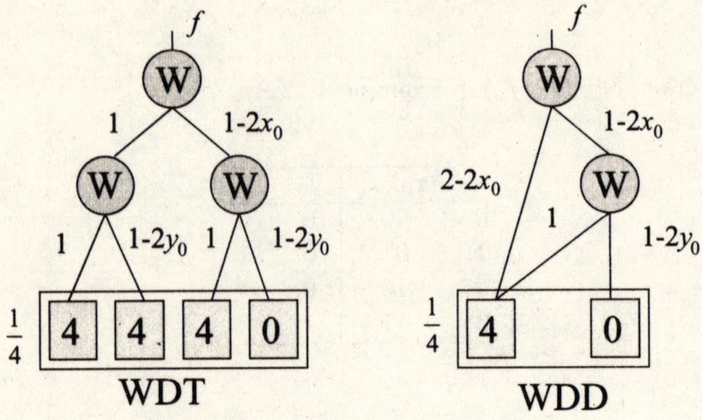

Figure 4.29. WDT and WDD for f in Example 4.17.

functions, it is convenient to perform encoding $(0,1) \to (1,-1)$, since in this case, values of constant coefficients are restricted to even numbers in the range -2^n to 2^n, which reduces the number of possible different constant coefficients.

EXAMPLE 4.18 *Encoded vectors of function values for* f_0 *and* f_1 *in the above example are* $\mathbf{F}_{0,(1,-1)} = [1,1,1,-1]^T$ *and* $\mathbf{F}_{1,(1,-1)} = [1,-1,-1,1]^T$, *whose Walsh transforms are* $\mathbf{W}_{f_{0,(1,-1)}} = \frac{1}{4}[2,2,2,-2]^T$ *and* $\mathbf{W}_{1,(1,-1)} = \frac{1}{4}[0,0,0,4]^T$. *Due to the linearity of the Walsh transform, the Walsh spectrum of* f_z *is* $\mathbf{W}_{f_z} = 2\mathbf{W}_{f_{1,(1,-1)}} + \mathbf{W}_{f_{0,(1,-1)}} = 2[2,2,2,-2]\ T + [0,0,0,4]^T = [4,4,4,0]^T$.

Fig. 4.29 shows WDT and WDD for the function f *in this example. Attention should be paid to the labels at the edges in this WDD, and for instance to the label at the left outgoing edge of the root node. It is determined as the sum of the outgoing edges of the left node at the level for* y_0 *multiplied by the label at the incoming edge to this node. This node can be deleted since both outgoing edges point to the same value 4, however, its impact has to be taken into account by changing the label at the incoming edge as described above.*

The example of WDDs shows that in the general case, the reduction rules for word-level decision diagrams should be modified compared to the BDD reduction rules, since relations involving binary-valued variables and constants 0 and 1 that are used in BDD and zero-suppressed reduction rules cannot be always used for various decomposition rules used in definition of STDDs. Fig. 4.30 shows the generalized BDD reduction rules which can be used for both bit-level and word-level decision diagrams, since they include the BDD reduction rules as a particular case.

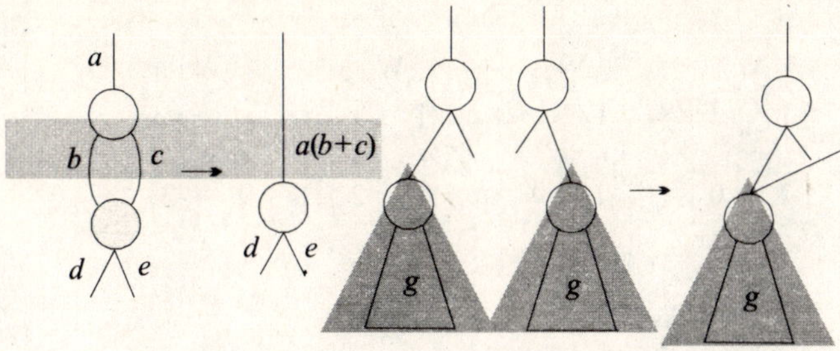

Figure 4.30. Generalized BDD reduction rules.

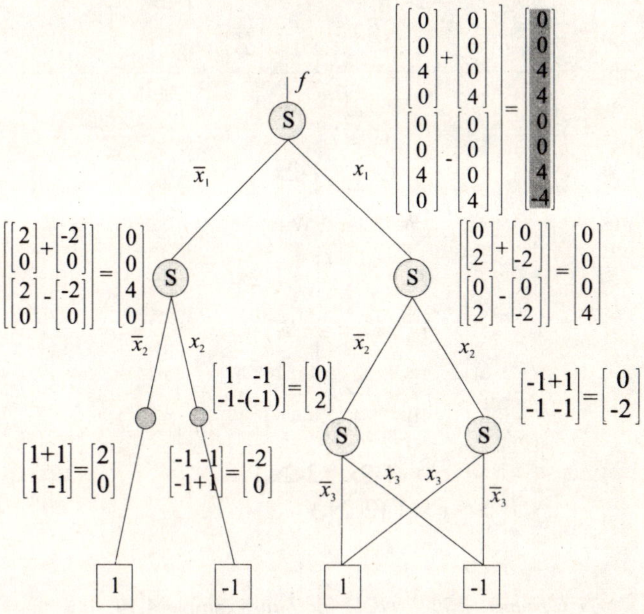

Figure 4.31. Calculation of the Walsh spectrum for f in Example 4.19.

The following example illustrates and explains the calculation of Walsh spectrum over a MTBDD, and the representation of a Walsh spectrum by a WDD. The method can be considered as a conversion of a MTBDD into a WDD.

EXAMPLE 4.19 *Consider the function* $f = \overline{x}_1 x_2 \oplus x_1 \overline{x}_2 x_3 \oplus x_1 x_2 \overline{x}_3$. *Fig. 4.31 shows a MTBDD for this function in* $(1, -1)$ *encoding with cross points indicated. If at each node and cross point the calculations determined by the basic Walsh matrix* $\mathbf{W}(1) = \begin{bmatrix} 1 & 1 \\ 1 & -1 \end{bmatrix}$ *are performed,*

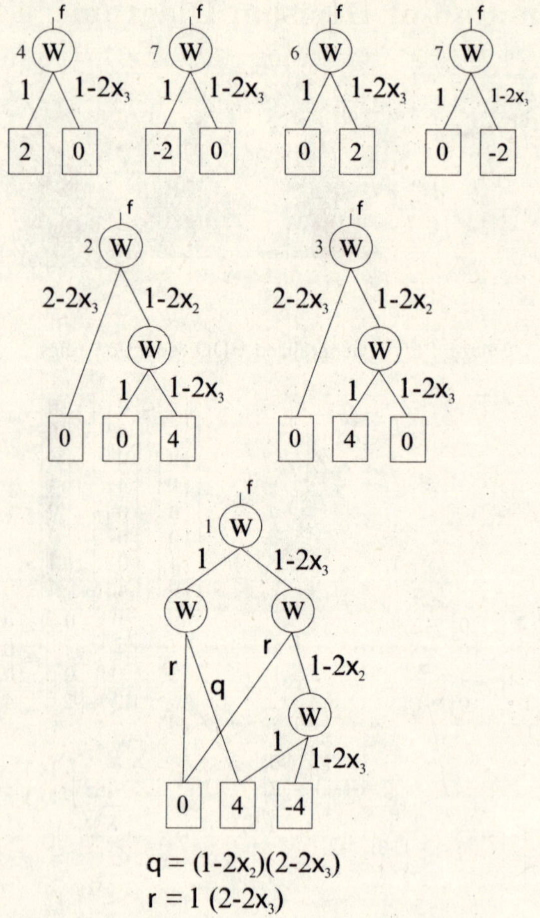

Figure 4.32. WDD for f in Example 4.19.

we get the Walsh spectrum at the root node. Notice that the calculations at the levels above the last level of non-terminal nodes are performed over subfunctions represented by the subtrees rooted in the processed nodes. This is the main difference to FFT-like algorithms where all calculations are over numbers representing function values. However, since we perform the calculations determined by the basic transform matrices, which determine butterfly operations in the FFT-like algorithms, it follows that in decision diagram methods for calculation of spectral transforms we actually perform FFT over decision diagrams instead of over vectors. If each step of the calculation is represented by a decision diagram, we get the Walsh decision diagram for f shown in Fig. 4.32.

10. Reduction of Decision Diagrams

In applications of decision diagrams, the following basic characteristics are most often considered

1 Size of DD, defined as the number of non-terminal nodes for bit-level diagrams and as the sum of non-terminal and constant nodes for word-level decision diagrams.

2 Depth of DD, defined as the number of levels,

3 Width of DD, defined as the maximum number of nodes per level,

4 Number of paths from the root node to the non-zero constant nodes.

There is a direct correspondence between these characteristic and the basic characteristics of logic networks that are derived from decision diagrams as it will be discussed further in this book. For instance, the number of non-terminal nodes corresponds to the number of elementary modules in the corresponding networks. When calculations are performed over decision diagrams, some calculation subprocedure should be performed at each non-terminal node. Therefore, reduction of non-terminal nodes is a chief goal in optimizing decision diagrams. The delay in a network is proportional to the depth of the decision diagram, which together with the width, determine the area occupied by the network. Edges in the diagram determine interconnections in the network. Thus, for applications where particular parameters in the networks are important, reduction of the corresponding characteristics of decision diagrams is useful. Considerable research efforts have been devoted to these problems, see for instance [36], [109], [113], [159], [175] and references therein.

In particular, selection of different decomposition rules, alternatively different spectral transforms to define various STDDs may be viewed as an approach to the optimization of decision diagram representations. Recall that the reduction in a BDT or MTBDT is possible if there are constant subvectors, the representation of which reduces to a single constat node, or identical subvectors, that can be represented by a shared subtree. In the case of Spectral transform decision diagrams, search for constant or identical subvectors is transferred to spectra instead of over the initial functions. It may happen that for an appropriately selected transform, the corresponding spectrum, that is, the vector of values of constant nodes, expresses more such useful regularity. Fig. 4.33 illustrates this statement, where a vector of 16 elements is split into four subvectors. The first field is a constant subvector, and the other two fields are identical subvectors and can be represented by a shared subtree, which can be at most a complete tree. The last field is an arbitrary

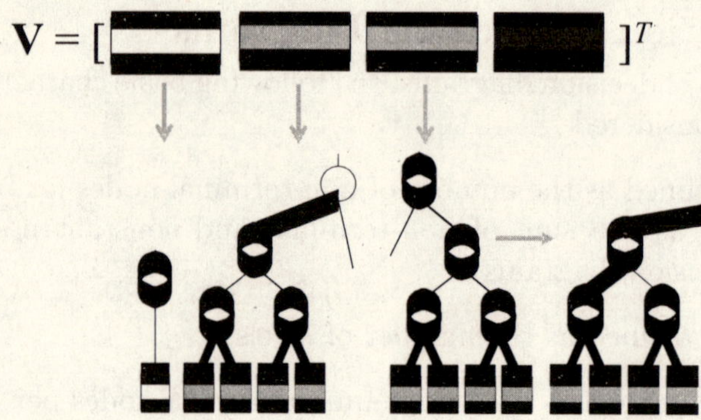

Figure 4.33. Reduction possibilities in a decision diagram.

subvector and has to be represented by a separate subdiagram, which, as the identical subvectors, could be at most a complete subtree with four different constant nodes.

A widely exploited method for reduction of the size of decision diagrams is reordering of variables in the functions represented, because the size of decision diagrams in usually strongly depends on the order of variables. Although introduced primarily for BDDs and MTBDDs, see for example, [144], [169], [170], the method can be equally applied to Spectral transform decision diagrams.

EXAMPLE 4.20 *Fig. 4.34 shows that the WDD for f in Example 4.19 which has four non-terminal nodes, can be converted in a WDD of the size three after permutation of variables* x_1 *and* x_2.

The determination of the best order of variables which produces the decision diagram of the minimum size is an NP-complete problem [13], [167]. There are many heuristic methods that often produce a nearly optimal diagram.

However, there are functions where reordering of variables is not efficient in reducing the size of decision diagrams or cannot applied. An example are symmetric functions whose value does not depend on the order of variables. For these reasons various methods to reduce the sizes of decision diagrams by linear combination of variables have been considered, see for example [53], [54], [78], [110]. The methods consists in mapping a given function f in primary variables x_i into a new function f_{lta} in variables y_i defined by a suitably determined linear transformation over the primary variables.

EXAMPLE 4.21 *Consider a two-output function* $f = (f_1, f_0)$, *which can be represented by an integer equivalent function* $f_z = 2f_1 + f_0$ *given by the*

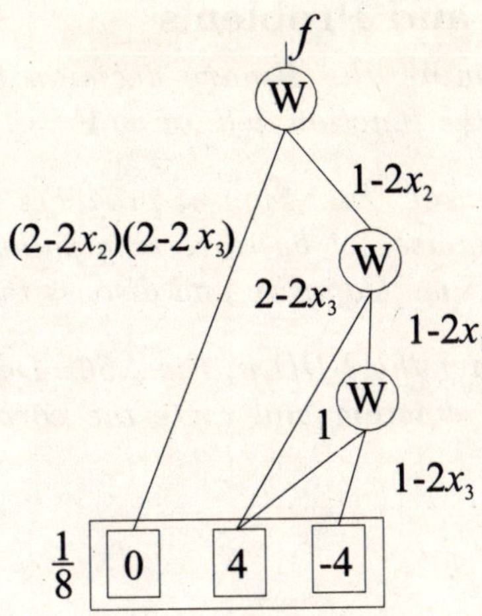

Figure 4.34. WDD with permuted variables for f in Example 4.19.

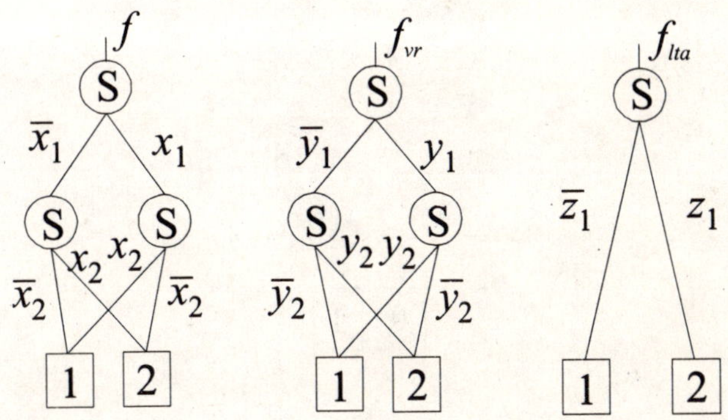

Figure 4.35. MTBDDs for initial order of variables, permuted, and linearly transformed variables in f in Example 4.21.

vector of function values $\mathbf{F} = [f(0), f(1), f(2), f(3)]^T = [1,2,2,1]^T$. *After reordering of variables, this vector is converted into the vector* $\mathbf{F}_{vr} = [f(0), f(2), f(1), f(3)]^T = [1,2,2,1]^T$. *Since this function is symmetric, reordering of variables* $y_1 = x_2$ *and* $y_2 = x_1$ *does not change the vector of function values. However, the linear transformation of variables* $z_1 = x_1 \oplus x_2$ *and* $y_2 = x_2$ *converts* $\mathbf{F}$ *into* $\mathbf{F}_{lta} = [f(0), f(3), f(2), f(1)]^T = [1,1,2,2]^T$.

Fig. 4.35 shows MTBDDs for f, f_{vr} *and* f_{lta}, *where* vr *and* lta *stand for reordering and linear transform of variables.*

11. Exercises and Problems

EXERCISE 4.1 *Determine the Binary decision tree and the Binary decision diagram for the function defined by* $\mathbf{F} = [0,1,1,1,0,1,1,0]^T$.

EXERCISE 4.2 *Determine the Sum-of-products expression for the function f in the Exercise 4.1 by traversing paths in the decision tree and the decision diagram. Compare and discuss these expressions.*

EXERCISE 4.3 *Consider the BDD in Fig.4.36. Determine the function f represented by this diagram and write the corresponding functional expression for f.*

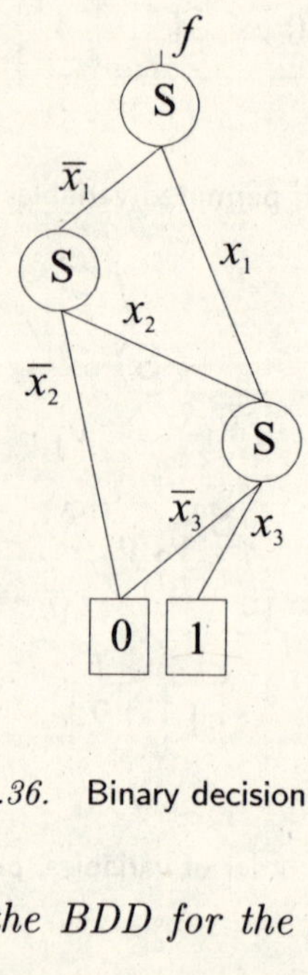

Figure 4.36. Binary decision diagram.

EXERCISE 4.4 *Construct the BDD for the function* $f(x_1,x_2,x_3,x_4) = \overline{x}_1x_2 \vee x_1x_3 \vee (x_1 \wedge x_4)$.

EXERCISE 4.5 *Represent the function given by the truth-vector* $\mathbf{F} = [1,0,0,1,1,1,1,1]^T$ *by decision trees on groups* C_2^3 *and* $C_2 \times C_4$. *Determine the corresponding decision diagrams.*

EXERCISE 4.6 *Table 4.4 shows a three-variable three-output function f. Represent f by a Shared BDD.*

EXERCISE 4.7 *Represent the multi-output function in Exercise 4.6 by an integer equivalent function* $f_Z = 2^2 f_0 + 2f_1 + f_2$ *and determine its MTBDD.*

Table 4.4. Multi-output function in Exercise 4.6.

	$x_1x_2x_3$	f_0	f_1	f_2
0.	000	1	0	1
1.	001	1	1	0
2.	010	1	1	1
3.	011	0	1	0
4.	100	0	0	0
5.	101	1	0	1
6.	110	1	1	1
7.	111	1	0	1

EXERCISE 4.8 *Draw the Positive and Negative Reed-Muller decision diagrams for the function f in Exercise 4.1.*

EXERCISE 4.9 *Compare the Positive and the Negative Reed-Muller diagrams in Exercise 4.8 with the BDD, and diagrams derived from the Positive and the Negative Reed-Muller trees by the BDD reduction rules.*

EXERCISE 4.10 *For the function in Exercise 4.1 draw Kronecker decision diagrams for the following assignment of decomposition rules per levels*

1.	*S, pD, nD*	*3.*	*S, nD, pD*
2.	*pD, S, nD,*	*4.*	*nD, S, pD.*

Determine the corresponding AND-EXOR expressions for f by traversing 1-paths in these diagrams and determine the Kronecker spectra.

EXERCISE 4.11 *Reduce the Kronecker decision tree in Fig. 4.37. Determine the function f represented by this diagram and write the functional expression for f corresponding to this diagram.*

EXERCISE 4.12 *Write the set of basis functions in terms of which the Kronecker decision tree in Exercise 4.11 is defined. Determine the corresponding transform matrix in terms of which the values of constant nodes are calculated.*

Calculate the values of constant nodes in the Kronecker decision tree with the same assignment of nodes for the function given by the truth-vector $\mathbf{F} = [1,1,0,1,1,1,0,0]^T$.

EXERCISE 4.13 *Consider the Kronecker decision tree in Fig. 4.37. Determine the function f represented by this diagram and write the corresponding functional expression for f.*

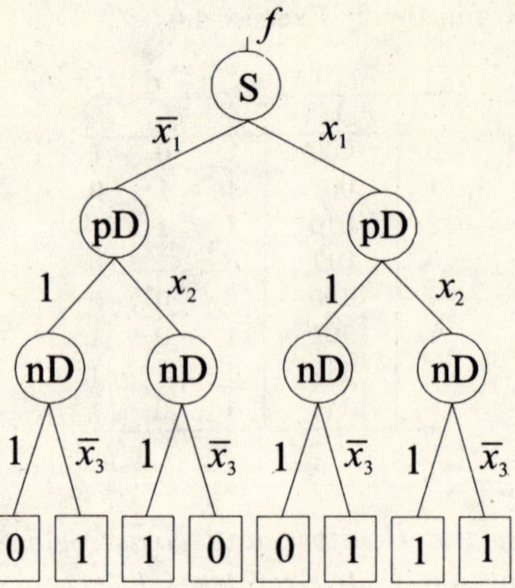

Figure 4.37. Kronecker decision tree in Exercise 4.11.

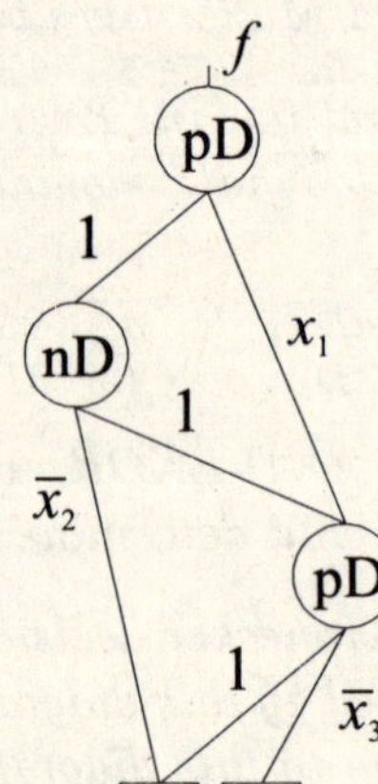

Figure 4.38. Kronecker decision diagram in Exercise 4.13.

EXERCISE 4.14 *For the function represented by the BDD in Fig. 4.31 calculate the arithmetic .spectrum over this BDD and show the corresponding ACDD.*

EXERCISE 4.15 *For the function* $f = x_1x_2 + x_2x_3 + x_1x_3$, *determine BDDs, and ACDDs for all possible ordering of variables. Compare the size, the width and the number of non-zero paths in these diagrams.*

Chapter 5

CLASSIFICATION OF SWITCHING FUNCTIONS

Classification of switching functions is among the most important problems in switching theory and closely related to their realizations. It is motivated by the desire to reduce the number of different networks in the modular synthesis of logic networks. There are 2^{2^n} different functions of n variables, which implies the same number of different logic networks to realize them. However, many of the functions are related in some sense. For instance, for each function f there is a logic complement of it, $\overline{f}$, which can be realized by adding an inverter at the output of the network that realizes f.

Fig. 5.1 illustrates that the classification task consists of the partition of the set SF of all switching functions of a given number of variables n into classes C_i of functions mutually similar with respect to some appropriately formulated classification criteria. Each class is represented by a *representative function* c_i, the *representative* of the class C_i. Functions that belong to the same class can be reduced to each other by applying the operations performed in the classification. These operations are usually called the *classification rules.* Thus, a function $f \in C_i$ can be reduced to the representative function c_i by the application of the classification rules. It follows that f can be realized by the same network as c_i modified as determined by the classification rules applied in order reverse the process in the classification.

There are several applications of the classification, and we point out two of them

1 Realization by prototypes, which assumes design of similar circuits for functions within the same class,

2 Standardization of methods for testing logic networks.

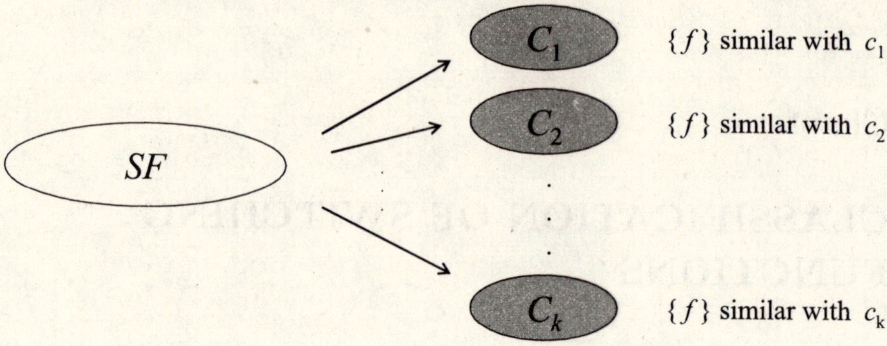

Figure 5.1. Classification of switching functions.

1. NPN-classification

Probably the most widely used is the *NPN-classification* due to the simplicity of the classification rules.

In NPN-classification, the classification rules are

1 Negation of input variables (N) $\overline{x}_i \leftrightarrow x_i$,

2 Permutation of input variables (P) $x_i \leftrightarrow x_j$,

3 Negation of the output (N) $f \rightarrow \overline{f}$.

If we only use a subset of these rules in the classification, we obtain several "subclassifications". The following cases are usually distinguished

1 N (rule 1),

2 P (rule 2),

3 NP (rules 1 and 2),

4 NPN (rules 1, 2 and 3),

with NP and NPN-classification the most often used in practice. Classifications with a larger number of classification rules produce a smaller number of classes, and thus are considered stronger classifications.

We say that two functions f_1 and f_2 of the same number of variables n belong to the same class, or are *equivalent*, if they can be reduced each to other by the classification rules allowed in the classification considered.

EXAMPLE 5.1 *(Equivalent functions)*
Consider the functions

$$\begin{aligned} f_1 &= x_1\overline{x}_2 + x_2x_3, \\ f_2 &= x_1x_2 + \overline{x}_2x_3, \\ f_3 &= x_1x_3 + x_2\overline{x}_3, \\ f_4 &= \overline{x}_1x_3 + \overline{x}_2\overline{x}_3, \end{aligned}$$

whose truth-vectors are

$$\begin{aligned} \mathbf{F}_1 &= [0,0,0,1,1,1,0,1]^T, \\ \mathbf{F}_2 &= [0,1,0,0,0,1,1,1]^T, \\ \mathbf{F}_3 &= [0,0,1,0,0,1,1,1]^T, \\ \mathbf{F}_4 &= [1,1,0,1,1,0,0,0]^T. \end{aligned}$$

P-equivalence

Functions f_1 and f_2 are P-equivalent, since they can be reduced each to other by the permutation $x_1 \leftrightarrow x_3$. Indeed, if the subscript P denotes the permutations, then $f_1^P = x_3\overline{x}_2 + x_1x_2 = f_2$. Similar, $f_2^P = x_3x_2 + \overline{x}_2x_1 = f_1$.

NP-equivalence

Functions f_1 and f_3 are NP-equivalent, since if $x_2 \leftrightarrow \overline{x}_2$, then $f_1^N = x_1x_2 + \overline{x}_2x_3$, where the subscript N denotes negation of variables. Further, if $x_2 \leftrightarrow x_3$, then $f_1^{NP} = x_1x_3 + \overline{x}_3x_2 = f_3$. Conversely, if $x_2 \leftrightarrow x_3$, then $f_3^P = x_1x_2 + x_3\overline{x}_2$. When $x_2 \leftrightarrow \overline{x}_2$, then $f_3^{PN} = x_1\overline{x}_2 + x_3x_2 = f_1$.

NPN-equivalence

We have shown that functions f_1 and f_3 are in the same NP-class. It is obvious from the truth-vectors of f_1 and f_4, that these functions are complements of each other. Thus, they can be reduced to each other by the negation of the output. It follows, that f_1 and f_4 belong to the same NPN-class.

Fig. 5.2 shows the representative functions for P, NP, and NPN-classes of switching functions for $n = 3$. In specifying the representative functions, we assume the canonic order of variables $x_1, \ldots, x_n$, and all the variables are written in positive literals, except in P-classification. In this figure, we have indicated the number of functions represented

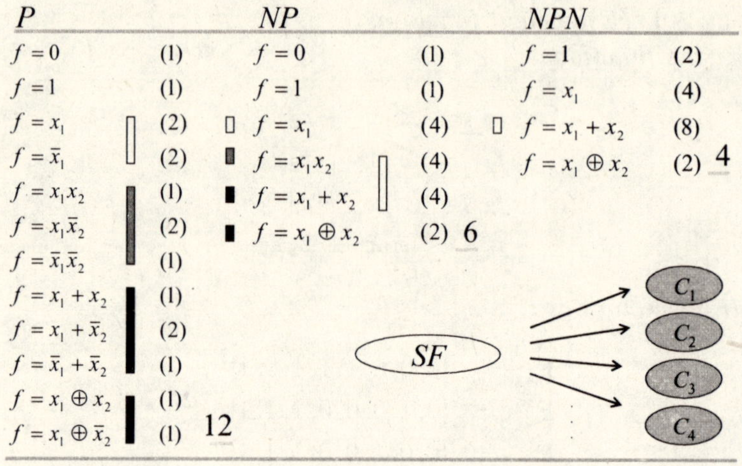

Figure 5.2. Representative functions in NPN-classification for $n = 3$.

Table 5.1. Number of functions of n variables ($\#f$), functions dependent on all n variables ($\#f(n)$), and representative functions in C_P, C_{NP} and C_{NPN} classes.

	n					
	1	2	3	4	5	6
$\#f$	4	1	256	65536	4.3×10^9	1.8×10^{19}
$\#f(n)$	2	10	128	64594	4.3×10^9	1.8×10^{19}
$\|C_P\|$	4	12	80	3984	3.7×10^7	-
$\|C_{NP}\|$	3	6	22	402	1228158	4.0×10^{14}
$\|C_{NPN}\|$	2	4	14	222	616126	2.0×10^{14}

by a single function and the bars show the functions represented by a single function in the next stronger classification by allowing successively another classification rule. P, NP, and NPN-classifications partition the set of all switching functions of a given number n of variables in disjoint classes, since each function is covered by a single representative function which implies that a function cannot belong to several classes. In particular, it can be shown that they are equivalence relations in the sense of Definition 1.5.

Table 5.1 compares the number of representative functions in different classes of functions. It shows the number of functions of n variables ($\#f$), functions that essentially depend on all n variables ($\#f(n)$), and representative functions in C_P, C_{NP} and C_{NPN} classes.

Table 5.2. Asymptotic number of functions per classes for n sufficiently large.

P	NP	NPN
$\frac{2^{2^n}}{n!}$	$\frac{2^{2^n}}{2^n n!}$	$\frac{2^{2^n}}{2^{n+1} n!}$

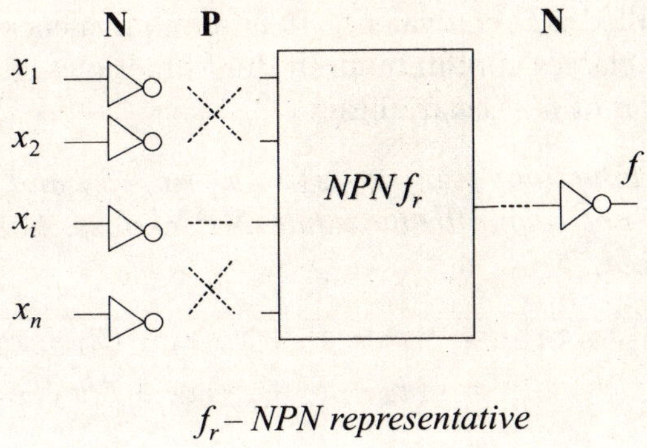

Figure 5.3. Realization of functions by NPN-classification.

Table 5.2 shows the asymptotic number of classes when n is sufficiently large.

Fig. 5.3 explains the basic principle of realization of logic functions by NPN-classification. Let there be a network that realizes an NPN-representative function c_i. Then, all other functions from the same NPN-class are realized by performing optionally negation and permutation of inputs, and negation of the output.

2. SD-Classification

A classification stronger than NPN-classification is defined in terms of *self-dual functions* and is, therefore, called the *Self-dual (SD) classification* of switching functions. It is based upon the following representation of switching functions.

Consider a function $f(x_1, \ldots, x_n)$ and its dual function $f^d(x_1, \ldots, x_n)$ defined by $f^d(x_1, \ldots, x_n) = \overline{f}(\overline{x}_1, \ldots, \overline{x}_n)$.

The function

$$f^{sd}(x_1, \ldots, x_n, x_{n+1}) = x_{n+1} f(x_1, \ldots, x_n) + \overline{x}_{n+1} f^d(x_1, \ldots, x_n),$$

is called its self-dualization.

Consider a self-dual function $f(x_1,\ldots,x_{n+1})$ of exactly $n+1$ variables. The nonself-dual functions $f(x_1,\ldots,x_n,1)$ and $f(x_1,\ldots,x_n,0)$ are called nonself-dualized function of $f(x_1,\ldots,x_n)$ and x_{n+1} the nonself-dualized variable.

Switching functions that become identical by self-dualization, nonself-dualization, negation of variables or the function, or permutation of variables are called SD-equivalent. It is an equivalence relation where the equivalence classes contain nonself dual functions of n variables and self-dual function of $n+1$ variables.

EXAMPLE 5.2 *Functions* $f_1(x_1,x_2,x_3)=x_1+x_2+x_3$ *and* $f_2(x_1,x_2,x_3)=x_1(x_2+x_3)$ *do not belong to the same* NPN*-class, however, are* SD*-equivalent. Indeed,*

$$\begin{aligned} f_1^{sd}(x_1,x_2,x_3,x_4) &= (x_1+x_2+x_3)x_4+\overline{(\overline{x}_1+\overline{x}_2+\overline{x}_3)\overline{x}_4} \\ &= (x_1+x_2+x_3)x_4+x_1x_2x_3. \end{aligned}$$

Similar,

$$\begin{aligned} f_2^{sd}(x_1,x_2,x_3,x_4) &= x_1(x_2+x_3)x_4+\overline{\overline{x}_1(\overline{x}_2+\overline{x}_3)\overline{x}_4} \\ &= x_1x_2x_4+x_1x_3x_4+(x_1+x_2x_3)\overline{x}_4 \\ &= x_1x_2x_4+x_1x_3x_4+x_1\overline{x}_4+x_2x_3\overline{x}_4 \\ &= (x_2+x_3+\overline{x}_4)x_1+x_2x_3\overline{x}_4, \end{aligned}$$

and after permutations $\overline{x}_4 \leftrightarrow x_4$ *and* $x_1 \leftrightarrow x_4$ *it follows*

$$f_2^{sd}(x_1,x_2,x_3,x_4)=f_1^{sd}(x_1,x_2,x_3,x_4).$$

Fig. 5.4 shows details in proving the equation

$$(x_1+x_2+x_3)x_4+x_1x_2x_3\overline{x}_4=(x_1+x_2+x_3)x_4+x_1x_2x_3,$$

with required Boolean relations explicitly shown and the terms that have been joined underlined. Fig. 5.5 shows verification of the expression

$$x_1x_2x_4+x_1x_3x_4+x_1\overline{x}_4=(x_2+x_3+\overline{x}_4)x_1,$$

through the equivalence of the truth-vectors for the expressions on the left and the right side of the sign of equality.

EXAMPLE 5.3 *The representative functions in SD-classification for* $n=3$ *are shown in Table 5.3.*

It should be emphasized that SD-classification creates an equivalence relation in the set of all Boolean functions and each class contains functions of n and $n+1$ variables. This is the reason why in Table 5.3

$$(x_1+x_2+x_3)x_4+x_1x_2x_3\bar{x}_4=(x_1+x_2+x_3)x_4+x_1x_2x_3$$

$$(x_1+x_2+x_3)x_4+x_1x_2x_3\bar{x}_4=x_1x_4+(x_2+x_3)x_4+x_1x_2x_3\bar{x}_4$$

$$=x_1x_4\cdot 1+(x_2+x_3)x_4+x_1x_2x_3\bar{x}_4 \qquad x\cdot 1=x$$

$$=x_1x_4(x_2+\bar{x}_2)+(x_2+x_3)x_4+x_1x_2x_3\bar{x}_4 \qquad x+\bar{x}=1$$

$$=x_1x_2x_4+x_1\bar{x}_2x_4+(x_2+x_3)x_4+x_1x_2x_3\bar{x}_4$$

$$=x_1x_2x_4\cdot 1+x_1\bar{x}_2x_4+(x_2+x_3)x_4+x_1x_2x_3\bar{x}_{4x\cdot 1=x}$$

$$=x_1x_2x_4(x_3+\bar{x}_3)+x_1\bar{x}_2x_4+(x_2+x_3)x_4+x_1x_2x_3\bar{x}_4$$

$$=x_1x_2x_3x_4+x_1x_2\bar{x}_3x_4+x_1\bar{x}_2x_4+(x_2+x_3)x_4+x_1x_2x_3\bar{x}_4 \qquad x+x=x$$

$$=x_1x_2x_3x_4+x_1x_2x_3x_4+x_1x_2\bar{x}_3x_4+x_1\bar{x}_2x_4+(x_2+x_3)x_4+x_1x_2x_3\bar{x}_4$$

$$=x_1x_2x_3x_4+x_1x_2\bar{x}_3x_4+x_1\bar{x}_2x_4+(x_2+x_3)x_4+x_1x_2x_3$$

$$=x_1x_2x_4+x_1\bar{x}_2x_4+(x_2+x_3)x_4+x_1x_2x_3$$

$$=x_1x_4+(x_2+x_3)x_4+x_1x_2x_3$$

$$=(x_1+x_2+x_3)x_4+x_1x_2x_3$$

Figure 5.4. Equivalence of expressions in Example 5.2.

$$x_1x_2x_4+x_1x_3x_4+x_1\bar{x}_4=(x_2+x_3+\bar{x}_4)x_1$$

$$\begin{bmatrix}0\\0\\0\\0\\0\\0\\0\\0\\0\\0\\0\\0\\0\\1\\0\\1\end{bmatrix}+\begin{bmatrix}0\\0\\0\\0\\0\\0\\0\\0\\0\\0\\0\\1\\0\\0\\0\\1\end{bmatrix}+\begin{bmatrix}0\\0\\0\\0\\0\\0\\0\\0\\1\\0\\1\\0\\1\\0\\1\\0\end{bmatrix}=\begin{bmatrix}0\\0\\0\\0\\0\\0\\0\\0\\1\\0\\1\\1\\1\\1\\1\\1\end{bmatrix} \qquad \left(\begin{bmatrix}0\\0\\0\\0\\1\\1\\1\\1\\0\\0\\0\\0\\1\\1\\1\\1\end{bmatrix}+\begin{bmatrix}0\\0\\1\\1\\0\\0\\1\\1\\0\\0\\1\\1\\0\\0\\1\\1\end{bmatrix}+\begin{bmatrix}1\\0\\1\\0\\1\\0\\1\\0\\1\\0\\1\\0\\1\\0\\1\\0\end{bmatrix}\right)\begin{bmatrix}0\\0\\0\\0\\0\\0\\0\\0\\1\\1\\1\\1\\1\\1\\1\\1\end{bmatrix}=\begin{bmatrix}0\\0\\0\\0\\0\\0\\0\\0\\1\\0\\1\\1\\1\\1\\1\\1\end{bmatrix}$$

Figure 5.5. Equivalence of expressions in Example 5.2 through truth-vectors.

Table 5.3. SD-representative functions for $n = 3$.

f	# of f
x_1	4
$x_1x_2 + x_2x_3 + x_1x_3$	32
$x_1 \oplus x_2 \oplus x_3$	8
$(x_1 + x_2 + x_3)x_4 + x_1x_2x_3\overline{x}_4$	128
$(x_1x_2x_3 + \overline{x}_1\overline{x}_2\overline{x}_3)x_4 + (x_1 + x_2 + x_3)(\overline{x}_1 + \overline{x}_2 + \overline{x}_3)\overline{x}_4$	64
$x_1(x_2x_3 + \overline{x}_2\overline{x}_3)x_4 + x_1 + x_2\overline{x}_3 + \overline{x}_2x_3)\overline{x}_4$	96
$(\overline{x}_1x_2x_3 + x_1\overline{x}_2x_3 + x_1x_2\overline{x}_3)x_4 + (x_1x_2 + x_2x_3 + x_1x_3 + \overline{x}_1\overline{x}_2\overline{x}_3)\overline{x}_4$	128

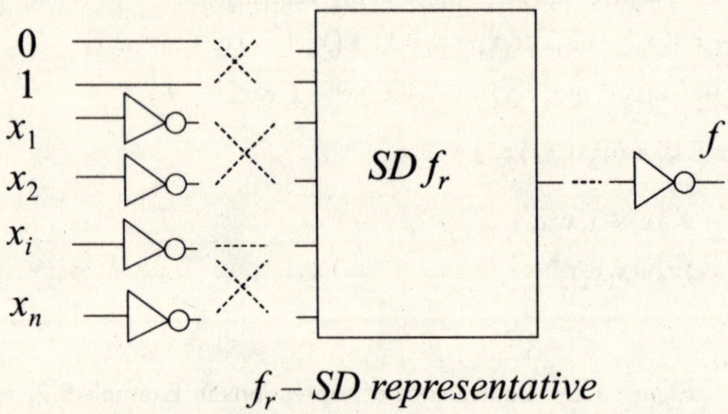

Figure 5.6. Realizations by SD-representative functions.

the sum of the number of functions representable by each representative function is greater than $256 = 2^{2^3}$. It follows that classes of SD-equivalent functions are not disjoint. It means that a given function f may be realized through several representative functions. In this case, a reasonable choice is to select the simplest representative function or the representative function to which f can be converted by the fewest number of applications of the classification rules.

Fig. 5.6 shows the basic principle of function realizations through SD-representative functions. In this case, transformations of the network at the inputs are

1 Selective application of constant 0 and 1, besides variables $x_1, \ldots, x_n$,

2 Permutation of input variables,

3 Negation of the output.

Table 5.4. Number of functions realizable by t products.

t	AND-OR	AND-EXOR
0	1	1
1	81	81
2	1804	2268
3	13472	21744
4	28904	37530
5	17032	3888
6	3704	24
7	512	0
8	26	0
av.	4.13	3.66

3. LP-classification

NPN and SD-classifications are intended for AND-OR synthesis, which means the representation of functions by AND-OR expressions. From 1990's, there has been an increasing interest in AND-EXOR synthesis, mainly after publication of [156], due to the feature that AND-EXOR expressions require on the average fewer product, accompanied by the technology advent which provided EXOR circuits with the same propagation delay and at about the same price as classical OR circuits with the same number of inputs.

EXAMPLE 5.4 *Table 5.4 shows the number of functions of four variables that can be realized with t products by AND-OR and AND-EXOR expressions, represented by SOPs and ESOPs, respectively. Notice that AND-OR expressions require on the average 4.13 compared with 3.66 products in AND-EXOR expressions.*

This consideration was a motive to introduce *LP-classification* adapted by the allowed classification rules to the AND-EXOR synthesis [82], [81]. In this classification, unlike NPN and SD-classification, transformations over constants, besides over variables, are also allowed.

LP-classification has been introduced by the following considerations.

Consider the following transformations that change a function f to (possibly) another function g

1 For $i \in \{1,\ldots,n\}$ and f written in the Shannon expansion with respect to the variable x_i

$$f = \overline{x}_i f_0 \oplus x_i f_1.$$

the function g is in the form

$$g = \begin{bmatrix} g_0 \\ g_1 \end{bmatrix} = \begin{bmatrix} a & b \\ c & d \end{bmatrix} \begin{bmatrix} f_0 \\ f_1 \end{bmatrix},$$

i.e.,

$$g = \overline{x}_i g_0 \oplus x_i g_1 = \overline{x}_i(af_0 \oplus bf_1) \oplus x_i(cf_0 \oplus df_1),$$

where $\begin{bmatrix} a & b \\ c & d \end{bmatrix}$ is a nonsingular matric over $GF(2)$.

2 g is obtained from f by permuting variables.

Functions f and g are called LP-equivalent if g is obtained form f by a sequence of (operations) transformations (1) and (2) above [81].

It is clear that the LP-equivalence is an equivalence relation.

EXAMPLE 5.5 *Consider the transformation by the matrix* $\begin{bmatrix} 1 & 0 \\ 1 & 1 \end{bmatrix}$. *Then,*

$$g = \begin{bmatrix} g_0 \\ g_1 \end{bmatrix} = \begin{bmatrix} 1 & 0 \\ 1 & 1 \end{bmatrix} \begin{bmatrix} f_0 \\ f_1 \end{bmatrix} = \begin{bmatrix} f_0 \\ f_0 \oplus f_1 \end{bmatrix},$$

and equivalently

$$g = \overline{x}_i g_0 \oplus x_i g_i = \overline{x}_i f_0 \oplus x_i(f_0 \oplus f_1) = (\overline{x}_i \oplus x_i)f_0 \oplus x_i f_1 = 1 \cdot f_0 \oplus x_i f_1.$$

Thus, g is obtained by the substitution $\overline{x}_i \rightarrow 1$ in the expression of f. Similarly, the matrix $\begin{bmatrix} 1 & 1 \\ 0 & 1 \end{bmatrix}$ *corresponds to the substitution $x_i \rightarrow 1$.*

Usually, the six transformations corresponding to the six different nonsingular matrices over $GF(2)$ are expressed in this substitution notation as shown in Table 5.5.

It is worth noticing that if f is represented by an ESOP with $|f|$ products, then $|g| = |f|$ [81].

EXAMPLE 5.6 *Functions $f(x,y) = x \oplus y$, $f(x,y) = x \oplus \overline{y}$, $f(x,y) = \overline{x} \oplus y$ and $f(x,y) = 1 \oplus xy$ are LP-equivalent.*

Indeed, $f(x,y) = x \oplus y$ converts into $f(x,y) = x \oplus \overline{y}$ by the transformation $y \rightarrow \overline{y}$, which can be written as $f(x,y) = x \cdot 1 \oplus 1 \cdot \overline{y}$. Transformation $x \rightarrow 1$ converts this function into $f(x,y) = 1 \oplus x\overline{y}$. If $1 \rightarrow \overline{x}$ and $x \rightarrow 1$, it follows $f(x,y) = \overline{x} \cdot 1 \oplus 1 \cdot \overline{y}$, which can be written as $f(x,y) = \overline{x} \oplus \overline{y}$. The transformation $\overline{x} \rightarrow x$ results in $f(x,y) = x \oplus \overline{y}$, and similar, $\overline{y} \rightarrow y$, produces $f(x,y) = \overline{x} \oplus y$, and similar for other functions.

Table 5.5. *LP*-classification rules.

1.	$LP_0(f) = \overline{x}_i f_0 \oplus x_i f_1$	Identical mapping	$\begin{bmatrix} 1 & 0 \\ 0 & 1 \end{bmatrix}$
2.	$LP_1(f) = \overline{x}_i f_0 \oplus 1 \cdot f_1$	$x_i \leftrightarrow 1$	$\begin{bmatrix} 1 & 1 \\ 0 & 1 \end{bmatrix}$
3.	$LP_2(f) = 1 \cdot f_0 \oplus x_i f_1$	$\overline{x}_i \leftrightarrow 1$	$\begin{bmatrix} 1 & 0 \\ 1 & 1 \end{bmatrix}$
4.	$LP_3(f) = x_i f_0 \oplus \overline{x}_i f_1$	$x_i \leftrightarrow \overline{x}_i$	$\begin{bmatrix} 0 & 1 \\ 1 & 0 \end{bmatrix}$
5.	$LP_4(f) = x_i f_0 \oplus 1 \cdot f_1$	$x_i \rightarrow 1$, and $\overline{x}_i \rightarrow x_i$	$\begin{bmatrix} 0 & 1 \\ 1 & 1 \end{bmatrix}$
6.	$LP_6(f) = 1 \cdot f_0 \oplus \overline{x}_i f_1$	$\overline{x}_1 \rightarrow 1$, and $x_i \rightarrow \overline{x}_i$	$\begin{bmatrix} 1 & 1 \\ 1 & 0 \end{bmatrix}$

Table 5.6. *LP*-equivalent functions.

Equivalent functions	Transformation
$\overline{x}y \equiv xy$	$\overline{x} \leftrightarrow x$,
$x \cdot 1 \equiv 1 \cdot y$,	$x \leftrightarrow y$,
$xy \equiv x \cdot 1$	$y \leftrightarrow 1$,
$1 \cdot y \equiv 1 \cdot 1$	$y \leftrightarrow 1$.

EXAMPLE 5.7 *Table 5.6 shows equivalent functions and the corresponding LP-transformations.*

Table 5.7 shows the *LP*-equivalence classes for functions of $n = 2$ variables. There are three *LP*-equivalence classes and functions are arranged in a way that simplifies transitions between functions in the same class.

Table 5.7. LP-equivalent functions for $n = 2$.

Class	Functions			
1	0			
2	$\overline{x}\overline{y}$	$\overline{x}y$	$x\overline{y}$	xy
	$\overline{x}$			
	1	x	$\overline{y}$	y
3	$x \oplus \overline{y}$	$x \oplus y$		
	$1 \oplus \overline{x}\overline{y}$	$1 \oplus \overline{x}y$	$1 \oplus x\overline{y}$	$1 \oplus xy$

Table 5.8. LP-representative functions for $n \leq 4$.

n	2	3	4		
	0	00	0000	016a	0678
	1	01	0001	0180	06b0
	6	06	0006	0182	06b1
		16	0016	0186	1668
		18	0018	0196	1669
		6b	0066	0660	1681
			0116	0661	1683
			0118	0662	168b
			012c	066b	18ef
			0168	0672	6bbd

For functions of $n = 3$ variables, there are 6 LP-representative functions

$$\begin{array}{ll} 0, & \overline{x} \cdot \overline{y} \cdot \overline{z}, \\ \overline{x} \cdot y \oplus \overline{x} \cdot z, & \overline{x} \oplus \overline{y} \cdot z \oplus \overline{x} \cdot y \cdot z, \\ x \cdot \overline{y} \cdot \overline{z} \oplus \overline{x} \cdot y \cdot z, & \overline{x} \oplus y \cdot \overline{z} \oplus x \cdot \overline{y} \cdot z. \end{array}$$

Table 5.8 shows the truth-vectors of LP-representative functions for $n = 2, 3, 4$ in hexadecimal encoding meaning that each character in the truth-vectors should be replaced by its binary representation as a sequence of four binary values.

Table 5.9 shows the number of LP-representative functions for up to 6 variables, which can be compared to data in Table 5.1. Since in any class there are $n!6^n$ functions, it follows that for n sufficiently large, the number of LP-classes approximates to $2^{2^n}/n!6^n$. It should be noticed

Table 5.9. Number of LP-classes.

n	1	2	3	4	5	6
$\|C_{LP}\|$	2	3	6	30	6936	$> 5.5 \times 10^{11}$

that LP-classification is the stronger than NPN and SD classifications, since considerably reduces the number of different classes.

4. Universal Logic Modules

Classification of switching functions has as one goal the reduction of the number of different logic networks to realize all the functions of a given number of variables. Further development of this idea leads to the *universal logic modules (ULMs)* defined as logic networks capable of realizing any of the 2^{2^n} logic functions of n variables. It is assumed that constants logic 0 and 1 and switching variables in positive and negative polarity are available at the inputs of ULMs. A ULM must have some control inputs to select which particular function the ULM realizes. The increased number of inputs, compared to the number of variables, is the price for the universality of the module. For example, a ULM for functions of three variables, has five inputs, two of which are the control inputs.

EXAMPLE 5.8 *Fig. 5.7 shows the ULM for $n = 2$. It may be shown that there are 6 essentially different ULMs for functions of two variables x_1 and x_2 and the control variable x_c [71]*

$$
\begin{aligned}
f_H &= x_1x_2 + \overline{x}_1\overline{x}_2x_c = \overline{(x_1 \oplus x_2)}(x_1 + x_c), \\
f_I &= \overline{x}_1x_2x_c + x_1\overline{x}_2x_c + x_1x_2\overline{x}_c = (x_1 \oplus x_2)x_c + x_1x_2\overline{x}_c, \\
f_J &= x_1x_2\overline{x}_c + x_1\overline{x}_2x_c = x_1(x_2 \oplus x_c), \\
f_K &= \overline{x}_1x_2\overline{x}_c + x_1\overline{x}_2x_c = (x_1 \oplus x_2)(x_2 \oplus x_c), \\
f_L &= x_1x_2 + \overline{x}_1x_c, \\
f_M &= x_1x_2\overline{x}_c + \overline{x}_2x_c + \overline{x}_1x_c = x_1x_2 \oplus x_c.
\end{aligned}
$$

The module described by f_L is a (2×1) multiplexer, which will be defined latter, and f_M is the Reed-Muller module, since realizes the positive Davio expansion rule. Fig. 5.8 shows logic networks which realizes the considered ULMs.

The concept and applications of ULMs have been already considered in [163] in the context of study of contact networks. Fig. 5.9 shows

Figure 5.7. ULM for $n = 2$.

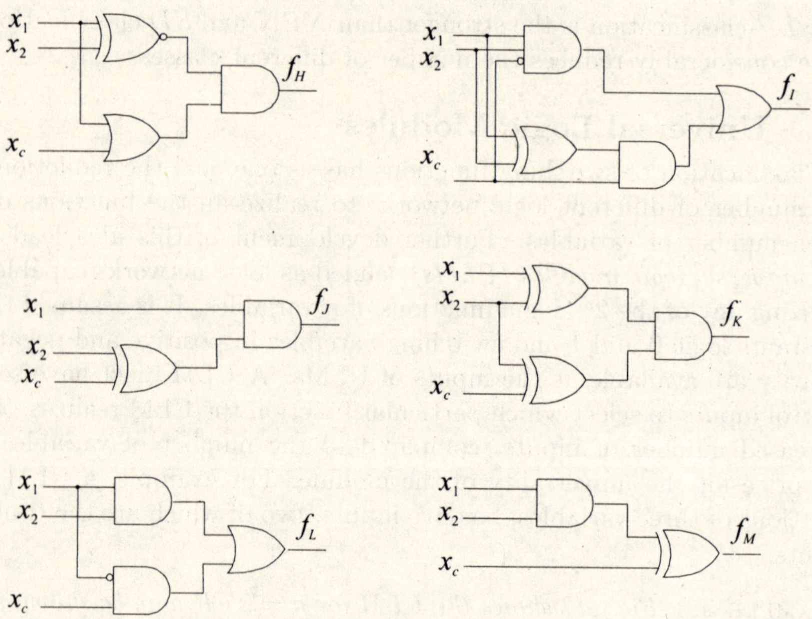

Figure 5.8. Realization of ULMs for $n = 2$.

the notation used by Shannon for basic logic elements implemented as contact networks.

EXAMPLE 5.9 *Fig. 5.10 shows realization of the function*

$$f = w(x + y(z + \overline{x}))$$

by a contact network.

In the same context, Shannon has shown that an arbitrary function of $n = 3$ variables can be written as

$$\begin{aligned} f(x,y,z) &= (x + y + f(0,0,z))(x + \overline{y} + f(0,1,z)) \\ &= (\overline{x} + y + f(1,0,z))(\overline{x} + \overline{y} + f(1,1,z)). \end{aligned}$$

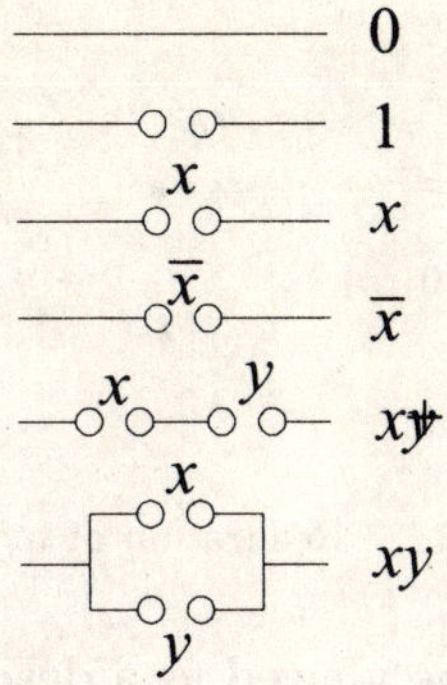

Figure 5.9. Basic logic circuits in contact networks.

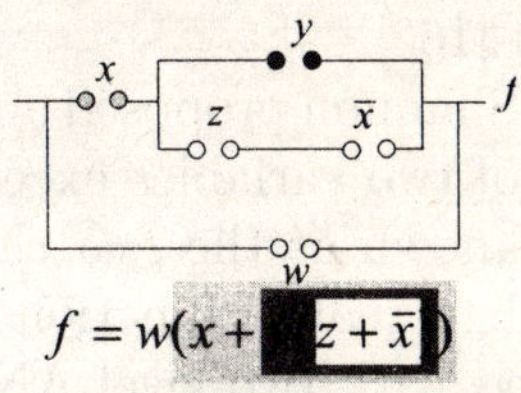

Figure 5.10. Realization of f in Example 5.9.

In the notation of Shannon, this expression can be written as

$$u_{ab} = f(x, y, z) = \prod_{k=1}^{4} (u_k + v_k),$$

where

$$\begin{aligned} u_1 &= x + y, \\ u_2 &= x + \overline{y}, \\ u_3 &= \overline{x} + y, \\ u_4 &= \overline{x} + \overline{y}, \end{aligned}$$

and

$$\begin{aligned} v_1 &= f(0, 0, z), \\ v_2 &= f(0, 1, z), \\ v_3 &= f(1, 0, z), \\ v_4 &= f(1, 1, z). \end{aligned}$$

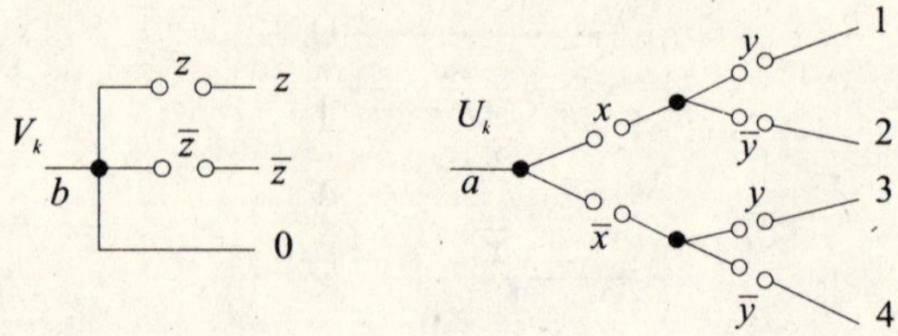

Figure 5.11. Realization of u_k and v_k.

This representation can be viewed as a description of a universal logic module to realize an arbitrary function of three variables. Fig. 5.11 shows realizations for u_k and v_k. Extension to functions of an arbitrary number of variables is straightforward, and the case of four variables has been discussed in detail in [163].

In the same technology, Shannon proposed a module shown in Fig. 5.12 that realizes all functions of two variables except the constants 0 and 1. This is a macro element, known as the *two variable function generator (TVFG)* that can be used to realize functions of an arbitrary number of variables when combined with two-level AND-OR networks. For instance, for a function f of an even number of variables $n = 2r$, the pairs of variables $X = (x, y)$ can be viewed as four-valued variables taking values $00, 01, 10, 11$. With this encoding, f can be represented by an SOP with four-valued variables. In this expression, each product requires an AND circuit, and it follows that the minimum SOP of four-valued variables provides for a network with minimum number of AND circuits. The method will be explained by the following example presented in [155]. In the usual notation for logic circuits, TVFG is shown in Fig. 5.13.

The following example [155] illustrates application of TVFGs as ULMs. The realization in this example by TVFGs will be compared with the realization by Reed-Muller modules in Example 5.11.

EXAMPLE 5.10 *([155])*
Consider a function given by the Karnaugh map in Fig. 5.15. If the binary variables are encoded as $X_1 = (x_1, x_2)$ and $X_2 = (x_3, x_4)$, then f can be expressed as

$$\begin{aligned} f &= X_1^{\{00\}}X_2^{\{00\}} \vee X_1^{\{00\}}X_2^{\{11\}} \vee X_1^{\{01\}}X_2^{\{01\}} \vee X_1^{\{01\}}X_2^{\{10\}} \\ & \quad X_1^{\{01\}}X_2^{\{11\}} \vee X_1^{\{10\}}X_2^{\{01\}} \vee X_1^{\{10\}}X_2^{\{10\}} \vee X_1^{\{10\}}X_2^{\{11\}}, \end{aligned}$$

which, after joining the common terms, is

$$f = X_1^{\{00\}}X_2^{\{00,11\}} \vee X_1^{\{01,10\}}X_2^{\{01,10,11\}}. \quad (5.1)$$

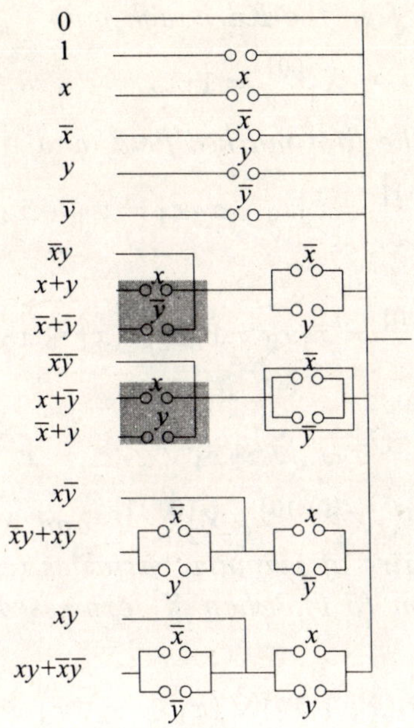

Figure 5.12. Two variable function generator by Shannon.

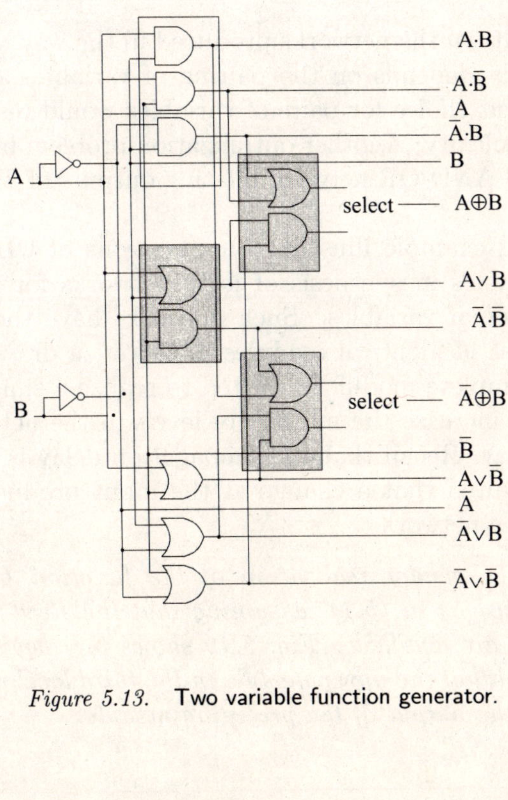

Figure 5.13. Two variable function generator.

From the definition of f in the Karnaugh map,

$$X_1^{\{00\}} = \overline{x}_1\overline{x}_2,$$

which corresponds to the first marked field, and

$$X_2^{\{00,11\}} = \overline{x}_3\overline{x}_4 \vee x_3x_4 = x_3 \oplus \overline{x}_4.$$

Similarly,

$$X_1^{\{01,10\}} = \overline{x}_1x_2 \vee x_1\overline{x}_2 = x_1 \oplus x_2,$$

and

$$X_2^{\{01,10,11\}} = \overline{x}_3x_4 \vee x_3\overline{x}_4 \vee x_3x_4 = x_3 \vee x_4.$$

The functions $X_1^{\{00\}}$, $X_1^{\{01,10\}}$, $X_2^{\{00,11\}}$ and $X_2^{\{01,10,11\}}$ can be realized by two TVFGs pairs of primary variables (x_1, x_2) and (x_3, x_4) at the inputs. Since, from (5.1), when X_i expressed in terms of primary variables,

$$f = (\overline{x} \cdot \overline{y})(x_3 \oplus \overline{x}_4) \vee (x_1 \oplus x_2)(x_3 \vee x_4),$$

the network that realizes f is as in Fig. 5.16. The required outputs of TVFGs can be realized as shown in Fig. 5.17, and, then, f can be realized by the network in Fig. 5.18.

The complexity of the networks produced in the way described in this example strongly depends on the pairing of variables at the inputs of TVFGs. Different choice for pairs of variables would result in networks of different complexity. Another optimization problem in this method is simplification of AND-OR network relating outputs of TVFGs to determine f [155].

The following example illustrates applications of ULMs for a small number of variables in synthesis of logic networks for functions of an arbitrary number of variables. Such networks have the useful feature that they consist of identical modules, however, a drawback is that in some cases a complete module is wasted to realize a simple subfunction which may also increase the number of levels in the network, thus, the propagation delay. Recall that the propagation delay is usually defined as the time required that a change at the input produces a change at the output of the network.

EXAMPLE 5.11 *Consider realization of the function f in the Example 5.10 expressed as in (5.1), assuming that the Reed-Muller modules with two inputs are available. Fig. 5.19 shows the required network. It should be noticed that the upper module in the third level realizes the logic complement of the output of the preceding module.*

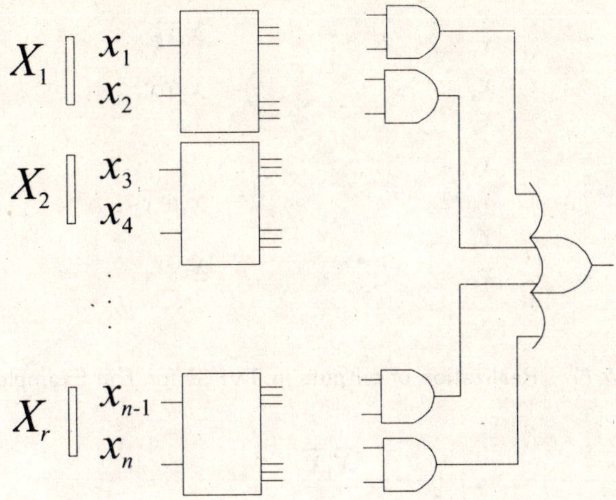

Figure 5.14. Realizations with TVFGs.

	00	01	11	10
00	1	0	0	0
01	0	1	0	1
11	1	1	0	1
10	0	1	0	1

Figure 5.15. Karnaugh map for f in Example 5.10.

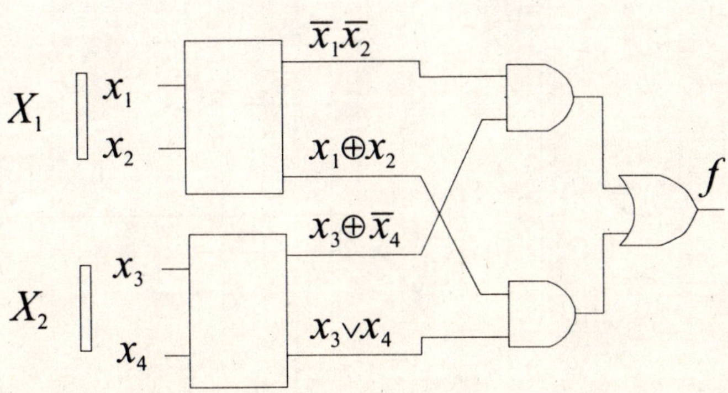

Figure 5.16. Realization of f in Example 5.10 by TVFGs.

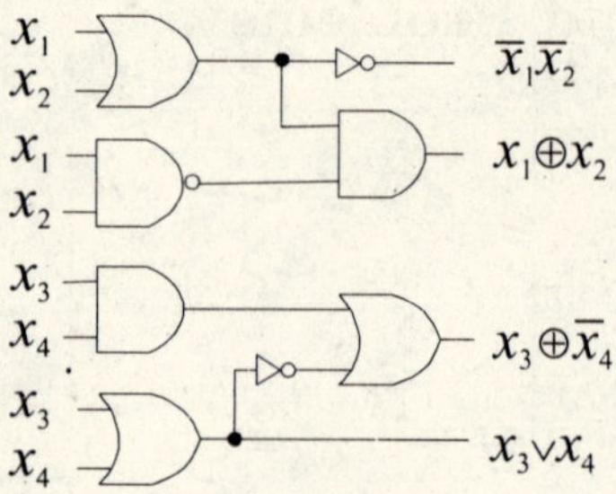

Figure 5.17. Realization of outputs in TVFGs for f in Example 5.10.

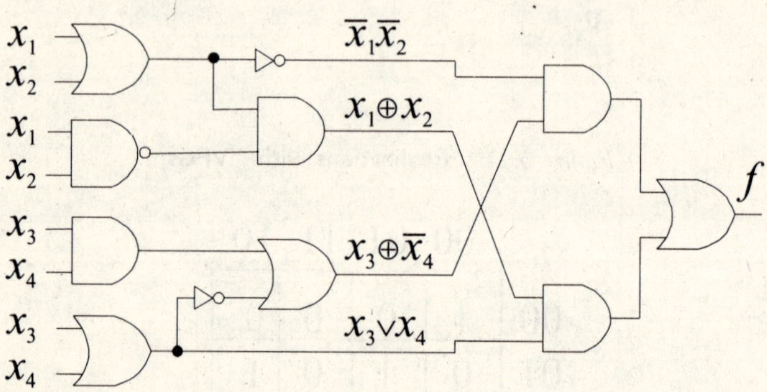

Figure 5.18. Realization of f in Example 5.10.

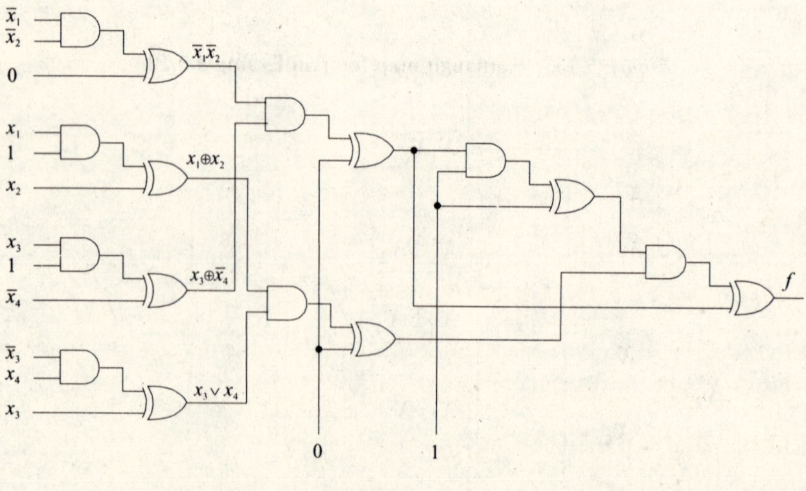

Figure 5.19. Realization of f in Example 5.10 with RM-modules.

5. Exercises and Problems

EXERCISE 5.1 *Check if the functions*

1 $f_1 = x_1 \vee x_2$,

2 $x_1 \rightarrow x_2$,

where $\rightarrow$ *denotes the implication, belong to the same*

1 *P-class,*

2 *NP-class,*

3 *NP = N-class.*

EXERCISE 5.2 *Enumerate all the functions of two variables that belong to the same*

1 *P-class,*

2 *NP-class,*

3 *NPN-class,*

to which belongs the function $x_1 \oplus x_2$.

EXERCISE 5.3 *Determine all functions of* $n \leq 2$ *variables that belong to the same NP class with the function* $f(x_1, x_2) = x_1$.

EXERCISE 5.4 *Determine all functions of* $n \leq 2$ *variables that belong to the same NPN class with the function* $f(x_1, x_2) = x_1 + x_2$.

EXERCISE 5.5 *Determine examples of functions that belong to the same*

1 *P-class,*

2 *NP-class,*

3 *NPN-class,*

with the function $f = x_1x_2 \vee x_1x_3 \vee x_2x_3$.

EXERCISE 5.6 *Determine examples of functions which belong to the same SD-class as the majority function of three variables.*

EXERCISE 5.7 *Check whether the functions*

1 $x_1 \wedge (\overline{x}_2 \vee x_3)$,

2 $x_1 \oplus x_2 \oplus x_3$,

belong to the same SD-class.

EXERCISE 5.8 *Determine all functions of two variables which belong to the same LP-class as the function* $x_1 \wedge x_2$, *and specify the corresponding LP transformations.*

EXERCISE 5.9 *Check if the functions* $x_1 \rightarrow x_2$ *and* $x_1 \vee x_2$ *belong to the same LP-class.*

EXERCISE 5.10 *Determine a function of three variables which belongs to the same LP-class as the function* $\overline{x}_1\overline{x}_2\overline{x}_3$.

EXERCISE 5.11 *Determine all functions of* $n \leq 2$ *variables that belong to the same NP-class with the function* $f(x_1, x_2) = x_1$.

EXERCISE 5.12 *Determine all functions of* $n \leq 2$ *variables that belong to the same NPN-class with the function* $f(x_1, x_2) = x_1 + x_2$.

Chapter 6

SYNTHESIS WITH MULTIPLEXERS

Multiplexers, abbreviated as MUXs, are basic circuits used in present logic design methods. They can be viewed as multi-input switches forwarding a particular input to the output depending on the values assigned to the control inputs. For instance, in [108] *mutiplexers* are formally defined as circuits that select a particular input out of several inputs and route it to a single output bit.

Therefore, multiplexers are data path connection elements, often used in synthesis of logic networks. Further, there are families of FPGAs based on multiplexers, as for example Actel ACT series and CLi 6000 series from Concurrent Logic.

If the number of data inputs is n, the number of control inputs is $k = \lceil \log_2 n \rceil$. In this book, we will mainly consider complete multiplexers, in which case $n = 2^k$. Each data input of a complete multiplexer is selected by a single binary k-tuple on the control inputs.

Fig. 6.1 shows the simplest multiplexer module with two inputs and a control input, thus, usually called (2×1) MUX. Fig. 6.2 shows a realization of this multiplexer in terms of NAND circuits with two inputs.

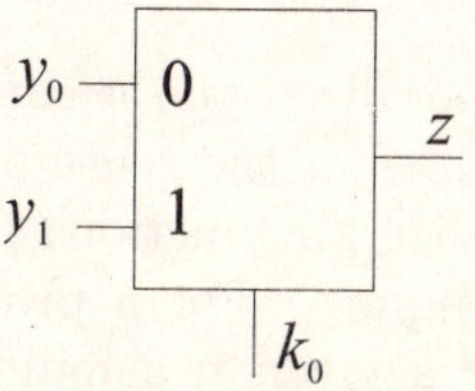

Figure 6.1. (2×1) multiplexer.

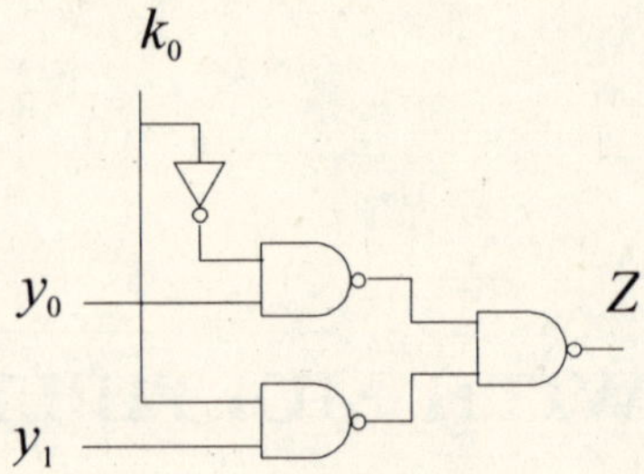

Figure 6.2. Realization of a (2×1) multiplexer by NAND circuits.

A (2×1) multiplexer can be described by the relation

$$z = y_0\overline{k}_0 \oplus y_1 k_0, \tag{6.1}$$

where the notation is as in Fig. 6.1.

It is obvious that a (2×1) multiplexer is a circuit realization of the Shannon expansion, since if $y_0 = f_0$ and $y_1 = f_1$, $k_0 = x_i$, then $z = f$, since $f = \overline{x}_i f_0 \oplus x_i f_1$.

In general, a multiplexer has 2^n inputs and n control inputs, which is called the size of the multiplexer. A good feature of multiplexers is that a multiplexer of a given size can be expressed, which also means realized, by a network with the structure of a tree of multiplexers of smaller size.

EXAMPLE 6.1 *Fig. 6.3 shows realization of a* (4×1) *multiplexer by* (2×1) *and* (3×1) *multiplexers, and the corresponding circuit realization by NAND circuits.*

Different assignments of logic constants and variables to control and data inputs realize different functions at the output of a multiplexer.

EXAMPLE 6.2 *Fig. 6.4 shows realization of four different functions by* (2×1) *multiplexers.*

This example can be generalized and it can be shown that multiplexers are NP-complete modules in the sense of NP-classification, i.e., a size n multiplexer can realize all functions of n variables by negation and permutation of data inputs. For a proof of this statement, it is sufficient to show that for a given n a multiplexer can realize all the NP-representative functions .

EXAMPLE 6.3 *Table 6.4 shows assignment of logic constant and variables for inputs in a* (2×1) *multiplexer to realize NP-representative*

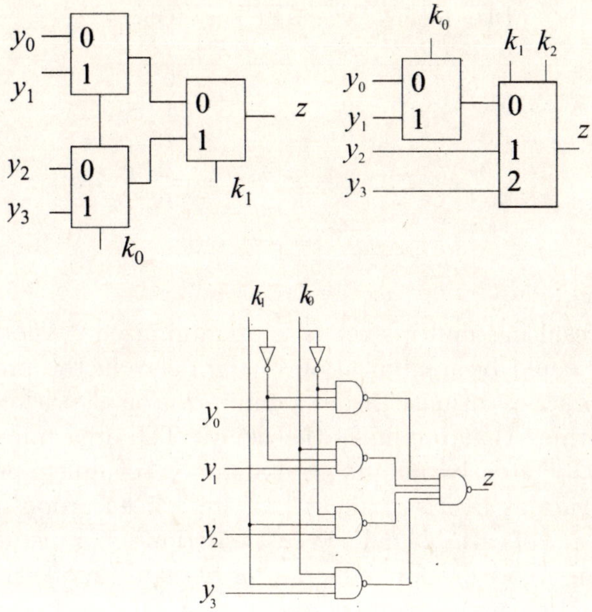

Figure 6.3. Realization of a (4×1) multiplexer by (2×1) and (3×1) multiplexers and NAND circuits.

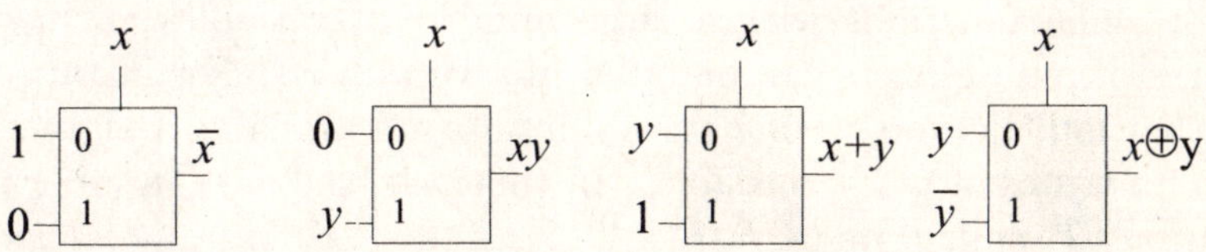

$$z = 1 \cdot \overline{x} \oplus 0 \cdot x = \overline{x} \qquad z = y \cdot \overline{x} \oplus 1 \cdot x = x + y$$

$$z = 0 \cdot \overline{x} \oplus y \cdot x = xy \qquad z = y \cdot \overline{x} \oplus \overline{y} \cdot x = x \oplus y$$

Figure 6.4. Realization of different functions by (2×1) multiplexers.

functions for $n = 2$. Therefore, combined with negation of permutation of inputs, a (2×1) mltiplexer can realize any of the 16 functions of two variables.

1. Synthesis with Multiplexers

The problem of multiplexer synthesis can be formulated as follows. Given a library of multiplexers, synthesize a larger multiplexer using a tree of multiplexer components from a library such that the total

Data Inputs y_0, y_1	Control Input k	Output f
$0, -$	0	0
$0, -$	0	1
$x_0, -$	0	x_0
$0, x_0$	x_1	x_0x_1
$x_1, 1$	x_0	$x_0 \vee x_1$
x_1, x_1	x_0	$x_0 \oplus x_1$

area of the resulting multiplexer is kept minimized. Another criteria of optimality could be minimization of the delay in the produced tree network. In practice, usually the area minimization algorithm is followed by the algorithms that minimize the delay. The area minimization is computationally intensive and, in general, an NP-complete problem. For that reason, various heuristic algorithms have been proposed based on the minimization of suitably defined cost functions. For instance, in [183] is proposed an algorithm for reduction of trees of (2×1) multiplexers. A more general algorithm is proposed in [115]. Some commercial tools for solving problems in multiplexer synthesis are available as provided for example by Ambit Design Systems [21], and Synopsis [30].

When multiplexers with the needed number of inputs are not available, or when functions with a large number of variables are needed, networks of multiplexers can be build in several ways. For instance, assume that multiplexers with k control inputs are available and we are to realize functions of $n > k$ variables. In this case, the data inputs can be the various 2^k co-factors of f, $f_i(x_1, \ldots, x_n) = f(x_1, \ldots, x_n)$ for fixed k variables and control inputs are arbitrary functions of k variables.

Consider a switching function $f(x_1, \ldots, x_k, x_{k+1}, \ldots x_n)$. Let the system of switching functions

$$\begin{gathered} g_1(x_1, \ldots, x_k), \\ g_2(x_1, \ldots, x_k), \\ \vdots, \\ g_k(x_1, \ldots, x_k), \end{gathered}$$

form a bijection $(g_1, \ldots, g_k)^T : \{0,1\}^k \to \{0,1\}^k$.

It is clear that because $(g_1, \ldots, g_k)$ is a bijection, we can write f in the form

$$\begin{aligned} f(x_1, \ldots, x_n) &= \overline{g}_1 \cdots \overline{g}_{k-1}\overline{g}_k h_{0\cdots 00}(x_{k+1}, \ldots, x_n) \\ &\quad \oplus \overline{g}_1 \cdots \overline{g}_{k-1} g_k h_{0\cdots 01}(x_{k+1}, \ldots, x_n) \\ &\quad \oplus g_1 \cdots g_{k-1} g_k h_{1\cdots 11}(x_{k+1}, \ldots, x_n). \end{aligned}$$

Actually, for the function f, the co-factors $h_{0\cdots 00}, h_{0\cdots 01}, \ldots, h_{1\cdots 11}$ with respect to $g_1, \ldots, g_k$ are just a permutation of the standard co-factors with respect to the Shannon expansion. However, determination of both co-factors of the given function for data inputs and functions for control inputs that will provide a network with minimum number of multiplexers is a very complex task. Therefore, in practice functions applied to control inputs are usually restricted to switching variables, which simplifies the determination of the co-factors of a given function f that are feed into data inputs. In this way, synthesis with multiplexers reduces to recursive application of the Shannon expansion and the networks produced have the structure of a tree. Depth of the network, i.e., number of levels can be controlled by selecting the number of variables in respect to which the decomposition is preformed at the price of complexity of generation of co-factors for f. If the Shannon decomposition is performed with respect to all the variables, the resulting multiplexer network is a complete tree and data inputs are elements of the truth-vector for the function realized.

EXAMPLE 6.4 *Fig. 6.5 illustrates realization of three-variable functions by a multiplexer network with the structure of a tree. Fig. 6.6 shows how to use the same network to realize functions of four variables.*

1.1 Optimization of Multiplexer Networks

The optimization of multiplexer networks is usually viewed as the reduction of the number of multiplexer modules. As noted above, this problem is closely related to the determination of data and control inputs. Even in the case of networks with the structure of a tree, the global optimization is difficult to perform. Therefore, the task is often simplified and reduced to the minimization of the number of multiplexers at the level $i+1$ by the consideration of modules at the level i. In this setting, a multiplexer at the level $i+1$ is redundant if the output of a multiplexer r at the i-th level is related to the output of another multiplexer j at the same level by any of the relations

1 $f_r = 0$, $f_r = 1$, $f_r = x_j$, $f_r = \overline{x}_j$,

2 $f_r = f_j$, $r \neq j$,

3 $f_r = \overline{f}_j$, $r \neq j$.

Fig. 6.7 shows realization of the complement of a function in the same way as the realization of the complement of a variable as shown in Fig. 6.4.

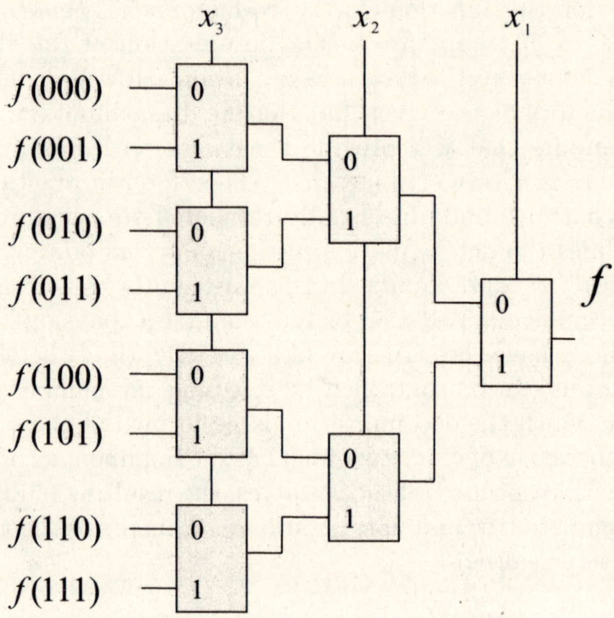

Figure 6.5. Network with the structure of a tree for $n = 3$.

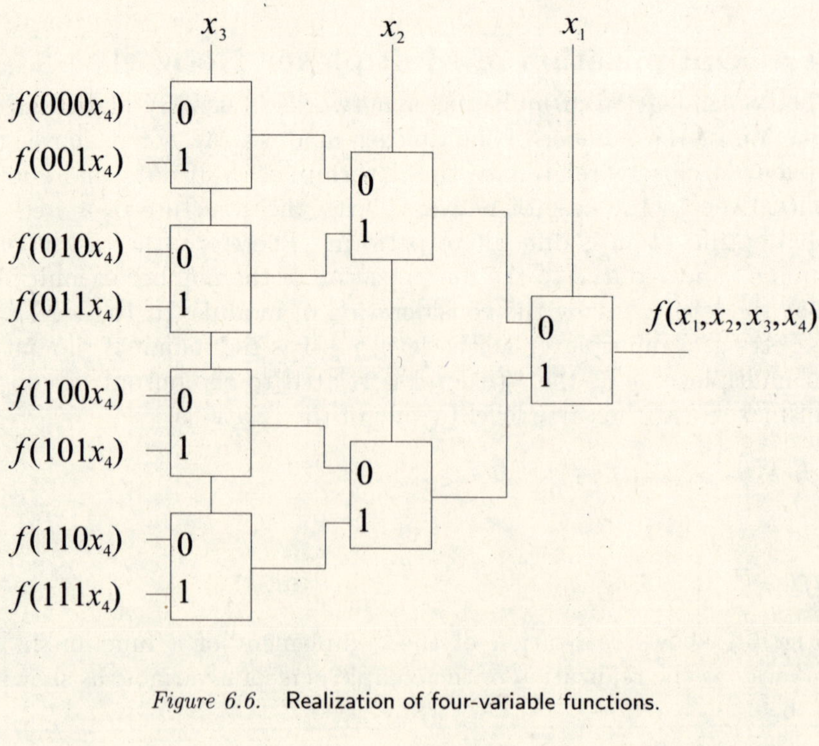

Figure 6.6. Realization of four-variable functions.

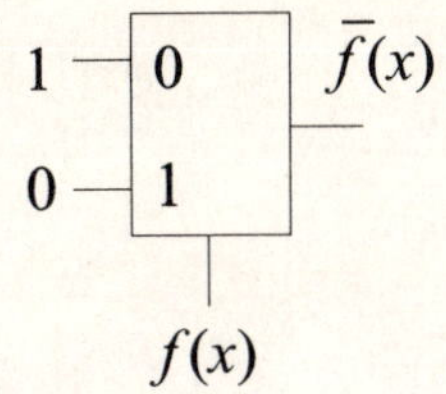

Figure 6.7. Realization of $\overline{f}$.

In [162], it is defined a spectral transform that permits efficient determination of redundant multiplexers in the way specified above. It is shown that in the case of realization of n-variable functions by multiplexers with k control inputs, the upper bounds of the number of levels is $L = \frac{n-1}{k}$, and the minimum number of modules is $M = \sum_{i=0}^{L-1} 2^{ik}$ [162].

A spectral method which guarantees a minimum network in the number of modules count uses the Walsh transform to determine the cofactors of a given function, called the residual functions, that will be applied on the data inputs of multiplexers [71].

1.2 Networks with Different Assignments of Inputs

Instead of networks with the structure of a tree, serial connections of multiplexers also realize arbitrary switching functions provided that a proper choice of functions is applied at control inputs of multiplexers. Such networks can be viewed as examples of universal logic networks.

EXAMPLE 6.5 *Fig. 6.8 shows a network consisting of seven* (2×1) *multiplexers connected serially. If at the control inputs elementary products of switching variables are applied, this network can realize an arbitrary switching function of* $n = 3$ *variables. In this figure, we show the values of product terms (the first and every second row further) and the outputs of each multiplexer for different assignments of switching variables. It can be seen from the rightmost column, that the output of the network produces the value of the function realized for each corresponding assignment of primary variables. Since elementary products are applied to control inputs, it is clear that the network realizes the positive polarity Reed-Muller expressions.*

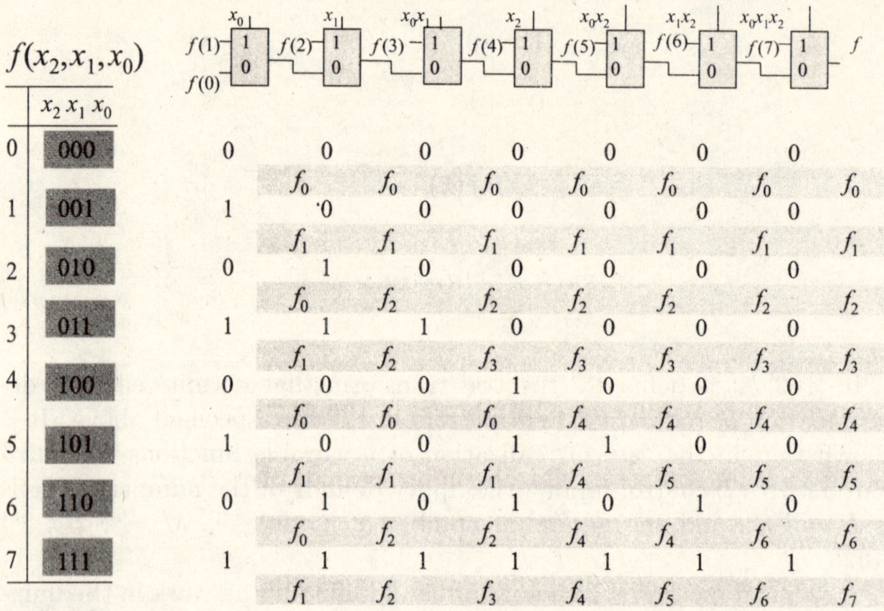

Figure 6.8. Multiplexer network with elementary product of variables at control inputs.

1.3 Multiplexer Networks from BDD

Non-terminal nodes in Binary decision diagrams are defined as graphic representations of the Shannon expansion, and since multiplexers are circuit realizations of this expansion, there is a direct correspondence between BDDs and multiplexer networks as specified in Table 6.1 and illustrated in Fig. 6.9. This correspondence determines a straightforward procedure for synthesizing of multiplexer networks from BDDs.

ALGORITHM 6.1 (Network from BDD)

1 *Given a BDD for f. Replace each non-terminal node including the root node by a (2×1) multiplexer.*

2 *Set interconnections of multiplexers as determined by the edges in the BDD.*

EXAMPLE 6.6 *Fig. 6.10 shows a BDD for the function $f = x_1x_2 \vee x_3$ and the corresponding multiplexer network for f.*

EXAMPLE 6.7 *Fig. 6.11 shows BDD for the function $f = \overline{x}_3\overline{x}_2\overline{x}_1\overline{x}_0 \oplus x_3x_2x_1x_0$, whose truth-vector is $\mathbf{F} = [1,0,0,0,0,0,0,0,0,0,0,0,0,0,0,1]^T$.*

Table 6.1. Correspondence between BDDs and (2×2) multiplexers.

BDD	Network
Non-terminal nodes	$MUX(2 \times 1)$
Edges	Interconections
Constant nodes	Inputs
Root node	Output

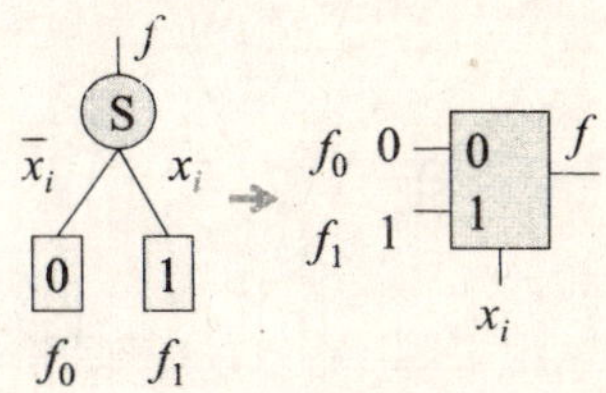

Figure 6.9. Correspondence between BDDs and $MUX(2 \times 1)$.

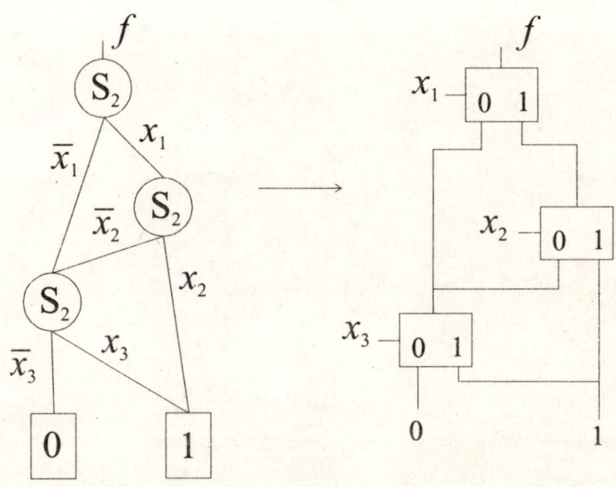

Figure 6.10. BDD and the multiplexer network for f in Example 6.6.

This function can be realized by the multiplexer network in Fig. 6.12 or alternatively by logic networks with AND-OR elements with four and two inputs. Table 6.2 compares the complexities of these three realizations.

EXAMPLE 6.8 *The function f in Example 6.7 can be realized by the network in Fig. 6.13 and it is shown [31] that it is optimal in both the*

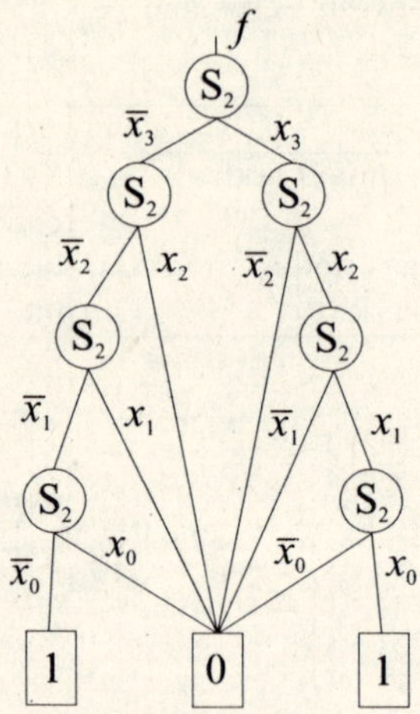

Figure 6.11. BDD for f in Example 6.7.

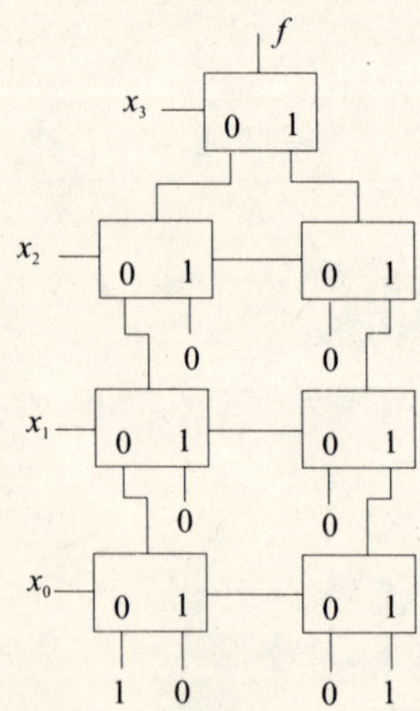

Figure 6.12. Multiplexer network for f in Example 6.7.

Table 6.2. Complexity of realization in Example 6.7.

Complexity	MUX	$AND - OR$ four-inputs	$AND - OR$ two-inputs
Levels	2	3	4
Circuits	3	7	7
Interconnections	10	14	21

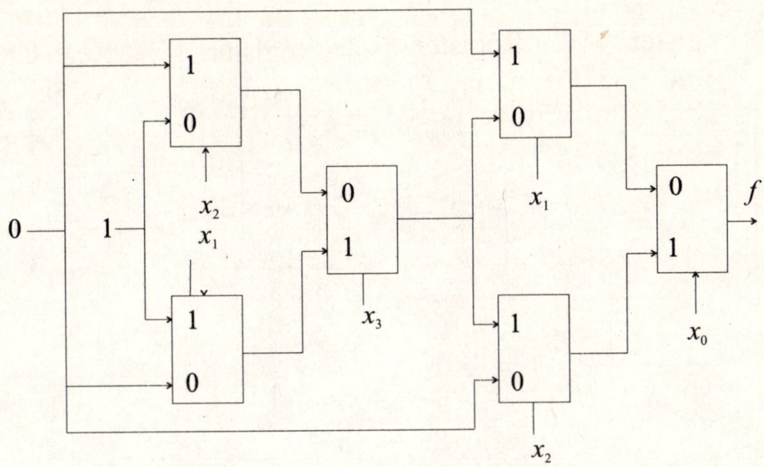

Figure 6.13. The optimized multiplexer network for f in Example 6.7.

number of multiplexers and the propagation delay, under the requirement that the realization is performed with (2×1) *multiplexers. Another good feature of this network is that the primary inputs are logic constants 0 and 1. However, in this realization, functions at the control inputs are determined separately for each module, which is not a simple task for larger networks, and can hardly be given an algorithm that can handle arbitrary functions.*

2. Applications of Multiplexers

There are some standard applications of multiplexers, and many of them are related to the manipulation of registers in a computer.

EXAMPLE 6.9 *Fig. 6.14 shows a memory with four registers A, B, C, and D, the contents of which should be transferred into a particular register E. The register whose contents is transferred into E is defined by a multiplexer network.*

Another important case is the selection of an m-bit word among the 2^n possible words.

EXAMPLE 6.10 *Fig. 6.15 shows a switch for words where* $m = 2$ *and* $n = 2$, *that is, the network performs selection of a four-bit word among four different words by transferring the corresponding bits of each given word to the outputs of the network.*

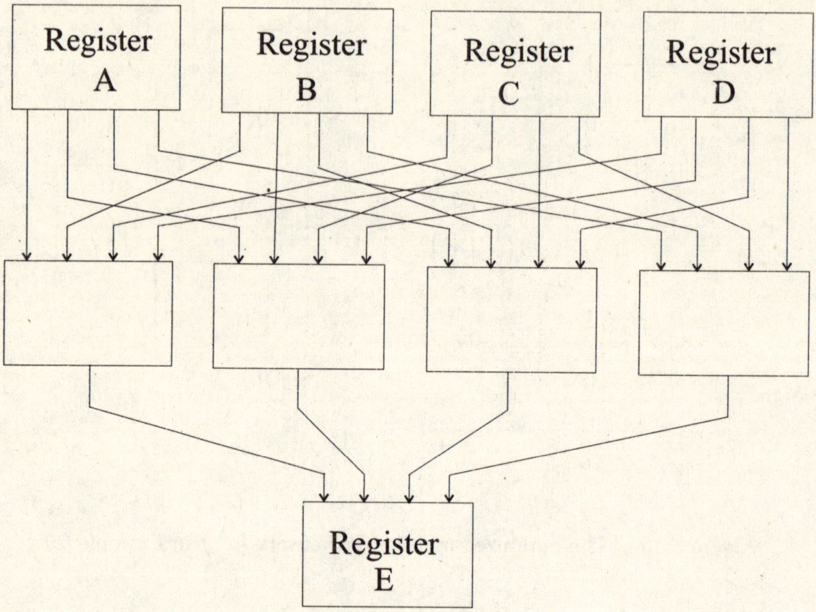

Figure 6.14. Application of multiplexers.

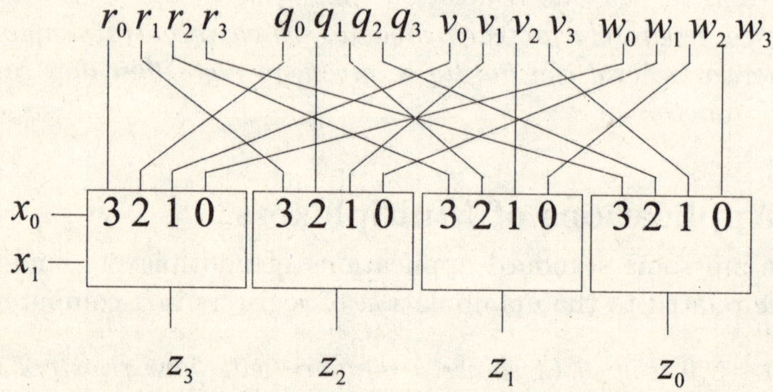

Figure 6.15. Switch for words realized as a network of multiplexers.

EXAMPLE 6.11 *A cross-bar switch is a two-input* x_0, x_1 *two-output* y_0, y_1 *device with a control input* w *that realizes the mapping* $y_0 = \overline{w}x_0 + wx_1$ *and* $y_1 = \overline{w}x_1 + wx_0$. *Fig. 6.16 shows a symbol and a realization of the cross-bar switch by* (2×1) *multiplexers.*

Cross-bar network is a network which performs arbitrary permutations between the inputs and the outputs.

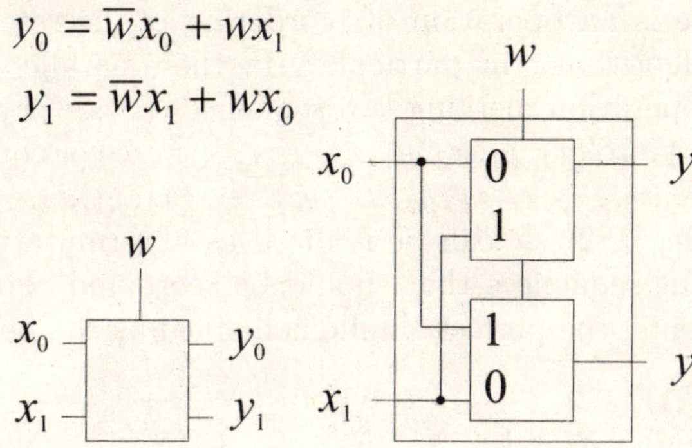

Figure 6.16. Cross-bar switch and realization with multiplexers.

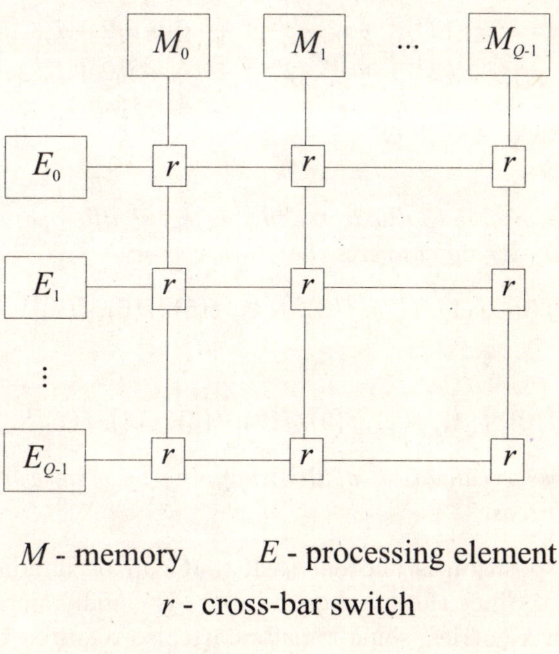

Figure 6.17. Cross-bar network for $Q = 4$.

EXAMPLE 6.12 *Consider Q processing elements that communicate with Q memory modules. The cross-bar network provides conflict-free communication paths such that a processing element can access any memory module if there is no other element reading or writing the same module. Fig. 6.17 shows the cross-bar network for $Q = 4$.*

Perfect shuffle is an operation of reordering of discrete data and is met in many algorithms, in particular, in their parallel implementations. It is the operation merging two sequences $(x_1, x_2, x_3, \ldots, x_r)$ and $(y_1, y_2, y_3, \ldots, y_r)$ into $(x_1, y_1, x_2, y_2, x_3, y_3, \ldots, x_r, y_r)$ or equivalently the permutation $(x_1, x_2, \ldots, x_r, y_1, y_2, \ldots, y_r) \rightarrow (x_1, y_1, x_2, y_2, \ldots, x_r, y_r)$, see, foer example, [182]. It can be realized as a permutation of indices of elements of the sequences that should be reordered. For a sequence of $N = 2^n$ elements, the perfect shuffle is defined as the permutation

$$
\begin{aligned}
P(i) &= 2i, & 0 \leq i \leq N/2 - 1, \\
P(i) &= 2i + 1 - N, & N/2 \leq i \leq N - 1.
\end{aligned}
$$

Notice that if the indices of elements that should be permuted are represented in binary form, then the i-th element is shuffled to the new position j determined by

$$
\begin{aligned}
i &= i_{n-1}2^{n-1} + i_{n-2}2^{n-2} + \cdots + i_1 2 + i_0, \\
j &= i_{n-2}2^{n-1} + i_{n-3}2^{n-2} + \cdots + i_0 2 + i_{n-1}.
\end{aligned}
$$

Multiplexers are a standard part of a network realizing the perfect shuffle.

EXAMPLE 6.13 *Fig. 6.18 illustrates the perfect shuffle operation for* $2^3 = 8$ *data. This reordering converts the truth-vector*

$$
\mathbf{F} = [f(0), f(1), f(2), f(3), f(4), f(5), f(6), f(7)]^T
$$

into

$$
\mathbf{F} = [f(0), f(4), f(1), f(5), f(2), f(6), f(3), f(7)]^T.
$$

Fig. 6.19 shows a realization of this mapping by a network containing (2×1) *multiplexers.*

Matrix transposition is another task that can be handled by multiplexer networks. Since the number of inputs is usually smaller than the number of matrix entries, some registers are also required to delay data before relocation and forwarding to the output. In two-dimensional networks, the delay is performed in parallel lines. Multiplexers as parts of networks are used to exchange data between different locations. Networks for matrix transposition form a subclass of permutation networks. In the design of such networks, the optimization goal is the minimization of the number of multiplexers or registers. In [10], [11] it is proposed a design methodology for two-dimensional networks for matrix transposition with minimum number of registers. These networks will be illustrated in the following example.

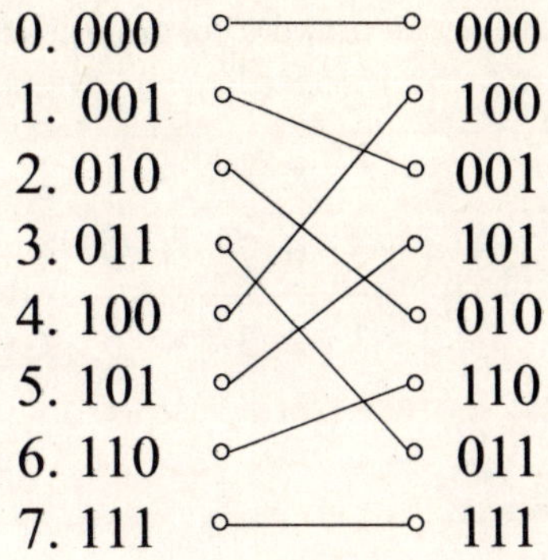

Figure 6.18. Perfect shuffle for $n = 3$.

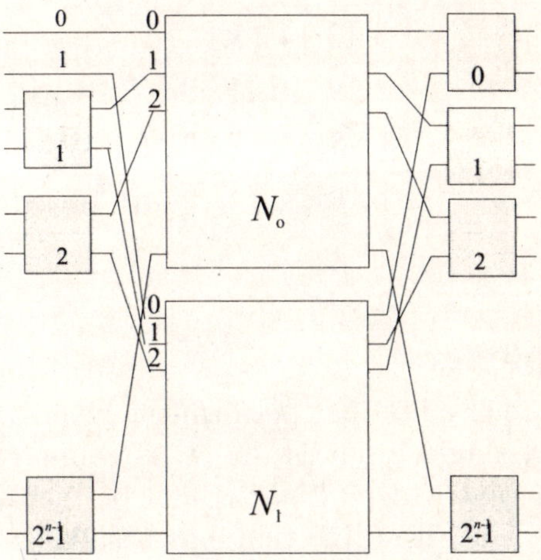

Figure 6.19. Realization of the perfect shuffle by multiplexers.

EXAMPLE 6.14 *Consider the design of a network for transposition of* (4×4) *matrices. The elements of these matrices are denoted by* 0, 1,...,15. *The data are allocated to the registers as specified in Table 6.3. At each clock cycle, data are shifted in parallel and sent to the output immediately when they become available. In Table 6.3 a backward allocation of the data elements is shown by the arrows. Circles denote data that are sent to the output. Fig. 6.20 shows the structure of the corresponding network for the transposition of* (4×4) *matrices.*

Table 6.3. Allocation of data in the network for transposition of a (4×4) matrix.

time	$t=1$	$t=2$	$t=3$	$t=4$
Input	0 1 2 3	4 5 6 7	8 9 10 11	12 13 14 15
$D_0D_1D_2D_3$		0 1 2 3	4 5 6 7	8 9 10 11
$D_4D_5D_6D_7$			0 1 2 3	4 5 6 7
$D_8D_9D_{10}D_{11}$				0 1 2 3
Output				0 4 8 12

	$t=5$	$t=6$	$t=7$
Input			
$D_0D_1D_2D_3$	3 13 14 15		
$D_4D_5D_6D_7$	2 9 10 11	3 7 14 15	
$D_8D_9D_{10}D_{11}$	1 5 6 7	2 6 10 11	3 7 11 15
Output	1 5 9 13	2 6 10 14	3 7 11 15

3. Demultiplexers

Demultiplexers are circuits that perform the inverse operation of multiplexers, that is, a single input is directed to one of the 2^n possible outputs. It follows that a *demultiplexer* can be viewed as a multilevel switch as illustrated in Fig. 6.15, that has a single input y, n control inputs, and 2^n outputs.

Similarly to multiplexers, a demultiplexer with a larger number of control inputs, can be realized by a combination of demultiplexers of the smaller size. Fig. 6.23 shows realization of a multiplexer with four control inputs, i.e., (1×4) demultiplexer, by three (1×2) demultiplexers arranged into a network with the structure of a tree. Fig. 6.24 shows realization of a (1×4) demultiplexer by NAND circuits.

4. Synthesis with Demultiplexers

Demultiplexers can be used in circuit synthesis in similar ways as multiplexers, however, their main use is as address decoders. In this case, the data input is set to the logic value 1, $y = 1$, and the control inputs to which switching variables $x_1, \ldots, x_n$ has been applied, are considered

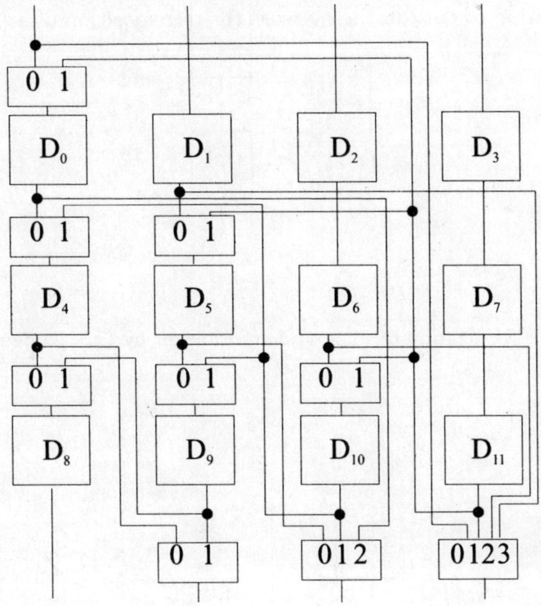

Figure 6.20. A network for transposition of (4×4) matrices.

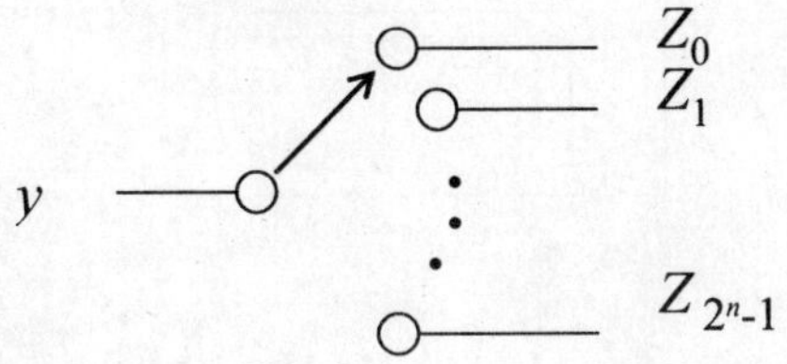

Figure 6.21. Principle of the demultiplexer.

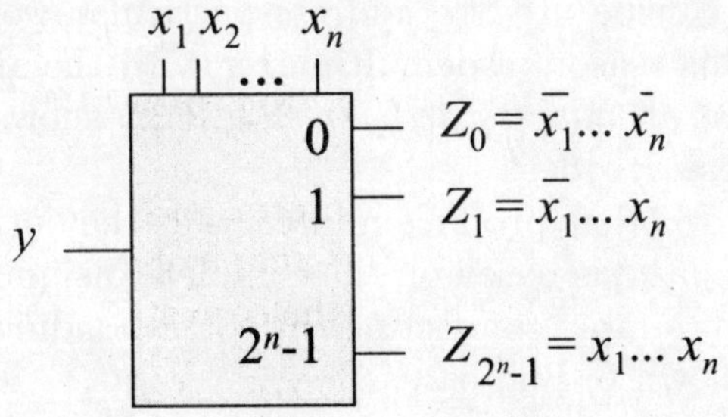

Figure 6.22. Demultiplexer.

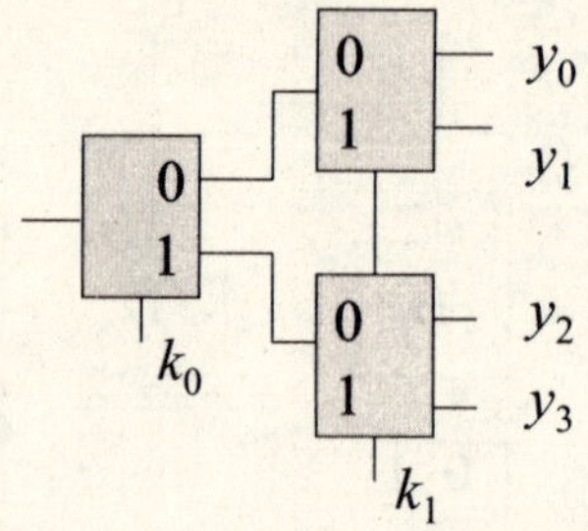

Figure 6.23. Realization of (1×4) demultiplexer by (1×2) demultiplexers.

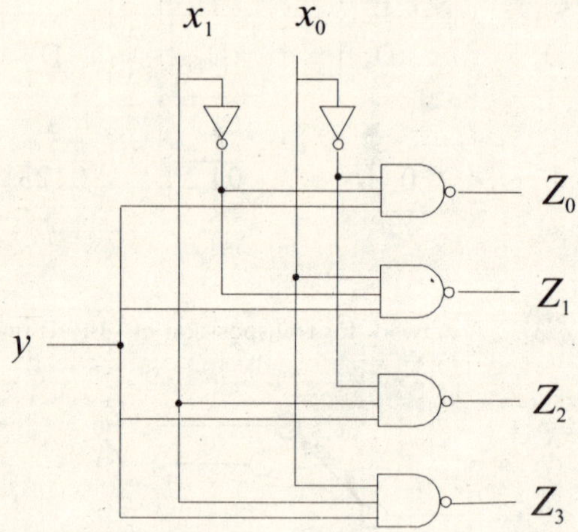

Figure 6.24. Realization of a (1×4) demultiplexer by NAND circuits.

as primary inputs. The minterms that are generated at the outputs of a demultiplexer can be used to address particular words in a memory structure. For this reason, a demultiplexer with the above assignments of inputs is called an *address decoder*. Fig. 6.25 shows a demultiplexer used as an address decoder.

Since address decoders produce minterms at the outputs, they can be used for circuit synthesis based on the complete disjunctive normal form representations by simply connecting the corresponding outputs by logic OR circuits as shown in Fig. 6.26.

EXAMPLE 6.15 *Fig. 6.27 shows realization of the function f from Example 6.7 by an address decoder with four inputs.*

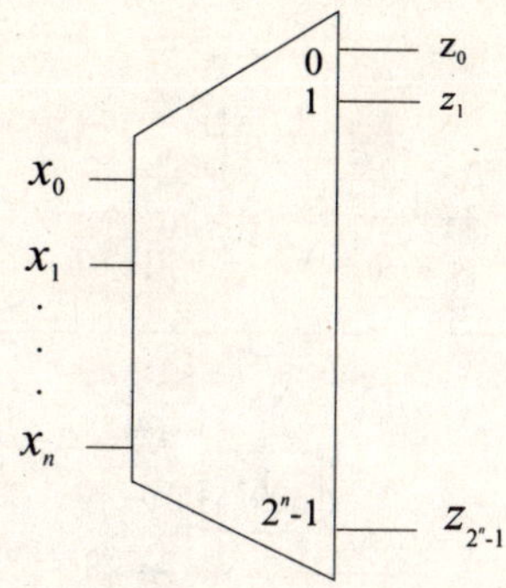

Figure 6.25. Address decoder.

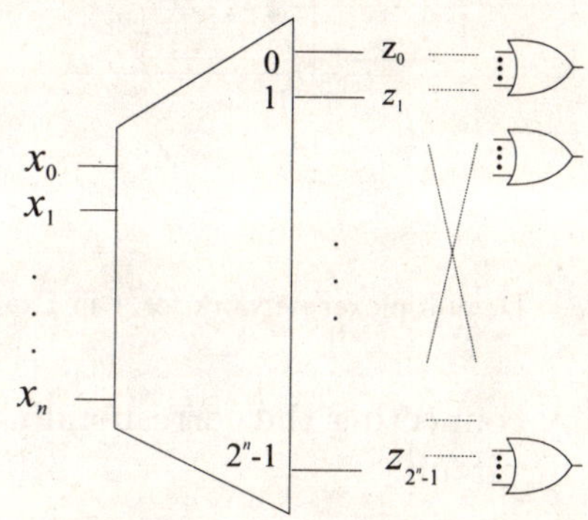

Figure 6.26. Synthesis from the complete disjunctive normal form by address decoders.

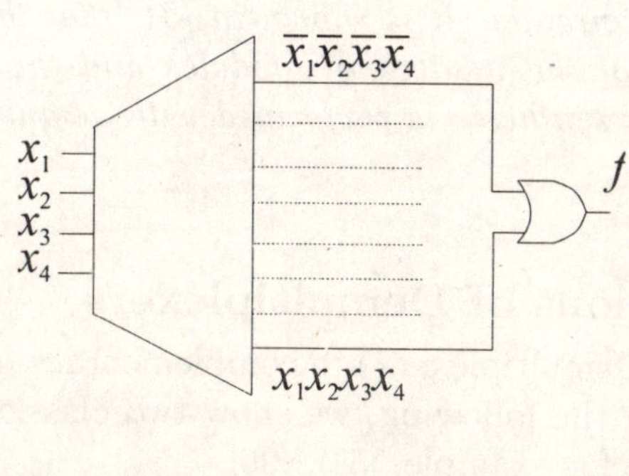

Figure 6.27. Synthesis with address decoder.

Due to the duality of the functions of multiplexers and demultiplexers, a network of multiplexers can be converted into an equivalent network

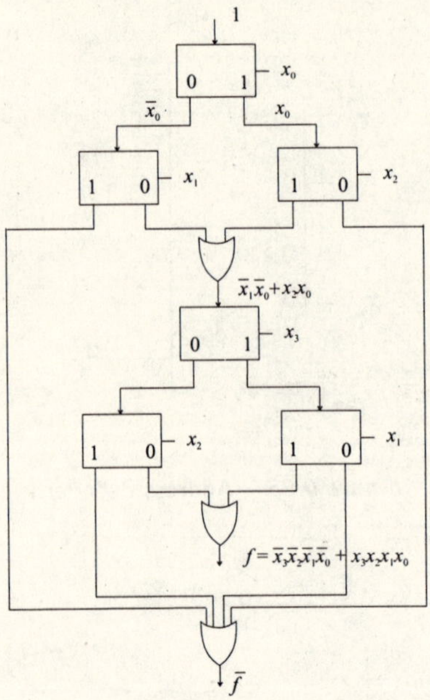

Figure 6.28. Demultiplexer network for f in Example 6.7.

with demultiplexers by connecting the corresponding outputs of demultiplexers with logic OR circuits.

EXAMPLE 6.16 *Fig. 6.28 shows the demultiplexer network realizing the function f in Example 6.7. This network is derived by replacing multiplexers in the network in Fig. 6.13 with demultiplexers and connecting the outputs by OR circuits. It is shown in [31] that this is the minimal network in terms of the number of modules and the delay, under the restriction that the synthesis is performed with demultiplexers with two control inputs.*

5. Applications of Demultiplexers

Applications of demultiplexers are complementary or similar to those of multiplexers. In the following, we show two classical applications of demultiplexers, see for example, [31], [96].

EXAMPLE 6.17 *Fig. 6.29 shows a network with demultiplexers used to transfer the contents of a register E to any of four available registers A, B, C, and D.*

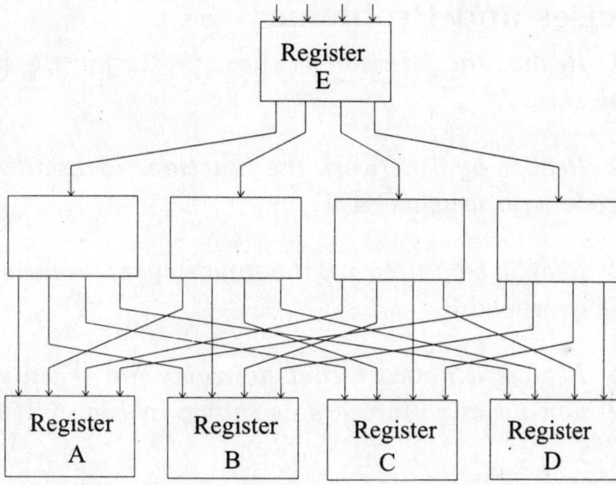

Figure 6.29. Demultiplexer network for transferring contents of registers.

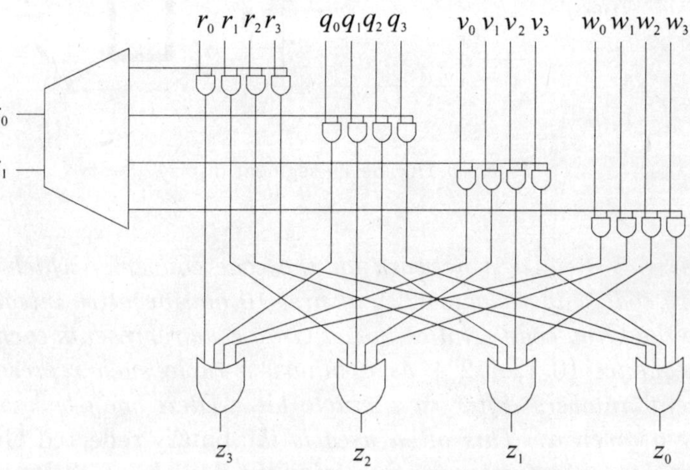

Figure 6.30. Switch for words by using address decoder.

EXAMPLE 6.18 *Fig. 6.30 shows a switch for words described in Example 6.10 realized by using an address decoder with two inputs.*

6. Exercises and Problems

EXERCISE 6.1 *Realize the function* $f(z) = z^2 + 2z$ *for* $z \in \{0, \ldots, 7\}$ *by* (4×1) *multiplexers.*

EXERCISE 6.2 *Realize by a network the function representing parity bit for the BCD code with weights* 8421.

EXERCISE 6.3 *Realize by a network the function representing odd parity bit for the code* overhead 3.

EXERCISE 6.4 *Realize a network that activates the seven-segment display of first 10 non-negative integers as shown in Fig. 6.31.*

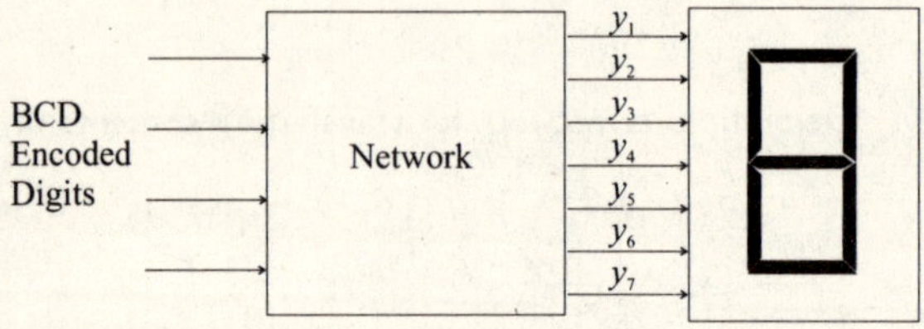

Figure 6.31. Seven-segment display.

EXERCISE 6.5 *Realize a network for the code converter which converts the binary code with weights* 4221 *of first 10 non-negative integers numbers into the Gray code. Notice that a Gray code represents each number in the sequence* $\{0, 1, \ldots 2^n\}$ *as a binary* n*-tuple such representations of adjacent numbers differ in a single bit. There may be many Gray codes for a given* n*. This often used is the* binary-reflected Gray code *which can be generated by starting from the* n*-tuple of all bits zero and successively flipping the right-most bit that produces a new sequence.*

EXERCISE 6.6 *Denote by* AB *and* CD *coordinates of two two-bit binary numbers. Realize a network whose output is* 1 *when the number* AB *is greater than* CD*.*

EXERCISE 6.7 *Realize a network whose input are first 10 non-negative integers* x *in the Gray code, and whose output has the value* 1 *when* $5 \leq x \leq 7$.

EXERCISE 6.8 *Realize a network which generates the output* $f(x) = x(\text{mod}3) + 4$ *for* $0 \leq x \leq 25$.

Table 6.4. BCD and Hamming code.

	BCD	Hamming
0	0000	0000000
1	0001	0000111
2	0010	0011001
3	0011	0011110
4	0100	0101010
5	0101	0101101
6	0110	0110011
7	0111	0110100
8	1000	1001011
9	1001	1001100

EXERCISE 6.9 *Realize the code converter which converts the binary (BCD) code into the Hamming code as specified in Table 6.4.*

EXERCISE 6.10 *[94]*
Consider the switching function $f(x_1, x_2, x_3)$ defined by the set of decimal indices corresponding to 1-minterms $f(1) = \{0, 4, 6, 7\}$. Realize f by an (8×1) decoder and an OR circuit. Repeat the realization with the same decoder and an NOR circuit. Compare the realizations in the number of required outputs of the decoder.

EXERCISE 6.11 *[94]*
The function $f(x_1, x_2, x_3)$ is given by the set of decimal indices of 1-minterms $f(1) = \{0, 3, 4, 5, 6\}$. Realize f by an (8×1) decoder and an AND circuit and the same decoder and a NAND circuit. Compare these realizations in the number of required nodes of the decoder.

EXERCISE 6.12 *[94]*
Realize the switching function $f = x_1\overline{x}_3 + x_1\overline{x}_2 + \overline{x}_1\overline{x}_2\overline{x}_3 + \overline{x}_1 x_2 x_3$ by an (8×1) multiplexer. Compare it with the realizations with (4×1) and (2×1) multiplexers. Use the Shannon expansions to determine the corresponding inputs.

EXERCISE 6.13 *Realize the switching function $f = x_1\overline{x}_2 x_5 + \overline{x}_2\overline{x}_3 x_5 + \overline{x}_2 x_3\overline{x}_5 + \overline{x}_2 x_4 x_5 + x_3 x_4\overline{x}_5$ by a (4×1) multiplexer and logic AND and OR circuits.*

Start by the Shannon expansion of f with respect to two variables that appear in the largest number of products.

EXERCISE 6.14 *[94]*
Realize the function $f = x_1\overline{x}_3x_4 + x_1\overline{x}_2x_4x_5 + x_1x_2x_4\overline{x}_5 + \overline{x}_1\overline{x}_2\overline{x}_3\overline{x}_4\overline{x}_5 + \overline{x}_1\overline{x}_2x_3\overline{x}_4x_5 + \overline{x}_1x_2\overline{x}_3\overline{x}_4x_5 + \overline{x}_1x_2x_3\overline{x}_4\overline{x}_5$ *by* (4×1) *multiplexers.*

EXERCISE 6.15 *Realize the function* $f(x_1, x_2, x_3) = x_1x_2 \vee x_1x_2x_3$ *by a* (4×1) *multiplexer network, with the minimum number of modules.*

EXERCISE 6.16 *From the BDD for the function* $f(x_1, x_2, x_3, x_4) = x_1x_2 \vee x_1x_3 \vee x_2x_3x_4$*, determine the corresponding* (2×1) *multiplexer network. Compare realizations with BDDs for a few different orders of variables.*

EXERCISE 6.17 *Realize the function* $f(x_1, x_2, x_3, x_4) = x_1 \oplus x_2 \oplus x_3 \oplus x_4$ *by a network of*

1. (2×1),
2. (4×1),
3. (8×1),

multiplexers.

EXERCISE 6.18 *Realize the function from Exercise 6.16 by* (4×1) *multiplexers using the following combination of variables at control inputs*

1. (x_1, x_3) *and* (x_2, x_4),
2. (x_1, x_4), *and* (x_2, x_3).

EXERCISE 6.19 *Realize the function in Exercise 6.16 by a network consisting of* (1×2) *demultiplexers.*

EXERCISE 6.20 *Determine the function* f *realized by the network in Fig. 6.32.*

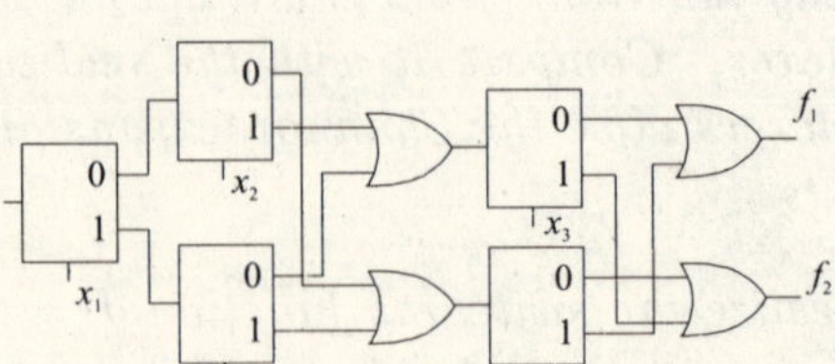

Figure 6.32. Network in Exercise 6.20.

Chapter 7

REALIZATIONS WITH ROM

A *Read Only Memory* (ROM) is a part of computer devices used to store data written by manufacturers that is only meant to be read by the user. It can be viewed as a two-dimensional array of cells $m_{i,j}$ with N inputs $y_1, \ldots, y_{N-1}$ and M outputs $z_1, \ldots, z_{M-1}$. Fig. 7.1 shows the structure of a ROM. When the input y_i is activated, it reads the contents of the cells $m_{i,j}$ in the i-th row and sends the content of each to the corresponding output z_j. The output $z_1, \ldots, z_{M-1}$, called the word in the memory, is therefore determined by

$$z_j = \bigvee_{i=0}^{N-1} y_i m_{i,j}, \quad 0 \leq j \leq M-1.$$

1. Realizations with ROM

ROMs can be used to realize multi-output functions with M outputs if the memory cell $m_{i,j}$ contains the i-th value of the j-th output when expressed in disjunctive normal form. Thus, if $m_{i,j} = f_j(i)$, then

$$z_j(y_1, \ldots, y_{N-1}) = \bigvee_{i=0}^{2^n-1} m_i(x) f_j(i) = f_j(x), \quad 0 \leq j \leq M-1.$$

In this case, the inputs y_i, $i = 0, \ldots, 2^n - 1$ are determined as outputs of an address decoder. Fig. 7.2 shows principle of the realization of an output function by ROM.

EXAMPLE 7.1 *The sum and carry bits of a three bit adder are represented by truth-vectors*

$$\mathbf{F}_0 = [0,1,1,0,1,0,0,1]^T,$$

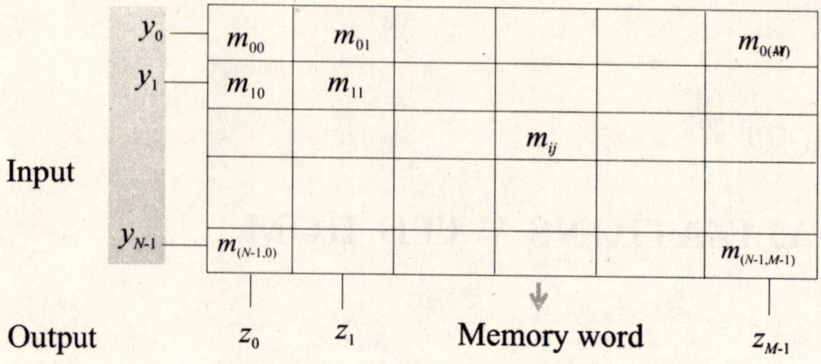

$$z_j = \bigvee_{i=0}^{N-1} y_j m_{ij} \qquad 0 \leq j \leq M-1$$

Figure 7.1. Structure of a ROM.

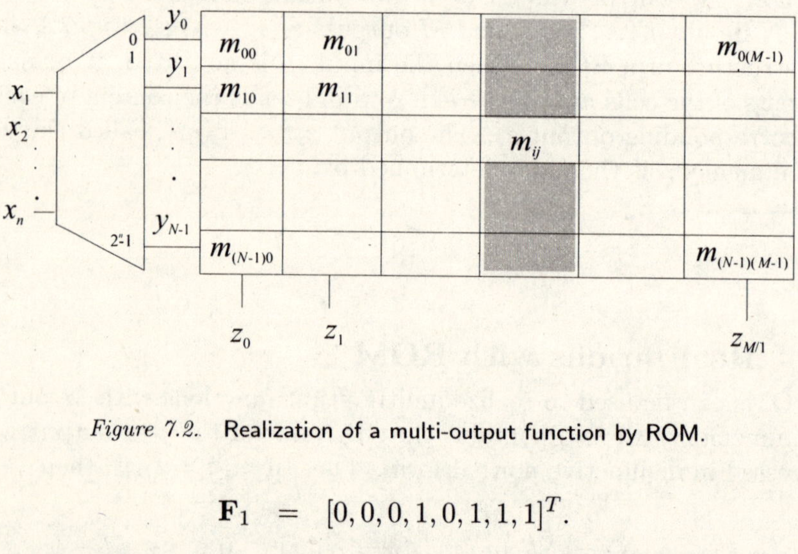

Figure 7.2. Realization of a multi-output function by ROM.

$$\mathbf{F}_1 = [0,0,0,1,0,1,1,1]^T.$$

This two-output function can be realized by a ROM as shown in Fig. 7.3. It is obvious that in this realization it is actually implemented the complete disjunctive normal form

$$\begin{aligned} f &= \overline{x}_1\overline{x}_2\overline{x}_3 f(0) \vee \overline{x}_1\overline{x}_2 x_3 f(1) \vee \overline{x}_1 x_2\overline{x}_3 f(2) \vee \overline{x}_1 x_2 x_3 f(3) \\ &\vee x_1\overline{x}_2\overline{x}_3 f(4) \vee x_1\overline{x}_2 x_3 f(5) \vee x_1 x_2\overline{x}_3 f(6) \vee x_1 x_2 x_3 f(7). \end{aligned}$$

Code converters are devices that perform conversion from one representation into another. The following example illustrates a converter from binary coded digits (BCD) into the Grey code, which is a code

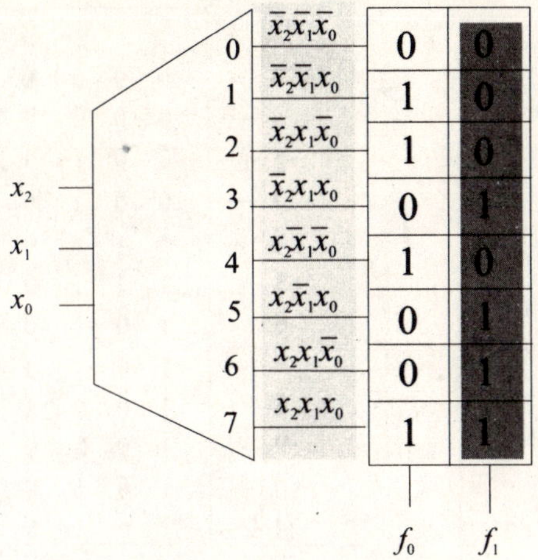

Figure 7.3. Realization of the three-bit adder by ROM.

where the successive code words differ in a single bit. Notice that there several ways to define a Gray code with this property and few of them are used in the practice.

EXAMPLE 7.2 *BCD to Gray code converter is a device whose input is a four-bit BCD number and the output is a four-bit Gray code number. It can be described by the following set of functions*

$$\begin{aligned} f_1 &= x_1 + x_2x_4 + x_2x_3, \\ f_2 &= x_2\overline{x}_3, \\ f_3 &= x_2 + x_3, \\ f_4 &= \overline{x}_1\overline{x}_2\overline{x}_3x_4 + x_2x_3x_4 + x_1\overline{x}_4 + \overline{x}_2x_3\overline{x}_4. \end{aligned}$$

Fig. 7.4 shows a realization of this code converter.

EXAMPLE 7.3 *Seven segment display is a standard way to write numbers in an electronic form. Segments are highlighted separately to form combinations that show digits. Each segment is controlled by a switching function and if these functions are written in terms of variables* x_3, x_2, x_1, x_0, *then functioning of the seven segment display can be descried by the set of functions*

$$\begin{aligned} f_0 &= x_3 \vee x_1 \vee \overline{x}_2\overline{x}_0 \vee x_2x_0, \\ f_1 &= \overline{x}_2 \vee \overline{x}_1\overline{x}_0 \vee x_1x_0, \\ f_2 &= x_3 \vee x_2 \vee \overline{x}_1 \vee x_0, \end{aligned}$$

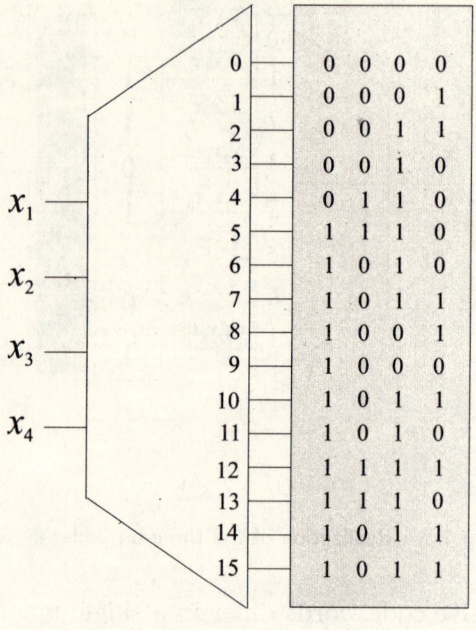

Figure 7.4. BCD to Gray code convertor.

$$
\begin{aligned}
f_3 &= x_3 \vee x_1\overline{x}_0 \vee \overline{x}_2 x_1 \vee \overline{x}_2\overline{x}_0 \vee x_2\overline{x}_1 x_0, \\
f_4 &= \overline{x}_2\overline{x}_0 \vee x_1\overline{x}_0, \\
f_5 &= x_3 \vee x_2\overline{x}_0 \vee \overline{x}_1\overline{x}_0 \vee x_2\overline{x}_1, \\
f_6 &= x_2\overline{x}_1 x_0.
\end{aligned}
$$

These functions can be efficiently realized by a programable logic device as shown in Fig. 7.5.

In [31], there is a realization of the seven segment display by classical logic circuits as shown in Fig. 7.6, achieving the minimal realization by exploiting the property that in f_0 the term x_2x_0 can be replaced by the term $x_2\overline{x}_1x_0$, which also appears in f_3.

Fig. 7.7 shows a realization of the seven segment display by ROM.

In the above examples, multiplexers are used to read the function values from ROMs with reduced dimensions. The realization with ROM can be efficiently combined with multiplexer synthesis, since inputs in a tree network of multiplexers can be generated by ROMs.

EXAMPLE 7.4 *[155]*
The majority function is a function that has the value 1 for all those assignments of binary variables where the number of 1 bits is larger than

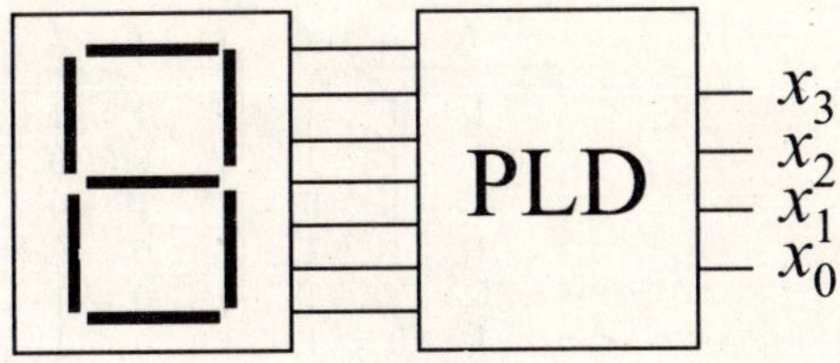

Figure 7.5. Seven segment display.

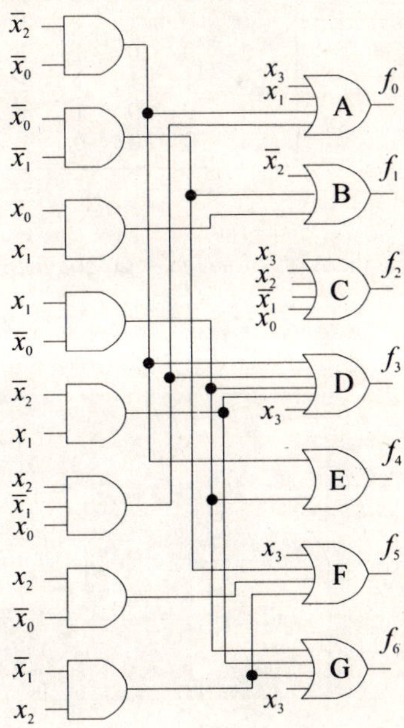

Figure 7.6. Minimal realization of seven segment display by classic logic elements.

or equal to the number of zero bits. For $n = 5$, the majority function can be expresses as

$$\begin{aligned} f(x_1, x_2, x_3, x_4, x_5) &= g_0(x_1, x_2, x_3)\overline{x}_4\overline{x}_5 \vee g_1(x_1, x_2, x_3)\overline{x}_4 x_5 \\ &\quad \vee g_2(x_1, x_2, x_3)x_4\overline{x}_5 \vee g_3(x_1, x_2, x_3)x_4 x_5 \end{aligned}$$

where

$$\begin{aligned} g_0 &= x_1 x_2 x_3, \\ g_1 &= g_2 = x_1 x_2 \vee x_2 x_3 \vee x_1 x_3, \\ g_3 &= x_1 \vee x_2 \vee x_3. \end{aligned}$$

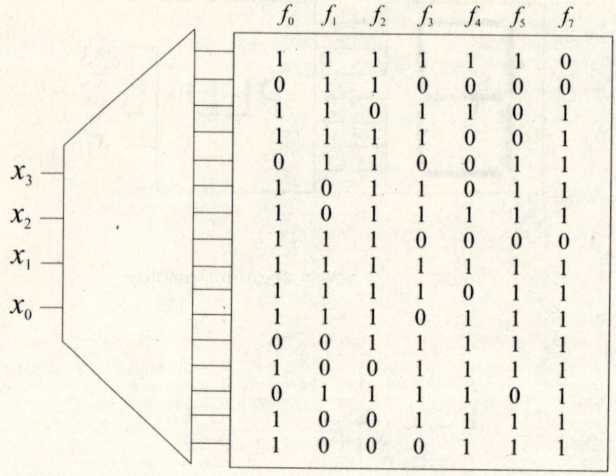

Figure 7.7. Realization of seven segment display by ROM.

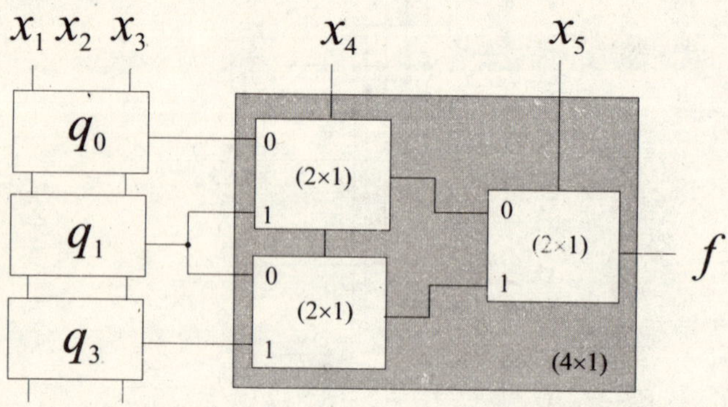

Figure 7.8. Realization of the majority function by ROM.

Due to this representation, f can be realized by a tree of multiplexers with x_4 and x_5 at control inputs and subfunctions g_i, $i = 0, 1, 2, 3$ realized by ROMs. Fig. 7.8 shows a realization of the majority function by a tree of multiplexers and ROMs.

2. Two-level Addressing in ROM Realizations

In realizations by ROM, the complete truth-vector is saved. It follows that classical minimization of functions does not have much sense in ROM realizations. However, in practical applications, it may happen that the size of memory required for a given function does not fit to standard ROM dimensions, or the available space does not allow to place the

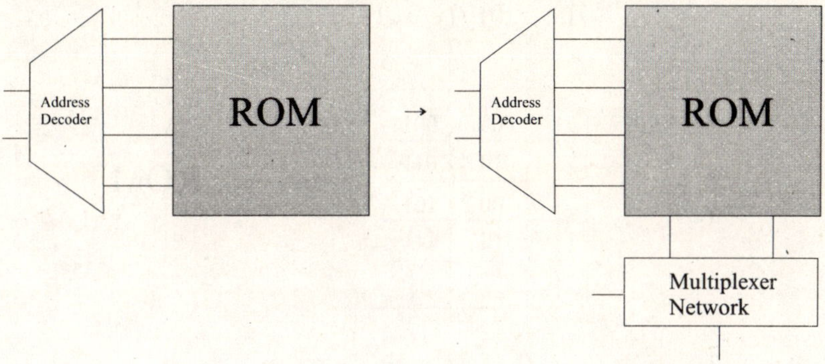

Figure 7.9. ROM with two-level addressing.

required ROM. Therefore, the optimization in synthesis by ROM may include a possibility to change the geometry of ROM. For instance order, two-level addressing can be applied, resulting in a circuit of the structure shown in Fig. 7.9. The set of variables $\{x_1, x_2, \ldots, x_n\}$ is split into two subsets $\{x_1, \ldots, x_r\}$ and $\{x_{r+1}, \ldots, x_n\}$. The optimization of ROM realizations consists of dividing the set of input variables $\{x_1, \ldots, x_n\}$ optimally into two subsets of variables that are applied at the inputs of address decoder and the multiplexer network.

Therefore, two-level addressing realization with ROM can be based on the following expressions derived for various combinations of k fixed variables, with $k = 1, 2, 3, \ldots, n$,

$$\begin{aligned}
f(x_1, \ldots, x_n) &= \overline{x}_1 f(0, x_2, \ldots, x_n) \vee x_1 f(1, x_2, \ldots, x_n) \\
& \quad f(0, 0, x_3, \ldots, x_n)\overline{x}_1\overline{x}_2 \\
& \quad \vee f(0, 1, x_3, \ldots, x_n)\overline{x}_1 x_2 \\
& \quad \vee f(1, 0 x_3, \ldots, x_n) x_1\overline{x}_2 \\
& \quad \vee f(1, 1 x_3, \ldots, x_n) x_1 x_2 \\
&= f(0, 0, 0, x_4, \ldots, x_n)\overline{x}_1\overline{x}_2\overline{x}_3 \\
& \quad \vee f(0, 0, 1, x_4, \ldots, x_n)\overline{x}_1\overline{x}_2 x_3 \\
& \quad f(0, 1, 0, x_4, \ldots, x_n)\overline{x}_1 x_2\overline{x}_3 \\
& \quad \vdots \\
& \quad f(1, 1, 1, x_4, \ldots, x_n) x_1 x_2 x_3 \\
&= f(0, 0, 0, \ldots, 0)\overline{x}_1\overline{x}_2 \cdots \overline{x}_n \vee f(1, 1, 1, \ldots, 1) x_1 x_2 \cdots x_n
\end{aligned}$$

Two-level addressing in ROM realizations provides the following features

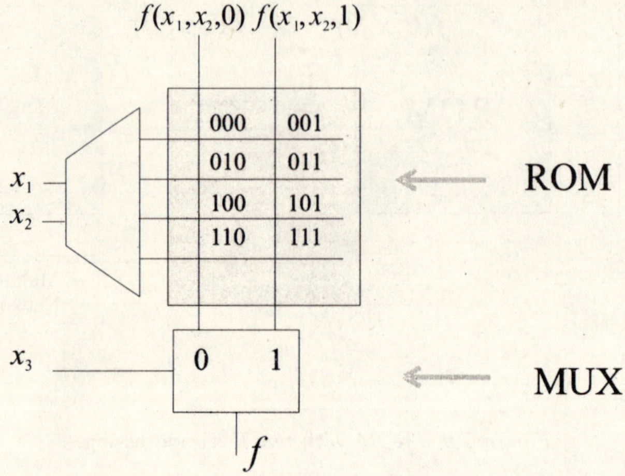

Figure 7.10. Realization by ROM with the decomposition with respect to x_1, x_2.

1 Reduced size of ROM by minimization of the number of rows,

2 Optimization of the address decoder, by replacing it with an optimized demultiplexer network.

3 Selection of an optimized multiplexer network at the output.

EXAMPLE 7.5 *Fig. 7.10 and Fig. 7.11 show ROM realizations for* $k = 2$ *and expansions with respect to* x_1, x_2 *and* x_1, x_3, *respectively. It is obviously a different geometry of ROM.*

EXAMPLE 7.6 *Sine is an important function often met in mobile devices. Due to the periodicity, it is sufficient to realize it for* $0 \leq x \leq 90°$. *If the variable* x *is expressed as* $x = (x_1 2^{-5} + x_2 2^{-4} + x_3 2^{-3} + x_4 2^{-2} + x_5 2^{-1})90$, *then* $sin(x) = y_1 2^{-8} + y_2 2^{-7} + \cdots + y_8 2^{-1}$ *and can be represented by truth-vectors as an five input eight output function and realized as shown in Fig. 7.12.*

EXAMPLE 7.7 *Consider a system of functions*

$$
\begin{aligned}
f_0 &= \overline{x}_2 + x_0 x_3 + x_1 x_3 + \overline{x}_0 x_1, \\
f_1 &= x_3 + \overline{x}_1 \overline{x}_2 + x_0 \overline{x}_2 + x_0 x_1, \\
f_2 &= x_0 + \overline{x}_2 x_3 + x_1 x_3 + x_1 x_2, \\
f_3 &= x_1 + x_0 \overline{x}_3 + \overline{x}_2 x_3 + x_0 \overline{x}_2.
\end{aligned}
$$

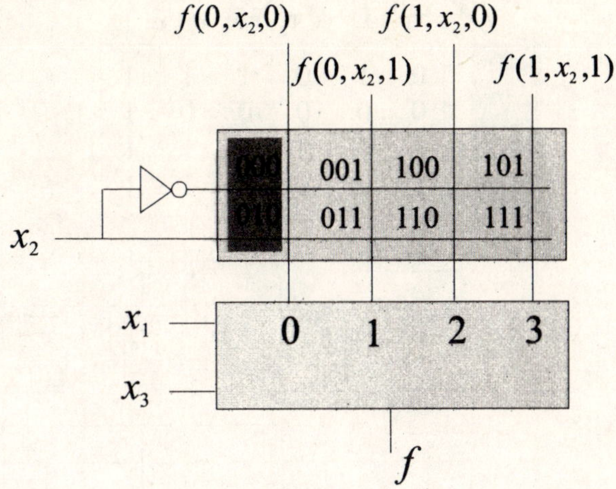

Figure 7.11. Realization by ROM with the decomposition with respect to x_1, x_3.

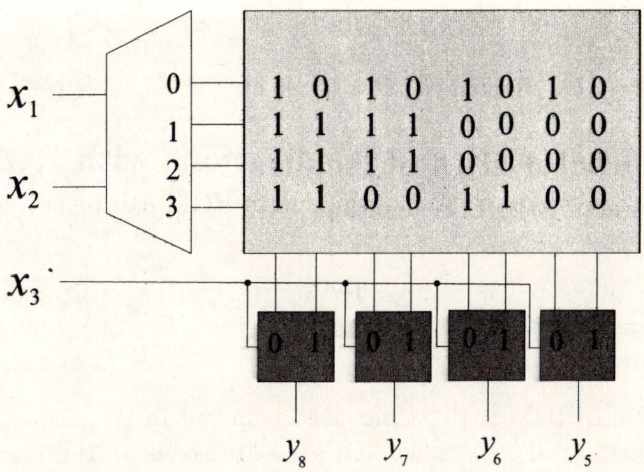

Figure 7.12. Realization of $sin(x)$ $0 \leq x \leq 90°$, by ROM.

Fig. 7.13 shows the optimal ROM realization of this system with respect to the demultiplexer network at the input and the multiplexer network at the output under the requirement that realization is done with four-input ROM.

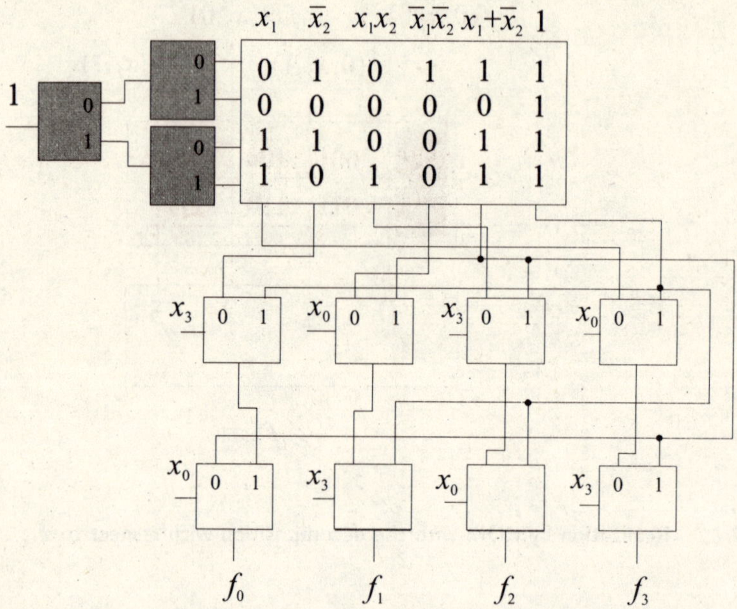

Figure 7.13. Realization of the system of functions in Example 7.7.

3. Characteristics of Realizations with ROM

Basic characteristics of realizations with ROM can be summarized as follows

1. A given function f is represented by the truth-vector, and therefore, there is no minimization in terms of the number of product terms in SOP representations.

2. Due to that, ROM realizations are inefficient in the case of functions that have many 0 or 1 values. This is a drawback of ROM realizations.

As convenient features, we point out

1. ROM realizations are useful in the cases when functions realized are described in a way that truth-tables are directly stored.

2. Such realizations are efficient for functions having many product terms in SOP representations. Examples are functions describing arithmetic circuits.

3. ROM are efficient when frequent change of the functioning of a network is required. Examples are converters of codes.

4. Exercises and Problems

EXERCISE 7.1 *Table 7.1 shows six different codes of the first 10 non-negative numbers. Realize the following code converters by ROM*

1 *BCD into the Gray code,*

2 *BCD into* $6, 3, 1, -1$,

3 *BCD into* $XS3$,

4 *BCD into* 2421,

5 *BCD into* 2 of 5.

Try realizations by ROM with different number of rows and columns.

Table 7.1. Codes in Exercise 7.1.

	BCD	*Gray*	$6, 3, 1, -1$	$XS3$	2421	*2 of 5*
0	0000	0000	0000	0011	0000	00011
1	0001	0001	0010	0100	0001	00101
2	0010	0011	0101	0101	0010	01001
3	0011	0010	0100	0110	0011	10001
4	0100	0110	0110	0111	0100	00110
5	0101	0111	1001	1000	1011	01010
6	0110	0101	1011	1001	1100	10010
7	0111	0100	1010	1010	1101	01100
8	1000	1100	1101	1011	1110	10100
9	1001	1101	1111	1100	1111	11000

EXERCISE 7.2 *Realize the system of functions* $f = (f_1, f_2)$ *specified in Table 7.2, by* (2×8) *and* (4×4) *ROMs.*

EXERCISE 7.3 *Realize the system of functions*

$$\begin{aligned}
f_1(x_1, x_2, x_3) &= x_1 + x_3 + x_1x_2 + x_1x_3, \\
f_2(x_1, x_2, x_3) &= x_2 + x_3 + x_1x_2 + x_2x_3, \\
f_3(x_1, x_2, x_3) &= \overline{x}_1x_2 + \overline{x}_2x_3 + \overline{x}_1\overline{x}_3, \\
f_4(x_1, x_2, x_3) &= \overline{x}_2\overline{x}_3 + \overline{x}_1\overline{x}_3,
\end{aligned}$$

by four-input ROM.

Table 7.2. System of functions in Exercise 7.2.

	$x_1x_2x_3$	f_1	f_2
1.	000	1	1
2.	001	0	1
3.	010	1	0
4.	100	1	1
5.	101	0	1
6.	110	1	0
7.	111	1	0

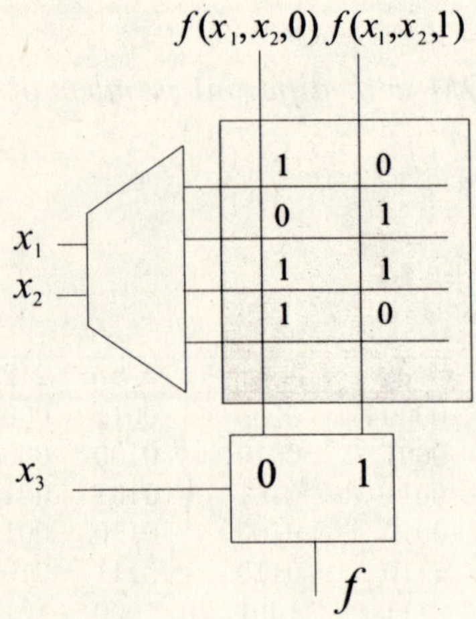

Figure 7.14. Network for the function f in Exercise 7.4.

EXERCISE 7.4 *Write the SOP-expression for the function f realized by the network in Fig. 7.14.*

EXERCISE 7.5 *Realize the function given by the truth vector* $\mathbf{F}=[1,0,0,1,1,0,0,0,1,0,0,1,1,0,0,0,1,1,1,1,1,0,0,1,1,1,1,1,0,0,0,1]^T$, *by a four input ROM. Try to minimize the number of required* (2×1) *multiplexers.*

EXERCISE 7.6 *Represent the integer-valued function* $\mathbf{F}=[2,1,0,1,1,2,1,2]^T$ *as a two-output binary-valued function $f = (f_0, f_1)$, where f_0 and f_1 are binary coordinates of entries in* $\mathbf{F}$, *and realize by ROM.*

Chapter 8

REALIZATIONS WITH PROGRAMMABLE LOGIC ARRAYS

The simplest form of *Programmable Logic Arrays* (PLAs) consists of two matrix-like elements where the first implements product terms of chosen variables and the second implements sums of chosen products. PLAs with input coding can be viewed as memory structures with addressing through associated or translation functions. Then, the input is an address and the outputs are function values for inputs specified by the addresses.

Fig. 8.1 shows the structure of a commercially available PLA. It consists of

1 AND matrix which realizes the logic AND operation and generates products (implicants) of input variables,

2 OR-matrix, alternatively EXOR-matrix, to perform addition of the outputs of the AND-matrix,

3 An input register to input data into the AND-matrix,

4 An output register to transfer the output of the OR-matrix to the output of the PLA,

5 A feedback register to connect the output of the OR (EXOR)-matrix to the input of the AND-matrix.

From the structure of a PLA it is obvious that PLAs can be used to realize combinational networks for switching functions in the SOP representations. The feedback register allows to realize also sequential networks. The realization is performed by establishing connections between horizontal and vertical lines in the AND and OR (EXOR) matrices. This

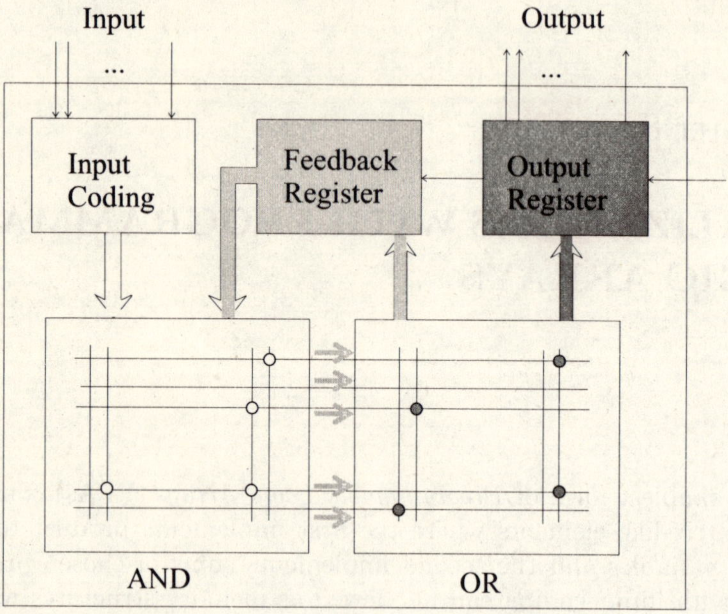

Figure 8.1. Structure of a PLA.

design methodology is called the personalization of a PLA and it is performed by arranging connections between the AND and OR matrices. There are several technological ways to determine links between lines in a PLA as a part of production procedure by mask programming or by fusible diodes. For example, in the case of a pioneering PLA 82S100 by Signetic Corporation, connections in the AND-matrix are established by Schottky diodes and in the OR-matrix by bipolar transistors.

Notice that besides PLA, some produces provide programmable devices with restricted programmability. For instance, Programmable Array Logic (PAL) devices have a programmable AND array, while the connections between products terms and specific OR circuits are hardwired. The number of product terms representing inputs in an *OR*-circuits are usually restricted to 2,4,8 and 16. Notice that unlike PLAs, in PALs sharing of product terms is not supported.

1. Realizations with PLA

The PLA realization of a switching function can be partitioned into three tasks [35]

1 Functional design, that consists of determination of a set of two-level sum-of-product representation of the given multiple-output functions.

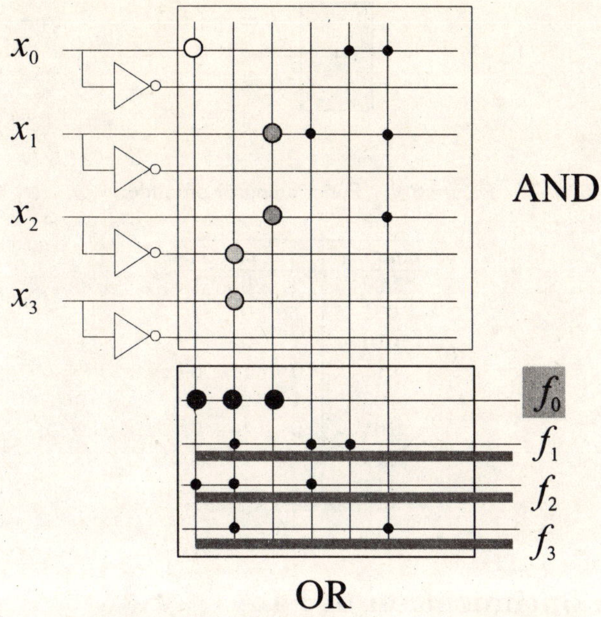

Figure 8.2. Realization of the system of functions in Example 8.1.

This procedure is followed by the logic minimization to reduce the number of implicants, which can be done by classical logic minimizers, as for instance, [17], [145].

2 Topological design, that involves the transformation of the set of implicants into a topological representation of the PLA structure, such as a symbolic table or a stick diagram.

3 The physical design to transfer the topological representation into the assumed technologic array.

EXAMPLE 8.1 *Fig. 8.2 shows realization of the following system of switching functions by a PLA*

$$\begin{aligned} f_0 &= x_0 + \overline{x}_2 x_3 + x_1 x_2, \\ f_1 &= \overline{x}_2 x_3 + x_1 + x_0 \overline{x}_3, \\ f_2 &= x_0 + x_1 + \overline{x}_2 x_3, \\ f_3 &= \overline{x}_2 x_3 + x_0 x_1 x_2. \end{aligned}$$

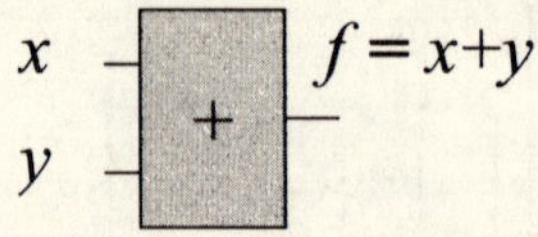

Figure 8.3. Functioning of an adder.

$x_i y_i c_{i-1}$	s_i	c_i	$\overline{c}_i$
000	0	0	1
001	1	0	1
010	1	0	1
011	0	1	0
100	1	0	1
101	0	1	0
110	0	1	0
111	1	1	0

2. The optimization of PLA

The complexity of a PLA, thus, its cost, is determined by the number of inputs and the area occupied. Therefore, the optimization is directed towards reduction of the number of inputs, when this is possible, since this usually also results in reduction of the number of outputs and the area. However, reduction of the number of inputs, which reduces the number of rows in AND-matrix, does not necessarily impliy reduction of the number of columns of the AND-matrix. There are examples, where reduction of the number of inputs increases the number of implicants. The reduction of implicants can be performed by the classical methods for minimzation of disjunctive normal forms. However, it can be shown that in practical applications, reduction of the number of inputs is more important than the reduction of implicants for the reduction of the area of PLA.

The optimization methods in synthesis with PLAs will be illustrated by an example of n-bit adders. Recall that an n-bit adder is a device that has two integers $x = (x_1, \ldots, x_n)$ and $y = (y_1, \ldots, y_n)$ as inputs, and produces their $(n+1)$-bits sum $z = x + y = (z_1, \ldots, z_{n+1})$ at the output. Notice, that z requires $(n+1)$ bits, due to the possible carry. Thus, an n-bit adder can be represented by a function with $2n$ inputs and $(n+1)$ outputs, $f(x_{n-1}, \ldots, x_0, y_{n-1}, \ldots, y_0)$. Fig. 8.3 shows basic principle of functioning of an adder.

EXAMPLE 8.2 *For $n = 3$, the sum s_i and carry c_i of an adder can be represented by the Table 8.3. The sum and carry bits can be expressed* *as the disjunctive normal forms*

$$\begin{aligned} s_i &= \overline{x}_i\overline{y}_ic_{i-1} + \overline{x}_iy_i\overline{c}_{i-1} + x_i\overline{y}_i\overline{c}_{i-1} + x_iy_ic_{i-1}, \\ c_i &= x_iy_i\overline{c}_{i-1} + x_i\overline{y}_ic_{i-1} + x_iy_ic_{i-1} + \overline{x}_iy_ic_{i-1}. \end{aligned}$$

Fig. 8.4 shows a PLA that realizes s_i and c_i. This realization requires a PLA with seven columns.

Notice that in the SOP for s_i the true minterms correspond to the decimal indices 1, 2, 4 and 7. True minterms in c_i are at decimal indices 3, 5, 6, and 7. Thus, there are a single joint minterm at the decimal index 7 for s_i and c_i. The union of true minterms in s_i and c_i is $s_i \cup c_i = \{1,2,3,4,5,6,7\}$. However, the disjunctive form for $\overline{c}_i$ is given by

$$\overline{c}_i = x_i\overline{y}_{i-1}\overline{c}_{i-1} + \overline{x}_iy_i\overline{c}_{i-1} + \overline{x}_i\overline{y}_i\overline{c}_{i-1} + \overline{x}_i\overline{y}_ic_{i-1}.$$

In this expression true minterms are at the decimal indices 0, 1, 2, and 4. Therefore, there are three joint minterms at decimal indices 1, 2 and 4. Thus, the union of true minterms in s_i and $\overline{c}_i$ is $s_i \cup \overline{c}_i = \{0,1,2,4,7\}$, and the number of columns in the resulting PLA would be five as shown in Fig. 8.5. In this figure, the logic complement of $\overline{c}_i$ is realized by a EXOR circuit with an input set to the logic constant 1, thus, left open as follows from

$$x_1\overline{x}_2 \oplus \overline{x}_1x_2 = \begin{cases} x_1, & x_2 = 0, \\ \overline{x}_1, & x_2 = 1. \end{cases}$$

It can be shown that the function expressions for s_i and c_i can be written as

$$\begin{aligned} s_i &= \overline{x}_i\overline{y}_ic_{i-1} + \overline{x}_iy_i\overline{c}_{i-1} + x_i\overline{y}_i\overline{c}_{i-1} + x_iy_ic_{i-1}, \\ &= (x_i\overline{y}_i + \overline{x}_iy_i)\overline{c}_{i-1} + (x_iy_i + \overline{x}_i\overline{y}_i)c_{i-1}, \end{aligned}$$

and

$$\begin{aligned} c_i &= x_iy_i\overline{c}_{i-1} + x_i\overline{y}_ic_{i-1} + x_iy_ic_{i-1} + \overline{x}_iy_ic_{i-1} \\ &= (x_i\overline{y}_i + \overline{x}_iy_i)\overline{c}_{i-1} + \overline{x}_i\overline{y}_i \\ &= (\overline{x}_i + \overline{y}_i)(x_i + y_i)\overline{c}_{i-1} + (\overline{x}_i + \overline{y}_i)(\overline{x}_i + y_i)(x_i + \overline{y}_i). \end{aligned}$$

In these expressions, the maxterms, i.e., sums of variables x_i and y_i for all possible combinations of polarities for variables appear. They can be realized by negating the outputs of an address decoder with these variables x_i and y_i at the inputs. Fig. 8.6 shows the realization of the three-bit adder with the address decoder at the input.

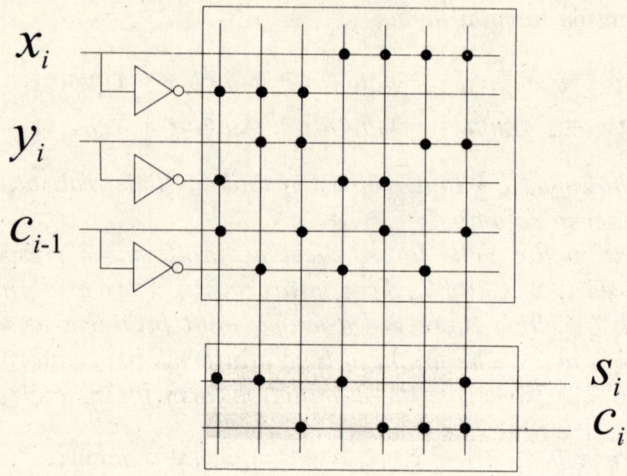

Figure 8.4. Direct realization of tree-bit adder by PLA.

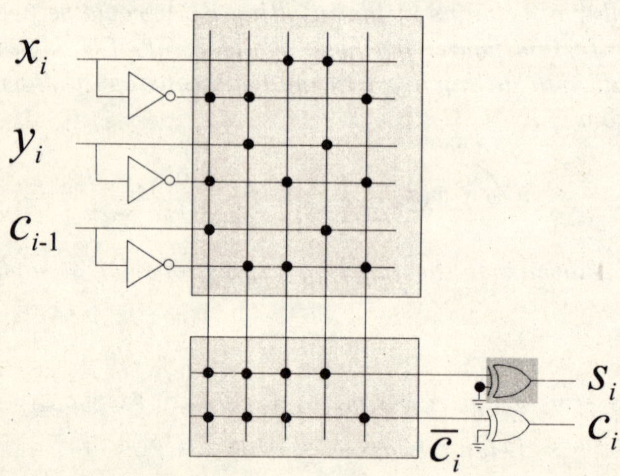

Figure 8.5. Realization of three-bit adder by using complement of carry.

Fig. 8.7 compares these three different realizations of the three-bit adder.

A spectral method utilizing logic autocorrelation functions calculated by the the Walsh transform for optimization of the AND-matrix in PLAs has been proposed in [95].

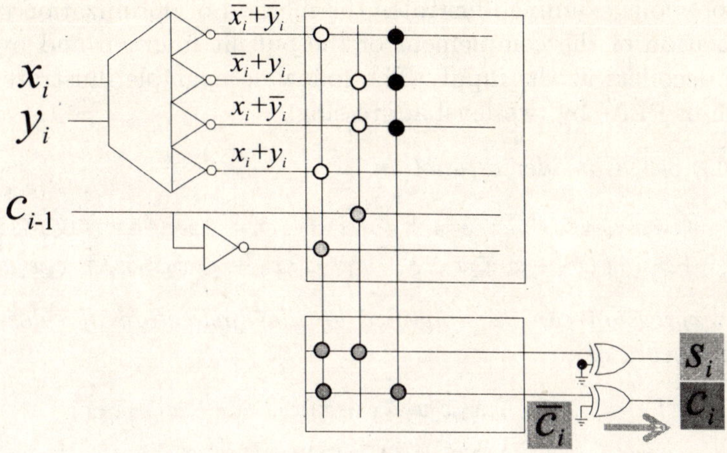

Figure 8.6. Realization of the three-bit adder with address decoder at the input of PLA and complemented carry.

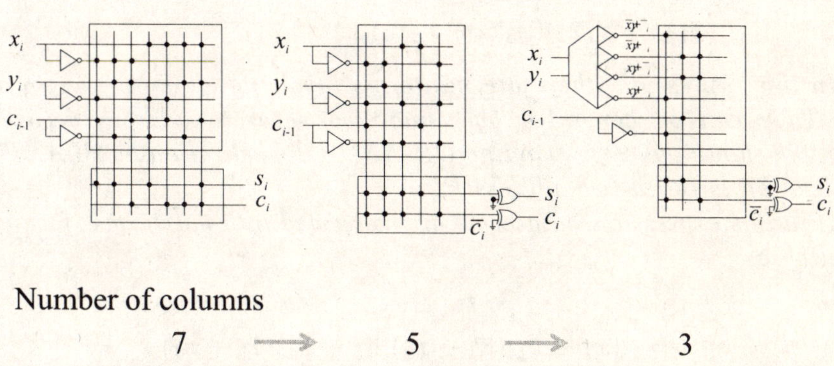

Figure 8.7. Comparison of different realizations of the three-bit adder.

3. Two-level Addressing of PLA

The optimization of PLA can be achieved by three-level PLAs, i.e., by two-level addressing in PLAs. In this approach, the set of input variables $(x_1, \ldots, x_n)$ is split into subsets, and an auxiliary matrix D generates minterms with respect to the variables in each of the subsets. The output of the D-matrix is the input in the AND-matrix, the output of which is the input in the OR-matrix. The matrix D can be conveniently realized by address decoder or can be replaced by another OR-matrix, which produces OR-AND-OR PLAs.

The previous example illustrates the method of optimization of PLA by realization of the complement of the output function and by using address decoders at the input. The following example illustrates optimization of PLAs by two-level addressing.

EXAMPLE 8.3 *Consider a function*

$$\begin{aligned} f &= \overline{x}_1\overline{x}_2\overline{x}_3\overline{x}_4 + \overline{x}_1\overline{x}_2\overline{x}_3x_4 + \overline{x}_1\overline{x}_2x_3\overline{x}_4 + \overline{x}_1x_2\overline{x}_3\overline{x}_4 + \overline{x}_1x_2\overline{x}_3x_4 \\ &+\overline{x}_1x_2x_3x_4 + x_1\overline{x}_2\overline{x}_3\overline{x}_4 + x_1\overline{x}_2x_3x_4 + x_1x_2\overline{x}_3x_4 + x_1x_2x_3\overline{x}_4. \end{aligned}$$

This expression can be simplified by the application of rules of the Boolean algebra as

$$\begin{aligned} f &= \overline{x}_1\overline{x}_3 + \overline{x}_1\overline{x}_2x_3\overline{x}_4 + \overline{x}_1x_2x_3x_4 + x_1\overline{x}_2\overline{x}_3\overline{x}_4 \\ &+x_1\overline{x}_2x_3x_4 + x_1x_2\overline{x}_3x_4 + x_1x_2x_3\overline{x}_4. \end{aligned}$$

If the set of input variables $\{x_1, x_2, x_3, x_4\}$ *is split into two subsets* $\{x_1, x_2\}$ *and* $\{x_3, x_4\}$, *then* f *can be written as*

$$\begin{aligned} f &= (\overline{x}_1\overline{x}_2 + \overline{x}_1x_2)(\overline{x}_3\overline{x}_4 + \overline{x}_3x_4) + (\overline{x}_1\overline{x}_2 + x_1x_2)(\overline{x}_3x_4 + x_3\overline{x}_4) \\ &+(\overline{x}_1x_2 + x_1\overline{x}_2)(\overline{x}_3\overline{x}_4 + x_3x_4). \end{aligned}$$

In this expression, there are minterms involving either x_1, x_2 *or* x_3, x_4. *They can be generated by using two separate address decoders. Fig. 8.8 shows the corresponding OR-AND-OR realization by PLA. This realization is called two-address PLA.*

If in this expression, minterms are converted into maxterms, f *can be written as*

$$\begin{aligned} f &= (\overline{x}_1 + \overline{x}_2)(\overline{x}_1 + x_2)(\overline{x}_3 + \overline{x}_4)(\overline{x}_3 + x_4) \\ &+(\overline{x}_1 + x_2)(x_1 + \overline{x}_2)(\overline{x}_3 + \overline{x}_4)(x_3 + x_4) \\ &+(\overline{x}_1 + \overline{x}_2)(x_1 + x_2)(\overline{x}_3 + x_4)(x_3 + \overline{x}_4). \end{aligned}$$

Fig. 8.9 shows a realization of f *derived from this expression and where minterms are realized by address decoders. Therefore, this is a D-AND-OR realization of* f.

However, if the set of input variables is decomposed into subsets $\{x_1,x_3\}$ *and* $\{x_2, x_4\}$, *then it is possible to represent* f *as*

$$f = g_0 + g_1,$$

where

$$\begin{aligned} g_0 &= (\overline{x}_1 + \overline{x}_3)(x_2 + \overline{x}_4)(\overline{x}_2 + x_4), \\ g_1 &= (x_1 + \overline{x}_3)(\overline{x}_1 + x_3)(x_2 + x_4)(\overline{x}_2 + \overline{x}_4). \end{aligned}$$

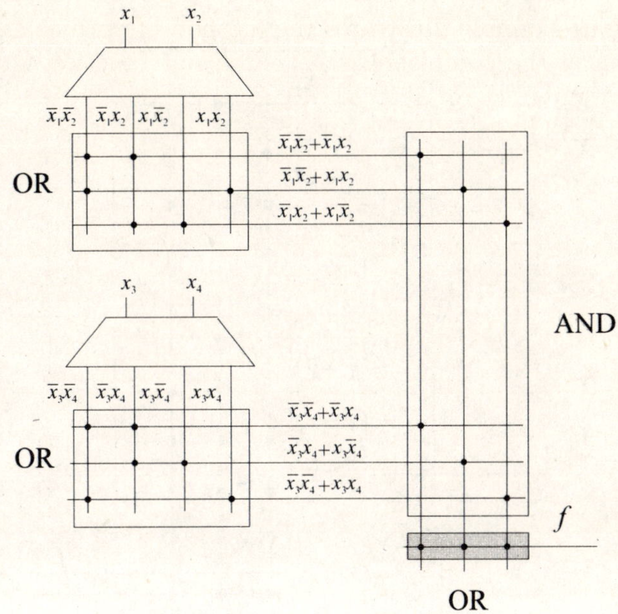

Figure 8.8. PLA for f in Example 8.3 with OR-AND-OR.

This representation provides the simplest realization shown in Fig. 8.10. The maxterms are generated by address decoders with negated outputs. Fig. 8.11 shows a realization of the same expression, where maxterms are generated by an OR-matrix at the input of the classical AND-OR PLA structure.

4. Folding of PLA

In practical implementations, AND and OR matrices in a PLA are usually sparse, since the logic minimization is performed. This sparsity can be utilized with an optimization technique called *PLA folding* to reduce the array occupied by a PLA, as well as the capacitance of the lines, which produces faster circuits. The technique consists of finding a permutation of the columns, and rows, or both, that produces the maximal set of columns and rows which can be implemented in the same column, respectively row, of the physical array. In this way, a PLA is split into a few AND and OR matrices. The splitting is possible when the product terms for different outputs are disjoint.

In the literature, the following cases have been considered

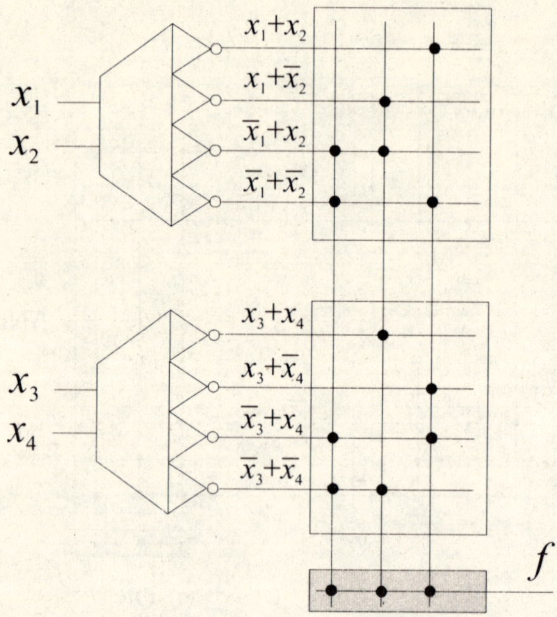

Figure 8.9. PLA for f in Example 8.3 with D-AND-OR.

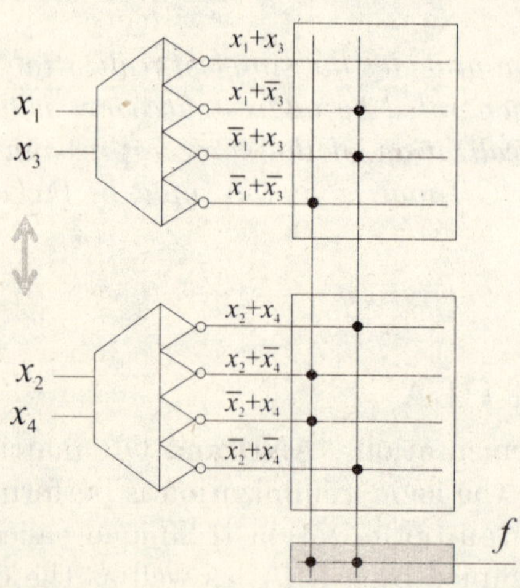

Figure 8.10. Reduced PLA for f in Example 8.3 with D-AND-OR structure.

1 Simple folding when a pair of inputs or outputs share the same column or row, respectively. It is assumed that the input lines and the output lines are either on the upper or lower sides of the columns,

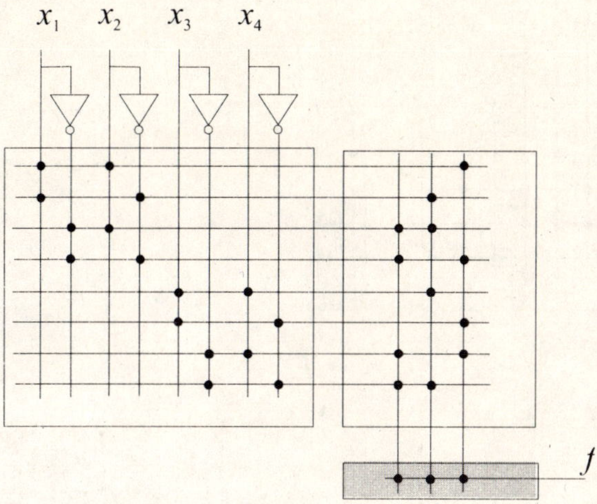

Figure 8.11. Reduced PLA for f in Example 8.3 with OR-AND-OR structure.

thus, there no intersections between folded lines. Most often, the input and output lines are folded in the AND and OR matrix, respectively, due to electrical and physical constrains.

2 Multiple folding is a more general technique where the input and output lines are folded as much as possible to minimize the number of columns, respectively rows, in AND and OR matrices. This method reduces the area. However, routing of the input and output lines is more complicated, and another metal or polysilicon layer may be required. Therefore, multiple folding is efficient when the PLA is a component of a large system where several metal or polysilicon layers are already required.

3 Bipartite folding is a special example of simple folding where column breaks between two parts in the same column must occur at the same horizontal level in either the AND or OR-matrix.

4 Constrained folding is a restricted folding where some constrains such as the order and place of lines are given and accommodated with other foldings.

It has been shown that PLA folding problems are NP-complete and the number of possible solutions approximates $c!$ or $r!$, were c and r are the number of columns and rows in the initial PLA, respectively. However, the procedure of folding can be automatized, and many algorithms have been proposed, by using different approaches, see for example [35], [42], [57], [58], [194], [200].

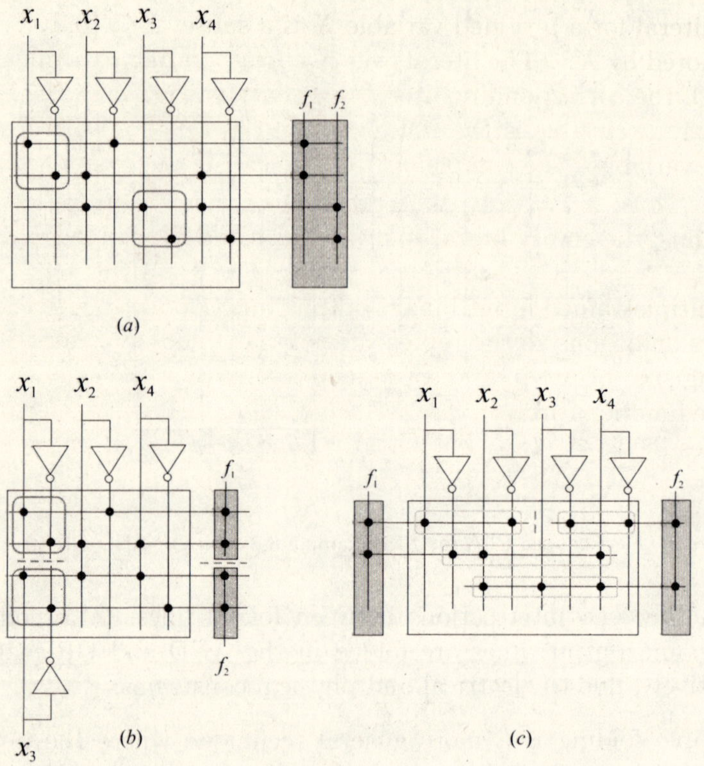

Figure 8.12. Realizations of f in Example 8.4, by (a) PLA, (b) PLA with folded columns, and (c) PLA with folded rows.

EXAMPLE 8.4 *Consider a four-variable two-output function* $f = (f_0, f_1)$, *where*

$$f_0 = x_1\overline{x}_2 + \overline{x}_1x_2x_4,$$
$$f_1 = x_2x_3x_4 + \overline{x}_3\overline{x}_4.$$

Fig. 8.12 shows (a) a PLA for this function f, *(b) the PLAs with columns folded, and (c) the PLA with rows folded.*

5. Minimization of PLA by Characteristic Functions

Multiple-valued (MV) functions are defined as mappings

$$f : \{0, 1, \ldots, p-1\}^n \to \{0, 1, \ldots, p-1\}^k,$$

where $p \neq 2$, n is the number of variables and k the number of outputs.

The literal for a p-valued variable X is a subset $S \subseteq \{0, 1, \ldots, p-1\}$, and denoted by X^S. The literal over X corresponding to a value j is X^j. If $S = \emptyset$, the corresponding literal is an empty literal and the literal for $S = \{0, 1, \ldots, p-1\}$ is the full literal and means don't care condition for that variable. The complement of a literal is the complementary set $\overline{S}$ for S. Thus, $\overline{X^S} = X^{\overline{S}}$. A literal is true when $X \in S$, otherwise it is false. Thus, the empty literal is always false and the full literal is always true.

A multiple-valued input binary output function can be represented in the ways analogous to the representations of binary switching functions including sum-of-product and product-of-sum representations.

These functions are used as mathematical models of signals with p stable states, however, can be efficiently applied in solving some problems in realizations of binary-valued functions. An example of such applications is reduction of the area in PLAs with address decoders as proposed in [149].

The method proposed in [149] exploits the feature that an n-variable binary-valued multiple-output function $f = (f_1, \ldots, f_k)$ can be represented by a single-output binary-valued function F with n binary-valued variables and the k-valued $(n+1)$-st variable. This function F is called the characteristic function for f and defined as follows [149].

DEFINITION 8.1 *(Characteristic functions)*
If $f = (f_1, \ldots, f_k)$, where $f_j = f_j(x_1, \ldots, x_n)$, $j = 0, \ldots, k-1$, then the characteristic function for f is $F : \{0,1\}^n \times \{0, 1, \ldots, k-1\}$ defined by $F(a_1, \ldots, a_n, j) = f_j(a_1, \ldots, a_n)$ for $(a_1, \ldots, a_n) \in \{0,1\}^n$ and $j \in \{0, 1, \ldots, k-1\}$.

Since each multiple-output binary-valued function can be expressed as a binary-valued function of multiple-valued inputs, minimization of the latter one leads to the minimization of the former one.

It can be shown [149] that in a two-level network derived from the minimum sum-of-product (MSOP) expression for F, the number of AND circuits will be minimum. However, the number of interconnections in the network produced is not always the minimum. Since reduction of AND-matrix is a main goal in PLA design, MSOPs for the characteristic functions F can be used to design PLAs with reduced arrays. The method will be explained by the following example taken from [155].

EXAMPLE 8.5 *Consider a function $f = (f_1, f_2, f_3)$ given by the Table 8.1. Then, the characteristic function $F = F(X_1, X_2, X_3, X_4)$ is given by the Table 8.2. The SOP expression for F is*

$$F = X_1^0 X_2^0 X_3^0 X_4^1 + X_1^0 X_2^0 X_3^0 X_4^2 + X_1^0 X_2^0 X_3^1 X_4^2 + X_1^0 X_2^1 X_3^1 X_4^2$$

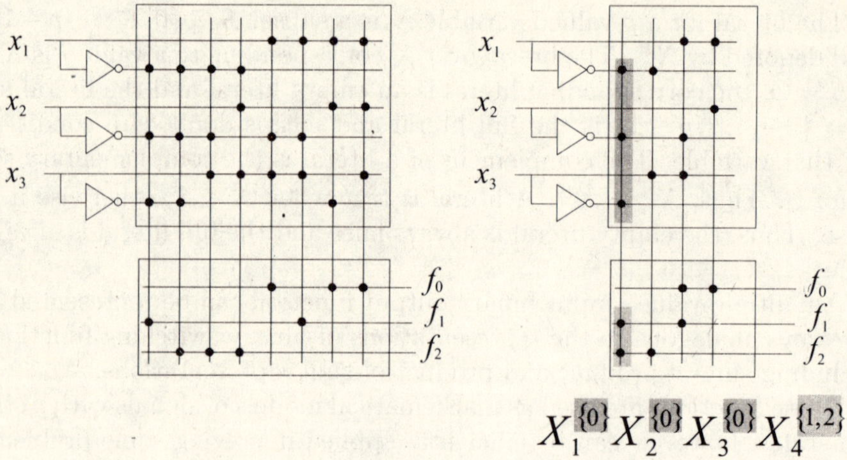

Figure 8.13. Realization of f in Example 8.5 (a) direct (b) MSOP for F.

$$+X_1^1X_2^0X_3^1X_4^0 + X_1^1X_2^0X_3^1X_4^1 + X_1^1X_2^1X_3^0X_4^0 + X_1^1X_2^1X_3^1X_4^0.$$

The correspondence between f and F is established by the variable X_4 and its superscript which shows the index of the output f_j which takes the value 1 at the assignment specified by the superscripts of X_i. For example, $X_1^0X_2^0X_3^0X_4^1$ shows that $f_1 = 1$ for $X_1 = X_2 = X_3 = 0$. Similarly, from $X_1^0X_2^0X_3^0X_4^2$, it follows $f_1 = 1$ for $X_1 = X_2 = X_3 = 0$.

The minimum SOP (MSOP) for F is determined by joining pairs of successive product terms. Therefore,

$$F = X_1^0X_2^0X_3^0X_4^{1,2} + X_1^0X_2^{0,1}X_3^1X_4^2 + X_1^1X_2^0X_3^1X_4^{0,1} + X_1^1X_2^1X_3^{0,1}X_4^0.$$

The products in the minimum SOP for F determine rows in the PLA for f. Fig. 8.13 shows PLAs for direct implementation of f and realization determined by the MSOP for f. In this example, the minimization by the characteristic function reduces the number of columns from 8 in direct realization to 4 in the minimized PLA.

6. Exercises and Problems

EXERCISE 8.1 *Realize by PLA a BCD to Gray code converter, where the BCD number is represented by x_1, x_2, x_3, x_4 and the four outputs for the Gray code word y_1, y_2, y_3, y_4 are defined as*

$$\begin{aligned} y_1 &= x_1 + x_2x_4 + x_2x_3, \\ y_2 &= x_2\overline{x}_3, \end{aligned}$$

Table 8.1. Truth-table for f in Example 8.5.

x_1, x_2, x_3	f_1	f_2	f_3
000	0	1	1
001	0	0	1
010	0	0	0
011	0	0	1
100	0	0	0
101	1	1	0
110	1	0	0
111	1	0	0

Table 8.2. Characteristic function F for f in Example 8.5.

	X_1, X_2, X_3, X_4	F
1	0000	0
2	0001	1
3	0002	1
4	0010	0
5	0011	0
6	0012	1
7	0100	0
8	0101	0
9	0102	0
10	0110	0
11	0111	0
12	0112	1
13	1000	0
14	1001	0
15	1002	0
16	1010	1
17	1011	1
18	1012	0
19	1100	1
20	1101	0
21	1102	0
22	1110	1
23	1111	0
24	1112	0

$$
\begin{aligned}
y_3 &= x_2 + x_3, \\
y_4 &= \overline{x}_1\overline{x}_2\overline{x}_3x_4 + x_2x_3x_4 + x_1\overline{x}_4 + \overline{x}_2x_3\overline{x}_4.
\end{aligned}
$$

Since there are no shared product terms, the PLA realization of these functions is convenient.

EXERCISE 8.2 *Realize the BCD to a Gray code converter specified by*

$$
\begin{aligned}
y_1 &= x_1, \\
y_2 &= x_1\overline{x}_2 \vee \overline{x}_1x_2, \\
y_3 &= x_2\overline{x}_3 \vee \overline{x}_2x_3, \\
y_4 &= x_3\overline{x}_4 \vee \overline{x}_3x_4.
\end{aligned}
$$

EXERCISE 8.3 *A two-bit magnitude comparator has four inputs x_1, x_2, x_3, x_4 representing two two-bit numbers at the inputs and four outputs taking the value 1 as specified as follows. The output*

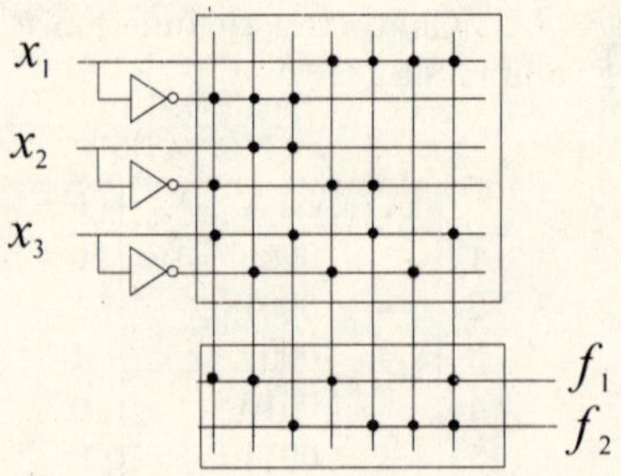

Figure 8.14. PLA for f_1 and f_2 in the Exercise 8.6.

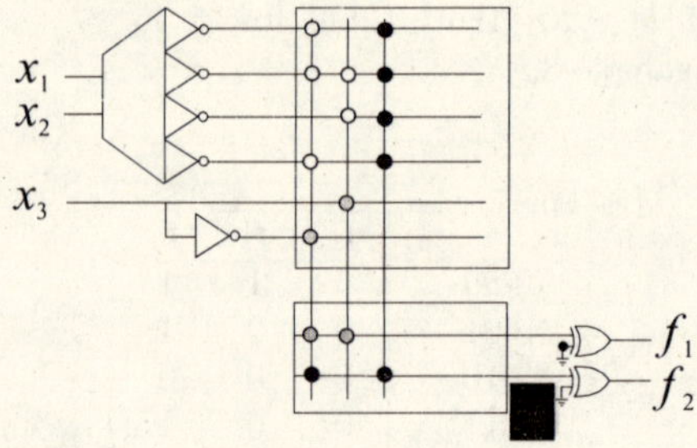

Figure 8.15. PLA for fPLA for f_1 and f_2 in the Exercise 8.7.

$$f_{eq} = 1 \textit{ when } x_1x_2 = x_3x_4,$$
$$f_{ne} = 1 \textit{ when } x_1x_2 \neq x_3x_4$$
$$f_{lt} = 1 \textit{ when } x_1x_2 < x_3x_4$$
$$f_{gt} = 1 \textit{ when } x_1x_2 > x_3x_4.$$

Show that the corresponding SOP-expressions for the outputs are

$$\begin{aligned} f_{eq} &= \overline{x}_1\overline{x}_2\overline{x}_3\overline{x}_4 + \overline{x}_1x_2\overline{x}_3x_4 + x_1x_2x_3x_4 + x_1\overline{x}_2x_3\overline{x}_4, \\ f_{ne} &= x_1\overline{x}_3 + \overline{x}_1x_3 + \overline{x}_2x_4 + x_2\overline{x}_4, \\ f_{lt} &= \overline{x}_1x_3 + \overline{x}_1\overline{x}_2x_4 + \overline{x}_2x_3x_4, \\ f_{gt} &= x_1\overline{x}_3 + x_1x_2\overline{x}_4 + x_2\overline{x}_3\overline{x}_4, \end{aligned}$$

and design the corresponding PLA realizing these functions.

EXERCISE 8.4 *Realize code converters in Exercise 7.1 by PLAs.*

EXERCISE 8.5 *Consider the function f of four variables defined by*

$$\begin{aligned} f(x_1,x_2,x_3,x_4) &= \overline{x}_1\overline{x}_2x_3 + \overline{x}_1x_2x_3 + \overline{x}_1\overline{x}_2x_4 + \overline{x}_1x_2x_4 \\ &\quad + x_1\overline{x}_2\overline{x}_4 + x_1x_2x_3 + x_3\overline{x}_4. \end{aligned}$$

Realize f by a PLA directly as defined, and when rewritten as

$$f(x_1,x_2,x_3,x_4 = (\overline{x}_1\overline{x}_2 + \overline{x}_1x_2)(x_3+x_4) + (x_1\overline{x}_2 + x_3)(x_1x_2 + \overline{x}_4),$$

by using address decoder for the inputs x_1 and x_2.

EXERCISE 8.6 *Determine the functions f_1 and f_2 realized by the PLA in Fig. 8.14.*

EXERCISE 8.7 *Consider PLA in Fig. 8.15 and determine functions f_1 and f_2. Realize these functions by a PLA directly and compare the complexities of the realizations in terms of the number of columns of the PLAs.*

Chapter 9

UNIVERSAL CELLULAR ARRAYS

Networks, often called modular networks, that consist of identical modules with simple interconnections, are certainly a target of many design procedures in various technologies. A solution is provided by the *universal cellular arrays* that are planar networks consisting of circuits from a few different classes distributed with a regular layout and with interconnections reduced to the links between neighboring modules. The term universal means that these structures can be applied to realize any of 2^{2^n} switching functions of a given number n of variables, when the dimension of the array is large enough.

Fig. 9.1 shows the symbol for a basic module in an universal cellular array and illustrates that the functioning of it will be determined by selecting the value of the control input k and depending also on the structure of the particular module considered.

1. Features of Universal Cellular Arrays

Universal cellular arrays can be classified with respect to different criteria. Depending on the number of interconnections between cells, they

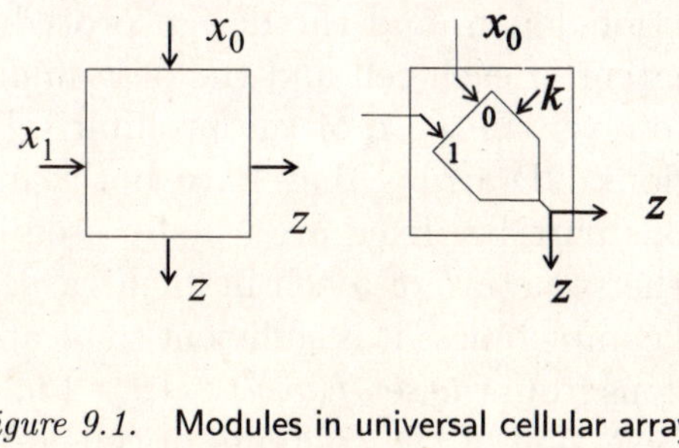

Figure 9.1. Modules in universal cellular arrays.

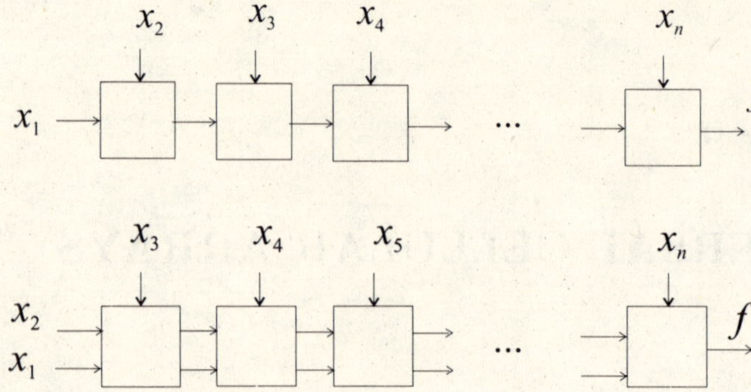

Figure 9.2. Single-rail and double-rail universal cellular arrays.

can be *single-rail*, *double rail*, and *multi-rail*. Fig. 9.2 shows the structures of single-rail and double-rail universal cellular arrays, also called cascades. If there are no feedback connections, the universal cellular arrays are called *unilateral*, otherwise *bilateral*. *Iterative cellular arrays* consists of identical cells. Restriction to iterative arrays and the number of interconnections is related to the functional completeness of the array, because of the limited amount of information that can be transferred through a small number of links. It is know that single-rail cascades are not functionally complete, which means cannot realize all the functions of n variables with n cells. Double rail universal cellular arrays are functionally complete if non-iterative. Iterative multi-rail cascades can be functionally complete.

Theoretically, besides these single-dimensional universal cellular arrays, two- and three-dimensional arrays can be used to provide compactness. However, in practice single-rail two-dimensional arrays are probably the most widely used due to the planarity, simplicity of connections. Fig. 9.3 illustrates the structure of a two-dimensional universal cellular array. In general, all the cells can be functionally different, and all the connections open, and the design procedure consists of the selection of the content of each cell and the determination of all the interconnections. However, because of the prohibitively large number of possible combinations, 2D-arrays that have both contents of the cells and interconnections partially fixed are usually used in practice.

Fig. 9.4 shows the structure of a cell in 2D-arrays. It may be proven that for functional completeness it is sufficient to be able to realize any of two-variable functions from the set $f(x, y) \in \{y, x+y, xy, x+\overline{y}, x\overline{y}, x\oplus\overline{y}\}$ at each cell [69]. Selection of the contents of cells depends on the analytical representations of function to be realized. Most often, universal

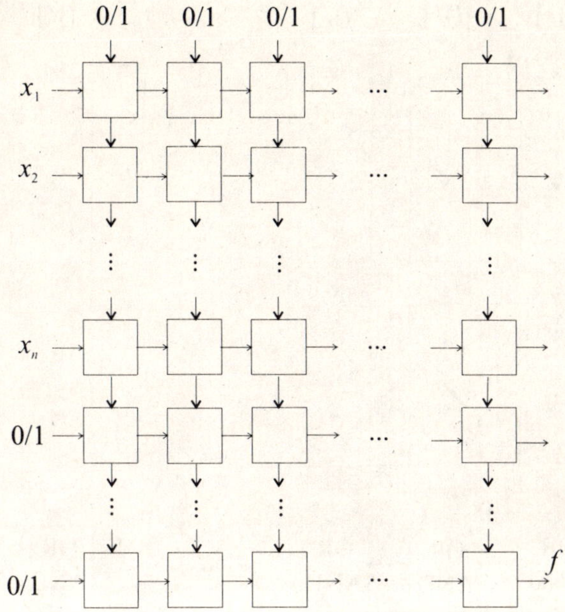

Figure 9.3. Two-dimensional single-rail universal cellular array.

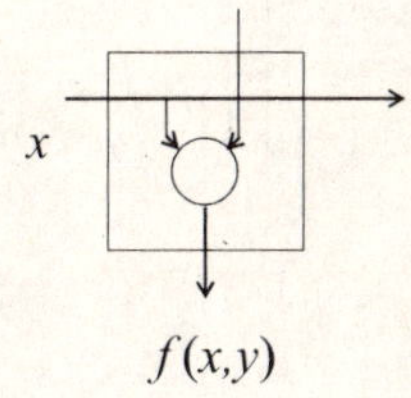

Figure 9.4. Structure of cells for realizations with 2D-arrays.

cellular arrays realize Sum-of-Products or Product-of-Sums and Reed-Muller expressions.

2. Realizations with Universal Cellular Arrays

Fig. 9.6 shows basic cells for realization of SOP/POS expressions by the universal cellular arrays whose structure is illustrated in Fig. 9.5. In this case, the interconnections and the operations in the cells of the upper part are fixed and only the last row depends on the function to be realized. The design procedure consists of the determination of the interconnections from the upper part to the last row in the array. It is obvious that the realization is based on the complete disjunctive

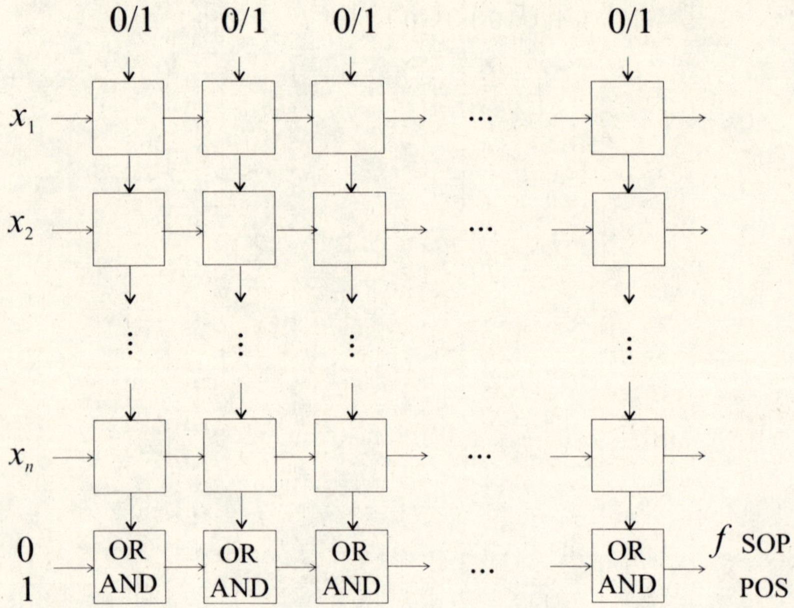

Figure 9.5. Realization of SOP and POS expressions by 2D-arrays.

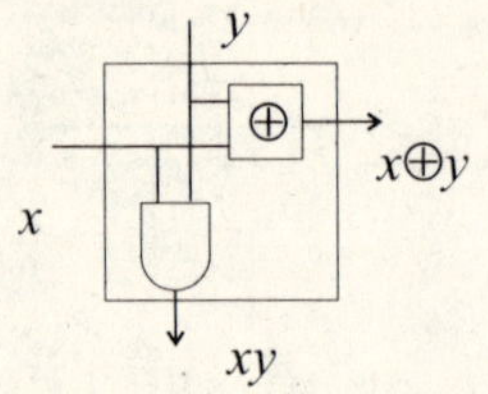

Figure 9.6. Module for realization of SOP and POS expressions.

form, and minterms are generated as the outputs from the upper part of the array. Therefore, the realization is universal in the sense that the same array can be used to realize all 2^{2^n} functions, by selecting interconnections towards the OR circuits in the last row. This realization is planar and modular, also called of homogenous structure, but these useful features are achieved at the price of the size of the array.

EXAMPLE 9.1 *Fig. 9.7 shows realization of the function* $f(x_1, x_2) = \overline{x}_1 + x_1x_2$ *by a 2D-array.*

Fig. 9.8 shows cells used to realize positive polarity Reed-Muller expressions by the arrays with the structure as in Fig. 9.9. These arrays

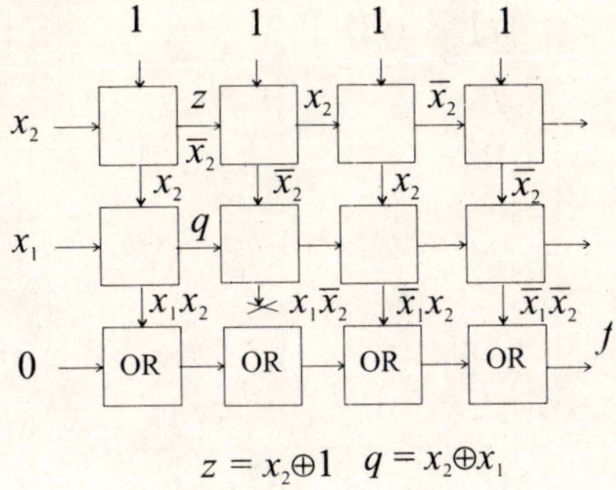

Figure 9.7. Realization of the function f in Example 9.1.

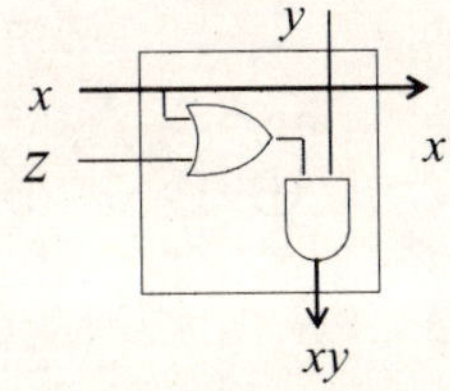

Figure 9.8. Modules for realization of PPRM-expressions.

also have partially fixed contents and interconnections and the design procedure consists of the determination of connections towards the last row of the array consisting of EXOR circuits. The outputs from the upper parts are elementary products of variables in terms of which PPRM-expressions are defined. The design procedure consists of determination which connections towards the last row of the array should be established, so that the PPRM-expression of the function is realized.

EXAMPLE 9.2 *Fig. 9.10 shows the realization of the function* $f(x_1, x_2) = \overline{x}_1 + x_1x_2$ *whose PPRM-expression is* $f(x_1, x_2) = 1 \oplus x_1 \oplus x_1x_2$.

Notice that there are switching functions which have a regular structure, for instance when written by truth-vectors, and therefore, are particularly suitable to be realized with logic networks of a regular form. In particular, functions that can be realized in the form of a single-dimensional iterative array are called *iterative functions.* These functions are naturally realized by iterative single-dimensional arrays. Examples of such functions are all totaly symmetric functions, detectors of fixed patterns, binary adders, etc., [196].

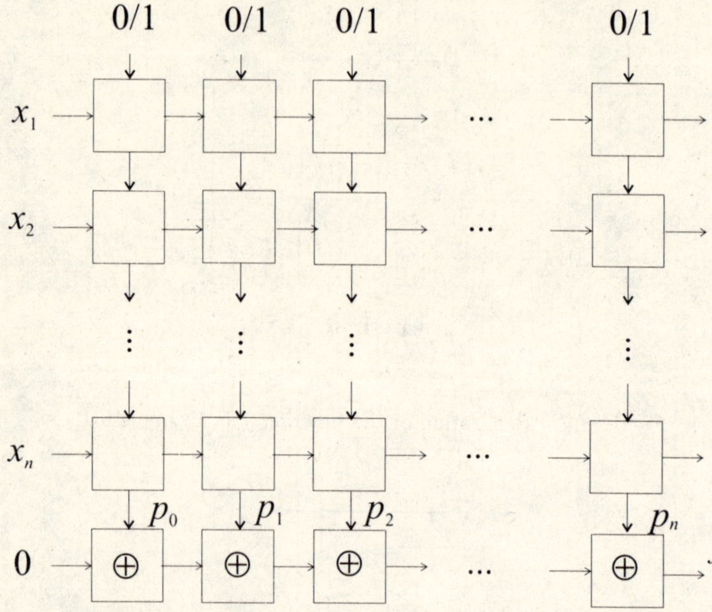

Figure 9.9. Realization of PPRM expressions by 2D-arrays.

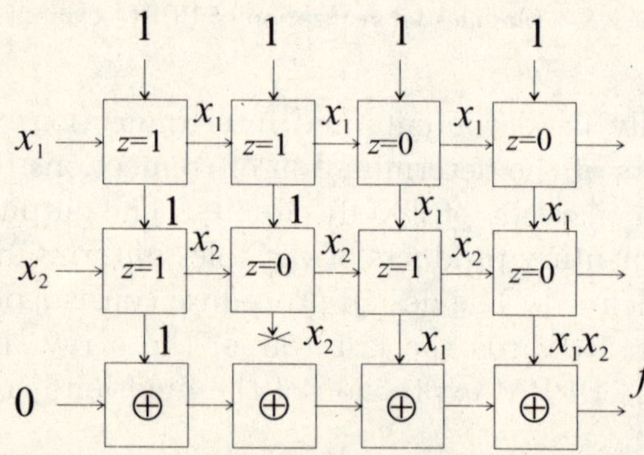

Figure 9.10. Realization of the function f in Example 9.2.

Many of these functions, as for instance symmetric functions, have SOPs that consist of many prime implicants, each covering a relatively small number of true minterms in the truth-vectors. Therefore, their two-level realizations by SOPs are very expensive in the number of gates. The same applies to the POS realizations for these functions. A supreme example are the n-variable XOR functions, which becomes obvious when, for example for $n = 4$ the XOR function $x_1 \oplus x_2 \oplus x_3 \oplus x_4$ is represented

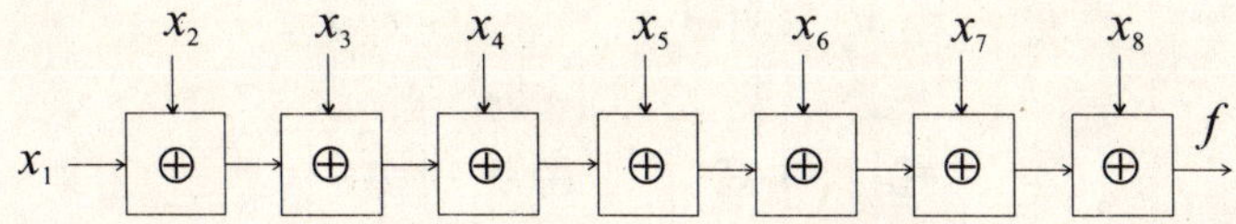

Figure 9.11. Realization of the parity function for $n = 8$.

by the Karnaugh map that resembles the chessboard, with black and white arrays corresponding to the logic 0 and 1. The cost of realization by iterative arrays for such functions is, however, linear in the number of variables.

The main disadvantage of realization by single-dimensional arrays is that the signal may have to pass through many, sometimes all of the cells, which results in the propagation delay linear in the number of inputs n. It can be shown that all iterative functions can be also realized by networks with the structure of a tree, with the worst case propagation delay proportional to $\log n$. The number of cells is linear in n, but they are generally more complex than cells in the single-dimensional circuits.

EXAMPLE 9.3 *Consider parity functions defined as functions whose output is 1 when the odd number of inputs is 1. For $n = 8$, the parity function can be written as [196]*

$$f = (((((((x_1 \oplus x_2) \oplus x_3) \oplus x_4) \oplus x_5) \oplus x_6) \oplus x_7) \oplus x_8),$$

and realized by a single-dimensional array as in Fig. 9.11. However, if due to the associativity of EXOR, f is written as

$$f = ((x_1 \oplus x_2) \oplus (x_3 \oplus x_4)) \oplus ((x_5 \oplus x_6) \oplus (x_7 \oplus x_8)),$$

it can be realized by an iterative network with the structure of a tree as in Fig. 9.12.

More information about iterative functions and their realizations can be found, for example, in [196].

3. Synthesis with Macro Cells

Synthesis with universal cellular arrays expresses some useful features, as universality, similar to universal logic modules, which ensures reusability of designed modules after simple modifications, reduced design procedure, regular layout, simple interconnections, etc. For these reasons, this approach to synthesis of logic networks, which can be viewed as synthesis with explicitly specified library of cells, has evolved into the two main approaches in *semicustom design* popular today

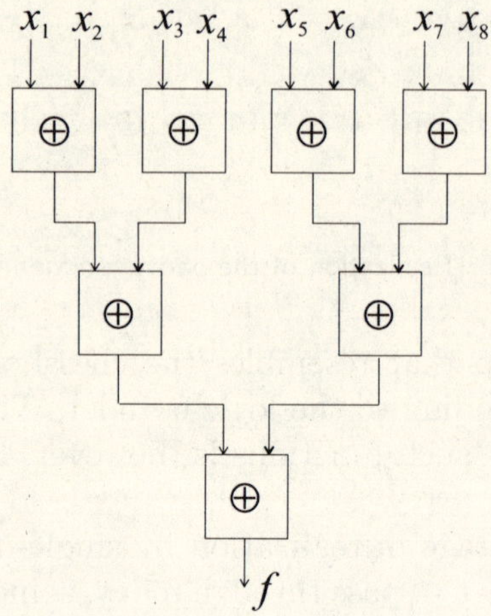

Figure 9.12. Realization of the parity function for $n = 8$ with reduced propagation delay.

1 *Cell-based design*, which can be design with *standard cells* and *macro-cells*, which will be discussed briefly in the following, and

2 Array-based design, where it may be distinguished the *predifused* (or *mask programmable*, *MPGA*) and *prewired* (or *field programmable*, *FPGA*) design.

Recall that, unlike the *custom design* where each part of the network produced is optimized to the maximum level at the high price of the complex and time consuming design procedure, semicustom design consists of assembling and interconnecting of predesign elements with verified and specified performances. Thus, it allows reusability of modules and reduce the design time. When during integration and system-level verification, the performance of each module preserved, the verification reduces to the verification of the system, and repeated verification of each component is not required. In custom design the high design cost is justified if re-compensated by the large production volume. The *application specific design of integrated circuits, (ASIC)* can be viewed as custom design where the high design cost is justified by the importance of the application intended.

In the case of MPGAs, programming is done during the fabrications of the chip, with programming consisting of application of metal and contact layers to connect entries of a matrix of uncommitted components often called the *sites*. In the FPGAs, the term field means that they can be programmed "in the field", i.e., outside of the factory, as will be discussed in Chapter 10.

The standard-cell based design is mainly intended to simplify the design procedure, as in universal cellular arrays above, which does not necessarily simplifies the manufacturing process. In this approach, a library of cells is provided and the designer has to confirm a logic scheme into the available cells in the library, which is called *library binding* or *technology mapping*, followed by cells allocation and establishing interconnections. In this approach, a hierarchical method is often used, where larger cells are derived as combinations of simpler cells from the library.

Design with macro-cells uses computer programs, *generators of modules*, which produce macro-cells for (optimized to some level) logic sub networks. Macro-cells are derived by connecting and distributing *functional cells* produced automatically from logic expressions. It is usually assumed a set of restrictions to starting logic expressions. These restrictions are mainly related to the area and performances of the cell that will be produced from logic expressions. For instance, restrictions could be the maximum number of inputs allowed for a cell, or the number of transistors within a cell that may be connected in parallel or in series. Logic expressions and cells that fulfil such functional restrictions form a *virtual library.* The design procedure consists of the manipulation of the network until the required performances achieved under the constrains imposed. Developing algorithms to solve various problems and tasks in these areas is subject to intensive research work. For example, there are several heuristic algorithms when the restrictions to functional cells are specified in terms of the number of transistors. If the restrictions are related to the number of inputs, the design is similar to that with FPGAs.

Both of these usually used approaches, design with macro-cells and FPGAs, can be viewed as the synthesis with an implicitly given library of cells.

Discussing universal cellular arrays is important, since provides foundations for analysis of properties of future technologies for system design and computing [16]. As it can be expected, in the future, regular structures will be highly prevalent, due to several reasons. First, the decrease of the minimum dimensions, as well as manufacturing variations, make the custom-made circuits difficult to produce. Effects like cross-talk noise, inductive effects, and prediction of the delay will run beyond the complexity bound for economic custom design.

Regular structures are more predicable in delays, and since the repeated patterns are relatively small, they can be hand-designed and extensively analyzed to avoid internal problems. Due to the uniform structure, manufacturing variations should decrease.

4. Exercises and Problems

EXERCISE 9.1 *[31]*

Analyze the cellular array in the Fig. 9.13 consisting of four different types of cells A, B, C, and D, and determine the output functions f and g. Fig. 9.14 shows a cell with two control inputs z_1 and z_0 to determine the contents of the cell which can replace any of these cells in this array

$$
\begin{aligned}
(z_1, z_0) &= (0,0) \rightarrow A, \\
(z_1, z_0) &= (0,1) \rightarrow B, \\
(z_1, z_0) &= (1,0) \rightarrow C, \\
(z_1, z_0) &= (1,1) \rightarrow D.
\end{aligned}
$$

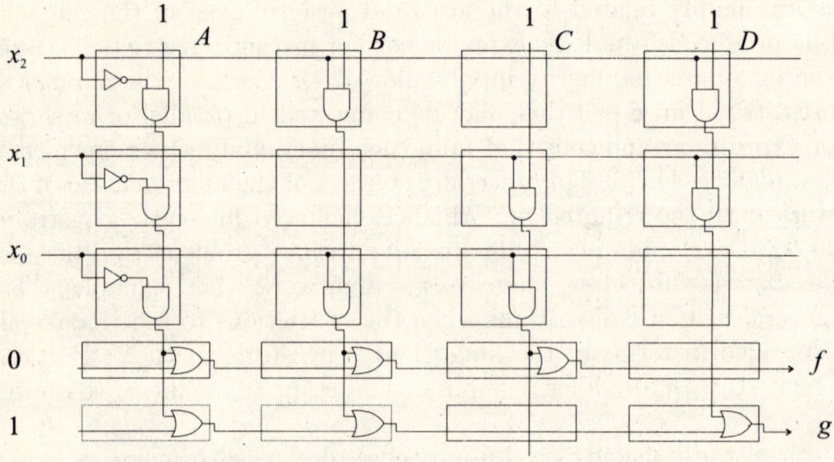

Figure 9.13. Array in Exercise 9.1.

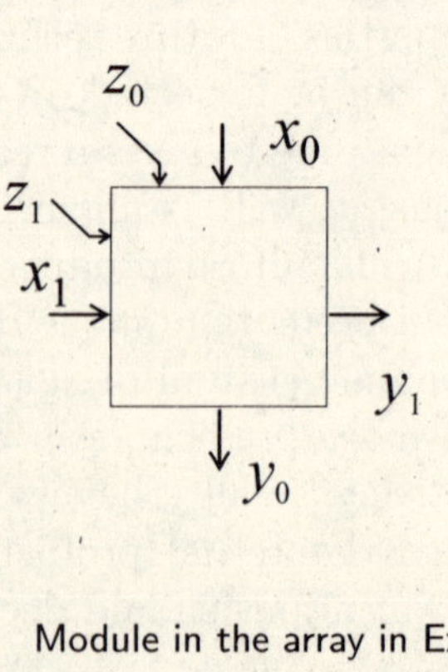

Figure 9.14. Module in the array in Exercise 9.1

EXERCISE 9.2 *[31]*
Determine the output of the array in Fig. 9.15, where each cell realizes the majority function of three variables $f(x_2, x_1, x_0) = x_1x_0 + x_0x_2 + x_1x_2$.

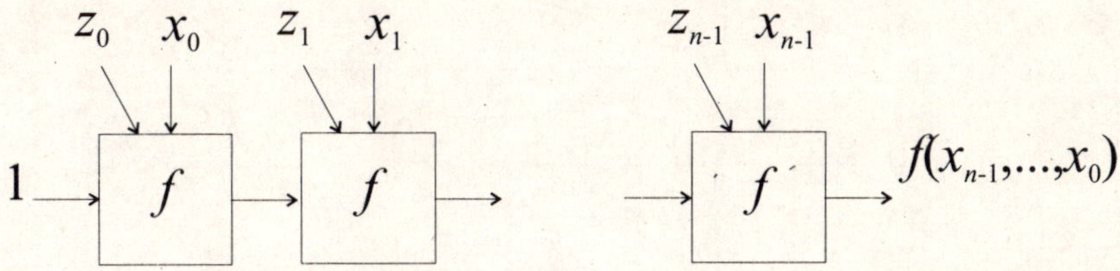

Figure 9.15. Array in Exercise 9.2.

EXERCISE 9.3 *Fig. 9.16 shows a module proposed in [74] for applications in universal cellular arrays with reduced routing. Show the assignments of inputs to realize the functions*

1 $\overline{x_1 \wedge x_2}$,

2 $\overline{x_1 \vee x_2}$,

3 $x_1 \vee \overline{x}_2 \wedge x_3$.

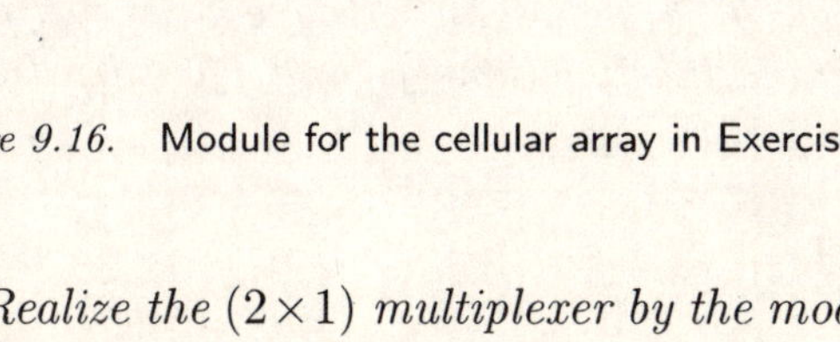

Figure 9.16. Module for the cellular array in Exercise 9.3.

EXERCISE 9.4 *Realize the* (2×1) *multiplexer by the module in Fig. 9.16.*

EXERCISE 9.5 *Consider the universal cellular array in Fig. 9.17. Determine the function realized by this array if*

1 *The first two rows are modules for realization of SOPs in Fig. 9.6, and the last row are the OR circuits,*

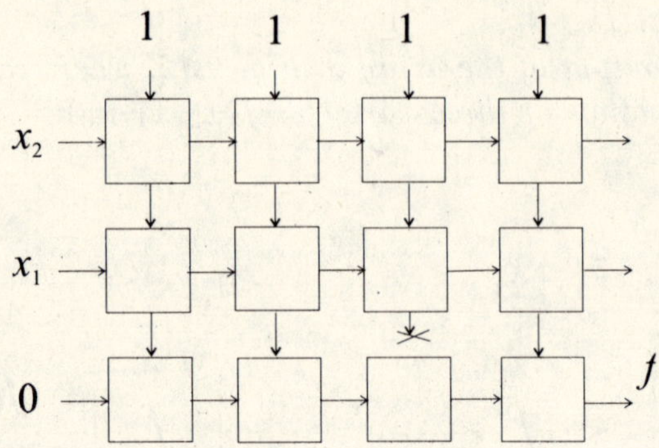

Figure 9.17. The cellular array in Exercise 9.5.

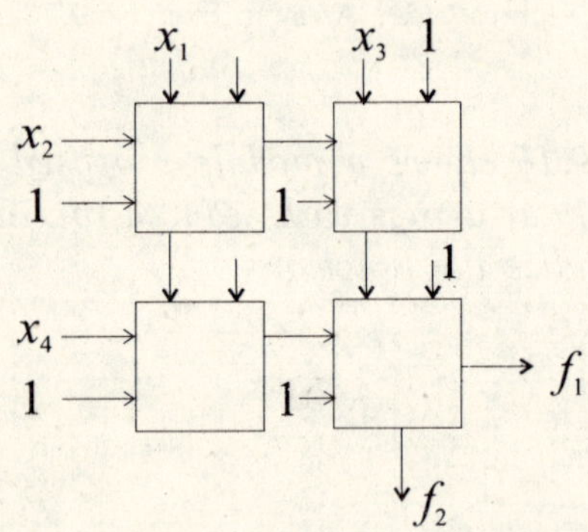

Figure 9.18. The cellular array in Exercise 9.6.

2 *The first two rows are the Reed-Muller modules in Fig. 9.8 and the last row are EXOR circuits.*

EXERCISE 9.6 *Fig. 9.18 shows an array consisting of the module in Fig. 9.16. Determine the functions f_1 and f_2 realized by this array for the given specification of inputs.*

Chapter 10

FIELD PROGRAMMABLE LOGIC ARRAYS

Field Programmable Logic Arrays (FPGA) are widely used in logic design, especially for fast prototyping and small series production, since they combine many nice features of other methods. In particular, FPGA provide both large scale integration and programmability by users. When compared for example with PLA realizations, we have the following basic features.

With PLAs

1 Basically two-level realizations are produced,

2 Realizations are based on AND-OR or AND-EXOR expressions, and

3 Large number of inputs in AND circuits is allowed.

With FPGAs

1 Multi-level realizations are produced,

2 The number of inputs in the circuits is smaller,

3 They are more compact than two-level realizations.

FPGAs can be viewed as programmable logic chips consisting of logic blocks, each capable of realizing a set of logic functions, programmable interconnections, and switches between blocks. Fig. 10.1 shows the structure of an FPGA.

Complexity of FPGAs is usually estimated by comparing their logic blocks, which can consist of

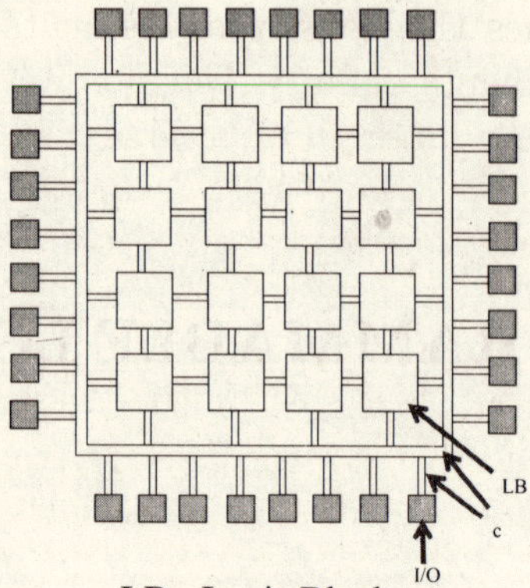

Figure 10.1. Structure of an FPGA.

1 A pair of transistors,

2 Basic logic circuits with few inputs (AND, OR, NAND, NOR),

3 Multiplexers,

4 Look-up tables (LUTs), often implemented as Static RAMs,

5 AND-OR structures with many inputs as PLAs, etc.

In this respect, FPGAs can be classified as *fine-grain* and *coarse-grain* arrays, and the comparison of logic blocks is performed with respect to the number of

1 Equivalent NAND circuits,

2 Transistors,

3 Normalized area defined as the ratio of the area occupied by a logic block and the total area of the FPGA, i.e., $n_a = a(LB)/a(FPGA)$,

4 Inputs and outputs.

The size of logic blocks influences considerably the performances of FPGAs [89], [142], since large logic blocks require less routing resources resulting in a smaller overall routing delay. On the other hand, larger logic blocks are slower and generally less efficiently exploited. Much research has been done to determine the optimal granularity of FPGAs [3], [89], [142].

In routing, the interconnections are established by connecting segments of lines in an FPGA by programmable switches. The number of segments determines the density of elements in an FPGA [193]. A small number of segments reduces the possibilities of interconnecting logic blocks. However, a large number of segments implies that many of them will remain unused, which wastes the area. The size of segments is another issue. Short segments require many switches, which causes delay, but long segments occupy area and also cause delay, because nowadays the delay in VLSI circuits is generally due to the interconnections more than logic circuits. Since this topics is strongly dependent on technology, a deeper analysis requires a more detailed specification of the architecture. It can be found in some overviews as, for example, [143].

With respect to the way of programming, FPGAs can be classified into *hard* and *soft programmable* FPGAs. In the first case, programming is performed thorough connecting segments of interconnections by *antifuses*, i.e., open circuits that are converted into short circuits by an appropriate current pulse or voltage. The second class involves FPGAs consisting of arrays of memory elements, called *look-up tables* (LUTs) that are programmed to store information about the module configuration and interconnections.

Look-up table based FPGAs are programmed in the same way as memory chips, and a word of configuration data is written into an addressed segment in the array. Every bit in the memory array controls a particular interconnecting element Several of these elements, up to the width of a data word, are programmed in parallel by applying voltages, usually 0 and 5 volts, to the FPGA in the correct programming sequence.

Antifuse based FPGAs are programmed with a mixed sequence of digital control and high voltage analog waveforms. Generally, antifuses are programmed separately each of them at a time within the full array of antifuses. An antifuse array can be viewed as a collection of vertical and horizontal wires with an antifuse at every wire crossing or intersection whenever it may appear a need to connect two lines. Many of them remain unused, however, since antifuses are small, this is a negligible and inexpensive overhead [105].

In general, an antifuse can exist in three states, off-state, on-state, and an off-on transition state. In the off-state, the antifuse consists of its original non-conducting amorphous (glass like - non-crystalline) state located between top and bottom metal electrodes. Application of the programming pulse across the metal electrodes leads to a transitional off-on state in which the amorphous silicon becomes a liquid and forms a complex metal-silicon composition. In the final on-state condition, the antifuse has become a conductive polycrystalline silicon-metal alloy

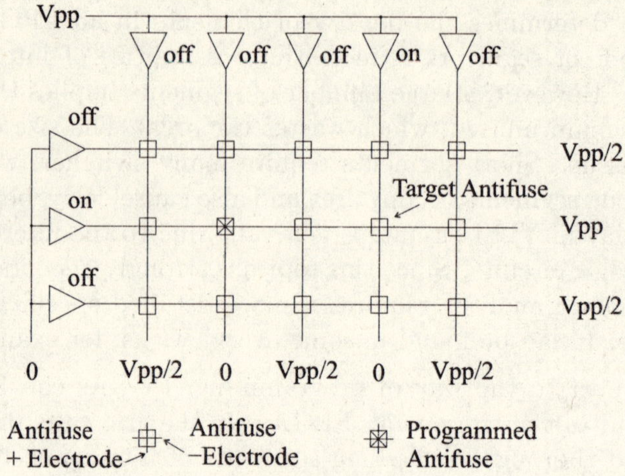

Figure 10.2. Distribution of antifuses in an FPGA.

with a low resistance. The programming process is irreversible. Fig. 10.2 shows an example of distribution of antifuses [105].

There are many FPGA families provided by different companies that differ in the technologies and structures of blocks. More details on each can be found e.g. on the Web pages of the producers.

EXAMPLE 10.1 *(Logic blocks in FPGA) [143]*
*Fig. 10.3 shows an example of a fine-grain FPGA (*Crosspoint Solutions, Ltd.*), realizing the function* $(a, b, c) = ab + \overline{c}$. *This is an example of FPGAs by the company* Crosspoint Solutions. Concurrent Logic *offers logic blocks containing a two-input AND circuit and a two-input EXOR circuit.* Toshiba *provides FPGAs with logic blocks containing NAND circuits. The company* Algotronix *produces FPGAs whose logic blocks are configurable multiplexers that can realize any function of two variables.*

Fig. 10.4 shows the realization of the same function by an Altera *5000 FPGA.*

Actel *offers FPGAs whose logic blocks are based on multiplexers. Fig. 10.5 shows the realization of the function in this example by an FPGA from the family* Act1.

Fig. 10.6 shows the logic blocks in FPGAs by Quick Logic.

Fig. 10.7 explains the basic principle of Look-up table FPGAs. Figs. 10.8 and 10.9 shows examples of logic blocks in Xilinix *3000 and* Plessey *FPGAs.*

The following examples, illustrate basic logic blocks in the family of FPGAs by *Xilinix* and *Altera*. The first is an example of devices that

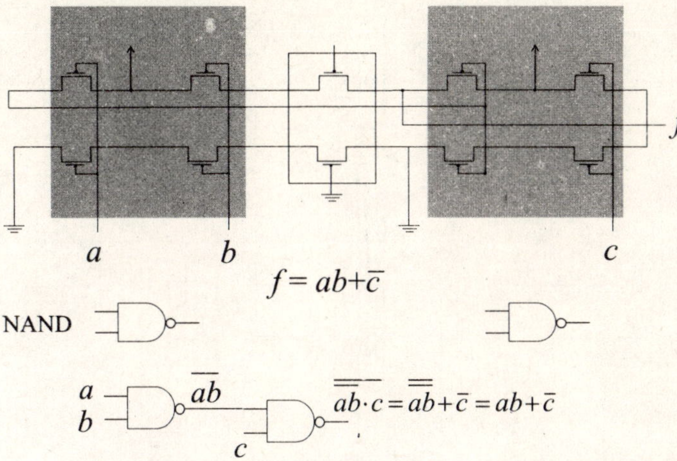

Figure 10.3. *Crosspoint* FPGA.

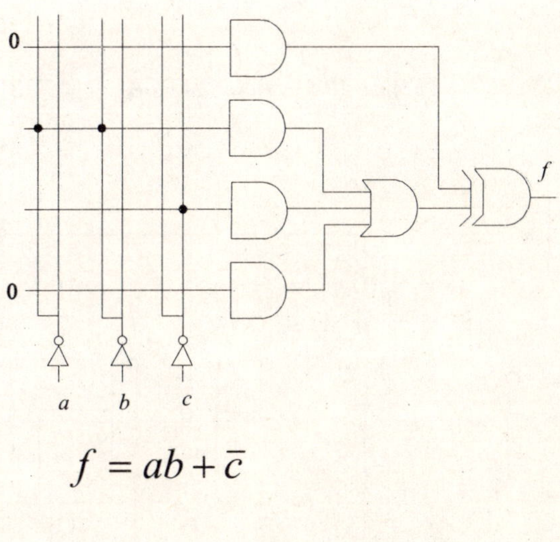

Figure 10.4. *Altera 5000* FPGA.

provide all key requirements for replacing application specific integrated circuits (ASIC) up to 40.000 gates, and may be suitable for production of high-volume series. The latter is an example of devices that offer up to 22 digital signal processing (DSP) blocks with up to 176 (9-bit × 9-bit) embedded multipliers, optimized for DSP applications that enable efficient implementation of high-performance filters and multipliers.

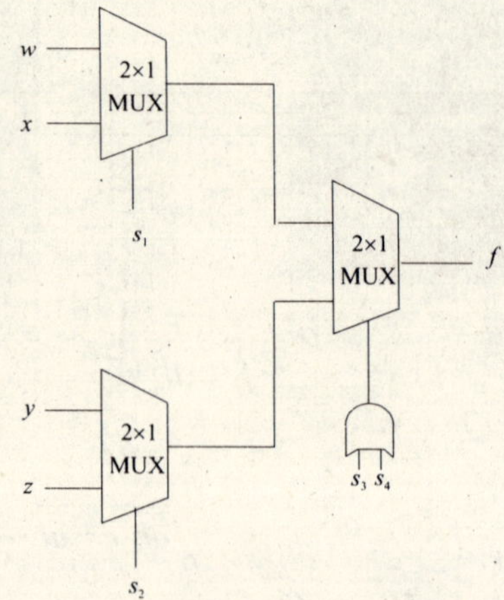

$$f = \overline{(s_3 + s_4)}(\bar{s}_1 w + s_1 x) + (s_3 + s_4)(\bar{s}_2 y + s_2 z)$$

$$f = ab + \bar{c}$$
$$w = 1, x = 1, s_1 = 0, y = 0$$
$$z = a, s_2 = b, s_3 = c, s_4 = 0$$

Figure 10.5. *Actel 1* FPGA.

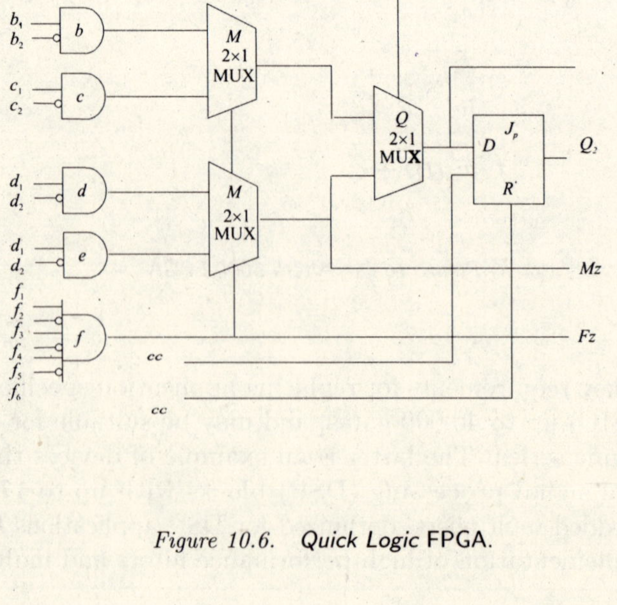

Figure 10.6. *Quick Logic* FPGA.

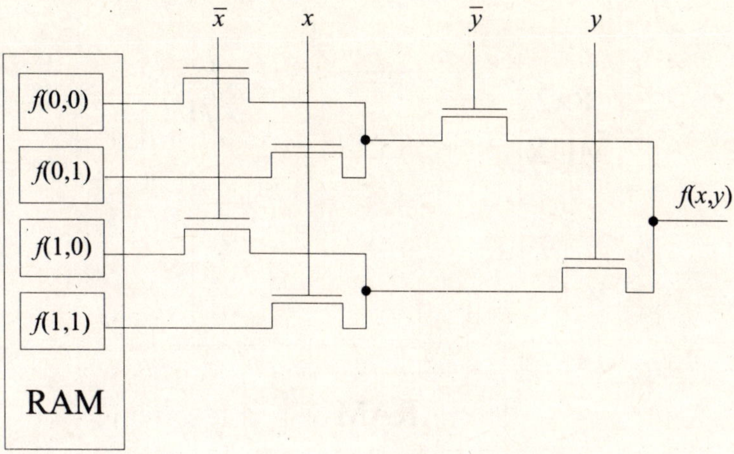

Figure 10.7. Look-up table FPGA principle.

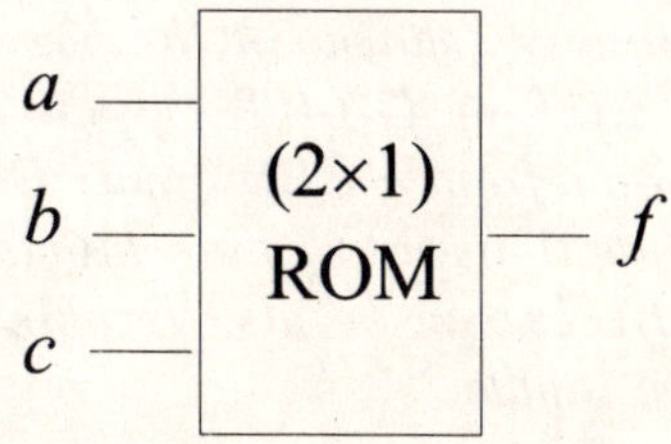

Figure 10.8. *Xilinix 3000* FPGA.

EXAMPLE 10.2 *Fig. 10.10 shows the structure of basic blocks in the FPGA family* Spartan-XL *by* Xilinix *as described in the corresponding data book. Fig. 10.11 shows in a simplified form the principal elements in configurable logic blocks (CLB) used in this FPGA. Each CLB consists of three LUTs used as generators of logic functions, two flip-flops and two groups of signal steering multiplexers.*

Two (16×1) *memory LUTs (F-LUT and G-LUT) may implement any switching function with no more than four inputs (F1 to F4 or G1 to G4). Since memory LUTs are used, the propagation delay is independent of the functions implemented.*

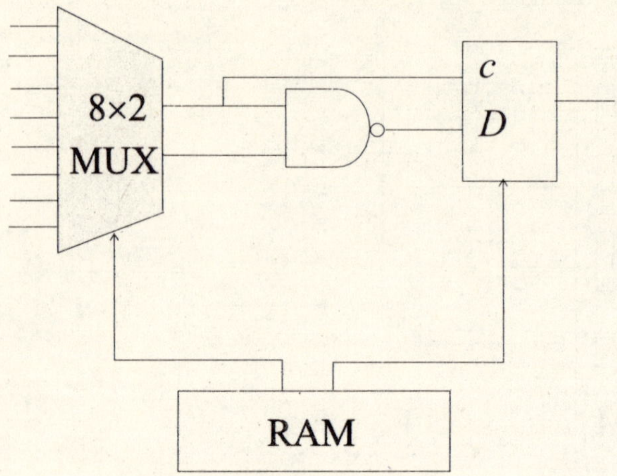

Figure 10.9. *Plessey* FPGA.

A third three input function generator (H-LUT) can implement any switching function of $n = 3$ *variables. Two of these inputs are controlled by programmable multiplexers (shown in the box A) These inputs can came from either the F-LUT or G-LUT outputs or from CLB inputs. The third input always come from a CBL input. Because of that, a CLB can implement certain functions up to nine inputs, for instance, parity checking. These three LUTs can be also combined to implement any switching function of five inputs.*

In summary, a CLB can implement any of the following functions

1 *Any function of up to four variables, and another function up to four unrelated variables, any additional function of up to three unrelated variables. Notice, that since there are available two unregistered function generator outputs from the CLB, when three separate functions are generated, a function must be captured in a flip-flop internal to the CLB.*

2 *Any single function of five variables.*

3 *Any function of four variables together with some functions of six variables.*

4 *Some functions of up to nine variables.*

EXAMPLE 10.3 Stratix *devices by* Altera *is a two-dimensional array intended to implement custom logic. It consists of array blocks (LABs),*

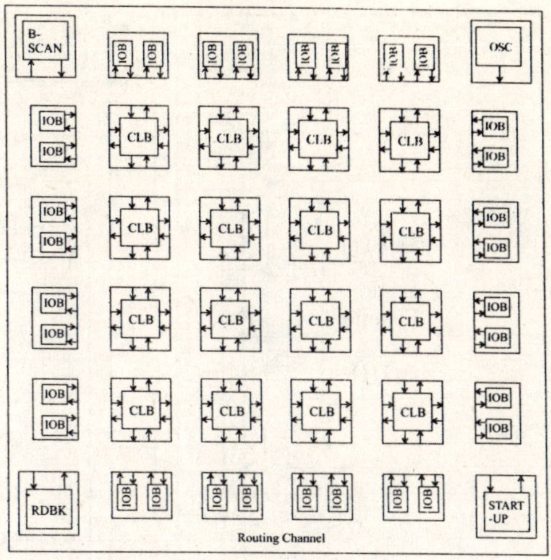

CLB - functional elements to implement logic

IOB - interface between the package pins and internal signal lines

Routing Channels - pats to interconnect the inputs and outputs of CLB and IOBs

RDBK - read back the content of the configuration memory and the level of certain internal nodes

START-UP - start-up bytes of data to provide four clocks for the start-up sequence at the end of configuration

Figure 10.10. Configurable logic block in *Spartan* FPGAs by *Xilinix.*

memory block structures, and DSP blocks connected with lines of varying length and speed. The logic array consists of LABs, with 10 logic elements (LEs) in each LAB. An LE is a small unit of logic providing efficient implementation of user logic functions. LABs are grouped into rows and columns across the device. Fig. 10.12 shows the structure of the Stratix *device.*

The smallest unit of logic in this architecture is the LE, that contains a four-input LUT, which is a function generator that can implement any function of four variables. In addition, each LE contains a programmable register and carry chain with carry select capability. A single LE also supports dynamic single bit addition or subtraction mode selectable by an LAB-wide control signal. Fig. 10.13 shows the structure of a LE.

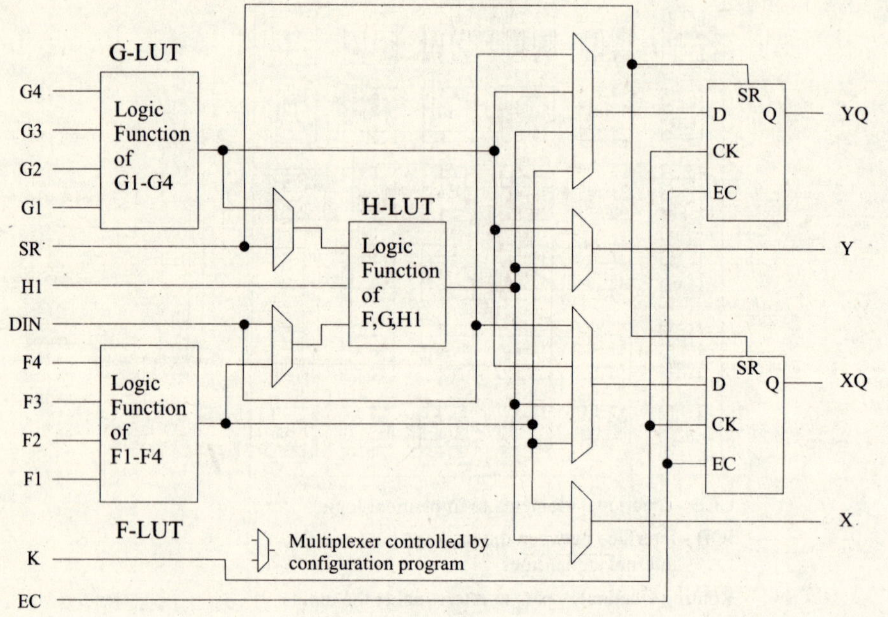

Figure 10.11. Components of the CLB in *Spartan* FPGAs.

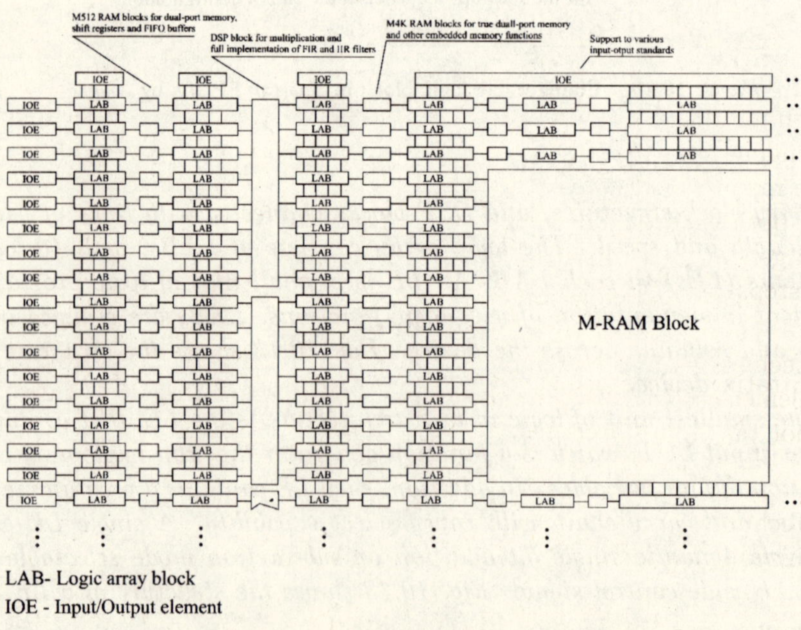

Figure 10.12. Structure of *Stratix* device by *Altera*.

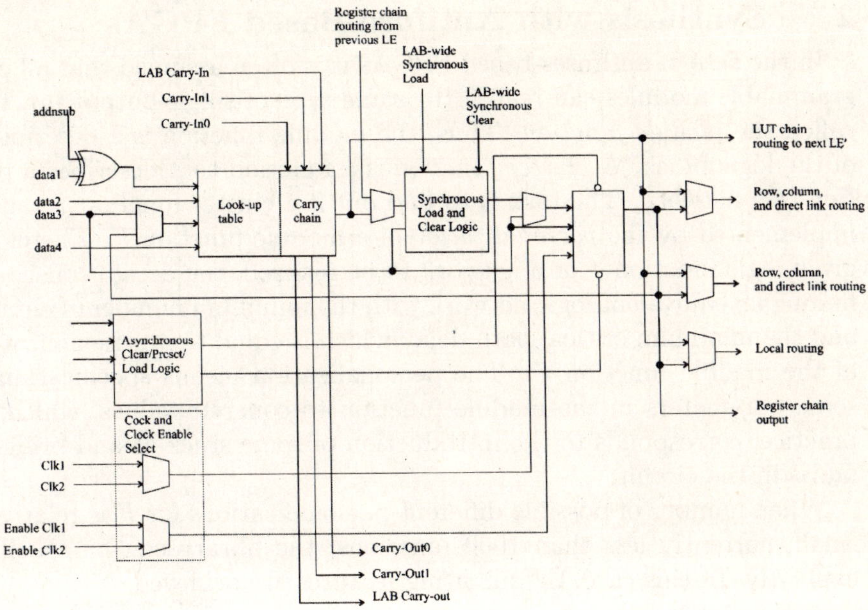

Figure 10.13. Logic element in *Stratix.*

1. Synthesis with FPGAs

Since FPGAs are a relatively new and fast evolving technology, the design methodologies are equally quickly developing and are technology dependent. Therefore, it is hard to present them in a rigorous and complete manner and, thus, provide here only some basic design guidelines with both antifuse and LUT-based FPGAs.

In general, the synthesis with FPGAs is a procedure that consists of two steps

1 Technology independent optimization, where the particular logic elements to be used in the implementations and their features are not taken into account,

2 Technology mapper, meaning the realization of the network optimized in the first step on a target FPGA.

Design with FPGAs can be viewed as the *personalization* of the programmable logic modules they consists of, to realize the functions required.

2. Synthesis with Antifuse-Based FPGAs

In the case of antifuses-based FPGAs it is often assumed that all programmable modules can realize the same type of single-output function called the *module function.* Thus, the module function is a description of the logic block. A *cluster function* is a function that describes a portion of a network. The task is to find out if a cluster function f can be implemented by the *personalization* of a module function F. Therefore, given logic function f or a network to be realized, the design consists of finding an equivalent logic network with the minimum number of circuits and the minimum critical path delay which is equal to a personalization of the module function F. The personalization means specification of some parameters in the module function to concrete values, which, in practice, corresponds to the introduction of some stuck-at and bridging faults in the circuit.

When number of possible different personalizations for F is relatively small, currently less than 1000 functions, the library can be specified explicitly. In this case, the following features are achieved

1 Application of standard library binding algorithms,

2 It is possible to eliminate gates with inconvenient delays or pin configurations,

3 Area and delay cost of each cell can be precisely determined.

EXAMPLE 10.4 *The module function for the* Act 1 *family of FPGAs in Fig. 10.5 is*

$$F = \overline{(s_3 + s_4)}(\overline{s}_1 w + s_1 x) + (s_3 + s_4)(\overline{s}_2 y + s_2 z),$$

and it can realize 702 different functions for different values of parameters. The personalization to realize the function $f(a, b, c) = ab + \overline{c}$ *is done by specifying the parameters as* $w = 1$, $x = 1$, $s_1 = 0$, $y = 0$, $z = a$, $s_2 = b$, $s_3 = c$, $s_4 = 0$.

Binary decision diagrams (BDDs) have proven useful in FPGA synthesis, especially when logic block are based on multiplexers, due among other features, also to the straightforward correspondence of nodes in BDDs and (2×1) multiplexers.

EXAMPLE 10.5 *[43]*
Consider the module function F for a logic block in a multiplexer based FPGA

$$F = (s_0 + s_1)(s_2 a + \overline{s}_2 b) + \overline{s}_0 \overline{s}_1 (s_3 c + \overline{s}_3 d).$$

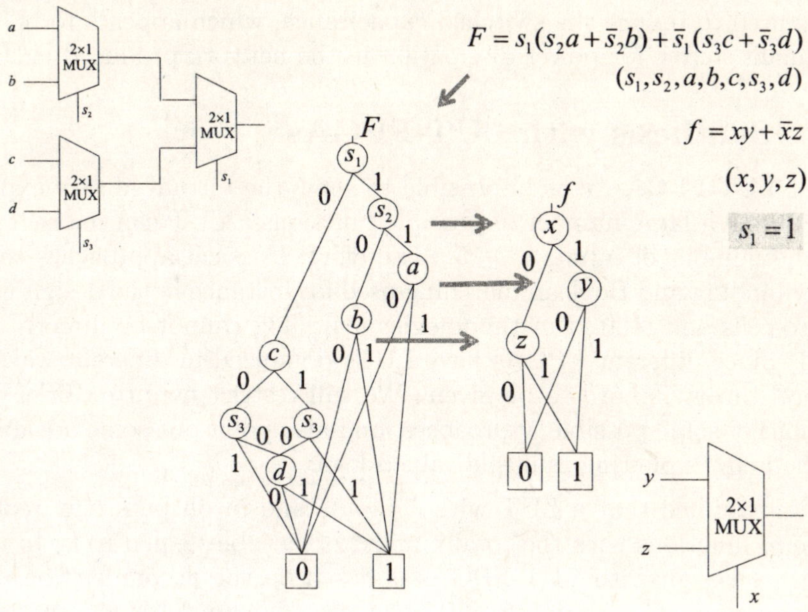

Figure 10.14. Module functions and cluster functions represented by BDDs.

This function can be represented by a BDD as in Fig. 10.14. If a cluster function f is given by $f(x,y,z) = xy + \overline{x}z$, then it can be represented by the corresponding BDD shown in the same figure. It is obvious that the BDD for f is a subtree in the BDD for F for the specification of the parameter $s_1 = 1$, which results in the realization of f by a (2×1) multiplexer.

Recall that BDDs are sensitive to the order of variables, and therefore, to cover all possible personalizations, the BDDs for all different orders of variables have to be considered. Therefore, a virtual library corresponding to a module function can be covered by a Shared BDD [34].

Various algorithms and techniques for efficient multiplexer synthesis can be efficiently combined with BDDs in synthesis with multiplexer-based FPGAs, as for instance, algorithms discussed in [55], [56], [128], [129]. In [104], it has been shown that by using some of these algorithms, BDDs with different order of variables along different paths can be produced and exploited efficiently in reducing the delay and power consumption in multiplexer-based FPGAs. It is worth noticing that techniques for splitting and duplicating of nodes can be used to reduce the delay and the number of FPGA nodes. These nodes are suitably configured to reduce the switched capacitance, which appears to be the dominant source for power dissipation in the network produced [104].

3. Synthesis with LUT-FPGAs

For LUT-FPGAs, it is impossible to show the virtual library explicitly, due to a large number of possible functions a LUT can realize even for the number of inputs $n \geq 5$. Therefore, classical approaches to library binding and Boolean matching used for instance in the design with macro-cells and related methodologies [34], [43], cannot be directly applied. Since different FPGAs have LUTs organized in different ways, a general theory is hard to be given. We will restrict here to a brief discussions of some possible approaches, and also point out some advanced methods by exploiting multiple-valued logic.

It is assumed that a LUT with k inputs and m outputs may realize up to m functions with the total number of variables equal to k. In this case, the design with LUT-FPGAs is based on the decomposition of a given function of n variables into no more than m subfunctions, each with at most k variables.

Similarly to the case of logic blocks in antifuses-based FPGAs, the size of LUTs considerably effects performances of FPGAs. Research has shown that wider LUTs offer higher performance, but narrower LUTs are more area and cost efficient [3], [142]. In the last decade, the development was primarily based on four-input LUTs to achieve the optimal trade-off. However, nowadays manufacturers offer, for various applications, different solutions giving predominance to performances or FPGA architectures targeted at specific applications. For instance, in the Stratix II devices by *Altera* various combinations or LUTs with 4,5,6, and 7 inputs are provided for efficient implementation of combined logic-arithmetic operations of complex arithmetic operations. At the same time, in Virtex devices by *Xilinix*, four-input LUTs are efficiently combined with various multiplexers of small orders to provide (16×1) and (31×1) multiplexers, or further with some additional and dedicated two-input multiplexers to perform operations involving wide AND and OR circuits, which may combine four-input LUT outputs. The idea of using universal logic modules within FPGAs [97], [184], [208], can be recognized in the so-called FXMUX logic, where for instance such modules for $X = 6, 7, 8$ capable to realize any function of 4,7, and 8 variables, are modules used in Virtex devices to implement custom Boolean functions up to 39 variables within the same logic bloc, or a function with 79 inputs in two blocks with dedicated connections in a single level of logic. An overview of these actual various solutions can be found in the specialized literature

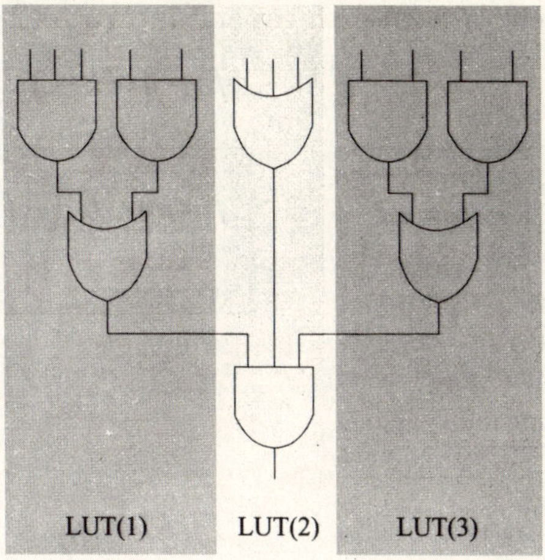

Figure 10.15. Covering of a network by LUTs.

as, for example, [90], [116]. More detailed information is available in the corresponding data books at the web pages of manufacturers.

3.1 Design procedure

There are several algorithms for design with LUT-FPGAs, see for example, [18], [47], [106], [121], [192], [201], [205].

Functions that should be realized are represented by an initial AND-OR multi-level network, a two-level specification as cubes, or BDDs, etc. The design consists of decomposing the initial network or other description of the given function into sub-networks or sub-functions, each realizable by a LUT.

The starting point of mapping a given function f to an LUT-FPGA with k inputs per LUT, is to decompose f into basic subfunctions with no more than k variables. It is usually convenient to use two-variable subfunctions to achieve a finer network granularity [34].

EXAMPLE 10.6 *[46], [34]*
Fig. 10.15 illustrates the basic principle of covering a network by the LUTs. It is assumed that a LUT has five inputs, and an network with 12 primary inputs is, therefore, covered by three LUTs.

The following example illustrates that a Sum-of-Product expression can be covered by LUTs in different ways.

EXAMPLE 10.7 *[46], [34]*
Consider realization of a function of four variables $f(a,b,c,d) = ab+cd$

$k=3 \quad n=4 \quad f=ab+cd \qquad |ab|=|cd|=2<k=3$

$|f|=4>k=3$

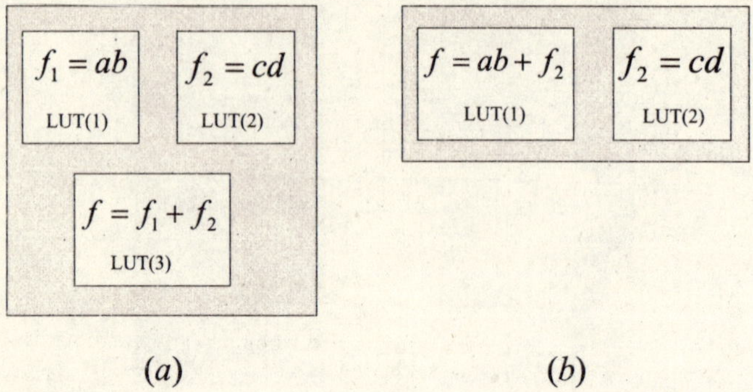

Figure 10.16. Covering of a SOP by LUTs.

by a LUT-FPGAs where LUTs have $k = 3$ inputs. Fig. 10.16a shows a direct assignment of product terms to LUTs. However, if f is written as $f = ab + f_2$, where $f_2 = cd$, then, two LUTs are sufficient as shown in Fig. 10.16b.

Assignment of SOPs to LUTs can be performed by the following algorithm.

A given function f of n variables is represented by a SOP consisting of r products P_i with $q_i = |P_i|$ literals. The task is to assign f to a LUT-FPGA with $k > max\{q_1, \ldots, q_r\}$ inputs per LUT by using the minimum number of LUTs. That means, few product terms can be realized by the same LUT, if the total number of variables in products q_i is smaller than the number of inputs k in the LUT.

1 Label available LUTs by assigning an identifier to each LUT. Create a list Q recording the labels of exploited LUTs and the number of used inputs v out of the total of k inputs. Set $Q = \emptyset$.

2 Select a product P_i with most literals, i.e., with $q_i = max\{q_1, \ldots q_r\}$, and assign to a LUT, where number of unused inputs is greater than q_i.

3 If there are no available LUTs with enough capacity, i.e., with the number of unused inputs $v > q_i$, add a new LUT to the present solution for the assignment, thus, increase the content of Q.

4 Declare as the final assignment of a P_i to a LUT, LUT_{P_i} the LUT with fewest number of unused variables v.

5 Associate a new variable z to this LUT_{P_i}, and assign it to the first LUT that accepts it, i.e., where $v < q_{LUT_{P_i}}$.

6 Repeat the procedure for all $i \in \{1, \ldots, r\}$.

7 Declare the last processed LUT as the output LUT.

If products in a SOP for a given function f are disjoint, then the algorithm ensures minimum number of LUTs for $k = 6$.

This algorithm is implemented in [46] with some modifications that allow sharing of variables between products and also duplicating products when this may reduce the number of LUTs.

The following example confirms that this algorithm will produce the optimal solution in Example 10.7.

EXAMPLE 10.8 *Since in the function f in Example 10.7, both products have the same number of variables, we randomly select the product cd and assign it to a $LUT(1)$ as specified in the Step 1, where a variable remains unused. The Step 2 does not apply, since $k = 3$ is greater than the number of variables in the product $v = 2$. By the Step 3, we assign the product ab to the $LUT(2)$. By the Step 4, since in both $LUT(1)$ and $LUT(2)$ a variable is unused, we select $LUT(1)$ as the LUT with the minimum number of unused variables, declare it as a final assignment and assign another variable z. By the Step 5, we assign this variable to the $LUT(2)$ that accepts it. Then, we declare the output of $LUT(2)$ as the final output. Fig. 10.17 illustrates this procedure.*

Application of decision diagrams in synthesis with LUT-FPGA is convenient, because then it is not necessary to construct the initial logic network [111]. Since a non-terminal node in a BDD is related to the Shannon expansion, which can be implemented by a (2×1) multiplexer, mapping of a BDD to a LUT-FPGA with $k = 3$ is straightforward and each non-terminal node requires a LUT that performs the function of a (2×1) multiplexer. It follows that when $k > 3$, LUTs are inefficiently used.

The routing architecture is an inherent necessary part of each FPGA. Reducing the area occupied by routing, would allow increasing the area devoted to the functionality of the FPGA. Reduced routing is often emphasized as an advantage of multiple-valued logic over the binary logic. LUT-FPGAs are pointed out in [111] as such an example.

With this motivation, a method for mapping a p-valued function represented by decision diagrams representing a straightforward extension

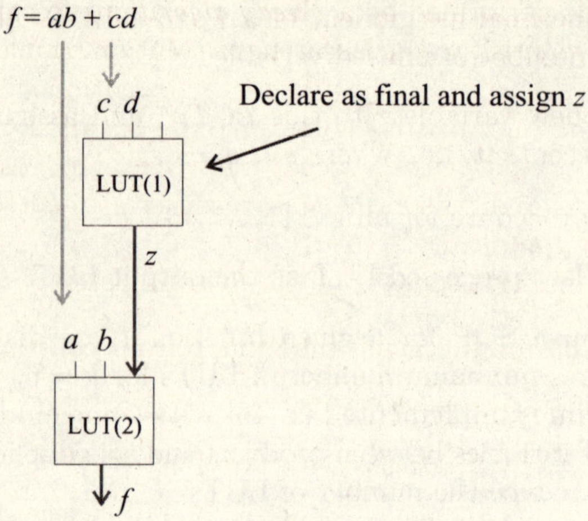

Figure 10.17. Assignment of the function f in Example 10.7 to LUTs.

of BDDs to multiple-valued functions, see, for example, [175], into a LUT-FPGAs has been presented in [111].

The method in [111] will be presented here for the case of binary-valued switching functions represented by BDDs.

Denote by $x_1, \ldots, x_n$ variables in a function f represented by a BDD. The variables x_{n+1} up to some x_r, where r depends on the given function f and the corresponding BDD, will be assigned to LUTs that will be used in the implementation of f.

For a non-terminal node to which the variable x_i is assigned, the dependency set D_i is the union of x_i and the dependency sets of descendant nodes, D_{i_0} and D_{i_1}, i.e., nodes to which point the outgoing edges i_0 and i_1 of the considered node [111]. Thus,

$$D_i = \{x_i\} \cup D_{i_0} \cup D_{i_1}.$$

The dependency set of a constant node is the empty set, since constant nodes show function values.

The method of mapping a BDD into a LUT-FPGA proposed in [111], can be described as follows. It is assumed that a given function of n variables has to be realized by a LUT-FPGA with k inputs per LUT. As in the other LUT-FPGA design methods, the procedure starts by decomposition of the BDD into subdiagrams representing subfunctions that can be realized by a LUT. The method should provide exploiting of as few of LUTs as possible which is viewed as increased functionality of FPGAs. Therefore, the assignment of subfunctions, i.e., subtrees to LUTs, will be performed by a *greedy algorithm.* Recall that a greedy algorithm is an algorithm which searches a solution by making a sequence of best local decisions based on the local information. Therefore, it is a heuristic method, and does not guarantee the optimality of the solution produced. The complexity of a greedy algorithm depends on the number of local decisions and, therefore, it is often implemented in a top dow way with linear complexity.

The method in [111] consists of the following steps.

1 Traverse BDD for the given function f from constant nodes to the root node.

2 Mark non-terminal nodes, by starting from nodes at the level $(n-k)$, where n is the number of variables and k number of inputs in LUTs.

3 Each marked non-terminal node is a root of a subdiagram and can be viewed as a pseudo constant node, since represents a subfunction that will be realized by a LUT.

4 Write a list of subdiagrams.

5 Assign subdiagrams rooted in the marked nodes into LUTs by using a greedy algorithm.

6 Process subdiagrams in order as generated.

7 If the number of variables v in a subdiagram is smaller that k, search for preceding subdiagrams with the number of variables u, such that $v+u \geq k$.

8 Make such combinations until list of subdiagrams traversed.

This method can be implemented by the following algorithm.

ALGORITHM 10.1 *(BDD into LUT-FPGA)*

1 Process a given BDD from the constant nodes to the root node and assign a dependency set D to each non-terminal node. The dependency set of a constant node is an empty set.

2 If for a node, the cardinality of D, $|D| < k$, no further processing of that node is required at the time.

3 If for a node $|D| = k$, mark this non-terminal node as the root of a subdiagram, assign to it a unique identifier q and set $D = [q]$. This node represents a subfunction that will be relied by a LUT.

```
Set LUTA(NODE, k)
  If (NODE = CONSTANT NODE)
    NODE → D = [∅]
    return NODE → D
  Else
    NODE→D where
    D=[NODE→ x, LUTA(NODE→L), LUTA(NODE→R)]
      If (|NODE → D| = k)
        Mark NODE as a root of a subtree representing a LUT
        assign that LUT a unique identifier q and
        set NODE → D = [q]
      End If
      If (|NODE → D| > k)
      DES = Max(|NODE → L → D|, |NODE → R → D|)
        Mark DES as a root of a subtree representing a LUT
        assign that LUT a unique identifier q and
        set NODE → D = [q]
      End If
    End If
  End Procedure
```

Figure 10.18. Mapping a BDD into a LUT-FPGA.

4 *If $|D| > k$, search the immediate descendants of this non-terminal node for that with the maximum $|D|$, mark this node as above, and reprocess the previous node.*

5 *If few of the descendant nodes have the dependency sets of the maximum cardinality, chose the first encountered.*

Fig. 10.18 describes this procedure in a pseudo code.

This algorithm will be illustrated by the following example [111].

EXAMPLE 10.9 *Consider a logic function called 2-of-5 checker, defined as a function of five variables $f(x_1, x_2, x_3, x_4, x_5)$ which takes the value 1 when two inputs have the values 1. Fig. 10.19 shows a BDD for f, which should be realized by a LUT-FPGA where LUTs have $k = 3$ inputs.*

We traverse this BDD up to the level for x_3, since $k = 3$, mark the non-terminal nodes at this level and assign to them unique identifiers $ID = (6, 7, 8)$. Then, we determine dependency sets for all the nodes at the levels below x_3 as shown by numbers in square brackets. The nodes

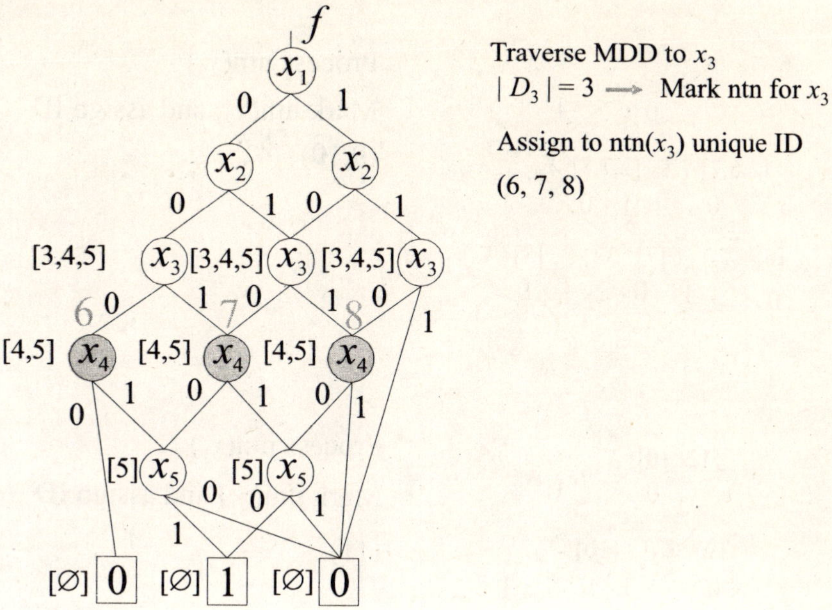

Figure 10.19. BDD for f in Example 10.9.

at the level x_3 are now considered as pseudo-constant nodes in a reduced diagram shown in Fig. 10.20(a).

Then, nodes at the level for x_2 are processed, identifiers $ID = (9, 10)$ are assigned and dependency sets determined. The root node is processed and, the identifier $ID = 11$ assigned, and the dependency set determined. Fig. 10.20(b) shows the reduced diagrams when these nodes considered as pseudo-constant nodes.

Each of the nodes with identifiers $ID = 6, 7, 8, 9, 10, 11$ is realized by a LUT. If labels at the edges of nodes 0 and 1 are written as $\overline{x}_i$ and x_i, respectively, it is possible to determine functional expressions for functions that will be realized by LUTs by traversing the the BDD for f.

These functions correspond to the products of labels at the edges in the paths from the pseudo-constant nodes at the level x_3 to the constant nodes in the BDD for f as shown in Fig. 10.21.

It has been pointed out in [73] that in mapping a BDD into a LUT-FPGA, it is usually more economic to put two four-input functions in a LUT table than a function of five inputs, since the former approach will cover more nodes.

More about synthesis with FPGAs can be found in the broad literature on this subject, see, for example, [18], [106], [121], [192], [201], [205].

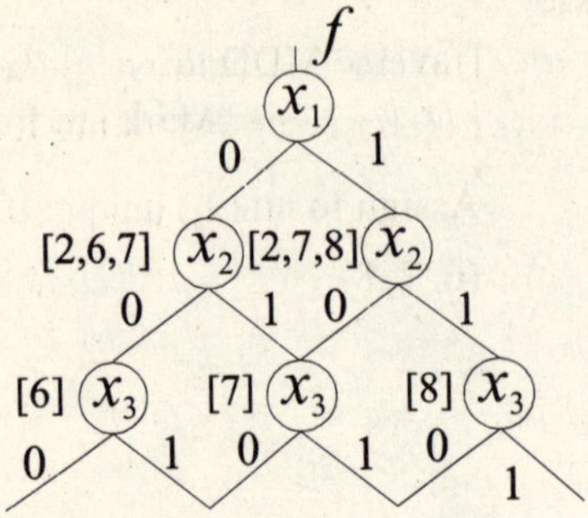

Process ntn(x_2)

Mark ntn(x_2) and assign ID

(9,10)

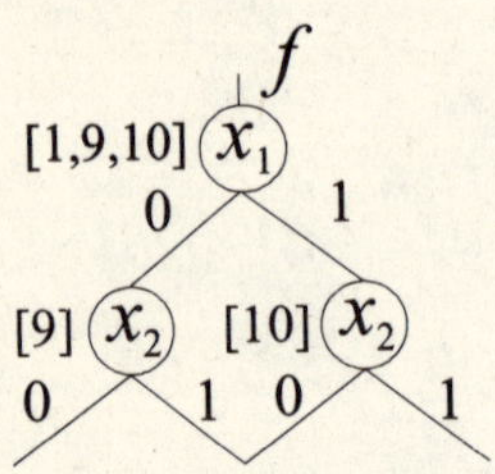

Process ntn(x_1)

Mark ntn(x_1) and assign ID

(11)

Figure 10.20. Reduced BDD for f after processing nodes for (a) x_3, (b) x_2.

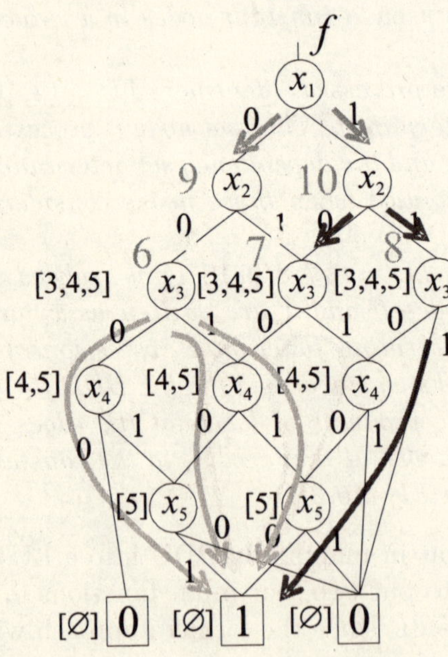

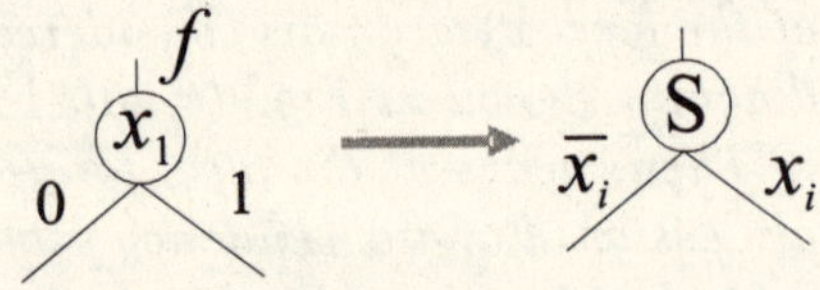

$$x_{11} = \bar{x}_1 x_9 + x_1 x_{10}$$

$$x_{10} = \bar{x}_2 x_7 + x_2 x_8$$

$$x_9 = \bar{x}_2 x_6 + x_2 x_7$$

$$x_8 = \bar{x}_3 \bar{x}_4 \bar{x}_5$$

$$x_7 = \bar{x}_3 \bar{x}_4 x_5 + \bar{x}_3 x_4 \bar{x}_5 + x_3 \bar{x}_4 \bar{x}_5$$
$$= \bar{x}_3 (x_4 \oplus x_5) + x_3 \bar{x}_4 \bar{x}_5$$

$$x_6 = \bar{x}_3 x_4 x_5 + x_3 \bar{x}_4 x_5 + x_3 x_4 \bar{x}_5$$
$$= \bar{x}_3 x_4 x_5 + x_3 (x_4 \oplus x_5)$$

Figure 10.21. Functions realized by LUTs for f in Example 10.9.

4. Exercises and Problems

EXERCISE 10.1 *Discuss the main features of FPGAs which make their application efficient, compared to PLAs and classical approaches to the synthesis of logic networks.*

EXERCISE 10.2 *Show the basic structure of an FPGA, and briefly discuss each of the main parts. Classify FPGAs with respect to the complexity.*

EXERCISE 10.3 *Classify and briefly discuss main features of FPGAs with respect of programmability.*

EXERCISE 10.4 *Discuss and show few examples of logic blocks in FPGAs.*

EXERCISE 10.5 *Describe the steps in synthesis with FPGAs and explain notions module function, cluster function and personalization of FPGA.*

EXERCISE 10.6 *Realize the functions*

$$f(x_1, x_2, x_3) = \overline{x}_1 x_2 + x_1 x_2 x_3$$

by personalization of the module function for the Act1 *family of FPGAs*

$$f = \overline{(s_3 + s_4)}(\overline{s}_1 w + s_1 x) + (s_3 + s_4)(\overline{s}_2 y + s_2 z),$$

EXERCISE 10.7 *Realize the functions*

$$\begin{aligned} f(x_1, x_2, x_3) &= \overline{x}_1 x_2 + x_1 x_3, \\ f(x_1, x_2, x_3, x_4) &= x_2 \overline{(x_1 + x_4)} + x_3 (x_1 + x_4). \end{aligned}$$

EXERCISE 10.8 *Personalize the module function*

$$F = (s_0 + s_1)(s_2 a + \overline{s}_2 b) + \overline{s}_0 \overline{s}_1 (s_3 c + \overline{s}_3 d).$$

to realize the functions

$$\begin{aligned} f_1(x_1, x_2, x_3, x_4) &= (x_1 + x_2)(x_3 + x_4) + \overline{x}_1 \overline{x}_2 x_4, \\ f_2(x_1, x_2, x_3, x_4) &= (x_3 + x_4)(x_1 x_2 + \overline{x}_2 x_4) + \overline{x}_1 \overline{x}_2 x_3. \end{aligned}$$

EXERCISE 10.9 *Realize the function* $f(x_1, x_2, x_3) = x_1x_3 + x_2x_4 + x_1x_2x_4 + x_2x_3x_4$ *by an FPGA with* $k = 3$ *input LUTs.*

EXERCISE 10.10 *Consider the function* $f(x_1, x_2, x_3, x_4, x_5) = \overline{x}_1 x_2 x_3 + x_1 x_2 x_4 + x_2 x_4 + \overline{x}_1 \overline{x}_2 x_5 + x_1 x_5$. *Represent* f *by a BDD and realize it*

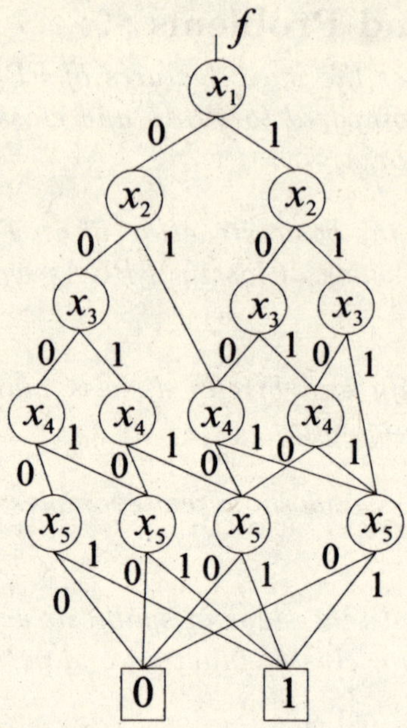

Figure 10.22. BDD for the function f in Exercise10.12.

with a LUT-FPGA, with $k = 3$ inputs per LUT. Try different order of variables and make conclusions.

EXERCISE 10.11 *Consider the function of eight variables*

$$\begin{aligned} f(x_1, \ldots, x_8) &= x_1x_2 + x_2x_3 + x_1\overline{x}_2\overline{x}_3 \\ & \quad x_1 + x_7 + x_6x_8 + \overline{x}_6x_7\overline{x}_8 + \overline{x}_7x_8 \\ & \quad x_1x_7 + x_2x_8 + x_8 + \overline{x}_2x_6x_8. \end{aligned}$$

Realize f by a LUT-FPGA with $k = 5$ inputs per LUT.

EXERCISE 10.12 *Consider the function f of five variables defined by the BDD in Fig. 10.22. Realize f by a LUT-FPGA with $k = 3$ inputs per LUT.*

EXERCISE 10.13 *Realize the function f of five variables defined by the truth-vector*

$$\mathbf{F} = [1,0,0,1,1,1,0,0,1,0,0,1,1,0,0,1,0,0,1,0]^T,$$

by a LUT-FPGA with $k = 3$ inputs per LUT.

Chapter 11

BOOLEAN DIFFERENCE AND APPLICATIONS IN TESTING LOGIC NETWORKS

Differential operators are a very important tool in science. Therefore, it has been quite natural to make attempts to extend the theory of differential calculus of functions on the real line R to switching functions.

The notion of the *partial derivative* has been introduced to get estimate the rate and the direction of the change of a function $f(x_1, \ldots, x_n)$ caused by an infinitesimal change of its argument x_i, as illustrated in Fig. 11.1. For a real function, i.e., $f : R^n \rightarrow R$, the *Newton-Leibniz derivative* is defined as

$$\frac{df}{dx} = \lim_{\Delta x \rightarrow 0} \frac{f(x + \Delta x) - f(x)}{\Delta x}.$$

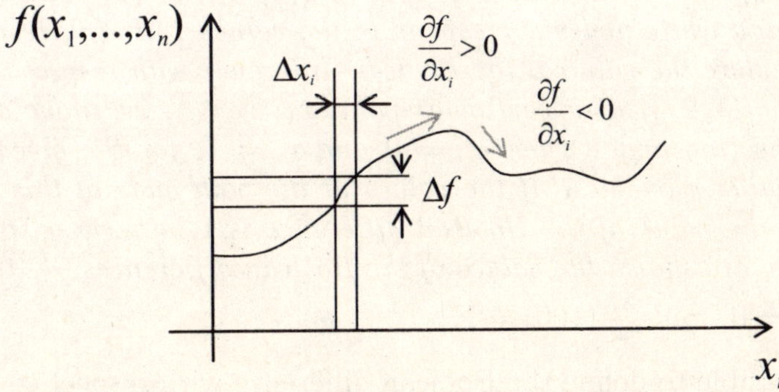

Figure 11.1. Illustration of the application of Newton-Leibniz derivative with respect to the variable x_i.

1. Boolean difference

Switching (Boolean) functions are defined as mappings $f : \{0,1\}^n \rightarrow \{0,1\}$ and, therefore, the smallest change in the argument and the function is equal to 1. Since the addition and subtraction modulo 2, which are used for switching functions coincide, and are viewed as logic EXOR, the definition of a differential operator for switching functions with respect to the variable x_i is

$$\frac{\delta f}{\delta x_i} = f(x_1, \ldots, x_i, \ldots, x_n) \oplus f(x_1, \ldots, \overline{x}_i, \ldots, x_n).$$

It is clear that due to the properties of EXOR, the Boolean difference cannot distinguish between the change of a function value from 0 to 1 or vice versa, since $1+0 = 0+1 = 1$. Thus defined operator expresses some of the properties of the classical Newton-Leibniz derivative, and is called the *Boolean derivative* [185]. However, to emphasize that it is defined on finite and discrete structures and is applied to discrete functions, the term *Boolean difference* is also used.

Since $x_i \oplus 1 = \overline{x}_i$, the definition of the Boolean difference can be written as

$$\frac{\delta f}{\delta x_i} = f(x_1, \ldots \overline{x}_i, \ldots, x_n) \oplus f(x_1, \ldots, x_i, \ldots, x_n)$$

It is obvious that $\frac{\delta f}{\delta x_i} = 1$ iff $f(x_1, \ldots, \overline{x}_i, \ldots, x_n) = \overline{f}(x_1, \ldots, x_i, \ldots, x_n)$. This property of the Boolean difference is used to check if a variable is an essential variable in a Boolean function f.

EXAMPLE 11.1 *Fig. 11.2 shows a Boolean cube specifying the function $f(x_1, x_2, x_3)$ whose truth-vector is $\mathbf{F} = [0,0,0,0,0,1,1,1]^T$. In this figure the dark and white nodes correspond to the values 1, and 0, respectively.*

To calculate the value of the Boolean difference with respect to a variable x_i, $i = 1,2,3$, at a particular point $x_1, x_2, x_3)$, we move along the edge connecting nodes where $x_i = 0$ and $x_i = 1$, for the given assignment of other variables. If the values at the both ends of this edge are different, the value of the Boolean difference is 1, otherwise it is 0. In this figure, are shown the values of the Boolean differences $\frac{\delta f}{\delta x_1}(000) = 0$, $\frac{\delta f}{\delta x_2}(101) = 0$, and $\frac{\delta f}{\delta x_3}(100) = 1$.

It is possible to define the Boolean difference with respect to a subset of m variables, which is called the multiple Boolean difference or the Boolean difference of higher order.

DEFINITION 11.1 *(Multiple Boolean difference)*
For a function of n variables $f(x_1,\ldots,x_n)$, the multiple Boolean difference

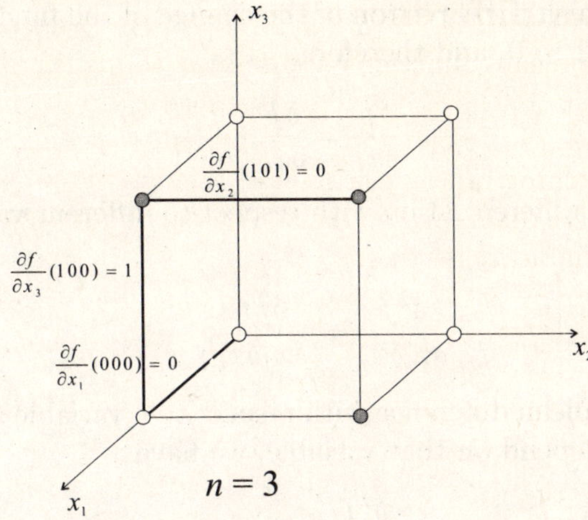

Figure 11.2. Illustration of the definition of the Boolean difference over a Boolean cube.

with respect to a subset of m variables is defined as

$$\frac{\delta^m f}{\delta x_1 \delta x_2 \cdots \delta x_m} = \frac{\delta}{\delta x_1}\left(\frac{\delta}{\delta x_2}\left(\cdots\left(\frac{\delta}{\delta x_m}\right)\cdots\right)\right).$$

The number of variables in terms of which the difference has been performed is called the order of the Boolean difference.

The Boolean difference has been introduced in [119], [141], for error-correction in communication channels transferring binary data. The theory of this differential operator has been developed by Akers [5], and further by Davio, Deschamps and Thayse in a series of publications reported and discussed in [185]. This theory has been a subject of a continuous interest mainly due to various applications in analyzing properties of switching functions, such as symmetry, decomposability, etc., as well as in fault detection in logic networks. Various generalizations for different classes of functions have been proposed in the literature, see, for example, [40], [41], [69], [172], [174], [178], [202] and references therein.

2. Properties of the Boolean Difference

Since, by the definition, in the Boolean difference we compare the function values for x_i and $\overline{x}_i$, and all the calculations are in $GF(2)$, it is obvious that the Boolean difference of a switching function of n variables is a switching function of $n-1$ variables. As noticed above, unlike the classical Newton-Leibniz derivative, the Boolean difference cannot distinguish the direction of the change of the function value form 0 to 1 or from 1 to 0, and therefore,

$$\frac{\delta \overline{f}}{\delta x_i} = \frac{\delta f}{\delta x_i}.$$

The order of differentiation with respect to different variables is irrelevant,

$$\frac{\delta^2 f}{\delta x_i \delta x_j} = \frac{\delta^2 f}{\delta x_j \delta x_i}.$$

Since the Boolean difference with respect to a variable x_i is a function that does not depend on that variable, we have

$$\frac{\delta^2 f}{\delta x_i \delta x_i} = 0.$$

The Boolean differentiation rules for basic logic operations are

$$\begin{aligned}
\frac{\delta(f \cdot g)}{\delta x_i} &= f \cdot \frac{\delta g}{\delta x_i} \oplus \frac{\delta f}{\delta x_i} \cdot g \oplus \frac{\delta f}{\delta x_i} \cdot \frac{\delta g}{\delta x_i}, \\
\frac{\delta(f + g)}{\delta x_i} &= \overline{f} \cdot \frac{\delta g}{\delta x_i} \oplus \frac{\delta f}{\delta x_i} \cdot \overline{g} \oplus \frac{\delta f}{\delta x_i} \cdot \frac{\delta g}{\delta x_i}, \\
\frac{\delta(f \oplus g)}{\delta x_i} &= \frac{\delta f}{\delta x_i} \oplus \frac{\delta g}{\delta x_i}.
\end{aligned}$$

It is interesting that the Boolean differences of the corresponding orders are the values of the coefficients in the Reed-Muller expressions. So also in this respect, the Reed-Muller expansions is analogous to the Taylor expansion of continuous functions.

EXAMPLE 11.2 *Fig. 11.3 shows the relationships between the coefficients of the positive polarity Reed-Muller expressions and the Boolean difference for functions of* $n = 3$ *variables.*

3. Calculation of the Boolean Difference

A straightforward way to compute the Boolean difference of a given function is to apply the definition of it and basic axioms and theorems from the Boolean algebra to simplify the expressions derived.

EXAMPLE 11.3 *Consider a function* $f(x_1, x_2, x_3) = x_1\overline{x}_2 + x_1x_3$. *From the definition of the Boolean difference,*

$$\begin{aligned}
\frac{\delta f}{\delta x_1} &= f(x_1, x_2, x_3) \oplus f(\overline{x}_1, x_2, x_3) = (x_1\overline{x}_2 + x_1x_3) \oplus (\overline{x}_1\overline{x}_2 + \overline{x}_1x_3) \\
&= \overline{x}_2 + x_3.
\end{aligned}$$

$$n = 3$$

$$f = r_0 \oplus r_1 x_3 \oplus r_2 x_2 \oplus r_3 x_2 x_3 \oplus r_4 x_1 \oplus r_5 x_1 x_3 \oplus r_6 x_1 x_2 \oplus r_7 x_1 x_2 x_3$$

$$\uparrow \quad \uparrow \quad \uparrow \quad \uparrow \quad \uparrow \quad \uparrow \quad \uparrow \quad \uparrow$$

$$f(0) \quad \frac{\partial f}{\partial x_3} \quad \frac{\partial f}{\partial x_2} \quad \frac{\partial^2 f}{\partial x_2 x_3} \quad \frac{\partial f}{\partial x_1} \quad \frac{\partial^2 f}{\partial x_1 x_3} \quad \frac{\partial^2 f}{\partial x_1 x_2} \quad \frac{\partial^3 f}{\partial x_1 x_2 x_3} \Bigg|_{x_1 x_2 x_3 = 0}$$

Figure 11.3. Relationships between the positive polarity Reed-Muller expressions and the Boolean differences for $n = 3$.

The complexity of calculations is a disadvantage of this approach, and we do not know in advance which manipulations are needed to simplify the expressions and in which order they should be performed. Therefore, in some cases tedious calculations may be required to determine the Boolean difference.

The following theorem can often simplify the calculations.

THEOREM 11.1 *The Boolean difference of a function $f(x_1, \ldots, x_n)$ with respect to the variable x_i can be expressed as*

$$\frac{\delta f}{\delta x_i} = f(x_1, \ldots, 1, \ldots, x_n) \oplus f(x_1, \ldots, 0, \ldots, x_n).$$

Proof. From the Shannon expansion we have

$$\begin{aligned} \frac{\delta f}{\delta x_i} &= (x_i f(x_1, \ldots, 1, \ldots, x_n) \oplus \overline{x}_i f(x_1, \ldots, 0, \ldots, x_n)) \\ &\quad \oplus(\overline{x}_i f(x_1, \ldots, 1, \ldots, x_n) \oplus x_i f(x_1, \ldots, 0, \ldots, x_n)) \\ &= (x_i \oplus \overline{x}_i)(f(x_1, \ldots, 1, \ldots, x_n) \oplus f(x_1, \ldots, 0, \ldots, x_n)) \\ &= f(x_1, \ldots, 1, \ldots, x_n) \oplus f(x_1, \ldots, 0, \ldots, x_n). \end{aligned}$$

When a function f is given by the truth-vector, it is convenient to use FFT-like algorithms to calculate the Boolean difference of f. From the definition of the Boolean difference, it is obvious that calculation of the difference with respect to the i-th variable corresponds to the implementation of the i-th step of a FFT-like algorithms where the basic butterfly operation is described by the matrix $\Delta(1) = \begin{bmatrix} 1 & 1 \\ 1 & 1 \end{bmatrix}$ with calculations over $GF(2)$. Notice that the singularity of this matrix is related with the fact that the Boolean difference of a function f with respect to the variable x_i is a function $\Delta_i f$ that does not depend on the variable in respect to which the differentiation has been performed.

The method of calculation of the Boolean difference by FFT-like algorithms is explained by the following example.

EXAMPLE 11.4 *Consider calculation of the Boolean difference of a two-variable function $f(x_1, x_2)$. By the definition,*

$$\frac{\delta f}{\delta x_1}(x_1, x_2) = f(x_1 = 0, x_2) \oplus f(x_1 = 1, x_2)).$$

Therefore,

$$\begin{aligned}
\left(\frac{\delta f}{\delta x_1}\right)(0,0) &= f(x_1 = 0, x_2 = 0) \oplus f(x_1 = 1, x_2 = 0) = f(0,0) \oplus f(1,0), \\
\left(\frac{\delta f}{\delta x_1}\right)(0,1) &= f(x_1 = 0, x_2 = 1) \oplus f(x_1 = 1, x_2 = 1) = f(0,1) \oplus f(1,1), \\
\left(\frac{\delta f}{\delta x_1}\right)(1,0) &= f(x_1 = 0, x_2 = 0) \oplus f(x_1 = 1, x_2 = 0) = f(0,0) \oplus f(1,0), \\
\left(\frac{\delta f}{\delta x_1}\right)(1,1) &= f(x_1 = 0, x_2 = 1) \oplus f(x_1 = 1, x_2 = 1) = f(0,1) \oplus f(1,1).
\end{aligned}$$

In matrix notation, where Δ_{x_1} stands for $\frac{\delta f}{\delta x_1}$,

$$\Delta_{x_1}\mathbf{F} = \begin{bmatrix} 1 & 0 & 1 & 0 \\ 0 & 1 & 0 & 1 \\ 1 & 0 & 1 & 0 \\ 0 & 1 & 0 & 1 \end{bmatrix} \begin{bmatrix} f(0,0) \\ f(0,1) \\ f(1,0) \\ f(1,1) \end{bmatrix} = \begin{bmatrix} f(0,0) \oplus f(1,0) \\ f(0,1) \oplus f(1,1) \\ f(0,0) \oplus f(1,0) \\ f(0,1) \oplus f(1,1) \end{bmatrix}.$$

It follows that the Boolean difference of $f(x_1, x_2)$ with respect to x_1 can be written as an operator in terms of the Kronecker product in a way similar to that used description of steps in FFT-like algorithms

$$\Delta_{x_1} = \begin{bmatrix} 1 & 0 & 1 & 0 \\ 0 & 1 & 0 & 1 \\ 1 & 0 & 1 & 0 \\ 0 & 1 & 0 & 1 \end{bmatrix} = \begin{bmatrix} 1 & 1 \\ 1 & 1 \end{bmatrix} \otimes \begin{bmatrix} 1 & 0 \\ 0 & 1 \end{bmatrix}.$$

Similarly, for the Boolean difference of $f(x_1, x_2)$ with respect to x_2, it will be

$$\frac{\delta f}{\delta x_2}(x_1, x_2) = f(x_1, x_2 = 0) \oplus f(x_1, x_2 = 1).$$

Therefore,

$$\left(\frac{\delta f}{\delta x_2}\right)(0,0) = f(x_1 = 0, x_2 = 0) \oplus f(x_1 = 0, x_2 = 1) = f(0,0) \oplus f(0,1),$$

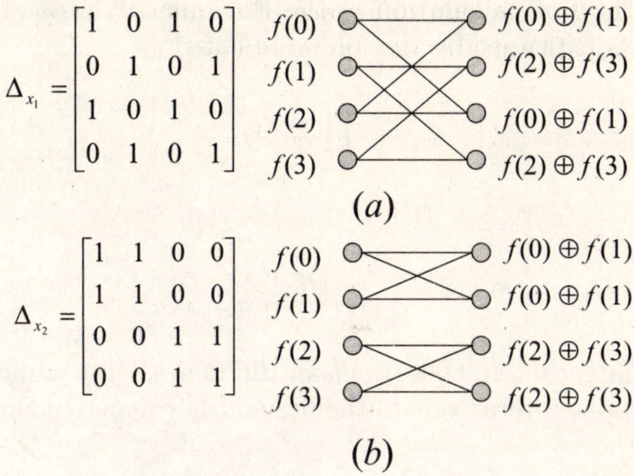

Figure 11.4. Flow-graphs of the fast algorithm for calculation of the Boolean difference of $f(x_1, x_2)$ with respect to (a) x_1, and (b) x_2.

$$\begin{aligned}
\left(\frac{\delta f}{\delta x_2}\right)(0,1) &= f(x_1 = 0, x_2 = 0) \oplus f(x_1 = 0, x_2 = 1) = f(0,0) \oplus f(0,1), \\
\left(\frac{\delta f}{\delta x_2}\right)(1,0) &= f(x_1 = 1, x_2 = 0) \oplus f(x_1 = 1, x_2 = 1) = f(1,0) \oplus f(1,1), \\
\left(\frac{\delta f}{\delta x_2}\right)(1,1) &= f(x_1 = 1, x_2 = 0) \oplus f(x_1 = 1, x_2 = 1) = f(1,0) \oplus f(1,1).
\end{aligned}$$

In matrix notation, where Δ_{x_2} stands for $\frac{\delta f}{\delta x_2}$,

$$\Delta_{x_2}\mathbf{F} = \begin{bmatrix} 1 & 1 & 0 & 0 \\ 1 & 1 & 0 & 0 \\ 0 & 0 & 1 & 1 \\ 0 & 0 & 1 & 1 \end{bmatrix} \begin{bmatrix} f(0,0) \\ f(0,1) \\ f(1,0) \\ f(1,1) \end{bmatrix} = \begin{bmatrix} f(0,0) \oplus f(0,1) \\ f(0,0) \oplus f(0,1) \\ f(1,0) \oplus f(1,1) \\ f(1,0) \oplus f(1,1) \end{bmatrix}.$$

When written as an operator in terms of the Kronecker product,

$$\Delta_{x_2} = \begin{bmatrix} 1 & 1 & 0 & 0 \\ 1 & 1 & 0 & 0 \\ 0 & 0 & 1 & 1 \\ 0 & 0 & 1 & 1 \end{bmatrix} = \begin{bmatrix} 1 & 0 \\ 0 & 1 \end{bmatrix} \otimes \begin{bmatrix} 1 & 1 \\ 1 & 1 \end{bmatrix}.$$

Fig. 11.4 shows the flow-graphs of the algorithm for calculation of the Boolean differences of $f(x_1, x_2)$ with respect to x_1 and x_2.

In general, the Boolean difference of a function of n-variables with respect to the i-th variable can be represented as

$$\Delta_{x_i} = \prod_{j=1}^{n} D_i(1),$$

where

$$D_i(1) = \begin{cases} \Delta(1) & \text{if } i = j, \\ \mathbf{I}(1) & \text{if } i \neq j. \end{cases}$$

To calculate the multiple Boolean differences, the same algorithms should be applied iteratively to the previously calculated Boolean differences.

From the theory of calculation of spectral transforms over decision diagrams, see, for example, [175], is know that FFT-like algorithms can be performed over decision diagrams instead of vectors. Therefore, the calculation of the Boolean difference can be also performed over decision diagrams due to the above FFT-like algorithms. To calculate the Boolean difference with respect to the i-th variable of a function represented by a BDD, the nodes and the cross points at the i-th level should be processed by the basic matrix $\Delta(1)$. The processing means performing calculations described by the matrix $\Delta(1)$. The nodes at the other levels remain unprocessed which corresponds to the identity matrices in the Kronecker product representing Δ_{x_i}.

EXAMPLE 11.5 *Fig. 11.5 shows calculation of the Boolean differences with respect to the variables x_1 and x_2 of a function $f(x_1, x_2)$ represented by the BDT.*

4. Boolean Difference in Testing Logic Networks

In this section, we present the principles of applying the Boolean difference in testing logic networks.

4.1 Errors in combinatorial logic networks

Although nowadays logic circuits are remarkably reliable in terms of the probability of a particular gate output being incorrect at any specific occasion, testing of logic circuits is among the hardest problems in this area. Different faults in logic networks can occur for a variety of reasons, as for instance shortcircuit, broken line, wrong value of the voltage threshold of a transistor, etc.

The failures in a logic network can be classified as

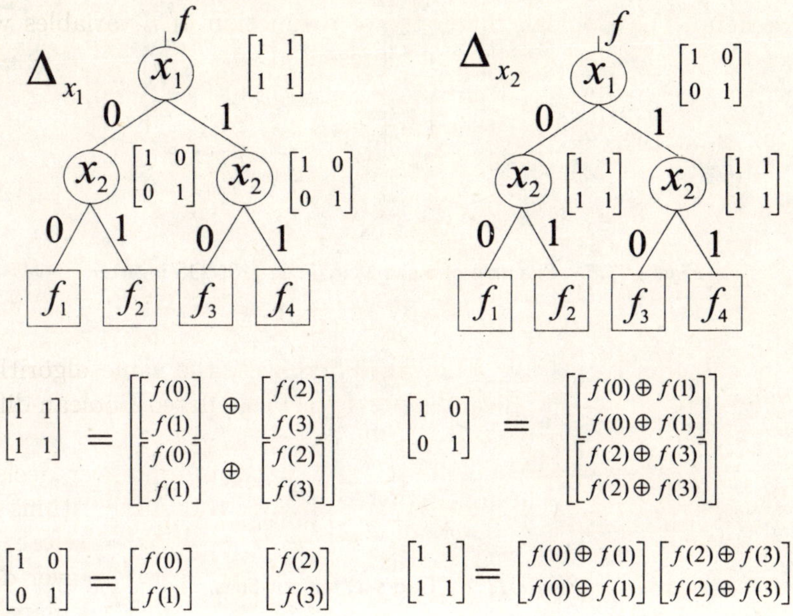

Figure 11.5. Calculation of the Boolean difference over BDT for $n = 2$.

1 *Soft errors* which are results from transient effects as, for instance, electrical noise entering through the power supply, or cosmic rays causing a burst of ions on a chip,

2 *Hard errors* which are permanent and may occur due to various mechanical effects such as vibration, long term corrosion, metal migration, etc.

Soft errors are hard to detect and are mainly handled by various software and overall system design techniques. Testing of logic networks mainly concerns hard errors.

At the logic level, we observe the influence of an error to the behavior of the circuit. Fig. 11.6 illustrates an example of a short circuit between the input of an invertor and the ground, which sets the value at the input to 0. At the logic level, such an error will be interpreted as the error input of the inverter set to 0.

There are various models of errors, however, the *single stuck-at 0/1 errors* (s-at 0/1) are probably the most often considered. It should be noted that a well determined test for these errors can discover at the same time many other errors. In the application of the stuck-at faults error model, we consider the cases when both input and output pins of a

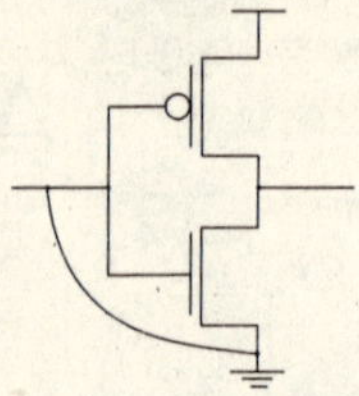

Figure 11.6. Example of a short circuit in a CMOS inverter.

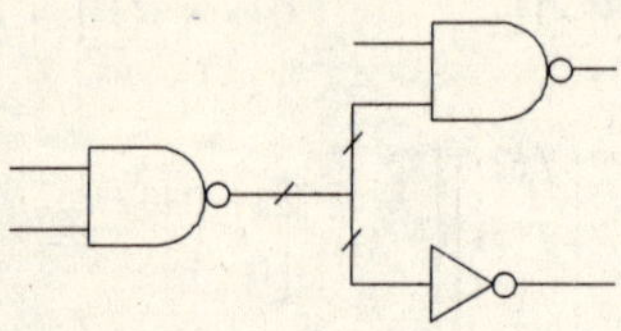

Figure 11.7. Errors at fan-out lines.

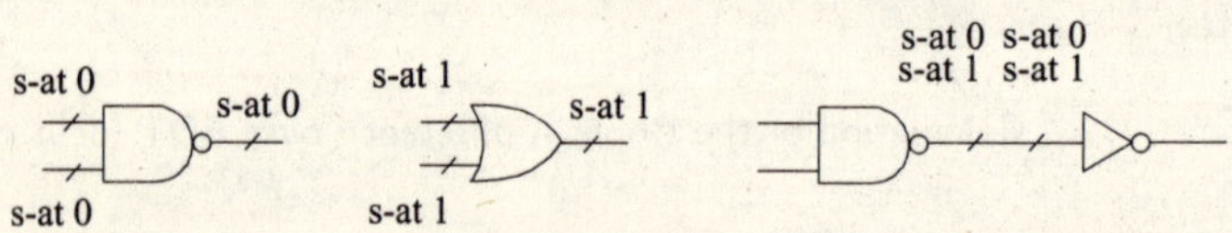

Figure 11.8. Examples of equivalent errors.

circuit are set to either value 0 or 1. However, if the same line drives few circuits, the number of errors is greater than 2 for this line. Fig. 11.7 illustrates this case.

The errors at both branches and streams in a network can be considered and it follows that the number of errors is $2c$ where c is the number of circuits in the *Device Under Testing* (DUT). However, the number of errors that have to be considered can be drastically reduced due to the notion of *equivalent errors.*

DEFINITION 11.2 *(Equivalent errors)*
Consider two errors e_1 and e_2 in a logic network N. Denote by f_{e_1} and f_{e_2} the outputs of N in the presence of the errors e_1 and e_2, respectively. The errors e_1 and e_2 are equivalent iff $f_{e_1} = f_{e_2}$.

It there are k equivalent errors $e_1, \ldots, e_k$, it is sufficient to generate the test for an error e_i to cover all other errors equivalent to e_i. Fig. 11.8 illustrates examples of equivalent errors. In an AND circuit, we cannot distinguish appearance of the error s-at 0 at any of the inputs and the output. It is the same with the error s-at 1 in the case of OR circuits. However, the same does not apply to the error st-at 0 in the case of OR circuits. Similarly, the error at the output of a NAND circuit is equivalent to the error at the input of an inverter.

In general, determination of pairs of equivalent errors is a complex task which, however, can be resolved by a consistent application of the considerations illustrated above. The procedure for determination of equivalent errors in a given circuit is called the *collapse of errors.* It is usually assumed that before testing a device, the collapse of errors has been performed.

It is possible to consider also *multiple errors* meaning simultaneous appearance of single errors. The basic problem in this case is the number of possible errors. If m is the number of places where errors may occur, then the number of multiple stuck-at j, $j = 0, 1$ errors is $3^m - 1$, since at each place it could be either no error, s-at 0, or s-at 1, which makes 3^n possibilities out of which we should exclude the case when no error at all m places.

If for an error e_1 the output of DUT is $f_{e_1} = f$, where f is the output of the fault free DUT, then e_1 cannot be detected, i.e., it is an *undetectable error.* Such errors are often called *redundant errors,* since are usually related to the appearance of some redundancy in the circuit (redundant gates or interconnections). Notice that an interconnection may be redundant for the logic behavior of the network, but is of essential importance for the functioning of it. Fig. 11.9 shows an example of undetectable errors. In this figure, the error line b s-at 1 cannot be detected, since to check this error we should eliminate the impact of the input c. Thus, it has to be $c = 0$, which requires $a = b = 1$, and to detect an error we should take the value opposite to that caused by the error, which is this case is $b = 0$. Therefore, there are contradictory requirements, and it follows that this error can be detected. In other words, this error cannot be detected since it influences both inputs of the NOR circuit at the same time. Notice that in this example, the output function is identically equal to 0, so neither a, b stuck-at errors can be detected. However, the c stuck-at 1 could be detected.

Test for error detection in a given DUT consists of the assignments of values at the inputs such that the value at the output is the opposite of the value for the fault free DUT. A *complete test* consists of test sequences capable of detecting all the assumed errors for a given network. It is clear that the test of all 2^n possible assignments of values for the inputs is complete. However, this is impractical for a large n. A

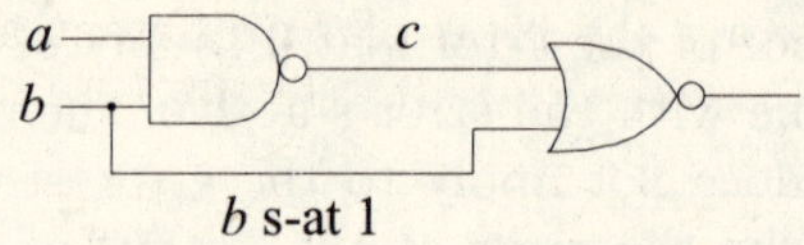

Figure 11.9. Example of an undetectable error.

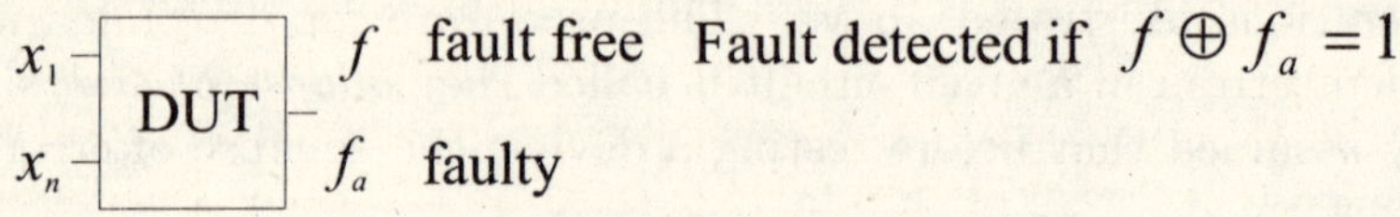

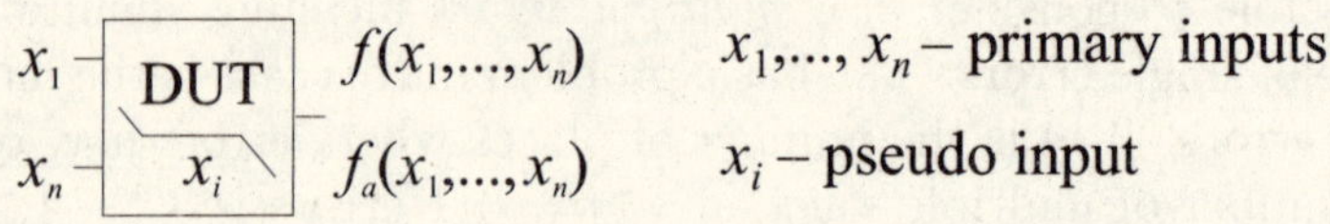

Figure 11.10. Fault free and faulty DUT.

minimum test is hard to determine, and, therefore, the problem of finding the detectable errors for a given input sequence is often considered.

There are various methods for automatic test pattern generation (ATPG), which can be basically classified as

1 Algebraic methods consisting of manipulation with the algebraic expressions describing the function realized by the DUT considered,

2 Topological methods related to dealing with circuits and their interconnections, thus, the topology of the DUT.

In the following section, we will consider ATPG for single errors by the application of the Boolean difference.

4.2 Boolean difference in generation of test sequences

The basic principle of application of the Boolean difference in testing of combinatorial circuits is illustrated in Fig. 11.10. If the output of the fault free DUT is f and the output in the presence of an error e_j is f_{e_j}, then the error is detected if $f \oplus f_{e_j} = 1$. For the fault free DUT, f is a function of primary inputs, i.e., $f = f(x_1, \ldots, x_n)$. The appearance of a stuck at error at a line q causes this line to behave as a pseudo-input x_q. The output of DUT becomes $f_{e_q} = F(x_1, \ldots, x_n, x_q)$.

It is clear that among the total of 2^n different assignments of logic values 0 and 1 for n primary inputs, for the test sequences we should select those which provide

1 *Excitation of the error* meaning that the value at the line q is the opposite to that caused by the error. Thus, to test an error which causes $x_q = j$, we select the assignments for which $x_q = \overline{j}$.

2 *Propagation of the error* which should ensure that occurrence of the error influences the output, i.e., produces output opposite to the value for the fault free DUT. In other words, x_q should be an essential variable for f_{e_q}, which can be expressed by the Boolean difference.

Therefore, the test for a stuck at error can be determined by using the following observation.

An assignment of input values $(a_1, \ldots, a_n)$ is a test sequence to detect the stuck at error $x_q = 0$, respectively 1, iff the minterm $x_1^{a_1}, \cdots x_n^{a_n}$ is a true minterm in the functions

$$x_q(x_1, \ldots, x_n)\frac{\delta F(x_1, \ldots, x_n, x_q)}{\delta x_q},$$

and

$$\overline{x_q(x_1, \ldots, x_n)}\frac{\delta F(x_1, \ldots, x_n, x_q)}{\delta x_q},$$

respectively.

The first part, x_q or $\overline{x}_q$, in these functions provides the value opposite to that caused by the error. The second part ensures that the error will propagate to the output, i.e., x_q is an essential variable of F. The test consist of the sequences that satisfy the above requirement.

Consequently, if

$$x_q(x_1, \ldots, x_n)\frac{\delta F(x_1, \ldots, x_n, x_q)}{\delta x_q} = 0,$$

and

$$\overline{x_q(x_1, \ldots, x_n)}\frac{\delta F(x_1, \ldots, x_n, x_q)}{\delta x_q} = 0,$$

the errors x_q stuck-at at 0, respectively 1, are undetectable. Moreover, in this case, we cannot even specify if the line x_q is stuck to the value equal to that caused by the error, or the error does not influence the output.

The application of the Boolean difference in generation of test sequences for combinatorial networks will be illustrated by the following example taken from [12].

EXAMPLE 11.6 *[12]*
Consider the network in Fig. 11.11. Analyzing the network we find that the network realizes the function $f(x_1, x_2, x_3, x_4) = x_2 + x_3$. *It is obvious that there is some redundancy in the network, which suggest that there may be undetectable faults. Fig. 11.12 shows the truth-table for* f.

We will apply the Boolean difference to generate test sequences for the four possible suck-at errors for the lines e and h in the network.

We first determine the outputs of the network for these errors as follows

$$\begin{aligned} F_e(x_1, x_2, x_3, x_4, e) &= (e + x_2) + x_3(x_3 + x_4) = (e + x_2) + (x_3 + x_3x_4) \\ &= (e + x_2) + x_3(1 + x_4) = e + x_2 + x_3, \\ F_h(x_1, x_2, x_3, x_4, h) &= (x_1x_2 + x_2) + hx_3 = x_2(x_1 + 1) + hx_3 \\ &= x_2 + hx_3. \end{aligned}$$

The Boolean differences for the outputs in the presence of the errors are

$$\begin{aligned} \frac{\delta F(x_1, x_2, x_3, x_4, e)}{\delta e} &= ((1 + x_2) + x_3) \oplus ((0 + x_2) + x_3) \\ &= (1 + x_3) \oplus (x_2 + x_3) \\ &= 1 \oplus (x_2 + x_3) = \overline{(x_2 + x_3)} = \overline{x}_2\overline{x}_3. \\ \frac{\delta F(x_1, x_2, x_3, x_4, h)}{\delta h} &= (x_2 + 1 \cdot x_3) \oplus (x_2 + 0 \cdot x_3) = (x_2 + x_3) \oplus x_2 \\ &= (x_2 + x_3)\overline{x}_2 + \overline{(x_2 + x_3)}x_2 \\ &= x_2\overline{x}_2 + \overline{x}_2x_3 + \overline{x}_2\overline{x}_3x_2 = \overline{x}_2x_3. \end{aligned}$$

For the error e stuck at 0, *from the network* $e = x_1x_2$, *and therefore,*

$$e\frac{\delta F(x_1, x_2, x_3, x_4, e)}{\delta e} = x_1x_2\overline{x}_1\overline{x}_2 = 0,$$

and it follows that this error is undetectable.

The explanation is that $e = x_1x_2 \neq 0$ *for the assignments at the decimal indices 12, 13, 14, and 15 as shown in the truth table for* f *in Fig. 11.12. However, for these assignments,* $x_2 = 1$ *and since* $f(x_1, x_2, x_3, x_4, e) = e + x_2 + x_3$, *the error* $e = 0$ *is covered by* $x_2 = 1$ *due to the properties of the logic OR, and thus, does not propagate to the output.*

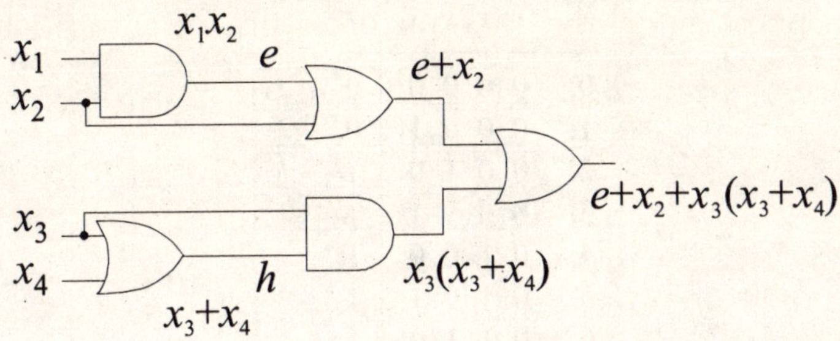

Figure 11.11. Network discussed in Example 11.6.

It can be shown in a similar way that the error h s-at 1 is also undetectable, since $\overline{h} = \overline{x}_3\overline{x}_4$ *and*

$$\overline{h}\frac{F(x_1, x_2, x_3, x_4, h)}{\delta h} = \overline{x}_3\overline{x}_4\overline{x}_2x_3 = 0.$$

Since,

$$\begin{aligned}\overline{e}\frac{\delta f(x_1, x_2, x_3, x_4, e)}{\delta e} &= \overline{(x_1x_2)}\overline{x}_2\overline{x}_3 = \overline{x}_2\overline{x}_3,\\ h\frac{\delta F(x_1, x_2, x_3, x_4, h)}{\delta h} &= (x_3 + x_4)\overline{x}_2x_3 = \overline{x}_2x_3,\end{aligned}$$

the errors e s-at 1, and h s-at 0 are detectable.

We determine the test sequences for these errors from the requirements $\overline{x}_2\overline{x}_3 = 1$ *and* $\overline{x}_2x_3 = 1$*, respectively, as*

$$\begin{aligned}e_1 &= \{0000, 0001, 1000, 1001\},\\ h_0 &= \{0010, 0011, 1010, 1011\}.\end{aligned}$$

The selection of these sequences is justified by the following considerations.

For the sequences in e_1*, since* $x_2 = 0$*, then* $x_1x_2 = 0$*. Similarly, since* $x_3 = 0$*, then* $x_3(x_3 + x_4) = 0$*, and, therefore, the output* $f = x_1x_2 + x_2 + x_3(x_3 + x_4) = 0$*. However, if* $e = 1$*, the output is* $f_{e_1} = e_1 + x_2 + x_3(x_3 + x_4) = 0 \neq f$*.*

For the sequences in h_0*, since* $x_2 = 0$*, it follows* $x_1x_2 + x_2 = 0$ *and the first input in the final OR circuit is 0. However,* $x_3 = 1$*, and, therefore,* $x_3(x_3 + x_4) = 1$*, which produces* $f = 1$*. If* $h = 0$*, then both inputs in the OR circuits are equal to 0, and the output is opposite of the expected value for* f*, which is 1 as it can be seen from Fig. 11.12.*

More information about testing and related subjects can be found, for example, in [1], [48], [49], [59].

	$x_1\,x_2\,x_3\,x_4$	f	
0.	0 0 0 0	0	e_1
1.	0 0 0 1	0	e_1
2.	0 0 1 0	1	h_0
3.	0 0 1 1	1	h_0
4.	0 1 0 0	1	
5.	0 1 0 1	1	
6.	0 1 1 0	1	
7.	0 1 1 1	1	
8.	1 0 0 0	0	e_1
9.	1 0 0 1	0	e_1
10.	1 0 1 0	1	h_0
11.	1 0 1 1	1	h_0
12.	1 1 0 0	1	
13.	1 1 0 1	1	
14.	1 1 1 0	1	
15.	1 1 1 1	1	

Figure 11.12. Truth-table of the function f realized by the network in Example 11.6.

5. Easily Testable Logic Networks

This Chapter discusses design of combinatorial logic networks that can be easily tested against errors. It presents main results in two papers [140] and [154], published in the period of 25 years. This is a good example showing the impact of technology to the acceptance of valuable theoretical research results. Theory presented in 1972 by S.M. Reddy [140], has not been applied in practice, since at that time realization of logic networks with EXOR circuits has been considered a tedious and costly task. Thanks to the advent of technology and due to the increasing demands of practice, these results has been revisited from nineties by several authors, as will be discussed below. In particular, we will present a further development provided in 1997 by T. Sasao [154], since nowadays design for testability and related easy testable realizations are of high importance in optimization of circuits. For these reasons, we present the results reported in [140] and [154]. We also provide references and a brief discussion of related recent research work.

5.1 Features of Easily Testable Networks

Reliability of a digital system can be achieved by introducing redundancy, which may be *static* or *dynamic.*

Static redundancy assumes that the system contains repeated parts (either hardware or software) and is designed to produce correct output even in the case of some errors.

In the case of dynamic redundancy, the system is tested with an appropriately selected frequency and in time intervals determined such that the appearance of an error can be detected and the system corrected by replacing the corresponding modules in a reasonably short time. Therefore, for such systems is is very desirable to design circuits which can be easily tested. Such circuits are usually called *easily testable circuits.*

It is assumed that the device under test (DUT) has primary inputs and outputs accessible. The testing is performed by the application of a set of test sequences, called the *test* for the network and a predefined set of possible errors.

An *easily testable network* should express the following properties

1 The set of test sequences should be as short as possible.

2 Network cannot be static redundant, since it may happen that existence of an error cannot be detected by the application of the test sequences.

3 The procedure for construction of the test should be simple, and, if possible, a part of the design method.

4 The test sequences should be easily generated, and the results obtained by the application of the test easily interpretable.

5 It is desirable that the test determines with certain precision also the location of the error.

6. Easily Testable Realizations from PPRM-expressions

It has been shown by S.M. Reddy [140] already in 1972 that easily testable combinatorial logic networks can be designed from Positive polarity Reed-Muller (PPRM) expressions. In the following, such an network will be called the *PPRM-network.* Fig. 11.13 shows the structure of a PPRM-network. It consists of the AND part realizing product terms that appear in the PPRM-expression of the function realized, and the EXOR performing EXOR over the products. Recall that, in matrix

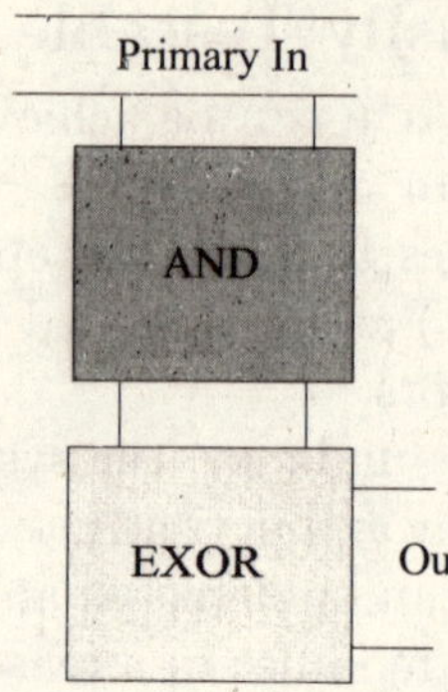

Figure 11.13. Structure of easy testable networks designed from PPRM-expressions.

notation, the product terms in the PPRM-expression for a function of n variables can be generated as

$$\mathbf{X}_{rm}(n) = \bigotimes_{i=1}^{n} \mathbf{X}_{rm}(1),$$

where $\otimes$ denotes the Kronecker product, and $\mathbf{X}_{rm}(1) = \begin{bmatrix} 1 & x_i \end{bmatrix}$, as defined in Section 2.

It is assumed that

1 At the inputs and outputs of AND circuits, single stuck-at 0/1 errors may occur,

2 If an error occurs at an EXOR circuits, then this circuit may produce any of the remaining 15 functions of two variables.

In this case,

1 If no error at the primary inputs in a PPRM-network allowed, then the test consists of $n+4$ test sequences, and the test does not depend on the function realized.

2 If an error at the primary inputs is allowed, the test consists of $n + 4 + e$ sequences, where e is the number of variables that appear in an even number of product terms in the PPRM-expression describing the network.

It is clear that in the second case, the test depends on the function realized by the network, since the number of test sequences is determined by the product terms and the number of appearance of variables in them.

With an additional dedicated AND circuit with accessible output, the test consists of $n + 4$ sequences, and does not depend on the function realized by the PPRM-network as in the previous case [140].

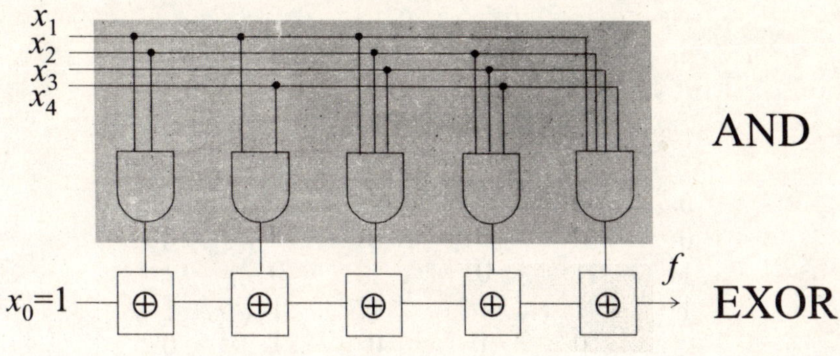

Figure 11.14. PPRM-network in Example 11.7.

This theory is illustrated by the following example [140].

EXAMPLE 11.7 *Consider the function f of four variables given by the truth-vector*

$$\mathbf{F} = [1,1,1,1,1,1,1,0,1,0,1,0,0,1,1,0]^T.$$

The PPRM-expression for f is

$$f = 1 \oplus x_1x_2 \oplus x_1x_4 \oplus x_1x_2x_3 \oplus x_2x_3x_4 \oplus x_1x_2x_3x_4.$$

Fig. 11.14 shows a PPRM-network realizing this function f. The variables x_1 and x_2 appear in an even number of products

$$\begin{array}{lll} x_1 & \text{appears in} & x_1x_2, x_1x_4, x_1x_2x_3, x_1x_2x_3x_4, \\ x_2 & \text{appears in} & x_1x_2, x_1x_2x_3, x_2x_3x_4, x_1x_2x_3x_4. \end{array}$$

Therefore, in this example, $e = 2$.

Test for EXOR part. *As mentioned above, it is assumed a single error in the EXOR circuits in the PPRM-network, and the faulty circuit may realize any two-variable switching function different from EXOR. The test should check the outputs of all the EXOR circuits for all possible combinations of values at their inputs. This can be achieved by the test T_1 specified as*

$$T_1 = \left\{ \begin{array}{c} (0\ \ 0\ \ 0\ \ 0\ \ 0) \\ (0\ \ 1\ \ 1\ \ 1\ \ 1) \\ (1\ \ 0\ \ 0\ \ 0\ \ 0) \\ (1\ \ 1\ \ 1\ \ 1\ \ 1) \end{array} \right\}$$

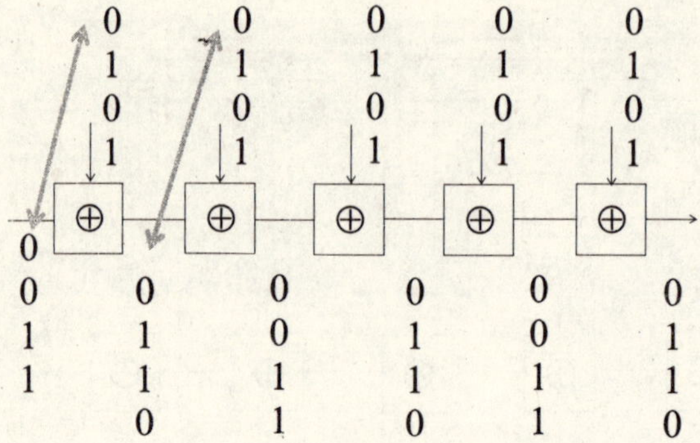

Figure 11.15. Test for EXOR part in Example 11.7.

Fig. 11.15 illustrates application of this test. When the first test sequence (00000) *applied to the primary inputs, the AND circuits will generate values of the product terms at the inputs of the EXOR circuits as shown in the first row at the upper part of the figure. The values at the outputs of the EXOR circuits are shown in the first row at the lower part of the figure. The application of other test sequences is shown in the same way.*

It is obvious that when all four test sequences are applied at the primary inputs, the inputs of all the EXOR circuits will be tested for all possible combinations of logic values 0 and 1.

Test for AND part. *To determine the test for the AND-part we first consider the single stuck-at 0 fault at an input of an AND circuit. This error is equivalent to the stuck-at 0 of the output, due to the properties of AND-circuits.*

The test in this case is $T_2 = \{\ (0 \quad 1 \quad 1 \quad 1 \quad 1)\ \}$, *since for this assignment of values at primary inputs* $f = 1$, *and in the case of the appearance of the error, the output will be* $f = 0$ *as shown in Fig. 11.16 by the example of the appearance of the error at the output of the second AND circuit.*

Alternatively, the same error can be checked by the test sequence $T_2 = \{\ (1 \quad 1 \quad 1 \quad 1 \quad 1)\ \}$, *as explained in Fig. 11.17 by the example of the appearance of the error at the output of the first AND circuit.*

Notice that both these test sequences are contained in the already determined test for the EXOR part T_1, *thus,* $T_2 \subset T_1$.

A similar consideration shows that the stuck-at 1 error at the output of the AND circuits can be tested by the sequences $T_3 = \{\ (0 \quad 0 \quad 0 \quad 0 \quad 0)\ \}$, *and* $T_3 = \{\ (1 \quad 0 \quad 0 \quad 0 \quad 0)\ \}$, *and* $t_3 \subset T_1$.

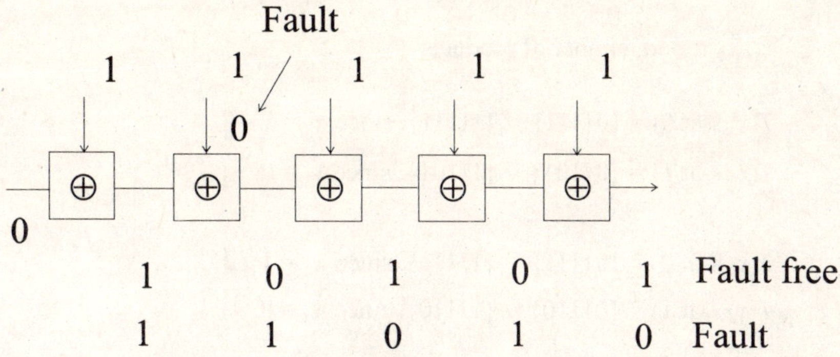

Figure 11.16. Test for AND part in Example 11.7.

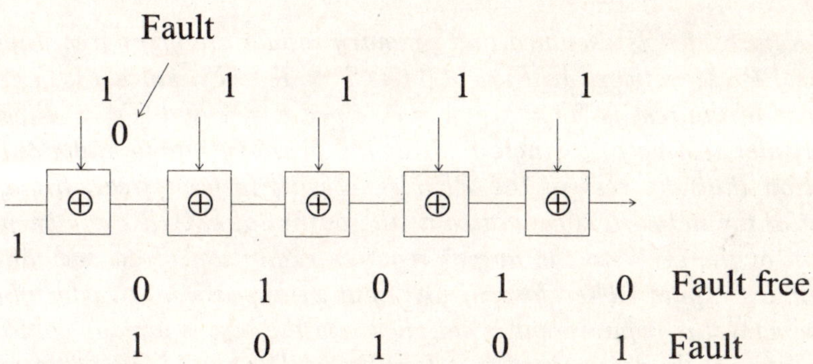

Figure 11.17. Alternative test for AND part in Example 11.7.

The stuck-at error 1 at an input of AND circuits requires the test

$$T_4 = \left\{ \begin{array}{c} (d \quad 0 \quad 0 \quad 0 \quad 0) \\ (d \quad 1 \quad 1 \quad 1 \quad 1) \\ (d \quad 0 \quad 0 \quad 0 \quad 0) \\ (d \quad 1 \quad 1 \quad 1 \quad 1) \end{array} \right\},$$

where d *can be either 0 or 1, thus,* $d \in \{0,1\}$. *For instance, if* $d = 0$, *and* $x_1 = x_2 = x_3 = 1$, *and* $x_4 = 0$, *then* $f = 0$, *in a fault free network. However, if* $x_4 = 1$, *the network will produce incorrect input* $f = 1$. *Similarly, if* $d = 1$, *and* $x_1 = x_2 = x_3 = 1$, *and* $x_4 = 0$, *then* $f = 1$ *in the fault free network. The error* $x_4 = 1$, *will produce the incorrect output* $f = 0$. *In a similar way, it can be shown that this test checks against all the stuck-at 1 errors for* x_i, $i = 1, 2, 3, 4$.

$x_3, x_4 \in$ odd number of products

$T(x_3$ s-at 0$) = \{01111\} \vee \{11111\}$, since $x_3 = 1$ ▮

$T(x_3$ s-at 1$) = \{01101\} \vee \{11101\}$, since $x_3 = 0$ ▯

▮ $\in T_1$

▯ $\in T_4$

$T(x_4$ s-at 0$) = \{01111\} \vee \{11111\}$, since $x_4 = 1$ ▮

$T(x_4$ s-at 1$) = \{01110\} \vee \{11110\}$, since $x_4 = 0$ ▯

Figure 11.18. Test for the primary inputs x_3 and x_4 in Example 11.7.

Therefore, if it is assumed that primary inputs are error free, the test for the PPRM-network in Fig. 11.14 is $T = T_1 \cup T_4$, since $T_2, T_3 \subset T_1$. The size of the test is $|T| = n + 4 = 8$, since $n = 4$ and $|T_1| = |T_4| = 4$.

Consider testing of a single fault at the primary inputs under the assumption that the rest of the PPRM-network is fault free. Since the output of the network is generated as the output of EXOR circuits, propagation of the error to the output requires excitation of an odd number of primary inputs. Therefore, if an input x_i appears in an odd number of products, this requirement is satisfied and the test is already contained in the previously determined test for the AND and EXOR parts of the PPRM-network. Fig. 11.18 illustrates this statement.

For the primary inputs the variables which appear in an even number of products, the test has to be extended by a some set of test sequences T_e determined as follows.

Consider a variable x_i appearing in an even number of products and denote by $P_i = x_i, x_j \cdots x_k$ the product which contains x_i and has the minimum number of literals. For instance, in this example, such products for the variable x_1 would be $P_1 \in \{x_1x_2, x_1x_4\}$.

For a product P_i, we select the assignments of input variables $V = (x_1, \ldots, x_n)$, where $x_i = 0$ and $x_i = 1$ such that the other variables in the product $x_j = \cdots = x_k = 1$, while the remaining variables $x_l \in \{x_1, \ldots, x_n\} \setminus \{x_i, x_j, \ldots, x_k\}$ take the value 0. We denote these assignments by V_i^1 and V_i^0 for $x_i = 1$ and $x_i = 0$, respectively.

For instance, if $P_1 = x_1x_2$, then $V_1^1 = d1100$ and $V_1^0 = d0100$.

For thus selected assignments of values at primary inputs corresponding to a product P_i, the AND circuit which produces P_i will be the single AND circuit whose output is 1. Therefore, if x_i stuck-at 0, the output will be 0, which is an incorrect value detectable at the output of the

	s-at 0	s-at 1
x_1	$V_1^1 = d1100$	$V_1^0 = d0100$
x_2	$V_2^1 = d1100$	$V_2^0 = d1000$

$$T_5 = \{d1100, d0100, d1000\}$$

$$T = T_1 \cup T_4 \cup T_5$$

For all single faults stuck at r, $r \in \{0,1\}$

Figure 11.19. Test for the primary inputs x_1 and x_2 in Example 11.7.

PPRM-network. It follows that sequences V_i^1 and V_i^0 are tests for the errors x_i stuck-at 0 and 1, respectively. Fig. 11.19 shows these test sequences for the PPRM-network considered in this example, which form the test for the primary inputs T_5.

Therefore, the complete test for the single stuck-at faults in this network is $T = T_1 \cup T_4 \cup T_5$.

7. Easily Testable Realizations from GRM-expressions

Easily testable realizations from PPRM-networks have soem drawbacks

1 The serial connection of EXOR circuits causes a large propagation delay.

2 For many functions the PPRM-expressions may contain a large number of products, which implies an equally large number of AND circuits.

3 Multiple faults cannot be detected.

With the motivation to avoid these bottlenecks and to improve the performances of related easily testable realizations, application of the generalized Reed-Muller (GRM) expressions has been proposed in [154].

The rationale for considering GRM-expressions is explained in [154] by an example showing the average number of product terms in different functional expressions required to represent functions of $n = 4$ variables. We show here just the main result of this example.

Table 11.1. Average number of products in SOP, PPRM. FPRM, GRM, and ESOP expressions for functions of $n = 4$ variables.

SOP	PPRM	FPRM	GRM	ESOP
4.13	8.00	5.50	3.68	3.66

EXAMPLE 11.8 *Table 11.1 shows the average number of products required in Sum-of-product (SOP), Positive-polarity Reed-Muller (PPRM), Fixed-polarity Reed-Muller (FPRM), Generalized Reed-Muller (GRM) and EXOR Sum-of-product (ESOP) expressions functions of $n = 4$ variables.*

It is pointed out that for $n = 4$, GRM-expressions require fewer products than PPRM-expressions. This number is comparable with the number of product in ESOPs, that is, however, much harder to determine for a given function.

Since, in GRM-expressions both positive and negative literals of variables are allowed, the structure of an easy testable GRM-network is as shown in Fig. 11.20. The part to generate literals consists of two-input EXOR circuits whose inputs are x_i and c, where c is a common control input for all these EXOR circuits. The Check part consists of additional two AND and two OR circuits with accessible outputs denoted as $AND(A)$, $AND(B)$, $OR(A)$, and $OR(B)$, respectively. The circuits denoted by A are intended to test the positive literals, which are, therefore, their inputs. Circuits B have $x_i^{\overline{c}}$ as inputs. The AND part is used to generate products in GRM-expressions, in the same way as in the PPRM-networks in [140]. Improvement comes from the reduced number of products, correspondingly, AND circuits. However, instead of a serial connection of EXOR circuits, the EXOR part can be a tree-network, which reduces the propagation delay and makes the network faster than a PPRM-network.

EXAMPLE 11.9 *[154]*
Fig. 11.21 shows an easily testable GRM-network realizing the function of $n = 4$ variables whose GRM-expression is

$$f = \overline{x}_2 \oplus \overline{x}_1\overline{x}_3x_4 \oplus x_2\overline{x}_3\overline{x}_4 \oplus \overline{x}_1x_2x_4.$$

Notice that the PPRM-expression for this function is

$$f = 1 \oplus x_4 \oplus x_3x_4 \oplus x_2x_3 \oplus x_2x_3x_4 \oplus x_1x_4 \oplus x_1x_3x_4 \oplus x_1x_2x_4,$$

which requires seven AND circuits in the PPRM-network.

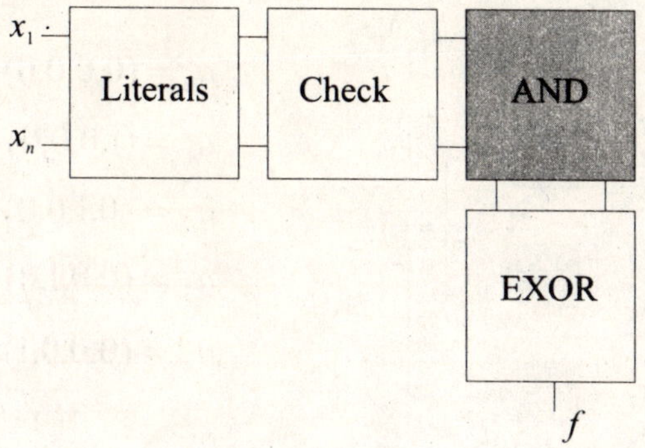

Figure 11.20. Structure of an easy testable GRM-network.

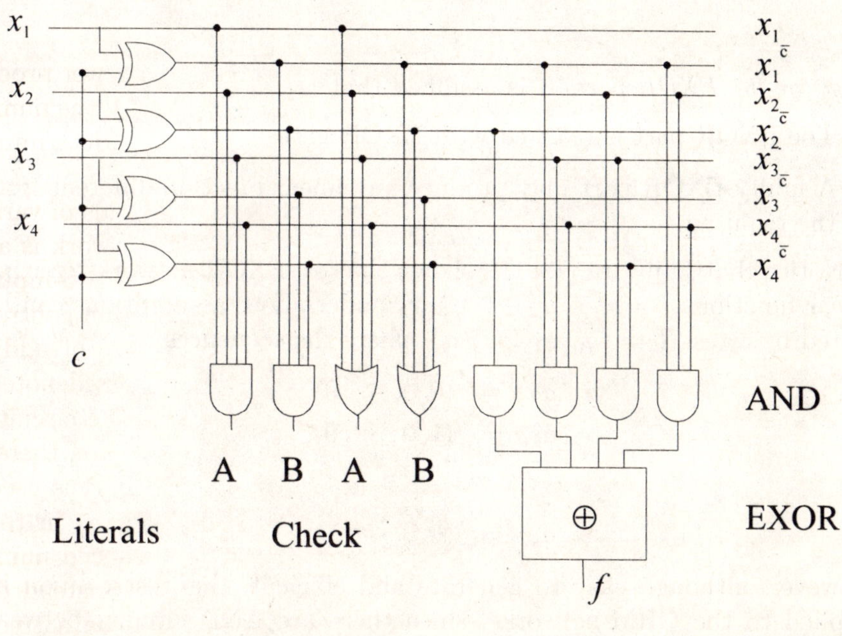

Figure 11.21. The GRM-network realizing the function f in Example 11.9.

It is assumed in [154] that multiple stuck-at errors can be detected, however, provided that errors appear in a single part of the network out of the four main parts of it, the literal part, the check part, AND and EXOR parts.

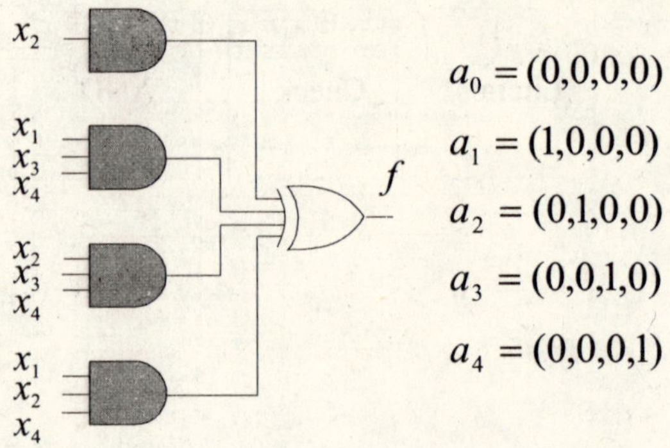

Figure 11.22. Example of a network where application of the Fujiwara method for testing of EXOR part is impossible.

Test for the EXOR part. It is assumed that

1 The EXOR part is realized with EXOR gates,

2 A faulty EXOR part may produce any linear function different from the required.

Notice that Fujiwara [48] has shown that an EXOR network realizing linear functions $f = x_1 \oplus x_2 \oplus \ldots \oplus x_s$ under above assumptions can be tested by a test $T = \{a_0, a_1, \ldots, a_s\}$ where the sequences

$$\begin{aligned} a_0 &= (0, 0, \cdots, 0), \\ a_1 &= (1, 0, \cdots, 0), \\ &\vdots \\ a_s &= (0, 0, \cdots, 1). \end{aligned}$$

However, although easy to generate and efficient, this test cannon be applied to the GRM-networks, since there are AND circuits between the primary inputs and the EXOR-part as shown in Fig. 11.22, which prevents propagation of the effect of test sequences to the inputs of the EXOR-part.

Therefore, it is proposed in [154] that the test for the EXOR part in GRM-networks consists of sequences $T = \{a_0, a_1, \ldots, a_s\}$, where $a_0 = (0, 0, \ldots, 0)$, and $a_i = (a_{i0}, a_{i1}, \ldots, a_{i_s})$, $i \in \{1, \ldots, s\}$, where sequences a_i are selected as rows of an $(s \times s)$ non singular matrix over $GF(2)$.

Actually, since each sequence corresponds to a product which is an input in the EXOR part, these test sequences are selected such that $a_{i_j} = 1$ if the variable x_j appears in the i-th product.

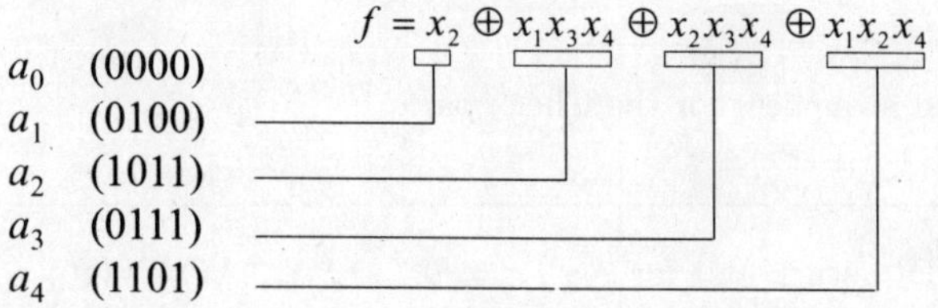

Figure 11.23. Test for the EXOR part of the GRM-network in Example 11.9.

EXAMPLE 11.10 *Fig. 11.23 shows determination of test sequences for the EXOR part of the GRM-network in Fig. 11.21. Notice that since we are interested just in the appearance of a variable in a product, not in its polarity, the product terms are written without specifying the polarity of variables.*

Test for the AND part. To determine the test for the AND part, the GRM-network is first simplified converting it into a PPRM-network by setting $c = 0$. It is assumed that t errors may appear simultaneously in the AND-part, but the rest of the network is fault free. Then, the test for the AND part consists of the sequences where the number of 0 values is smaller than or equal to $\lfloor \log_2 2t \rfloor$, where $\lfloor x \rfloor$ is the integer part of x. The number of such sequences, i.e., the size of the test is $|T_{AND}| = \sum_0^r \binom{n}{i}$, where $r = \lfloor \log_2 2t \rfloor$.

EXAMPLE 11.11 *For $n = 4$, if $t = 2$, the test for the AND-part is*

$$T_{AND} = \{(0011), (0101), (0110), (1001), (1010), (1100), (0111), (1011), (1101), (1110), (1111)\}.$$

Test for the Literal part. The Literal part is checked by observing outputs of the Check part. In the Check part the inputs of AND(A) and OR(A) are x_i. The inputs of AND(B) and OR(B) are $x_i^{\overline{c}}$.

The stuck-at 0 faults for x_i and $x_i^{\overline{c}}$ are tested by the test sequence $(c, x_1, \ldots, x_n) = (0, 1, \ldots, 1)$, and the error is detected when the output of AND(A) has the value 0, since for this sequence, in a fault free network all the literal lines have the value 1.

The test for stuck-at 1 faults for x_i is the test sequence $(c, x_1, \ldots, x_n) = (0, 0, \ldots, 0)$, since for this sequence OR(A) will produce the value 1 in the case of an error.

Similarly, the test for stuck-at faults 1 for $x_i^{\overline{c}}$ is the test sequence $(c, x_1, \ldots, x_n) = (1, 1, \ldots, 1)$, and the fault will be detected when the output of OR(B) has the value 1.

Table 11.2. Test sequences for the Check part.

AND	stuck-at 1 for x_i	$x_i = 0$,	$\{x_1, \ldots, x_n\} \setminus \{x_i\} = 1$
	stuck-at 0 for x_i	$x_i = 1$,	$\{x_1, \ldots, x_n\} \setminus \{x_i\} = 1$
OR	stuck-at 1 for x_i	$x_i = 0$,	$\{x_1, \ldots, x_n\} \setminus \{x_i\} = 0$
	stuck-at 0 for x_i	$x_i = 1$,	$\{x_1, \ldots, x_n\} \setminus \{x_i\} = 0$

Therefore, the complete test for the primary input lines, which also tests the EXOR circuits in the Literal part consists of three sequences $T_{Literal} = \{(0,1,\ldots,1),(0,0,\ldots,0),(1,1,\ldots,1)\}$.

Test for the Check part. The errors may appear also in the parts of the network intended for testing, i.e., the Check part should be also tested. Table 11.2 specifies the test sequences for the Check part in a GRM-network.

Size of the Test. Table 11.3 summarizes the number of test sequences for different parts of an easy testable GRM-network with the structure as in Fig. 11.21. The test for the network is the union of tests for these parts. Therefore, the total size of the test for the complete network satisfies

$$|T| \leq s + n + 4 + \sum_{i=1}^{r} \binom{n}{s},$$

where n is the number of variables, s the number of product in the GRM-expression for the function realized, $r = \lfloor \log_2 2t \rfloor$ and t is the number of multiple errors to consider.

EXAMPLE 11.12 *[154]*
Fig. 11.24 shows the test sequences for the GRM-network used as the example in [154]. Sequences which repeat in tests for different parts are marked. The test is determined as the union of tests for all the parts of the GRM-network, i.e.,

$$T = T_{EXOR} \cup T_{AND} \cup T_{Literal} \cup T_{Check}.$$

The size of the total test is $|T| = 17$.

Table 11.3. Size of the test.

Test	Size
$\lvert T_{EXOR}\rvert = s+1$	s - number of products in GRM(f)
$\lvert T_{AND}\rvert = \sum_{i=0}^{r} \binom{n}{i}$	$r = \lfloor \log_2 2t \rfloor$, t - number of multiple errors
$\lvert T_{Literal}\rvert = 3$	
$\lvert T_{Check}\rvert = 2n+2$	

The main features of the easily testable realizations proposed in [154] can be summarized as follows

1 GRM-expressions are used which reduces the number of AND circuits.

2 EXOR part is a tree network, which reduces the propagation delay and makes the network faster.

3 The test can be easily generated, however, it is dependent on the function realized.

4 Multiple errors are detectable, provided that they appear in a single part of the network of the assumed structure.

The overhead is an additional input for the control signal c and four extra outputs for the Check part.

7.1 Related Work, Extensions, and Generalizations

The method by Reddy has been extended to Fixed-polarity Reed-Muller expressions in [148], and ESOP expressions in [134], [160], [203]. In general, ESOPs require fewer products. However, the problem with ESOPs, as pointed out in [154], is that when the number of minterms in the function represented is odd, any ESOP expression contains a minterm, i.e., a product term containing all the variables, which implies that the test is exhaustive. For almost all functions the test has the length near 2^n for a large n. In [203], the overhead is five additional inputs, an extra output, and another dedicated EXOR part.

Extensions to GRM-expressions in [130], suggest decomposition into several FPRM-expressions and then exploiting the method in [148].

$$f = \bar{x}_2 \oplus \bar{x}_1\bar{x}_3x_4 \oplus x_2\bar{x}_3\bar{x}_4 \oplus \bar{x}_1x_2x_4$$

T(EXOR)	*T(AND)*	*T(Check)*	*T(Literal)*
(00000) ▨	(01111) □	(00000) ▨	(01111) □
(00100)	(00111) ■	(01000)	(00000) ▨
(01011)	(01011) ■	(00100)	(11111)
(00111)	(01101) ■	(00010)	
(01101)	(01110) ■	(00001)	
	(00011)	(01111) □	
	(00101)	(00111) ■	
	(00110)	(01011) ■	
	(01001)	(01101) ■	
	(01010)	(01110) ■	$\|T\| = 17$
	(01100)		

Figure 11.24. Test sequences for the network in Example 11.9.

Detecting multiple-errors has been discussed in [147] for networks derived from PPRM-expressions, and [134] for ESOPs. Bridge errors have been discussed in [203] for both PPRMs and ESOPs.

All these extensions assume that the EXOR part is realized as a serial connection of EXOR circuits. Exception is [139], where tree EXOR network has been considered. In this case, if $m + 1$ extra inputs are provided, where m is an even number, the test will be independent on the function realized, and will have the length $2^m + n$.

In [38] and [39], a generalization to multiple-valued logic functions has been presented.

The above discussions concern the so-called *deterministic testing*, i.e., when the test sequences are explicitly determined. In [37], it has been shown that networks based on PPRM and FPRM expressions can be easily modified to have also good properties when tested by randomly generated test sequences, i.e., a *random pattern test.* However, the experimental results reported in [37] do not indicate the same for networks derived from other AND-EXOR expressions, including ESOPs.

8. Exercises and Problems

EXERCISE 11.1 *Determine the Boolean difference* $\frac{\delta f}{\delta x_i}$ *and all multiple Boolean differences of functions*

$$\begin{aligned} f(x_1, x_2, x_3) &= \overline{x}_1\overline{x}_2 + x_2x_3 + x_1x_3, \\ f(x_1, x_2, x_3, x_4) &= x_1x_3 + \overline{x}_2x_4 + \overline{x}_1\overline{x}_3\overline{x}_4 + x_2\overline{x}_3, \end{aligned}$$

EXERCISE 11.2 *Discuss complexity of calculation of the Boolean difference of a function of n variables by FFT-like algorithms and through decision diagrams. Illustrate the considerations by the example of functions* f_1 *and* f_2 *defined by the truth-vectors*

$$\begin{aligned} \mathbf{F}_1 &= [1,0,0,1,0,1,1,1]^T, \\ \mathbf{F}_2 &= [1,0,0,0,0,1,0,1]^T, \end{aligned}$$

and determine the number of EXOR operations required in FFT-like algorithms and decision diagram methods.

EXERCISE 11.3 *Show analytically that the order of processing variables in calculation of the Boolean difference of order two with respect to the variables* x_i *and* x_j *is irrelevant, i.e.,* $\frac{\delta^2 f}{\delta x_i \delta x_j} = \frac{\delta^2 f}{\delta x_j \delta x_i}$.

Illustrate the considerations by determining the Boolean difference $\frac{\delta^2 f}{\delta x_1 \delta x_2}$ *of the function* $f(x_1, x_2, x_3) = x_1x_2 + x_1x_3 + x_2x_3$.

EXERCISE 11.4 *Discuss the relationships between the Boolean differences and coefficients in the Reed-Muller expressions. Illustrate the considerations by the example of the function* $f(x_1, x_2, x_3) = x_1 + x_2 + x_1x_2x_3$.

EXERCISE 11.5 *Does the change of polarity of a variable* x_i *influence the calculation of the Boolean difference with respect to this variable? What the are relationships between the Boolean differences and coefficients in the Fixed-polarity Reed-Muller expressions?*

EXERCISE 11.6 *For two switching functions f and g, what is the Boolean difference of the first order of* $f + g$, $f \cdot g$, *and* $f \oplus g$?

EXERCISE 11.7 *Write the matrix relations for calculation of the Boolean differences of first order for a function of* $n = 3$ *variables. Form their Kronecker product structure, determine the matrix relations for calculation of higher order Boolean differences.*

EXERCISE 11.8 *Draw the flow-graphs of FFT-like algorithms for calculation of the first order Boolean differences for functions of* $n = 3$ *variables by using matrix relations in the previous exercise.*

EXERCISE 11.9 *Represent the function* $f(x_1,x_2,x_3) = x_2+x_1\overline{x}_2+\overline{x}_1x_2x_3$ *by the BDD and calculate the Boolean differences of the first order by processing nodes in this diagram.*

EXERCISE 11.10 *Check if the functions*

$$\begin{aligned} f(x_1,x_2,x_3,x_4) &= x_2x_3+\overline{x}_2+\overline{x}_1\overline{x}_3x_4+x_2\overline{x}_3, \\ f(x_1,x_2,x_3,x_4) &= \overline{x}_1\overline{x}_4+\overline{x}_2x_3+\overline{x}_3x_5+x_2\overline{x}_3\overline{x}_4, \end{aligned}$$

have fictive variables by using the Boolean difference.

EXERCISE 11.11 *Check if the function* $f(x_1,x_2,x_3)$ *defined by the set of decimal indices* $f^{(1)} = \{0,3,4,7\}$ *has fictive variables.*

EXERCISE 11.12 *For the function* $f(x_1,x_2,x_3,x_4) = x_1 + x_1x_2x_3 + \overline{x}_1x_2x_4x_2\overline{x}_3x_4$ *calculate the Boolean difference of the first and the second order with respect to the variables* x_1, x_2, x_4 *and* x_1x_3 *and* x_2x_3.

EXERCISE 11.13 *Draw an easily testable network for the function specified by the positive-polarity Reed-Muller expression*

$$f(x_1,x_2,x_3,x_4) = 1 \oplus x_1 \oplus x_1x_2 \oplus x_1x_3 \oplus x_2x_4 \oplus x_2x_3x_4 \oplus x_1x_2x_3x_4.$$

Show the number of tests for this network against stuck-at faults in the case of error free primary inputs and in the presence of errors at the primary inputs.

EXERCISE 11.14 *Consider the network in Fig. 11.25. Determine the set of test for the error the line e stuck-at* 0 *and* 1.

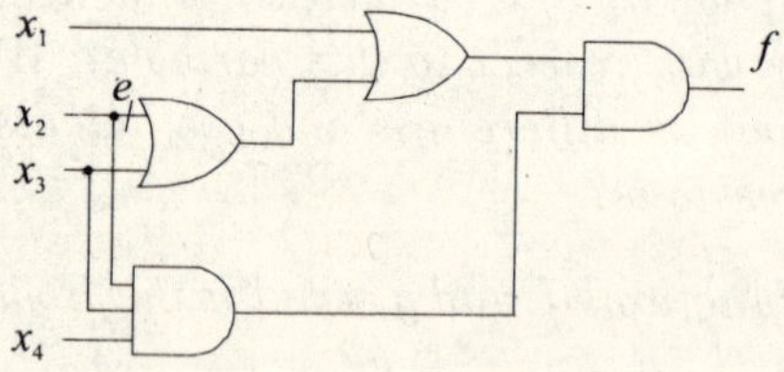

Figure 11.25. Network in the Exercise 11.14.

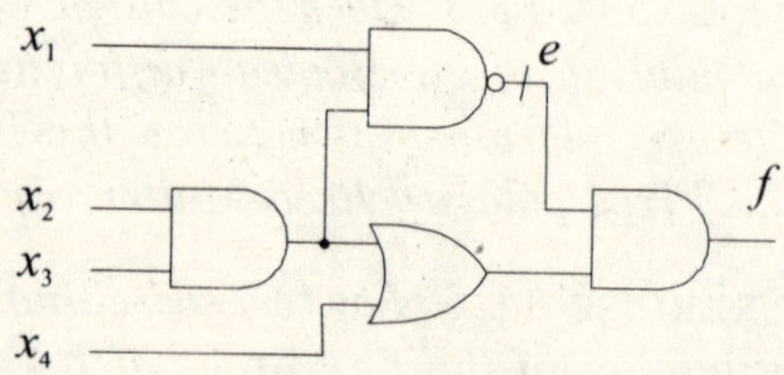

Figure 11.26. Network in the Exercise 11.15.

EXERCISE 11.15 *For the network in Fig. 11.26, determine the set of test for the error line e stuck-at* 0 *and* 1.

EXERCISE 11.16 *Consider the network in Fig. 11.27 realizing the two-bit binary adder. Determine the set of test for the error line e stuck-at 0 and 1. Specify some other errors at internal lines of the circuit and show examples of tests.*

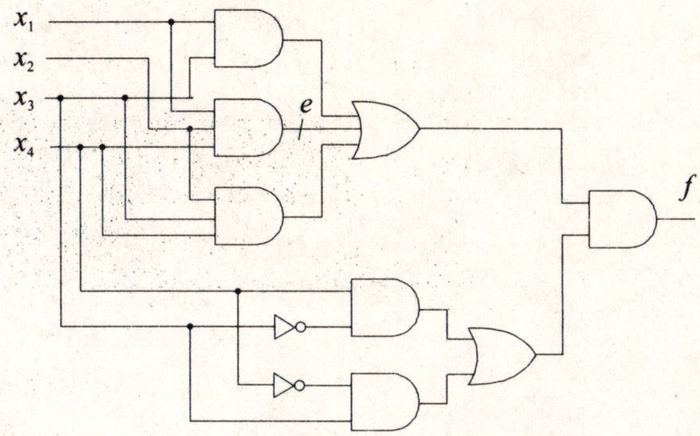

Figure 11.27. Network in the Exercise 11.16.

EXERCISE 11.17 *For the function specified by the GRM-expression*

$$f(x_1, x_2, x_3, x_4) = \overline{x}_1 \oplus x_1x_2 \oplus x_2\overline{x}_4 \oplus x_2x_3x_4$$

determine an easily testable network.

EXERCISE 11.18 *Determine the easily testable network for a four-variable function given by the truth-vector*

$$\mathbf{F} = [1, 0, 1, 1, 0, 0, 0, 1, 1, 1, 1, 1, 0, 0, 1, 1]^T.$$

Chapter 12

SEQUENTIAL NETWORKS

The output of a combinatorial logic network depends on the values of input signals at the time. On the other hand, the output of a sequential network is determined by the present input and current *state* of the network. Thus, the output depends on the history of the system. From the constructional point of view, sequential networks differ from the combinatorial networks in the memory elements used to record the previous state of the network.

The functional behavior of a combinatorial network is described by the truth-tables specifying the outputs of the network for all possible combinations of the input signals. The behavior of a sequential network is described by a mathematical model called *sequential machine*, *finite-state machine* or *finite automaton*, and can be represented by a *state table* or *state diagram.* Notice that the notions *sequential machine*, *finite machine*, *state machine*, *finite automaton*, *automaton*, are synonyms.

Sequential machines can be defined by *state (transition) tables* or *state (transition) diagrams*, or their behavior can be specified by two functions: the *state function* that determines the next state of the sequential machine, and the *output function*, that defines the corresponding output.

In this book, we will discuss finite and deterministic sequential machines, i.e., machines where for each pair of present state and input symbol, there is a deterministic next state. In the case of non-deterministic machines, there may be several possible next states for each pair.

DEFINITION 12.1 *A deterministic finite sequential machine is defined by the quintuple* $M = (\Sigma, Q, Z, f, g)$, *where*

1 Σ *- finite non-empty set of input symbols* $\sigma_1, \ldots, \sigma_l$, *also called the input alphabet,*

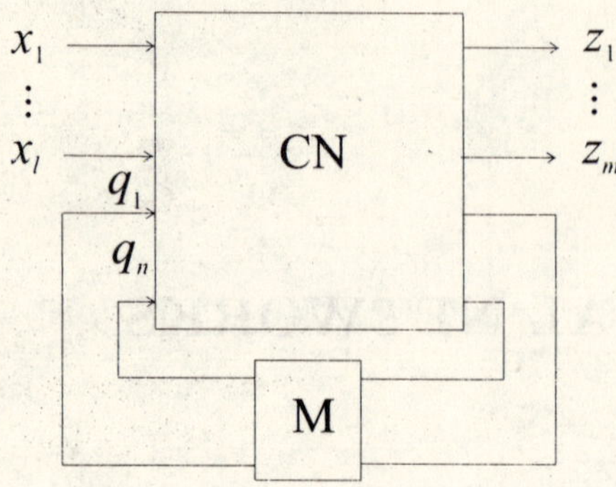

Figure 12.1. Sequential machine.

2 *Q - finite non-empty set of states $q_1, \ldots, q_n$, the state alphabet*

3 *Z - finite non-empty set of output symbols $z_1, \ldots, z_m$, the output alphabet,*

4 *f - state function,*

5 *g - output function.*

Fig. 12.1 shows the basic structure of a sequential machine. It consists of the combinatorial network (CN), realizing the state and output functions and, the memory (M) to keep information about the state.

In the set Q, a state is selected as the *initial state* and marked with a special symbol, usually by encircling the symbol for the state.

Elements of Σ are often called *input symbols*, *inputs*, or *letters*. The *length* of a word is the number of letters it consists of. The *empty word* is a word that contains any letter. It is usually denoted by λ and also called the *empty letter*. We will denote the set of all possible words over an alphabet A by $W(A)$.

EXAMPLE 12.1 *Over an input alphabet $\Sigma = \{\sigma_1, \sigma_2\}$, possible words are λ, σ_1, then σ_2, and $\sigma_1\sigma_1$, $\sigma_1\sigma_2$, $\sigma_1\sigma_1\sigma_2$ and belong to $W(\Sigma)$. The lengths of these words are 0, 1, 1, 2, 2, and 3, respectively.*

Notice that although all three alphabets are finite, and in particular, the input alphabet is finite, the number of possible input signals is infinite, since concatenation of input symbols in an arbitrary order and their repetition arbitrarily many times is allowed.

From the design point of view, the most important task is the minimization of a sequential network. A particular function can be realized

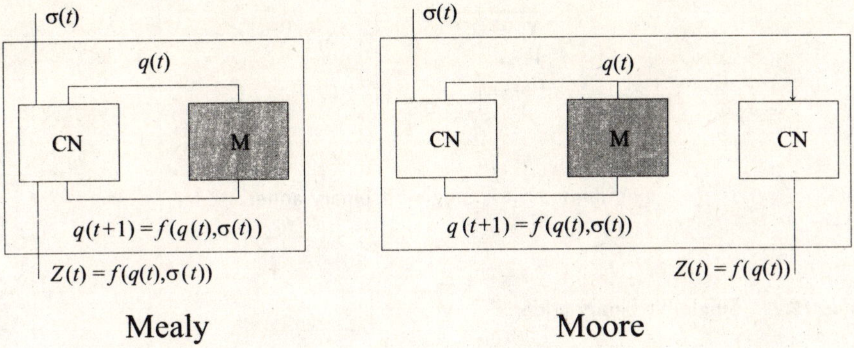

Figure 12.2. Elementary sequential machines (a) Mealy, (b) Moore.

by an infinite number of machines and the task is to find a machine that minimizes the number of states.

Two states in a sequential machine are equivalent if starting from either of the states the same input word produces exactly the same output. In the minimization, we need to identify equivalent states and then eliminate the redundant ones.

Another important task is to find binary encodings for inputs, outputs, and states such that the realizing binary representation is as simple as possible.

A third important task is to hierarchically decompose a complex sequential machine into smaller submachines that can be analyzed and optimized separately.

1. Basic Sequential Machines

There are two basic deterministic sequential machines *Mealy* and *Moore* sequential machines.

DEFINITION 12.2 *(Mealy machine)*
A deterministic sequential machine is the Mealy machine if

1. *The state function is* $f : Q \times \Sigma \to Q$ *and,*

2. *The output function is* $g : Q \times \Sigma \to Z$.

DEFINITION 12.3 *(Moore machine)*
A deterministic sequential machine is the Moore machine if

1. *The state function is* $f : Q \times \Sigma \to Q$ *and,*

2. *The output depends on the present state, but not the input, i.e.,* $g : Q \to Z$.

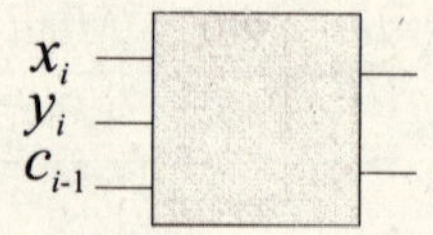

Figure 12.3. Single-bit binary adder.

Table 12.1. Single-bit binary adder.

$c_{i-1}x_iy_i$	c_is_i	Z
000	00	0
001	01	1
010	01	1
011	10	2
100	01	1
101	10	2
110	10	2
111	11	3

Denote by $\sigma(t)$, $q(t)$, and $z(t)$, the input, state, and output of a sequential machine at the instant $t = 1, 2, \ldots$. Then, for the state function f and the output function g we have the relations

$$\begin{aligned} f(q(t), \sigma(t)) &= q(t+1), \\ g(q(t), \sigma(t)) &= Z(t), \end{aligned}$$

where $\sigma(t)$, $q(t)$ are the input, the present state, $z(t)$ is the output, and $q(t+1)$ is the next state. In the case of Moore machines, $z(t) = g(q(t))$.

Notice that selection of instants when values of states, input and output signals, are determined may be specified differently. For instance, sometimes the value of the output signal $z(t)$ is determined by the state at the moment $t+1$. Thus, in this case, the output function is $z(t) = g(q(t+1), \sigma(t))$. Similarly, the state function is often given by $q(t) = f(q(t-1), \sigma(t))$. The overall properties remain the same.

Fig. 12.2 shows the structure of the Mealy and Moore finite sequential machines.

EXAMPLE 12.2 *Fig. 12.3 shows a single-bit serial binary adder, which is a device with two inputs x_i and y_i for operands, and the carry input c_{i-1}, and outputs for the sum s_i and the carry bit c_i. Table 12.1 defines behavior of the binary adder.*

It is clear that, when considered as a Mealy sequential machine, two states are needed to describe the binary adder

1 q_0 - *no carry,*

2 q_1 - *carry.*

Therefore, the set of states is $Q = \{q_0, q_1\}$. *The input and the output symbols are* $\Sigma = \{x_i y_i\} = \{00, 01, 10, 11\}$, *and* $Z = \{s_i\} = \{0, 1\}$, *respectively.*

A simple analysis of the impact of all possible combinations of values at the inputs $x_i y_i$, *that can be* 00, 01, 10, *and* 11, *to the next state of the adder, can be described by the following state function* f

$$\begin{aligned} f(q_0, 11) &= q_1, \\ f(q_0, 00) = f(q_0, 01) = f(q_0, 10) &= q_0, \\ f(q_1, 01) = f(q_1, 10) = f(q_1, 11) &= q_1, \\ f(q_1, 00) &= q_0. \end{aligned}$$

Indeed, for instance, if the initial state is q_0, *i.e., there is no carry, and the input is* $x_i y_i = 11$, *the result will be* $1 + 1 = 2$, *which in binary notation is* $s_i c_i = 10$ *meaning that the sum is* 0 *and the carry is* 1. *Thus, the machine changes to the state* q_1, *and we write* $f(q_0, 11) = q_1$.

Similarly, since the output of the binary adder is determined as $x_i \oplus y_i \oplus c_{i-1} = z$, *it can be specified by the output functions*

$$\begin{aligned} g(q_0, 00) = g(q_0, 11) &= 0, \\ g(q_0, 01) = g(q_0, 10) &= 1, \\ g(q_1, 00) = g(q_1, 11) &= 1, \\ g(q_1, 01) = g(q_1, 10) &= 0. \end{aligned}$$

Therefore, the binary adder can be defined as a Mealy sequential machine $M = (\{00, 01, 10, 11\}, \{q_0, q_1\}, \{0, 1\}, f, g)$, *where* f *and* g *are as defined above.*

However, if the states should take into account not just carry, but also the sum, then four states are needed $q_{00}, q_{01}, q_{10}, q_{11}$. *The state* q_{00} *denotes the combination when there is no carry and sum is 0. Similarly, the state* q_{01} *denotes that there is no carry, but the sum is 1, etc.*

In this case, since the states q_{sc} *include both carry and the sum, which are uniquely determined by the inputs* $x_i y_i$, *the output will depend just on the state and not the inputs. Therefore, the corresponding sequential machine will be a Moore machine with the state function*

$$
\begin{aligned}
f(q_{00},00) = f(q_{01},00) &= q_{00}, \\
f(q_{00},11) = f(q_{01},11) &= q_{10}, \\
f(q_{00},01) = f(q_{00},10) = f(q_{01},01) = f(q_{01},10) &= q_{01}, \\
f(q_{10},00) = f(q_{11},00) &= q_{01}, \\
f(q_{10},11) = f(q_{11},11) &= q_{11}, \\
f(q_{10},01) = f(q_{10},10) = f(q_{11},01) = f(q_{11},10) &= q_{10}.
\end{aligned}
$$

The output function is

$$
\begin{aligned}
g(q_{00}) &= q(q_{10}) = 0, \\
g(q_{01}) &= g(q_{11}) = 1.
\end{aligned}
$$

Therefore, the single-bit serial binary adder can be equivalently represented by either a Mealy or Moore sequential machine. In general, two sequential machines defined over the same input and output alphabets are equivalent if for any input word they produce the same output. Machines can be different in the number of states, and the selection of the one most appropriate for a given task depends on the application and other possible requirements.

For each Moore machine there is an equivalent Mealy machine with the same number of states. The output function is just viewed as a function $Q \times \Sigma \rightarrow Z$. For each Mealy machine with $|\Sigma|$ states, there is an equivalent Moore machine with $|Q| \times |\Sigma|$ states.

2. State Tables

To specify a deterministic sequential machine we need to give the sets of states, input symbols, output symbols, and output and state transition functions. This information can be presented conveniently in the form of a table, called the *state table* or *state transition table.*

EXAMPLE 12.3 *Fig. 12.4 shows the state table for the binary adder in Example 12.2 considered as the Mealy machine. The first row shows the possible input signals* $00, 01, 10, 11$. *The left most column shows the present states* q_0 *and* q_1, *and the remaining part of the table shows the next states and the corresponding outputs.*

For instance, the last row shows that if the present state is q_1, *the next states and outputs for the corresponding inputs will be* $q_0, 1$, $q_1, 0$, $q_1, 1$, *and* $q_1, 1$, *respectively.*

Fig. 12.5 shows the state table for the equivalent Moore machine. In this table, the output is separately shown in the column Z, *since does not depend on the present inputs.*

$q \backslash x_i y_i$	00	01	11	10
q_0	q_0,0	q_0,1	q_1,0	q_0,1
q_1	q_0,1	q_1,0	q_1,1	q_1,0

Figure 12.4. State table for the binary adder realized as a Mealy machine.

$q \backslash x_i y_i$	00	01	11	10	Z
q_{00}	q_{00}	q_{01}	q_{10}	q_{01}	0
q_{01}	q_{00}	q_{01}	q_{10}	q_{01}	1
q_{10}	q_{01}	q_{10}	q_{11}	q_{10}	0
q_{11}	q_{01}	q_{10}	q_{11}	q_{10}	1

Figure 12.5. State table for the binary adder realized as a Moore machine.

Alteratively, the information in a state table can be presented in the form of a *state diagram.*

EXAMPLE 12.4 *Fig. 12.6 shows the state diagram for the single-bit binary adder considered as the Mealy machine. In this diagram, the directed edge* $q_0 \overset{11/0}{\rightarrow} q_1$ *shows that the machine goes from the state* q_0 *into the state* q_1 *under the input* 11 *and the output is* 0*. Such representation indicates that the output depends on the input and the state.*

Fig. 12.7 shows the state diagram when binary adder is considered as the Moore machine. In this diagram, the values for the output are shown in the states.

State diagrams are useful for visualizing various properties of sequential machines.

If some of the functions that define a sequential machine, the state function or the output function, are incompletely specified, then the sequential machine is also *incompletely specified.*

EXAMPLE 12.5 *A Mealy machine with the input alphabet* $\Sigma = \{0, 1\}$*, the state alphabet* $q = \{1, 2, 3, 4\}$*, and the output alphabet* $Z = \{0, 1\}$*,*

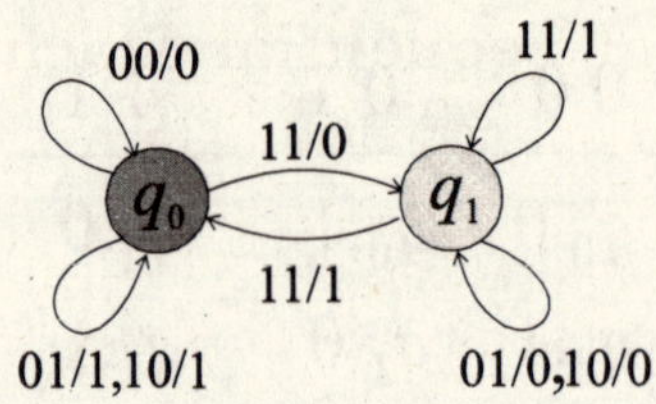

Figure 12.6. State diagram for the binary adder realized as a Mealy machine.

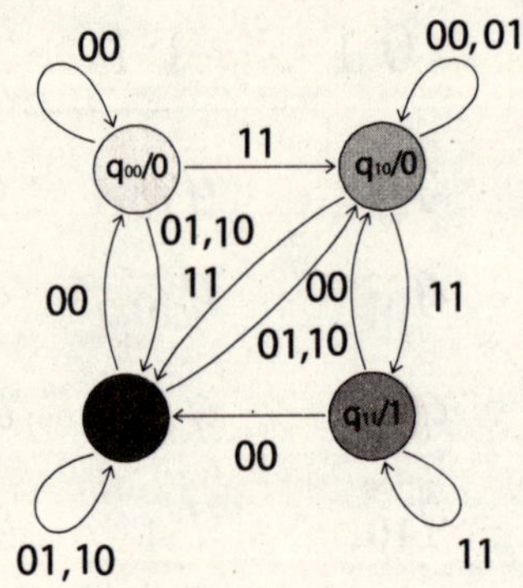

Figure 12.7. State diagram for the binary adder realized as a Moore machine.

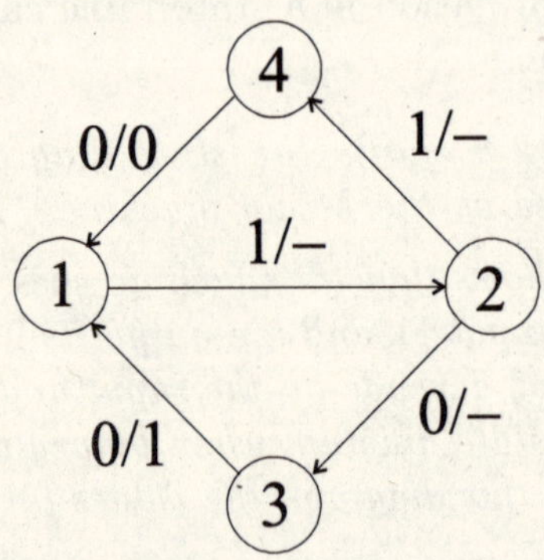

Figure 12.8. State diagram of an incompletely specified sequential machine.

given by the state diagram is Fig. 12.8 is an incompletely specified sequential machine.

3. Conversion of Sequential Machines

For a particular input-output relation, there are many (infinite number) of different sequential machines realizing the relation. In the design process, it is often desirable to convert a sequential machine to another equivalent one that is more suitable to the technology at hand. Also, from the set of suitable sequential machines, the designer should find the simplest one. We shall consider two examples of the above tasks and while doing so, also give a more precise meaning to the words "equivalent" and "simplest" in this context.

DEFINITION 12.4 *The state transition function is extended from* $Q \times \Sigma$ *to* $Q \times W(\Sigma)$ *by*

$$\begin{aligned} f(q, \lambda) &= q, \textit{for all } q \in Q, \\ f(q, w\sigma) &= f(f(q, w), \sigma), \textit{for all } q \in Q, \sigma \in \Sigma, w \in W(\Sigma). \end{aligned}$$

If f is clear from the context, we can write qw for $f(q, w)$.

DEFINITION 12.5 *The response function* $r_q(w)$ *induced by the input word* w *is defined by*

$$\begin{aligned} r_q(\lambda) &= \lambda, \\ r_q(\sigma w) &= g(q, \sigma) r_{q\sigma}(w), \textit{for a Mealy machine}, \\ r_q(\sigma w) &= g(q) r_{q\sigma}(w), \textit{for a Moore machine}, \end{aligned}$$

where $\sigma \in \Sigma$, $w \in W(\Sigma)$ *and* $q \in Q$.

DEFINITION 12.6 *Two states* q *and* q' *(from the same or two machines) are called equivalent if* $r_q(w) = r_{q'}(w)$*, for all* $w \in W(\Sigma)$*, and the two machines* M_1 *and* M_2 *are equivalent if for each state of* M_1 *there is an equivalent state in* M_2 *and vice versa.*

THEOREM 12.1 *For any Moore machine there is an equivalent Mealy machine with the same number of states. For each Mealy machine* $M_e = (\Sigma, Q, Z, f, g)$ *there is an equivalent Moore machine with* $|Q| \times |Z|$ *states.*

Proof. Let $M_o = (\Sigma, Q, Z, f, g)$ be a Moore machine. Consider the quintuple $M_e = (\Sigma, Q, Z, f_1, g_1)$, where $q_1(q, \sigma) = g(f(q, \sigma))$. Clearly, M_e is equivalent to M_o.

Let $M_e = (\Sigma, Q, Z, f, g)$ be a Mealy machine. Consider the quintuple $M_o = (\Sigma, Q \times Z, f_1, g_1)$, where

$$\begin{aligned} f_1((q, z), \sigma) &= (f(q, \sigma), g(q, \sigma)), q \in Q, z \in Z, \sigma \in \Sigma, \\ g_1((q_1, z)) &= z, q \in Q, z \in Z. \end{aligned}$$

As f_1 maps $(Q \times Z) \times \Sigma$ to $(Q \times Z)$ and g_1 maps $Q \times Z$ to Z, the quintuple M_o defines a Moore machine. Let then $q_0 \in Q$ be an arbitrary state of M_o and $w = \sigma_1\sigma_2 \cdots \sigma_n \in W(\Sigma)$. Denote $f(q_{i-1}, \sigma_i) = q_i$ and $g(q_{i-1}, \sigma_i) = z_i$ for $i = 1, 2, \ldots, n$. Let $z_0 \in Z$ and consider the state s_0 of M_e and (s_0, z_0) of M_o. Since

$$f_1((q_{i-1}, z_{i-1}), \sigma_i) = (f(q_{i-1}, g(q_{i-1}, \sigma_i))) = (q_i, z_i),$$

and

$$g_1((q_i, z_i)) = z_i,$$

for $i = 1, \ldots, n$, we have

$$r_{q_0}(\sigma_1\sigma_2 \cdots \sigma_n) = r_{(q_0, z_0)}(\sigma_1\sigma_2 \cdots \sigma_n) = z_1 z_2 \cdots z_n.$$

We can conclude that q_0 and (q_0, z_0) are equivalent, which implies the theorem.

4. Minimization of States

Consider a sequential machine $M = (\Sigma, Q, Z, f, g)$. It may be possible to find another machine that has identical performance with regard to output response to an input, but which has a smaller number of states. It is of considerable importance to be able to find the "simplest" machine. For completely specified machines there is a unique solution for this problem and an algorithm for finding it. To present it formally, we need first some definitions.

DEFINITION 12.7 *Let q and q' be two states in the same sequential machine or in two distinct machines that have the same input alphabet Σ, and let σ be a word over Σ. We say that σ distinguishes q and q' iff*

$$resp_q(\sigma) = resp_{q'}(\sigma),$$

where resp denotes the response of the machine.

Two states are equivalent if are indistinguishable for all words.

THEOREM 12.2 *Consider a sequential machine $M = (\Sigma, Q, Z, f, g)$ where $|Q| \geq 2$. For a positive integer l, define an equivalence relation R_l over Q by: qR_lq' iff q and q' are not distinguishable by any word of length at most l. Then, there is $k < |Q|$ such that $R_k = R_{k+1}$. Furthermore, any states q and q' are equivalent iff qR_kq'.*

Proof. It is straightforward to verify that R_l is an equivalence relation. If q and q' satisfy $qR_{l+1}q'$, then also qR_lq' which shows that R_{l+1} is a refinement of R_l, i.e., every equivalence class of R_{l+1} is a subset of an equivalence class of R_l. We denote this by

$$R_{l+1} \subset R_l.$$

For the numbers of equivalence classes S_l of R_l we obviously have the corresponding inequalities

$$S_{l+1} \geq S_l.$$

Let us now show that if $R_l = R_{l+1}$ for some l, then $R_l = R_{l+j}$ for $j = 1, 2, \ldots$.

Assume that $R_l = R_{l+1}$ and $j > 1$ is smallest value such that $R_l \neq R_{l+j}$. Then, there are states q and q' and $\sigma_1\sigma_2 \cdots \sigma_{l+j}$ such that qR_lq'

$$q\sigma_1\sigma_2 \cdots \sigma_{l+1} \neq q'\sigma_1\sigma_2 \cdots \sigma_{l+1}. \tag{12.1}$$

Since $R_l = R_{l+j-1}$ we must have

$$[q\sigma_1\sigma_2 \cdots \sigma_{j-1}]R_l[q'\sigma_1\sigma_2 \cdots \sigma_{j-1}],$$

which, by $R_l = R_{l+1}$, implies

$$q\sigma_1\sigma_2 \cdots \sigma_{j-1} \underbrace{\sigma_j \cdots \sigma_{l+j}}_{l+1} = q'\sigma_1\sigma_2 \cdots \sigma_{j-1} \underbrace{\sigma_j \cdots \sigma_{l+j}}_{l+1}$$

which is a contradiction.

It immediately follows that if $R_l = R_{l+1}$, for some l, then q and q' are equivalent if qR_lq'.

As long as $R_l \neq R_{l+1}$ the number of blocks S_l n the partition defined by the equivalence relations must satisfy

$$S_{l+1} > S_l,$$

and since it cannot be longer than the number of states $|Q|$ we see that there must be an integer $k < |Q|$ such that $R_k = R_{k+1}$.

DEFINITION 12.8 *A Mealy machine is called* reduced *if it has no distinct equivalent states.*

The above equivalence relation R_l satisfying $R_l = R_{l+1}$ is the key to determining the minimal Mealy machine M_1 equivalent to a given Mealy machine $M = (\Sigma, Q, Z, f, g)$.

We first determine the smallest l satisfying $R_l = R_{l+1}$. Denote $R = R_l$ and by $[q]$ the block containing q. Denote the set of blocks by Q_1 and define the Mealy machine $M_1 = (\Sigma, Q_1, Z, f_1, g_1)$ by

$$f_1([q], \sigma) = [f(q, \sigma)], \tag{12.2}$$

$$g_1([q], \sigma) = g(q, \sigma). \tag{12.3}$$

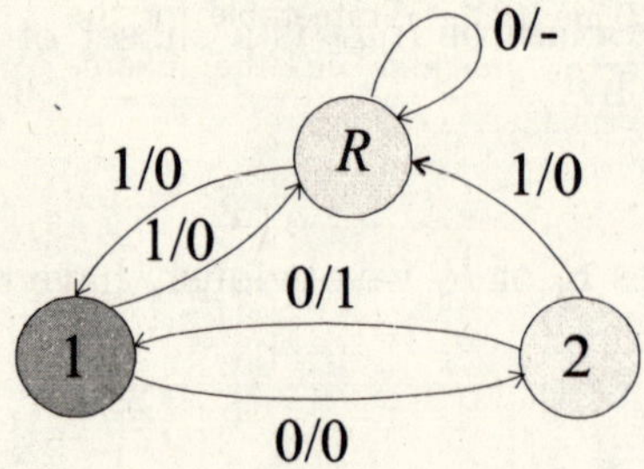

Figure 12.9. State diagram of the sequential machine in Example 12.6.

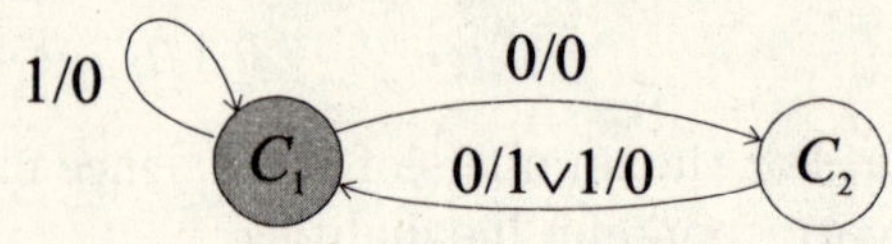

Figure 12.10. State diagram of the factor machine in Example 12.6.

$f(R,0) = R,-$ $\quad f(2,0) = 1,1$ $\quad f(1,1) = R,0$

$f(1,0) = 2,0$ $\quad f(2,1) = R,0$ $\quad f(R,1) = 1,0$

$C_1 \quad C_2 \qquad C_2 \quad C_1 \qquad C_1 \quad C_1$

Figure 12.11. Equivalent states in the sequential machine in Example 12.6.

Let $q', q'' \in [q]$. Since $q'Rq''$, we have

$$f(q', \sigma)Rf(q'', \sigma) \qquad \text{for all } \sigma,$$

and

$$g(q', \sigma) = g(q'', \sigma) \qquad \text{for all } \sigma.$$

Thus, the functions f and g are well defined and for any q the states q and $[q]$ are equivalent.

It appears evident and can be rigorously shown that there is no Mealy machine equivalent to M that has fewer states than M_1.

Similar results can be also shown to hold also for Moore machines.

EXAMPLE 12.6 *[31]*
Consider the sequential machine given by the state diagram in Fig. 12.9 and the state Table 12.2. Fig. 12.11 shows the state function for this machine and explains that there are equivalent states. A closed covering is $\{C_1 = \{R, 1\}, C_2 = \{R, 2\}\}$, *and the corresponding factor machine is defined by the state table in Table 12.3, which is determined from the requirements* $f(C_1, \sigma) = C_2$, $f(C_2, \sigma) = C_1$ *or* $f(C_1, \sigma) = C_1$ *and* $f(C_2, \sigma) = C_2$ *for all* $\sigma \in \Sigma$. *Fig. 12.10 shows the state diagram for this factor machine.*

Table 12.2. State table for the sequential machine in Example 12.6.

	0	1
R	$R,-$	$1,0$
1	$2,0$	$R,0$
2	$1,1$	$R,0$

Table 12.3. State table for the factor machine in the Example 12.6.

	0	1
C_1	$C_2,0$	$C_1,0$
C_2	$C_1,1$	$C_1,0$

5. Incompletely Specified Machines

The minimization of Mealy and Moore machines is straightforward, in principle, and yields a unique minimal machine. However, in practice, sequential machines are often incompletely specified. For instance, when the machine is in a certain state, then a particular input cannot occur and state transition and output corresponding to the input are left unspecified. Also, for certain state/input combinations it may not matter what is the output and so it can be left unspecified.

The minimization of completely specified machines used the equivalence relation R. A similar relation, *compatibility relation*, is used in the minimization of incompletely specified machines. The difficulty is that the compatibility relation is not an equivalence relation and, thus, the classes of mutually compatible states do not form a partition of the set of states. It follows that these classes cannot be directly used to construct a minimal machine.

DEFINITION 12.9 *Two states q_1 and q_2 are compatible if for each input word r, the outputs $g(q_1, r)$ and $g(q_2, r)$ are equal, whenever the outputs $g(q_1, r)$ and $g(q_2, r)$ are specified.*

The compatibility relation is reflexive and symmetric, however, in general, it is not transitive. For a given machine, a *compatibility class* is a set of mutually compatible states.

DEFINITION 12.10 *(Covering of states)*
A covering of a set of states Q is the set $\mathcal{B} = \{C_1, C_2, \ldots, C_q\}$ of compatibility classes whose union is Q, i.e., $C_1 \cup C_2 \cup \ldots \cup C_q = Q$.

DEFINITION 12.11 *(Closed covering)*
A covering $\mathcal{B} = \{C_1, C_2, \ldots, C_q\}$ is closed if for each index $i \in \{1, 2, \ldots, q\}$ and each symbol $\sigma \in \Sigma$, there exists an index $j \in \{1, 2, \ldots, q\}$ such that

$$f(C_i, \sigma) \subset C_j. \tag{12.4}$$

If $\mathcal{B}$ is a closed covering, then it is possible to define a *factor machine* $A/\mathcal{B} = (\Sigma, b, Z, f', g')$, where $f'(C_i, \sigma) = C_j$, with the class C_j determined by (12.4), and $g'(C_i, \sigma) = g(C_i, \sigma)$. It is clear that $g(C_i, \sigma)$ is either a singleton set or the empty set, since C_i is an compatibility class.

Consider a state q in a sequential machine A, and the compatibility class C_i which contains q. If q and C_i are the initial states for the machine A and the factor machine $A/\mathcal{B}$, and to them both same input word r is applied, then A and $A/\mathcal{B}$ generate the same output word whenever the output is defined in the machine A. Thus, the factor machine $A/\mathcal{B}$ behaves exactly as the initial machine A.

It follows that minimization of the number of states can be performed in two steps

1 Determine compatibility classes,

2 Construct a closed covering for the initial machine.

For both steps, there have been developed explicit algorithms [83], [122], [196].

EXAMPLE 12.7 *[31]*

Consider a systems for transmission of binary messages encoded such that appearance of two consecutive values 1, *or four consecutive values* 0 *is forbidden. The task is to construct a system that detects faulty messages.*

We define a sequential machine with the input and output alphabets $\Sigma = Z = \{0, 1\}$. *The machine generates the output* 1 *when the string* 11 *or* 0000 *appears at the input. Fig. 12.12 shows the state table of this sequential machine. In this table, indices are selected such that the machine goes into the state* s_{ijk} *when* j, j, *and* k, *are the three last symbols at the input.*

To minimize this state table, we first search for equivalent states under R_1. *The state* s_{000} *has different output for both inputs* 0 *or* 1. *Thus, it cannot be a candidate for equivalent states under* R_1. *States* s_{001}, s_{010}, *and* s_{011} *have the same output for both input symbols and belong to the same class of equivalent states under* R_1. *Similarly, states* s_{100}, s_{101}, s_{110} *and* s_{111} *have the same outputs for the both input symbols,* 0 *and* 1, *but the outputs are different for different symbols, and they form a separate equivalence class under* R_1. *Thus, the equivalence classes of* R_1 *are*

$$\{s_{000}\}, \{s_{001}, s_{010}, s_{011}\}, \{s_{100}, s_{101}, s_{110}, s_{111}\}.$$

The equivalence under R_2 *is determined within these equivalence classes. It has to be checked if the output is the same for all the inputs of the*

q	0	1
s_{000}	s_{000},1	s_{100},0
s_{001}	s_{000},0	s_{100},0
s_{010}	s_{001},0	s_{101},0
s_{011}	s_{001},0	s_{101},0
s_{100}	s_{010},0	s_{110},1
s_{101}	s_{010},0	s_{110},1
s_{110}	s_{011},0	s_{111},1
s_{111}	s_{011},0	s_{111},1
y	Y/Z	

Figure 12.12. State table for the sequential machine in Example 12.7.

length 2. For instance, it easily follows that the states s_{001} and s_{010} are not in the same equivalence class under R_2, since have different outputs for the input 00.

When 0 *is applied to* 001, *it is converted into* 000 *and the output is* 0, *since this is the third* 0 *in a row. When the second* 0 *is applied,* 000 *is again* 000, *however, the output is* 1, *since this is the fourth* 0 *in a row.*

The first 0 *converts* 010 *into* 001 *and the output is* 0, *The second* 0 *at the input, converts* 001 *into* 000, *however, the output is still* 0, *since this is the third* 0 *in a row.*

In this way it can be shown that the equivalence classes of R_2 are

$$\{s_{000}\}, \{s_{001}\}, \{s_{010}, s_{011}\}, \{s_{100}, s_{101}, s_{110}, s_{111}\}.$$

Checking for the equivalence classes under R_3 shows that $R_2 = R_3$. Therefore, the blocks of R_2 form the states of the minimal machine. Fig. 12.13 which shows also the state diagram of this sequential machine. Thus, we have the from 8 states in the initial sequential machine to four states.

6. State Assignment

Sequential machines are defined by using different symbols for the input, output alphabets, and states. However, for realization by binary components which are nowadays prevalent circuitry, these symbols have to be encoded by binary sequences. Usually, the encoding of input and output signals depends on the application and the particular task the

q	0	1
q_1	q_1,1	q_4,0
q_2	q_1,0	q_4,0
q_3	q_2,0	q_4,0
q_4	q_3,0	q_4,1

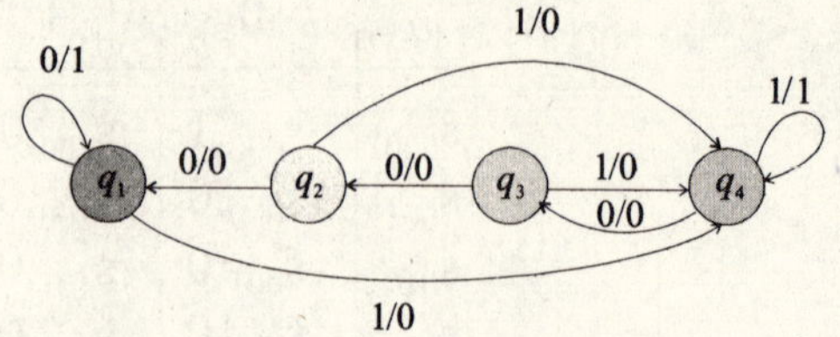

Figure 12.13. State table and state diagram for the minimized sequential machine in Example 12.7.

sequential machine performs, and so a priori determined. However, *state encoding* or *assignment* is mainly left to the designer and different encodings may significantly reduce complexity of state and output functions as will be illustrated by the following example.

State assignment is also very important to avoid problems related to proper functioning of sequential machines in some modes of realization as will be discussed in Section 7.

EXAMPLE 12.8 *[96]*
Consider a sequential machine defined by the state table in Fig. 12.14. For simplicity, the outputs are omitted since we discuss just the state assignment. There are 8 states which can be encoded by sequences of three bits (y_1, y_2, y_3)*, which results in three state functions* Y_1, Y_2, Y_3 *determining the bits of next states. In this figure, three possible encodings are shown. The encoding in the first column is the direct encoding of integers by binary sequences with weight coefficients* 2^i*,* $i = 0, 1, 2$*. Fig. 12.15 shows the state table of the sequential machine with this direct encoding of states. The other two encodings are arbitrarily chosen.*

Consider, for instance, the state function Y_2*, which takes the value* 1 *for the input signal* 11 *at the present states* $q = 1, 4, 5, 8$*. Therefore,*

$$\begin{aligned} Y_2 &= x_1x_2(\overline{y}_1\overline{y}_2y_3 + y_1\overline{y}_2\overline{y}_3 + y_1\overline{y}_2y_3 + \overline{y}_1\overline{y}_2\overline{y}_3) \\ &= x_1x_2(\overline{y}_1\overline{y}_2 + y_1\overline{y}_2) = x_1x_2\overline{y}_2. \end{aligned}$$

In the same way we determine the other two state functions Y_1 *and* Y_3*, and we repeat this for the three encodings in Fig. 12.14. The corresponding state functions are shown in Fig. 12.16. Fig. 12.17 compares the number of elementary logic circuits required to realize state functions for these three encodings.*

Notice that overall measure of complexity of a state assignment is related to the number of encoding bits, i.e., encoding length, which determines the complexity of required registers to store the states, and the

$q \backslash x_1x_2$	00	01	11	10
1	1	4	3	1
2	1	4	4	1
3	1	4	5	8
4	1	4	6	8
5	8	8	7	8
6	8	8	8	8
7	1	1	1	1
8	1	1	2	1

q	$y_1y_2y_3$	$y_1y_2y_3$	$y_1y_2y_3$
1	001	000	000
2	010	001	001
3	011	010	011
4	100	011	010
5	101	100	110
6	110	101	111
7	111	110	101
8	000	111	100

Figure 12.14. State table for the sequential machine in Example 12.8.

q	$y_1y_2y_3 \backslash x_1x_2$	00	01	11	10
1	001	001	100	011	001
2	010	001	100	100	001
3	011	001	100	101	000
4	100	001	100	110	000
5	101	000	000	111	000
6	110	000	000	000	000
7	111	001	001	001	001
8	000	001	001	010	001

x_1	x_2	y_1	y_2	y_3
1	1	0	0	1
1	1	1	0	0
1	1	1	0	1
1	1	0	0	0

y_2

$$Y_2 = x_1x_2\bar{y}_2$$

$$x_1x_2(\bar{y}_1\bar{y}_2 + y_1\bar{y}_2) = x_1x_2\bar{y}_2$$

$$x_1x_2(\bar{y}_1\bar{y}_2y_3 + y_1\bar{y}_2\bar{y}_3 + y_1\bar{y}_2y_3 + \bar{y}_1\bar{y}_2\bar{y}_3)$$

$y_1\bar{y}_2$ $\quad$ $\bar{y}_1\bar{y}_2$

Figure 12.15. State table for the sequential machine in Example 12.8 with direct encoding and determination of the next state function Y_2.

number of literals used in the description of the combinatorial part of the sequential machine. This latter complexity is measured in a different way for two-level and multi-level realizations, and correspondingly state assignment techniques are developed separately for these two approaches, see for example, [34].

The state assignment known as the 1-*hot code* assumes that encoding of states is performed by binary sequences with a single non-zero bit.

EXAMPLE 12.9 *For a state table with four states q_0, q_1, q_2, q_3, the 1-hot code produces the following encoding*

$$q_0 = (1000),$$

$$Y_1 = \bar{y}_1 y_2 x_2 + y_1 \bar{y}_2 \bar{y}_3 x_2 + \bar{y}_1 y_3 \bar{x}_1 x_2 + y_1 \bar{y}_2 x_1 x_2$$

$$Y_2 = \bar{y}_2 x_1 x_2$$

$$Y_3 = \bar{y}_1 \bar{y}_3 \bar{x}_2 + y_1 y_2 y_3 + \bar{y}_2 \bar{y}_3 \bar{x}_1 \bar{x}_2 + y_3 x_1 x_2 + \bar{y}_1 \bar{x}_1 \bar{x}_2 + \bar{y}_1 \bar{y}_2 \bar{y}_3 \bar{x}_1 + \bar{y}_1 \bar{y}_2 y_3 x_1$$

$$Y_1 = y_1 \bar{y}_2 + \bar{y}_1 y_2 x_1$$

$$Y_2 = y_1 \bar{y}_2 + \bar{y}_2 x_2 + \bar{y}_1 \bar{x}_1 x_2 + \bar{y}_1 y_2 x_1 \bar{x}_2$$

$$Y_3 = y_1 \bar{y}_2 \bar{x}_2 + y_3 x_1 x_2 + \bar{y}_1 \bar{x}_1 x_2 + \bar{y}_1 y_2 + x_1 \bar{x}_2 + \bar{y}_2 \bar{x}_1 x_2$$

$$Y_1 = y_1 y_2 + y_2 x_1$$

$$Y_2 = \bar{y}_1 x_2$$

$$Y_3 = \bar{y}_3 x_1 x_2$$

Figure 12.16. State functions for different encodings.

	C_1	C_2	C_3
AND	12	11	4
OR	2	3	1
NOT	5	4	2
Gates	19	18	7
In	47	36	11

Figure 12.17. Comparisons of the number of circuits to realize state functions in Example 12.8 with different encodings.

$$q_1 = (0100),$$
$$q_2 = (0010),$$
$$q_3 = (0001).$$

It is clear that the number of bits required for encoding is equal to the number of states. This results in larger registers.

In 1-hot code encoding, the logic is more complex, but generally comparable to some other methods, especially in the case of sequential machines with a small number of transitions [34].

The approach using 1-hot code simplifies the design. However, all the transitions are necessarily done in two steps, since to change from a state in the i-th row of the state table into a state in the j-th row, first the y_j is set to 1, and then y_i is reset to 0, where y_i and y_j are hot bits in these two state encodings. It follows that the circuit is slower than it could be by using a single-transition-time assignment. For more details, see for example, [196].

The selection of the best encoding is a difficult task, since there are $2^r!/(2^r - s)$ possible encodings, where r is the number of bits and s number of states. Since in two-level realizations, the size of sum-of-product expressions is invariant under permutation and complementation of encoding bits, the number of possible combinations reduces to $(2^r - 1)!/(2^r - s)!r!$. That is still large [34]. Therefore, most of the state assignment algorithms are heuristic and often related to the targeted technology. Due to its importance, state assignment is a subject of extensive research [22], [24], [28], [68], [75], [188], [197].

7. Decomposition of Sequential Machines

Rationales for decomposition of a sequential machine are identical to these used generally in engineering practice when a complex system is decomposed into simpler subsystems

1 The organization of a given complex system becomes more obvious when decomposed into smaller subsystems, which is important for description, design, and maintaining.

2 Each subsystem can be optimized separately, when the optimization of the entire system is hard to perform due to large space and time requirements.

In the case of sequential machines, decomposition is usually performed when the initial machine has many states. The first question is when the decomposition of a given sequential machine is possible? To provide an answer to this question, we first need some basic definitions, see for example, [62], [96].

7.1 Serial Decomposition of Sequential Machines

DEFINITION 12.12 *(Serial connection of sequential machines)*
Serial connection of two sequential machines $M_1 = (Q_1, \Sigma_1, Z_1, f_1, g_1)$ *and* $M_2 = (Q_2, \Sigma_2, Z_2, f_2, g_2)$ *where* $\Sigma_2 = Z_1$ *is the sequential machine* $M = (Q_1 \times Q_2, \Sigma_1, Z_2, f, g)$, *where the state function* f *and the output function* g *are*

$$\begin{aligned} f((q,p),\sigma) &= (f_1(q,\sigma), f_2(p, g_1(q,\sigma))), \\ g((q,p),\sigma) &= g_2(p, g_1(q,\sigma)). \end{aligned}$$

$$A_1 = (Q_1, \Sigma_1, Z_1, f_1, g_1)$$
$$A_2 = (Q_2, \Sigma_2, Z_2, f_2, g_2)$$
$$\Sigma_2 = Z_1$$
$$A = (Q_1 \times Q_2, \Sigma_1, Z_2, f, g)$$

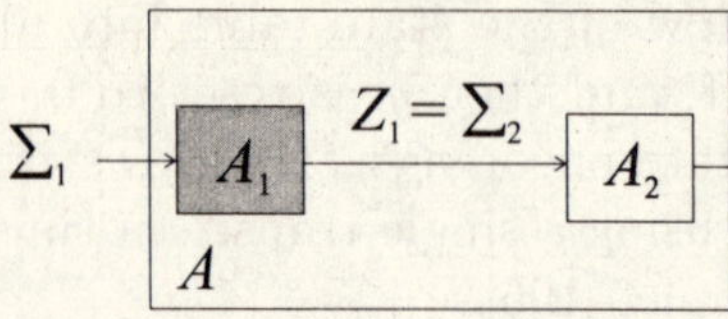

A_1 - Master
A_2 - Slave

$$f((q,p),\sigma) = (f_1(q,\sigma), f_2(p,\sigma))$$
$$g((q,p),\sigma) = g_2(p, g_1(q,\sigma))$$

Figure 12.18. Serial decomposition of a sequential machine M.

A sequential machine $M_1 - M_2$, that is serial connection of M_1 and M_2, is a serial decomposition of a given sequential machine M iff $M_1 - M_2$ realizes M. The decomposition is non-trivial iff the total number of states in M_1 and M_2 is smaller than the number of states in M.

Fig. 12.18 shows the basic principle of the serial decomposition of sequential machines.

Example 12.10 *[96]*

Consider a sequential machine that generates the parity bit to the end of a binary sequence of three bits. Recall that the parity bit in the end of the sequence makes the number of ones in the sequence even. Thus, this machine accepts four binary digits and generates the output of the length four where the last is the parity bit of he three.

Table 12.4 shows an example of the input and output sequences for the parity bit generator for three bit sequences.

Table 12.5 shows the state table of the parity bit generator for sequences of three bits. Fig. 12.19 shows the state diagram for this machine.

It can be shown that the partition $\{(A)(B,C),(D,E),(F,G)\}$ *is an SP-partition. Table 12.6 shows the state table of the factor machine with respect to this partition. From this table, it is obvious that this is an autonomous system, i.e., its output is independent on the input signals. Thus, the output of the master machine is, by definition, equal to the present state.*

The slave machine has two states, which we denote by q_1 *and* q_2*, since the largest block in the partition contains two states.*

Table 12.7 shows the encoding of states in the initial machine by the states of the master and slave machines. These states are determined

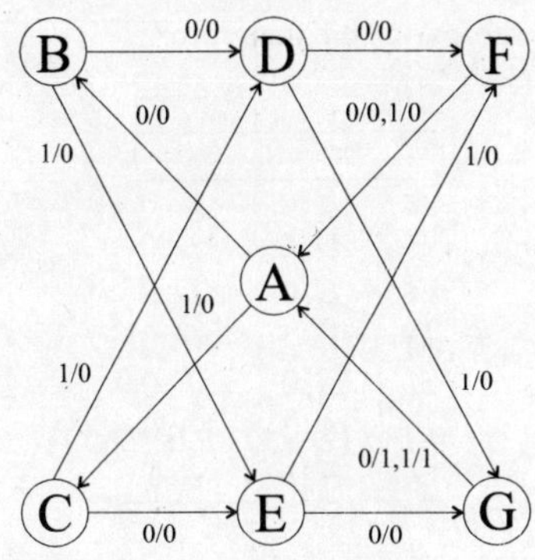

Figure 12.19. State diagram for the parity bit generator in Example 12.10.

Table 12.4. Example of input and output sequences of a parity-bit generator.

Input	0001	0000	0110	0100	1010	1011
Output	0000	0000	0000	0001	0000	0000

	0				1			
	P_1	P_2	P_3	P_4	P_1	P_2	P_3	P_4
q_1	q_1,0	q_1,0	q_1,0	-,0	q_2,0	q_2,0	q_2,0	-,0
q_2	q_1,0	q_2,0	q_2,0	-,1	q_2,0	q_1,0	q_1,0	-,1

Figure 12.20. State table for the serial decomposition of the initial machine in Example 12.10.

by an analogy to the group operation table, since states of the initial machine are dependent on the states of master and slave machines.

It remains to determine the state function and output function of the slave machine. For instance, we calculate $f((q_1, p_1), 0)$ *and* $g((q_1, p_1), 0)$.

From Table 12.7 $(p_1, q_1 \rightarrow A$, *and from Table 12.6,* $f^A(A, 0) \rightarrow B$, *and* $g^A(A, 0) \rightarrow 0$. *Since,* B *is obtained from* (p_2, q_1), *it follows* $f((q_1, p_1), 0) = q_1$, *and* $g((q_1, p_1), 0) = 0$.

In a similar way, the complete state table is determined as shown in Fig. 12.20. Fig. 12.21 illustrates this procedure.

Table 12.5. State table for the parity bit generator.

	$x = 0$	$x = 1$
A	$B, 0$	$C, 0$
B	$D, 0$	$E, 0$
C	$E, 0$	$D, 0$
D	$F, 0$	$G, 0$
E	$G, 0$	$F, 0$
F	$A, 0$	$A, 0$
G	$A, 1$	$A, 1$

Table 12.6. State table of the factor machine in Example 12.10.

		$x = 0$	$x = 1$
(A)	P_1	P_2, P_2	P_2, P_2
(B, C)	P_2	P_3, P_3	P_3, P_3
(D, E)	P_3	P_4, P_4	P_4, P_4
(F, G)	P_4	P_1, P_1	P_1, P_1

Table 12.7. Encoding of states in the initial machine in Example 12.10.

	q_1	q_2
P_1	A	A
P_2	B	C
P_3	D	E
P_4	F	G

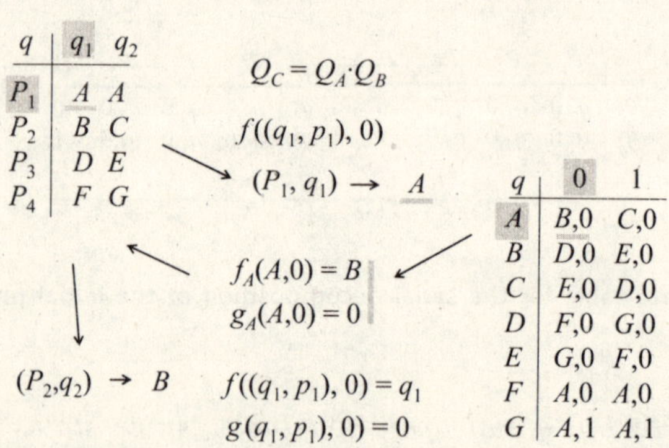

Figure 12.21. Determination of the state table for the serial decomposition of the initial machine in Example 12.10.

7.2 Parallel Decomposition of Sequential Machines

In this section, we discuss parallel decomposition of sequential machines.

$$M_1 = (\Sigma_1, Q_1, Z_1, f_1, g_1)$$

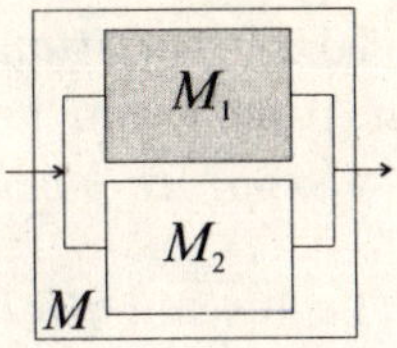

$$M_2 = (\Sigma_2, Q_2, Z_2, f_2, g_2)$$

$$M = M_1 \cdot M_2 = (\Sigma_1 \times \Sigma_2, Q_1 \times Q_2, Z_1 \times Z_2, f, g)$$

$$f((q_1, q_2), (x_1 x_2)) = (f_1(q_1, x_1), f_2(q_2, x_2))$$

$$g((q_1, q_2), (x_1, x_2)) = (g_1(q_1, x_1), g_2(q_2, x_2))$$

Figure 12.22. Parallel decomposition of sequential machines.

DEFINITION 12.13 *(Parallel connection of sequential machines)*
A parallel connection of two sequential machines $M_1 = (\Sigma_1, Q_1, Z_1, f_1, g_1)$ *and* $M_2 = (\Sigma_2, Q_2, Z_2, f_2, g_2)$ *is a sequential machine* $M = M_1|M_2 = (\Sigma_1 \times \Sigma_2, Q_1 \times Q_2, Z_1 \times Z_2, f, g)$*, where the state function* f *and the output function* g *are*

$$\begin{aligned} f((q_1, q_2), (x_1, x_2)) &= (f_1(q_1, x_1), f_2(q_2, x_2)), \\ g((q_1, q_2), (x_1, x_2)) &= (g_1(q_1, x_1), g_2(q_2, x_2)). \end{aligned}$$

DEFINITION 12.14 *(Parallel decomposition of sequential machines)*
A sequential machine $M_1|M_2$ *is a parallel decomposition of a sequential machine* M*, iff* $M_1|M_2$ *realizes* M*. The decomposition is non-trivial iff the total number of states in* M_1 *and* M_2 *is smaller than the number of states in* M*.*

Fig. 12.22 shows the basic principle of parallel decomposition of sequential machines. In the case of parallel decomposition, the submachines M_1 and M_2 have equal role and may be both considered as master sequential machines. Therefore, the parallel decomposition requires existence of two SP-partitions.

To formulate necessary and sufficient conditions for existence of a non-trivial parallel decomposition of a sequential machine, the following notions are needed.

DEFINITION 12.15 *(Product of partitions)*
The product $P_1 \cdot P_2$ *of two partitions* P_1 *and* P_2 *of a set* Q*, is a partition derived as the intersections of blocks of the partition* P_1 *with blocks of the partition* P_2*.*

EXAMPLE 12.11 *Consider two partitions* $P_1 = \{\{1, 2\}, \{3, 4, 5, 6, 7, 8\}\}$*, and* $P_2 = \{\{1, 2, 3, 4\}, \{5, 6, 7, \}\}$*, then* $P_1 \cdot P_2 = \{\{1, 2\}, \{3, 4\}, \{5, 6, 7\}\}$*.*

DEFINITION 12.16 (*0-partition*)
For a set Q, the 0-partition (zero-partition) is a partition where each element of Q is a separate block.

STATEMENT 12.1 *A sequential machine M has non-trivial parallel decomposition iff there exist two non-trivial SP-partitions P_1 and P_2 for M such that $P_1 \cdot P_2 = 0$.*

The following example illustrates determination of a parallel decomposition of a sequential machine.

EXAMPLE 12.12 *Consider a sequential machine described by the state table in Table 12.8. There are two non-trivial SP-partitions*

$$
\begin{aligned}
P_1 &= \{\{1,2,3\},\{4,5,6\}\} = \{A,B\} = \{B_{P_1}\}, \\
P_2 &= \{\{1,6\},\{2,5\},\{3,4\}\} = \{C,D,E\} = \{B_{P_2}\}
\end{aligned}
$$

where B_{P_1} and B_{P_2} denote blocks of these partitions.

We associate the machines M_{P_1} and M_{P_2} to these partitions, which are defined by the state tables Table 12.9 and 12.10. These tables are determined by the inspection of the state table for the initial machine. For instance, for M_1, the state $A = \{1,2,3\}$ and from Table 12.8 the corresponding next states for the input 0 are 4, 5, and 6, which belong to the block B. Therefore, the nest state for A under the input 0 is B.

The outputs in these tables are determined by the definition of parallel decomposition, i.e., providing that for the state q, the output $g(q) = g_1(B_{P_1}) \cdot g_2(B_{P_2})$. For instance, the output from the state 3 is determined by the requirement that $g(3) = g_1(B_{P_1}) \cdot g_2(B_{P_2}(3))$, where $B_{P_1}(3)$ is the block of P_1 containing the state 3, and similar for $B_{P_2}(3)$. Therefore, $g(3) = g_1(A) \cdot g_2(E) = 1 \cdot 1 = 1$.

The output from the state 4 is determined in the same way as $g(4) = g_1(B_{P_1}(4)) \cdot g_2(B_{P_2}(4)) = g_1(B) \cdot g_2(E) = 0 \cdot 1 = 0$.

It should be pointed out that although the presented algebraic structure theory of decomposition provides solutions, it is in practice hard to apply, since requires considerable calculations, except in trivial cases. Therefore, in practice, often heuristic methods based on some a priori knowledge about functioning and peculiar features of the sequential machine that should be realized may exhibit. For instance, the master sequential machine in the parity bit generator is an autonomous system, i.e., does not depend on the input signals, and actually this is a binary counter with four states. Existence of such a counter within the system considered is quite natural, since it can be decomposed into four cycles.

Table 12.8. State table for the sequential machine in Example 12.12.

q	0	1	Z
1	4	3	0
2	6	3	0
3	5	2	1
4	2	5	0
5	1	4	0
6	3	4	0

Table 12.9. State tables of the component sequential machines M_1 in Example 12.12.

q	0	1	Z
A	B	A	1
B	A	B	0

Table 12.10. State table of the component sequential machine M_2 in Example 12.12.

q	0	1	Z
C	E	E	0
D	C	E	0
E	D	D	1

In the first three cycles the values of input bits are checked, and during the fourth cycle, the value of the output bit is calculated.

In practice, often algebraic structure theory methods are combined with various heuristic methods to achieve efficiency and implemented in different programming systems for decomposition of sequential machines, see, for example, [6], [7], [8], [50], [120], [131], [132], [165]. Some methods are related to targeted technologies [137], [138], [204], or low-power consumption [72], [117], [118].

In [9], it is proposed a method for decomposition of sequential machines by exploiting similar disjoint subgraphs in a state diagram. The method is reported as the factorization of state diagrams, and the exact factorization assumes search for subdiagrams with the identical nodes, edges, and transitions. Such subgraphs are realized as a slave machine that is invoked by a master machine. This provides reduced complexity, since some states and transitions are shared. Some generalizations to exploit non-identical subdiagrams providing required corrections are also discussed [9]. In [98], it is discussed a method for realization of sequential machines that exploits both decomposition of and the so-called wave steering, i.e., by allowing several signal waves to coexist in a circuit.

8. Exercises and Problems

EXERCISE 12.1 *Show that each Mealy sequential machine can be converted into a Moore sequential machine and vice versa. Provide an example.*

EXERCISE 12.2 *Determine the state transition graph for the sequential machine which recognizes the set S of binary sequences consisting of n zero values followed by m values equal to 1, i.e., $S = \{0^n1^m\}$, where $n \geq 1$, and $m \geq 0$.*

EXERCISE 12.3 *Table 12.11 shows the state transition table of a sequential machine. Show that there exist few serial decompositions of this sequential machine.*

Table 12.11. State-transition table for the sequential machine in Exercise 12.3.

q, x	0	1
1	3,1	1,0
2	3,1	1,0
3	2,0	1,1
4	1,0	3,0
5	6,1	4,0
6	5,0	4,1

Table 12.12. State-transition table for the sequential machine in Exercise 12.4.

q, x	α	β	γ	δ	z
1	1	5	7	4	0
2	2	6	8	3	1
3	1	7	5	2	0
4	2	8	6	1	1
5	2	1	2	8	0
6	2	2	1	7	0
7	1	3	4	6	0
8	1	4	3	5	0

EXERCISE 12.4 *Check if is possible to preform parallel decomposition of the sequential machine specified by the state-transition table in Table 12.12.*

EXERCISE 12.5 *Determine the state table for a Mealy sequential machine specified by the state diagram in Fig. 12.23.*

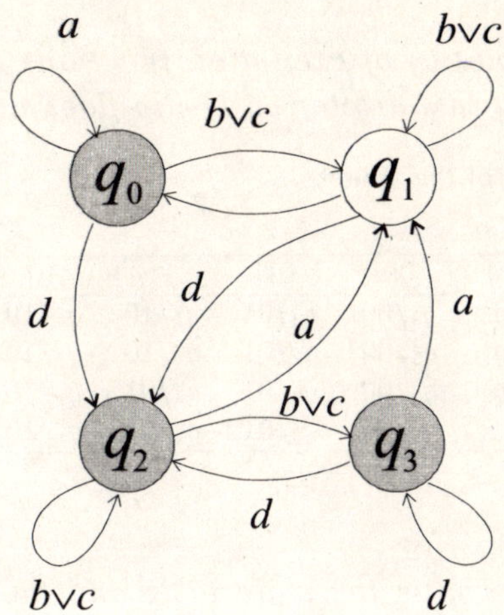

Figure 12.23. State diagram for the sequential machine in Exercise 12.5.

EXERCISE 12.6 *Determine the state diagram of a Mealy sequential machine which controls the entrance of a garage with four parking places. The garage accepts both trucks and cars, but a truck occupies two parking places. The machine should generate the outputs corresponding to the combinations*

1 *Free entrance for both cars and trucks,*

2 *Free entrance for cars,*

3 *No free places.*

EXERCISE 12.7 *Table 12.13 shows the state transition table of an arbiter, which is a device controlling the use of a facility required by two users. The user x_i requires the facility by setting the input bit x_i to* 1, *and release it by returning the input to* 0. *It is assumed that if both users require the facility simultaneously, it will be granted to the user which did not use it last. When granted, the facility cannot be taken from a user before it releases the facility converting the input from* 1 *to* 0. *The following encoding of states is assumed in this table*

1 q_0 - *the initial state,*

2 q_1 - *the user x_1 requires the facility,*

3 q_2 - the user x_2 requires the facility,

4 q_3 - the user released the facility, but there is no request from the other user.

Compare the complexity of excitation functions and output functions for the realizations of this arbiter by D-flip-flops and JK-flip-flops.

Table 12.13. State table of the arbiter.

q	00	01	11	10
q_0	$q_0/00$	$q_2/01$	$q_1/10$	$q_1/10$
q_1	$q_3/00$	$q_2/01$	$q_1/10$	$q_1/10$
q_2	$q_0/00$	$q_2/01$	$q_2/01$	$q_1/10$
q_3	$q_3/00$	$q_2/01$	$q_2/01$	$q_1/10$

EXERCISE 12.8 *Determine the state table and the state diagram for a sequential machine at which input an arbitrary sequence of letters a, b, c, and d can occur. Machine produces the output* 1 *when the sequence contains the string aba.*

EXERCISE 12.9 *The input in a sequential machine is a binary sequence. The machine recognizes successive appearance of two or more* 1 *values. The output is specified as follows*

1 even, when the number of 1 *is even,*

2 odd, when the number of 1 *is odd,*

3 0, *otherwise.*

Show that the machine can be realized with four states. Determine the state table and state diagram for this machine.

EXERCISE 12.10 *A vending machine sales candies at the price of 70 cents. The machine accepts coins of 10, 20, and 50 cents. When the amount of inserted coins is equal or greater than 70 cents, the candy is offered and change, if any, returned. Then, machine waits for another customer.*

Determine the state table and draw the corresponding state table for this vending machine.

Chapter 13

REALIZATIONS OF SEQUENTIAL NETWORKS

Sequential machines are realized by sequential logic networks, that can be constructed in different ways. As pointed out in [96], sequential networks may be classified with respect to the construction or their functional features. Fig. 13.1 shows a classification of sequential networks with respect to these criteria.

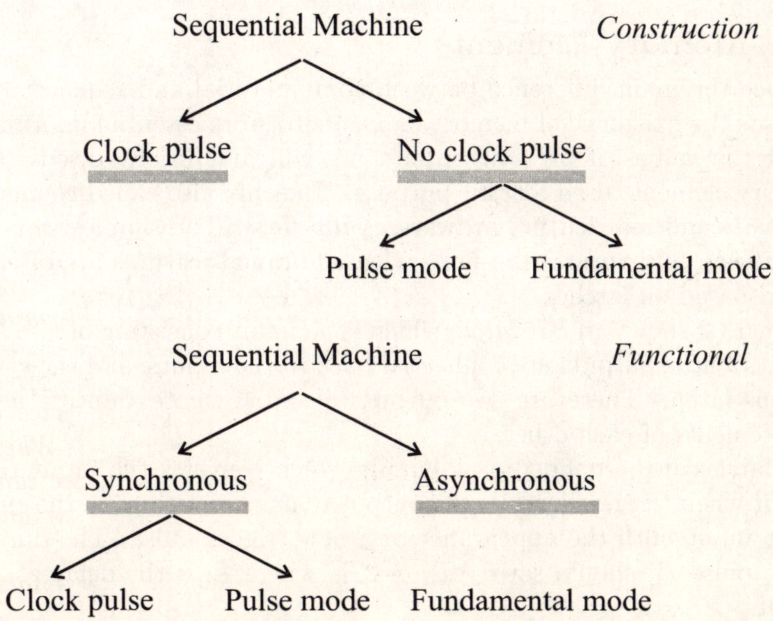

Figure 13.1. Classification of sequential networks.

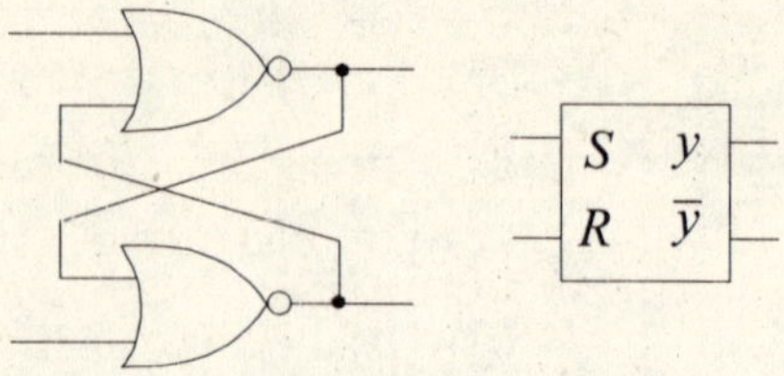

Figure 13.2. SR-latch.

If the transitions in sequential networks are synchronized by clock pulses, they are called *clocked networks.* Sequential machines may also work without such external synchronization. In the latter case, sequential machines may be realized as networks working in the *pulse mode* or the *fundamental mode.*

From the functional point of view, both clocked and pulse mode networks are *synchronous* sequential networks. The fundamental mode networks are *asynchronous* networks.

1. Memory Elements

Since the main difference between combinatorial and sequential networks is the existence of memory elements to store essential information about the values of previous inputs, we will first briefly discuss basic memory elements used for this purpose. They are also called *elementary automata* and realized in hardware as *flip-flops.* The simplest flip-flops are *latches*, and various flip-flops with additional features are often designed based on latches.

Fig. 13.2 shows an SR-*latch*, which is a circuit consisting of two NOR circuits whose outputs are connected back to the inputs, and the symbol for this latch. There are two outputs y and $\overline{y}$ whose values are logic complements of each other.

A latch can be defined as a circuit which converts the input to the output when triggered, while the output remains invariant to the change of the input until the appearance of a new trigger pulse. The duration of the pulse T_w should satisfy $T_w > 2T_0$, where T_0 is the delay of NOR circuits.

Recall that a two-input NOR circuit works as an inverter when an input is set to the logic value 0. Since the output of a NOR circuit with inputs x_1 and x_2 is $y = \overline{(x_1 + x_2)} = \overline{x}_1\overline{x}_2$, if for instance, $x_1 = 0$, then $y = \overline{0 + x_2} = \overline{0} \cdot \overline{y} = 1 \cdot \overline{y} = \overline{y}$.

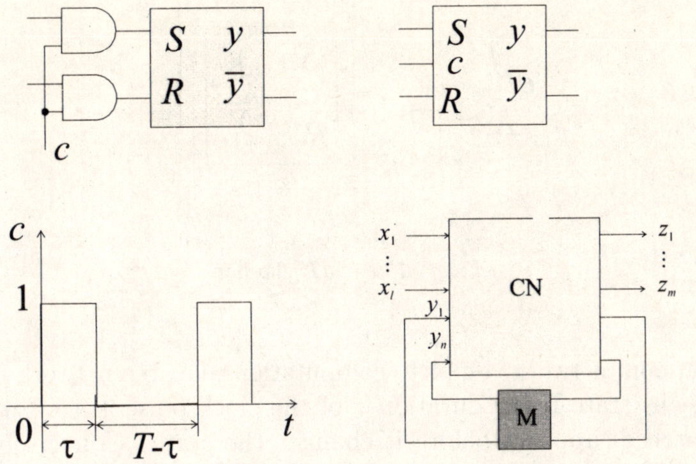

Figure 13.3. Clocked SR-latch and its application as the memory element in a sequential network.

Since the output of an SR-latch can be described as $y(n+1) = \overline{\overline{R}(n)\overline{S}(n)\overline{y}(n)}$, when $R = S = 0$, we have $y(n+1) = \overline{1 \cdot 1 \cdot \overline{y}(n)} = y(n)$. Thus, for $R = S = 0$, the SR-latch keeps the present state.

Similarly, when $R = 1$ and $S = 0$, we have $y(n+1) = \overline{\overline{R}(n)\overline{\overline{S}}(n)\overline{y}(n)} = \overline{0 \cdot 1 \cdot \overline{y}(n)} = 0$, which causes that the output is $y(n+1) = 0$ whence the other output $\overline{y}(n+1) = 1$ Thus, the lower input in the upper NOR circuit has the value 1, while the upper input of the same circuit is $S = 0$, resulting that the output y keeps the value 0.

The combination $R = 0$, $S = 1$ has the opposite effect, the output takes the value 1 and keeps it.

The combination $R = S = 1$ is forbidden, since causes both outputs to take the value 0, which is a well defined state, except that outputs are not complements of each other. If after using $R = S = 1$ the inputs change to $R = S = 0$, the circuit keeps the former state with outputs that are complements of each other. Therefore, it is unpredictable which output will be complemented.

When sequential networks are to be clocked, it is convenient to use latches that are controlled by clocks. Fig. 13.3 shows a clocked SR-latch and its symbol. It changes the state when the clock pulse $c = 1$.

There are some restrictions that should be appreciated when using clocked SR-latches as memory elements in sequential networks. In particular, when $c = 0$, the output is determined by the input in the combinatorial part that calculates the next state $q(n+1)$. If the interval $T - \tau$ between two clock pulses is short, the state changes before the

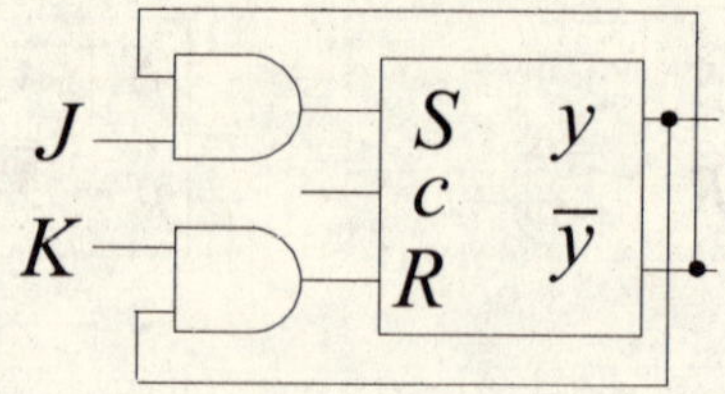

Figure 13.4. JK-flip-flop.

combinational network complete computations, i.e., the network goes into an erroneous state. If the duration τ of the clock pulse is short, the input in the latch disappears before it changes the state. Conversely, if τ is long, the latch will change the state twice during the same clock pulse.

The clocked SR-latch is also called SR-flip-flop. There are many variants of flip-flops with different additional functions. For instance, in some applications it is inconvenient that the output of the SR-flip-flop is undefined for $R = S = 1$, and flip-flops with outputs defined for any combination of the inputs may be preferred. For this reason, the JK-flip-flops have been introduced by adding two AND circuits to the inputs of an SR-flip-flop as shown in Fig. 13.4. The difference to the SR-flip-flop is that the output, i.e., next state, is defined for $J = K = 1$ as the logic complement of the present state.

Notice that the circuit in Fig. 13.4 oscillates if the clock pulse and $J = K = 1$ stands for long, and it is necessary to provide a short clock pulse or a signal source that generates a short signal 1. For that reason, in practice more sophisticated implementations of flip-flops the so-called *raceless flip-flops* are used. They can be implemented as *master-slave* (MS) flip-flops or *edge-triggered* flip-flops.

The behavior of MS-flip-flops is controlled by the leading and trailing edges of a clock pulse. The leading edge isolates the slave from the master and reads in the input information to the master. The trailing edge isolates the J and K inputs from the master and then transfers the information to the salve.

Master-slave flip-flops can be viewed as flip-flops triggered by both leading and trailing edges of clock pulses. In edge-triggered flip-flops, either the leading or the trailing edge, but not both, causes the flip-flop to respond to an input and then immediately disconnect the input from the flip-flop by the feedback of some gate output to its input gates. The behavior of edge-triggered flip-flops is more reliable than the behavior of networks using master-salve flip-flops, since inputs do not influence edge-triggered flip-flops after the flip-flop accepts its new input value

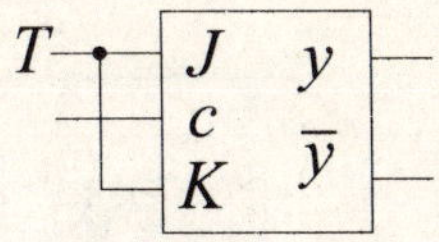

Figure 13.5. T-flip-flop.

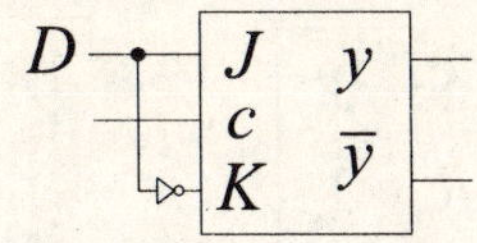

Figure 13.6. D-flip-flop.

at the edge of a clock pulse. The inputs remain disconnected from the flip-flops until the edge of the next clock pulse.

For applications at the logical level it is important to notice that the relationships between the combinations of values at the J,K inputs and the outputs of a master-slave JK-flip-flop are identical to that in the JK-flip-flop, which is also called a JK-latch.

The so-called *taggle flip-flop*, or *trigger flip-flop*, in short T-flip-flop, is a modification derived by connecting the J and K inputs into a single input T as shown in Fig. 13.5.

D-flip-flop is another modification as shown in Fig. 13.6 and is also called D-latch, polarity-hold latch, transparent latch, and Earle latch. The value at the input during a clock pulse, completely determines the output until the next clock pulse, i.e., $Y(k+1) = D(k)$, where Y is the next state and D the input in the D-flip-flop. For example, if $D=1$, the next state of the D-flip-flop will be $Y=1$ when the clock pulse appears, regardless the value for Y before the clock pulse.

There are some restrictions that have to be appreciated in application of flip-flops as memory elements in sequential machines. To point out them, denote by

1 T_p - minimum time for propagation of an input signal to the output of a flip-flop.

2 τ - duration of a clock pulse.

3 T_0 - minimum time for propagation of an input signal to the output of a sequential machine.

Then, the following condition must be satisfied

$$2T_p > \tau > max(T_p, T_0).$$

The first part in this inequality, $2T > \tau$ ensures a single transition per clock pulse. The other requirement is related to the construction sequential networks and takes into account the delay of circuits in feedback connections.

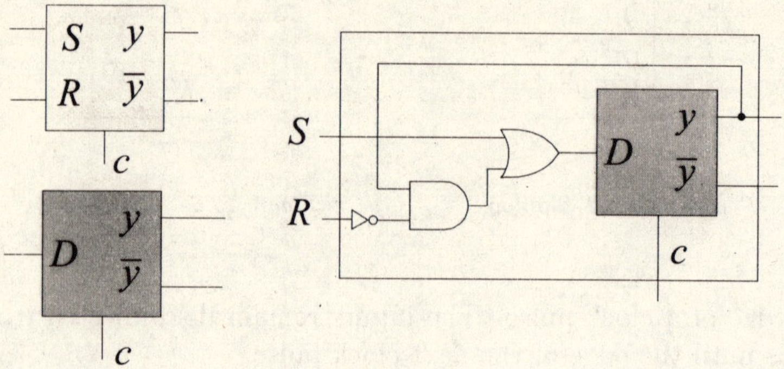

Figure 13.7. Realization of a SR-flip-flop with a D-flip-flop.

Another important feature is that a flip-flop can be realized by other flip-flops.

EXAMPLE 13.1 *Fig. 13.7 shows realization of the SR-flip-flop with a D-flip-flop.*

Flip-flops can be viewed as elementary sequential machines, and therefore, may be described by state tables. Fig. 13.8 shows state tables and output functions for the flip-flops considered above. The state tables are written as Karnaugh maps, and the output functions are derived in the minimum form by joining the corresponding minterms where possible. However, for practical applications, it is convenient to rewrite these state tables into *application tables* of flip-flops, where the present state y and the next state Y are selected as arguments in functions determining the inputs of flip-flops. For example, in the state table for the SR-flip-flop, if the present state $y = 0$ and the next state $Y = 0$, the inputs can be 00 as in the second column, and 01 in third column. Therefore, for $yY = 00$, the inputs $SR = 0-$, where bar means unspecified value, which can be either 0 or 1. In the same way, we determine other rows in the application tables of flip-flops. Fig. 13.9 shows application tables of the flip-flops considered.

2. Synthesis of Sequential Networks

The synthesis of sequential networks can be performed by the following general algorithm.

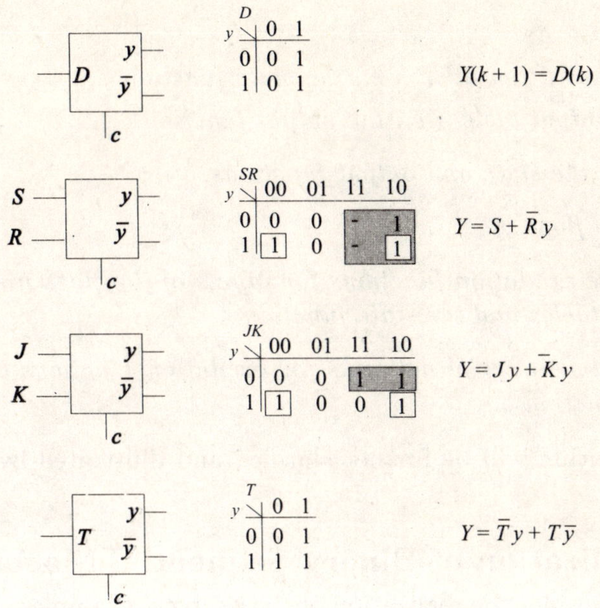

Figure 13.8. State tables and output functions of D, SR, JK and T-flip-flop.

$y \backslash D$	0	1
0	0	1
1	0	1

$Y(k+1) = D(k)$

yY	D
00	0
01	1
10	0
11	1

$y \backslash SR$	00	01	11	10
0	0	0	-	1
1	1	0	-	1

$Y = S + \overline{R}\,y$

yY	SR
00	0-
01	10
10	01
11	-0

$y \backslash JK$	00	01	11	10
0	0	0	1	1
1	1	0	0	1

$Y = J\,y + \overline{K}\,y$

yY	JK
00	0-
01	1-
10	-1
11	-0

$y \backslash T$	0	1
0	0	1
1	1	0

$Y = \overline{T}\,y + T\,\overline{y}$

yY	T
00	0
01	1
10	1
11	0

Figure 13.9. Application tables of D, SR, JK and T-flip-flop.

ALGORITHM 13.1 *(Synthesis of sequential networks)*

1 *Derive the state table from the functional description of the sequential machine.*

2 *Simplify the state table whenever possible.*

3 *Add codes to the states.*

4 Derive

(a) The transition table, i.e., the state function f,

(b) The output table, i.e., the output function g.

5 Minimize the state and output functions.

6 Select flip-flops.

7 Derive the excitation functions for inputs of flip-flops from their application tables and the state function f.

8 Realize combinatorial networks for excitation functions and and the output function g.

This algorithm will be further clarified and illustrated by the examples.

3. Realization of Binary Sequential Machines

We first consider the realization of the simplest examples, i.e., realization of binary sequential machines where the input symbols, states and output symbols are binary numbers, by D-flip-flops. Therefore, there is no need for encoding. Binary counters and shift registers are classical examples of binary sequential machines.

EXAMPLE 13.2 *(Shift register)*
Realize a three-bit register executing shift to the right with a serial input and output by using D-flip-flops.

This sequential machine has a single input x which can take values in $\{0,1\}$, and 8 states $(y_1y_2y_3)$, $y_i \in \{0,1\}$. The output $(Y_1Y_2Y_3)$ is equal to the present state, therefore, symbolically, $Y_i = f(x, y_1, y_2, y_3)$. Fig. 13.10 shows the corresponding state table, from where

$$
\begin{aligned}
Y_1 &= [0000000011111111]^T, \\
Y_2 &= [0000111100001111]^T, \\
Y_3 &= [0011001100110011]^T.
\end{aligned}
$$

Therefore, $Y_1 = x$, $Y_2 = y_1$, and $Y_3 = y_2$. From the state function of D-flip-flop, it follows $D_1 = x$, $D_2 = y_1$, and $D_3 = y_2$. Fig. 13.11 shows the corresponding network, where the outputs y_1, y_2, y_3 for different combinations of values 0 and 1 represent 8 possible states of the shift to the right register.

EXAMPLE 13.3 *(Binary counter)*
A binary counter is a circuit that starts from 0 and counts until $2^n - 1$,

$y_1y_2y_3 \backslash \sigma$	0	1
000	000	100
001	000	100
010	001	101
011	001	101
100	010	110
101	010	110
110	011	111
111	011	111
	$Y_1Y_2Y_3$	

Figure 13.10. State table of the three-bit shift to the right register.

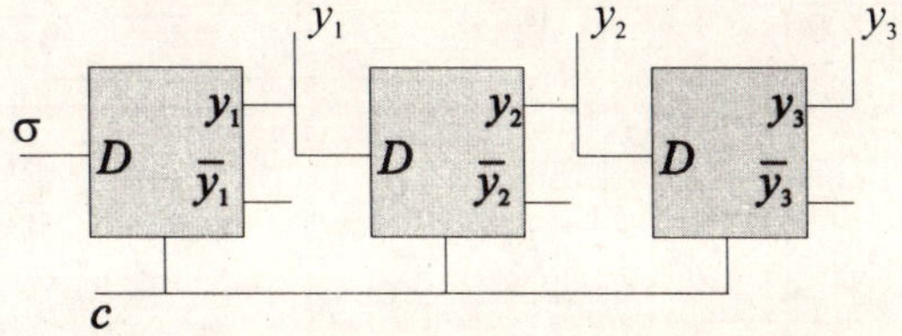

Figure 13.11. Realization of the three-bit shift to the right register.

when returns to 0. For example, if $n = 3$, the counter runs through binary encoded numbers 0 to 7, and therefore, when viewed as a sequential machine, has 8 states. The output is equal to the state. Fig. 13.12 shows the state table of a three-bit binary counter. There are three state functions Y_1, Y_2, and Y_3, which from the state table are determined as

$$\begin{aligned} Y_1 &= [00011110]^T, \\ Y_2 &= [01100110]^T, \\ Y_3 &= [10101010]^T. \end{aligned}$$

When minimized these functions are

$$\begin{aligned} Y_1 &= y_1\overline{y}_2 + y_1\overline{y}_3 + \overline{y}_1y_2y_3, \\ Y_2 &= \overline{y}_2y_3 + y_2\overline{y}_3, \\ Y_3 &= \overline{y}_3. \end{aligned}$$

Three D-flip-flops are needed to realize these state functions and since $Y(k+1) = D(k)$, the excitation functions for inputs of D-flip-flops are $D_1 = Y_1$, $D_2 = Y_2$, and $D_3 = Y_3$. Fig. 13.13 shows the corresponding sequential network.

$y_1y_2y_3$ \ σ	1
000	001
001	010
010	011
011	100
100	101
101	110
110	111
111	000
	$Y_1Y_2Y_3$

Figure 13.12. State table for the three-bit binary counter.

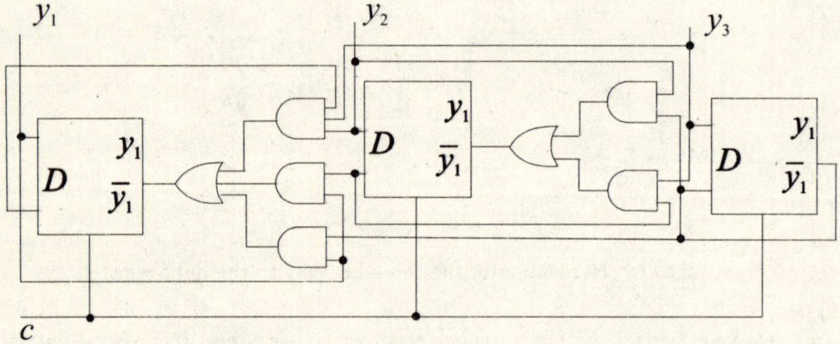

Figure 13.13. Realization of the three-bit binary counter by D-flip-flops.

4. Realization of Synchronous Sequential Machines

Fig. 13.14 shows the model of a sequential network that can realize an arbitrary synchronous sequential machine by using clocked flip-flops.

The synthesis of such sequential networks can be performed by the Algorithm 13.1 as will be illustrated by the following example.

EXAMPLE 13.4 *Consider realization of the binary adder in Example 12.2 by clocked JK-flip-flops.*

When considered as the Mealy sequential machine, the state table of the binary adder is given in Fig. 12.4. Since there are just two states, a single JK-flip-flop is sufficient. The states q_0 and q_1 should be encoded by binary symbols, which in this case, can be done by just keeping their indices. In this way, the encoded state table in Fig. 13.15 is derived. For convenience in minimization, the output is shown separately. This

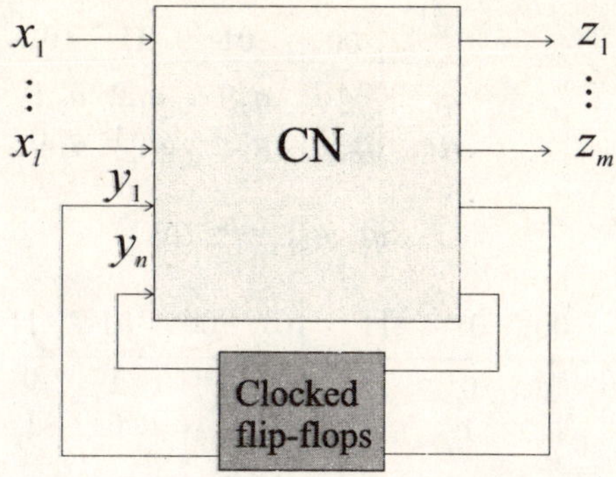

Figure 13.14. Model of a synchronous sequential machine with clocked flip-flops.

table is converted into an excitation table *for the J and K inputs of the JK-flip-flop. This table shown in Fig. 13.16 is derived by the following considerations. In the encoded state table, for the input* $x_1x_2 = 00$*, the present and the next states are* $yY = 00$*, and from the application table for the JK-flip-flop in Fig. 13.9, the corresponding values for the J and K inputs are* $0-$*. Therefore, in the excitation table the first element in the column for the input 00 is* $0-$*. The same inputs are determined for the input signals* $x_1x_2 = 01$*. However, for* $x_1x_2 = 11$*, the present state is* $y = 0$ *and the next state is* $Y = 1$*, and from the application table of the JK-flip-flop, the inputs* $JK = 1-$*. Therefore, in the column for the input 11, the corresponding JK inputs are* $1-$*. In the same way, the complete excitation table is determined. Fig. 13.17 shows that the excitation functions J and K, and the output function Z can be determined by considering this table and the table specifying the output as Karnaugh maps with variables* x_1x_2 *for inputs and y for the present state. In this way,*

$$\begin{aligned} J &= x_1x_2, \\ K &= \overline{x}_{12}\overline{x}_2, \\ Z &= x_1x_2y + x_1\overline{x}_2\overline{y} + \overline{x}_1x_2\overline{y} + \overline{x}_1\overline{x}_2y. \end{aligned}$$

Fig. 13.18 shows the corresponding sequential network where the combinatorial part is realized as a PLA.

If considered as a Moore sequential machine, the binary adder is described by the state table in Fig. 12.5. Since there are four states, two JK flip-flops are required. Again, if we keep just indices of states q_{00}*,* q_{01}*,* q_{10} *and* q_{11}*, the encoded state table in Fig. 13.19 is derived. In the same figure, it is shown also the excitation table derived by using the application table for JK-flip-flops as explained above. In this case, for*

$y \backslash x_1x_2$	00	01	11	10
q_0	q_0,0	q_0,1	q_1,0	q_0,1
q_1	q_0,1	q_1,0	q_1,1	q_1,0

$\{q_0, q_1\} \longrightarrow \{0,1\}$

$y \backslash x_1x_2$	00	01	11	10	00	01	11	10
0	0	0	1	0	0	1	0	1
1	0	1	1	1	1	0	1	0

Figure 13.15. Encoded state table for the binary adder.

each input x_1x_2, a pair of values for J_1K_1 and J_2K_2 is shown. These pairs are determined for the first and the second bits in the binary code for the present and the next states for the corresponding inputs. For example, consider the present state $q_1q_2 = 00$ for the input $x_1x_2 = 01$. Then, from the encoded state table, the next states are $Y_1Y_2 = 01$. For the first pair $q_1Y_1 = 00$, from the application table for the JK-flip-flops, the inputs $J_1K_1 = 0-$. For the second pair $q_2Y_2 = 01$, and the same input $x_1x_2 = 01$, the inputs $J_2K_2 = 1-$. Therefore, in the excitation table, for the input $x_1x_2 = 01$ the pair $0-, 1-$ is written. In the same way, the complete excitation table is determined. Fig. 13.20 shows the separated tables for each input, which when considered as the Karnaugh maps with variables x_1x_2 for inputs and y_1y_2 for the present states, yield the following functions excitation functions

$$
\begin{aligned}
J_1 &= x_1x_2, \\
K_1 &= \overline{x}_1\overline{x}_2, \\
J_2 &= \overline{x}_1\overline{x}_2y_1 + \overline{x}_1x_2\overline{y}_1 + x_1x_2y_1 + x_1\overline{x}_2\overline{y}_1, \\
K_2 &= \overline{x}_1\overline{x}_2\overline{y}_1 + \overline{x}_1x_2y_1 + x_1x_2\overline{y}_1 + x_1\overline{x}_2y_1.
\end{aligned}
$$

The output function is determined from Fig. 13.19 as $Z = \overline{y}_1y_2 + y_1\overline{y}_2$.

Fig. 13.21 shows the corresponding sequential network. Notice that a different and simpler realization will be produced for the encoding of states as q_{00}, q_{01}, q_{10}, q_{11} as 00, 01, 11, and 10, respectively.

A problem which should be taken into account when working with sequential network is caused by the delay in propagation of clock pulses to all the flip-flops in the network. The discrepancies between arrival

yY	JK
00	0,-
01	1,-
10	-,1
11	-,0

$y \backslash x_1x_2$	00	01	11	10
0	0	0	1	0
1	0	1	1	1

$y \backslash x_1x_2$	00	01	11	10
0	0,-	0,-	1,-	0,-
1	-,1	-,0	-,0	-,0

JK

Figure 13.16. Excitation table for the binary adder with JK-flip-flop.

$y \backslash x_1x_2$	00	01	11	10
0	0	0	1	0
1	-	-	-	-

$J = x_1x_2$

$y \backslash x_1x_2$	00	01	11	10
0	-	-	-	-
1	1	0	0	0

$K = \overline{x}_1\overline{x}_2$

$y \backslash x_1x_2$	00	01	11	10
0	0	1	0	1
1	1	0	1	0

$$Z = \overline{x}_1\overline{x}_2y + \overline{x}_1x_2\overline{y} + x_1x_2y + x_1\overline{x}_2\overline{y}$$

Figure 13.17. Excitation functions for the binary adder with JK-flip-flop.

of the corresponding edges to flip-flops are called *clock pulse skew* or in short skew. There are methods to design synchronous sequential machines taking the skew into account [196].

5. Pulse Mode Sequential Networks

A sequential network working in *pulse mode* is a synchronous, but unclocked sequential network.

DEFINITION 13.1 *(Pulse mode sequential networks)*
A sequential network works in pulse mode if the following requirements are satisfied

1. *Input signals are pulses of the duration τ sufficient to allow the state change of all flip-flops in the network.*
2. *Pulses are applied just to a single input.*

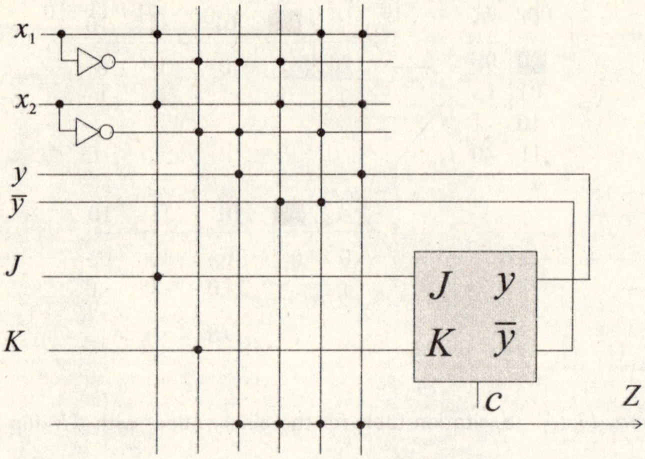

Figure 13.18. Realization of the binary adder as the Mealy sequential machine with JK-flip-flop.

yY	JK
00	0,-
01	1,-
10	-,1
11	-,0

q_1q_2 \ x_1,x_2		01	11	10	Z
00	00	01	10	01	0
01	00	01	10	01	1
10	01	10	11	10	0
11	01	10	11	10	1

q_1q_2 \ x_1,x_2		01	11	10	Z
00	0-,0-	0-,1-	1-,0-	0-,1-	0
01	0-,-1	0-,-0	1-,-1	0-,-0	1
10	-1,1-	-0,0-	-0,1-	-0,0-	0
11	-1,-0	-0,-1	-0,-0	-0,-1	1

J_1K_1, J_2K_2

Figure 13.19. Encoded state table and the excitation table for the binary adder considered as the Moore sequential machine.

3 *States change in response to the appearance of a pulse at an input, and each pulse causes just a single state change. In practice, this requirement is provided by using pulses of small width so that they are no longer present after the memory elements changed their states.*

Therefore, in a pulse mode sequential network, appearance of a pulse at any of the inputs causes a state change. Since simultaneous pulses are

q_1q_2 \ x_1,x_2	00	01	11	10
00	0	0	1	0
01	0	0	1	0
10	-	-	-	-
11	-	-	-	-

$J_1 = x_1x_2$

q_1q_2 \ x_1,x_2	00	01	11	10
00	-	-	-	-
01	-	-	-	-
10	1	0	0	0
11	1	0	0	0

$K_1 = \bar{x}_1\bar{x}_2$

q_1q_2 \ x_1,x_2	00	01	11	10
00	0	1	0	1
01	-	-	-	-
10	-	-	-	-
11	1	0	1	0

$J_2 = \bar{x}_1\bar{x}_2y_1 + \bar{x}_1x_2\bar{y}_1 + x_1x_2y_1 + x_1\bar{x}_2\bar{y}_1$

q_1q_2 \ x_1,x_2	00	01	11	10
00	-	-	-	-
01	1	0	1	0
10	0	1	0	1
11	-	-	-	-

$K_2 = \bar{x}_1\bar{x}_2\bar{y}_1 + \bar{x}_1x_2y_1 + x_1x_2\bar{y}_1 + x_1\bar{x}_2y_1$

Figure 13.20. Excitation functions for the binary adder considered as the Moore machine.

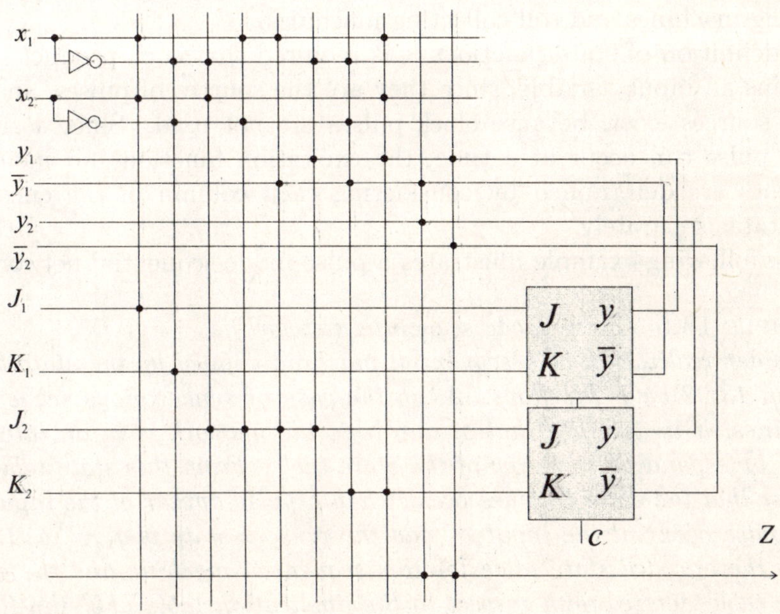

Figure 13.21. Realization of the binary adder as the Moore sequential machine with JK-flip-flops.

forbidden, the number of possible input signals is equal to the number of columns in the state table, which is at the same time the number of inputs in the sequential network. In the case of Mealy machines, the

y	x_1	x_2
q_0	q_0,0	q_1,0
q_1	q_0,1	q_1,0

Figure 13.22. State table of the sequential machine in Example 13.5.

outputs are pulses. However, in Moore machines, they can be also level signals whose value is defined in the intervals between pulses. In this case, the number of different outputs cannot be greater that the number of possible different states of clocked sequential circuits. Recall that a level signal is a signal that can take two different values, a value is preserved for an arbitrary number of periods and may be changed at an integer multiple of periods.

Pulse mode sequential networks are generally confined to special purpose circuits that are not parts of larger systems. Classical examples are vending machines and toll-collecting machines.

In definition of state functions it is required that each product term contains an input variable, since they are the sources of pulses, and no other sources exist, because clock pulses are not used. Since a single input pulse can occur at a time, the excitation functions for memory elements are determined by considering each column of the encoded state table separately.

The following example illustrates a pulse-mode sequential network.

EXAMPLE 13.5 *(Pulse-mode sequential network)*

Consider realization of a sequential machine defined by the state table in Fig. 13.22 by T-flip-flops. As in the case of synchronous sequential machines, it is assumed that at any time the network is in an internal state corresponding to a row of the state table. From this state table, it is clear that the state changes occur when a pulse appear at the input x_2 *or a pulse occur at the input* x_1 *and the present state is* q_1. *Fig. 13.23 shows the encoded state table for this sequential machine and the excitation table derived with respect to the application table of T-flip-flops. We consider this table as Karnaugh map and perform the minimization under the restriction specified above, i.e., by considering each column separately. In this way, the state function is* $T = x_1y + x_2$, *and the output function is* $Z = x_1y$. *Notice again that the minimum expression* $T = x_2 + y$ *cannot be used, since it contains a product term where no input variables appear. Fig. 13.24 shows the realization of the sequential machine considered.*

yY	T
00	0
01	1
10	1
11	0

y	x_1	x_2	x_1	x_2
0	0	1	0	0
1	0	1	1	0
	Y		Z	

y	x_1	x_2	x_1	x_2
0	0	1	0	0
1	1	1	1	0
	T		Z	

forbidden

Figure 13.23. Encoded state table and excitation table for sequential machine in Example 13.5.

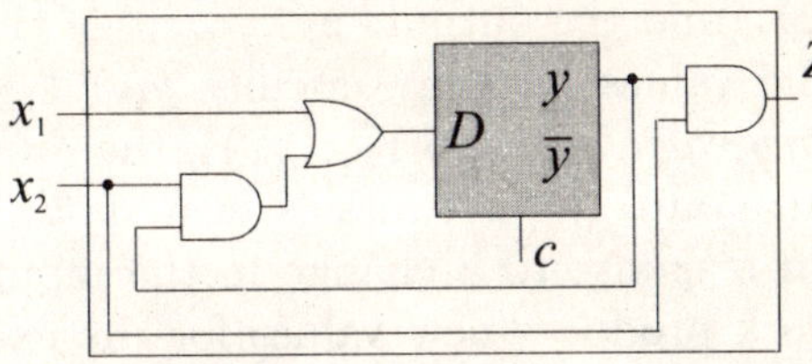

Figure 13.24. Realization of the pulse mode sequential network in Example 13.5.

6. Asynchronous Sequential Networks

Asynchronous sequential networks are used in the cases when synchronizing clock pulses are not available. Notice that provision of clocks in logic networks is often very expensive in terms of area. Asynchronous networks are also often preferred within large synchronous systems where some subsystems can operate asynchronously to increase the overall speed of the entire system.

The first systematic discussion of asynchronous sequential circuits is provided by Huffman [66] who proposed a model for such networks as shown in Fig. 13.25.

In an asynchronous sequential network, the input can change at any time, and inputs and outputs are represented by level signals rather that pulses. Their internal structure is characterized by using delay circuits, usually denoted by Δ, as memory devices. The combination of level signals at the inputs and the outputs of the delay circuits determines pairs called the *total* states of the network. The values of input level signals $x_1, \ldots, x_l$ are called the *input states* or *primary variables*. The level outputs by the combinatorial part of the network determine the

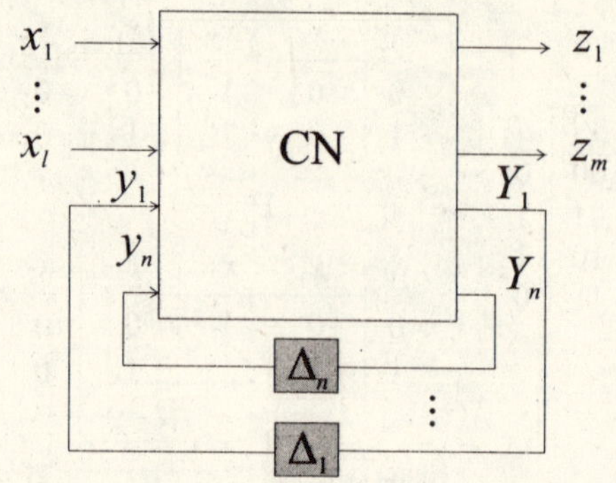

Figure 13.25. Huffman model of asynchronous sequential circuits.

next states $Y_1, \ldots, Y_n$ and the outputs $z_1, \ldots, z_m$ of the entire network. In this settings, the values of delay circuits $y_1, \ldots, y_n$ are called the *internal* or *secondary variables*, and $Y_1, \ldots, Y_n$ the *excitation variables.*

For a given input state, the network is in a *stable* state iff $y_i = Y_i$, for $i = 1, \ldots, n$. In response to a change in the input state, the combinatorial subnetwork produces new values for the excitation variables and it may happen that some of internal variables y_i are not equal to the changed values of the corresponding excitation variables Y_i due to the influence of the delay circuits Δ_i. Then, the network goes to an *unstable state.* When again y_i becomes equal to Y_i after the time equal to the delay in the Δ_i, the combinatorial subnetwork generates new output. This need not necessarily be a stable state, and the network may continue to traverse through different states, until enters the next stable state. Therefore, unlike sequential networks, the transition between two stable states goes though a series of unstable states. For that reason, the state table in synchronous networks is replaced by the *flow table* in asynchronous sequential networks. The flow table defining functioning of an asynchronous sequential machine has the same form as the state table of an synchronous machine. The columns are labelled by input signals, and rows correspond to the states. The entries of the table are the next states and the outputs. However, the difference is that there are stable and unstable, also called *quasi-stable* states. A transition to another state occurs in response to a change in the input state. It is assumed that after a change in an input, no other changes in any input occurs until the networks enters a stable state. This way of functioning is called *fundamental mode* [66], [67], [107], [195].

In a fundamental mode network, when due to a change of the input state, the machine goes from a stable state, it will move within the

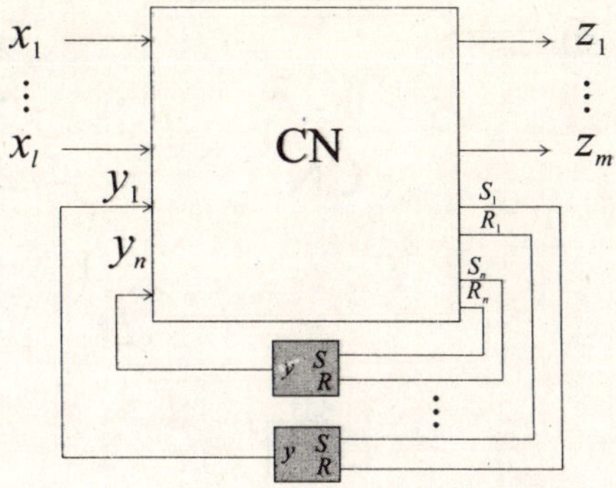

Figure 13.26. Asynchronous sequential network with SR-latches.

current row of the flow table to the new input column, and then if the state arrived at is unstable, the network will move along that column to the next internal state.

Internal states in an asynchronous sequential circuit may be clearly expressed if to each state variable a separate memory element is assigned to save the state. Fig. 13.26 shows the model of an asynchronous sequential network with SR-latches used to save states [15].

Notice that in this network there are twice more excitation variables, since each latch has two inputs, S and R, and saves a single state. This circuit is asynchronous, and the state can change in response to a change at the input. This network can be converted into a synchronous network by adding clock pulses which will allow the state change when the clock pulse occurs. If the SR-latches are replaced by D-flip-flops which have a single input, the clock pulse will determine when the change is possible, and the output will be equal to the input value keeping it until the new clock pulse occurs. Therefore, this will be a synchronous sequential circuit whose model is shown in Fig.13.27 [15].

As explained above, a synchronous sequential machine may be stable in any defined state and this will last at least during a clock cycle, which means until appearance of another clock pulse. Asynchronous machines are stable just in these states where the next state Y_i is equal to the present state y_i, since there are no any break in the feedback loops which contains just delay circuits. We will discuss the flow tables by the example of D-latch.

EXAMPLE 13.6 *(D-latch)*
Fig. 13.28 shows the flow table of a D-latch derived by analyzing its behavior. In this table, there is a stable state in each row, and it is

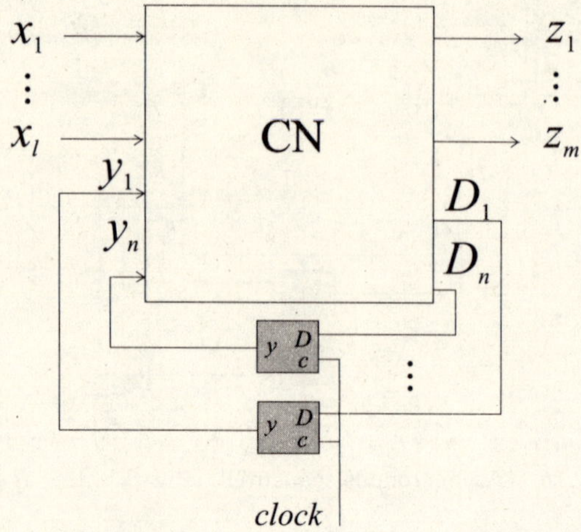

Figure 13.27. Synchronous sequential network with D-flip-flops.

denoted by encircling the symbol of the state. Therefore, it is called the simple *flow table. This table is defined in the following way.*

Assume that both inputs have the value 0*, and that the output is also* 0*. These are conditions what corresponds to the upper left entry of the table. Each entry defines a total state determined by the pair consisting of the value at the input and a state. A change at the input causes a change of the total state by shifting it in the next block in the same row. An internal state cannot be changed instantaneously, which means the row cannot be changed. For that reason, it was necessary to impose the restrictions defining the fundamental mode. Without this restriction, we cannot be sure in the effective order of simultaneous changes at the input.*

Assume that the D-input changes the value to 1*. This leads to the second total stable state which corresponds to the input* 01 *and has the output* 0*. This new state is in the second row, where it is labeled as a stable state. When the D-input returns to* 0*, we get back into a unstable state shown as the first entry in the second row.*

Notice that in the first row, the entry which corresponds to the input 11 *is undetermined, since it requires simultaneous change of both input bits from* 00 *to* 11*, which is forbidden in the fundamental mode. In this way, the complete flow table is derived.*

Further, in each row there is is an unspecified entry, which corresponds to the change from a stable state requiring simultaneous change of two bits of input signals. For instance, in the second row, the rightmost entry is unspecified since it corresponds to the input signal 01*, while the stable state, encircled* 2*, in this row corresponds to the input signal* 01.

q \ C,D	00	01	11	10
1	(1),0	2,0	-,-	3,0
2	1,0	(2),0	4,0	-,-
3	1,0	-,-	4,0	(3),0
4	-,-	(5),1	(4),1	3,1
5	6,1	5,1	4,1	-,-
6	(6),1	5,1	-,-	3,1

Figure 13.28. Flow table for D-latch.

It is obvious from the inspection of the simple flow table, that there are identical rows in it. Since unspecified entries may contain any next state and the output, the first three rows can be replaced by a single row viewing states 1, 2, *and* 3 *as equivalent states. In the same way, the states* 4, 5, *and* 6 *are equivalent, and these three rows can be replaced by a single row. In this way, the* reduced *flow table is derived shown in Fig. 13.29. The reduction is possible due to an appropriate specification of unspecified states. Since unspecified states are transient states, the specification is equally good if, for example, for the change* $0 \rightarrow 1$ *between the stable states for the output sequence it is selected* $0 \rightarrow 0 \rightarrow 1$ *or* $0 \rightarrow 1 \rightarrow 1$, *while the combinations* $0 \rightarrow 1 \rightarrow 0$ *and* $1 \rightarrow 0 \rightarrow 1$ *are unacceptable.*

This reduction of the flow table corresponds directly to the reduction of state tables in the case of synchronous sequential machines. There are methods to perform it [83], [122], [196].

When reduced flow table has been determined, the synthesis of the D-latch can be performed in the same way as in the case of synchronous sequential networks.

Since there are just two stable states, a single variable y *is sufficient. If the values* $y = 0$ *and* $y = 1$ *correspond to the states* 1 *and* 2, *we get the encoded excitation table as in Fig. 13.30. When the function in this table minimized, we get a function that is realized by a circuit which corresponds to the Huffman model of asynchronous sequential networks. Fig. 13.31 shows the model of the circuit and the corresponding realization of it. The lowest AND circuit corresponds to the two encircled entries in columns* 01 *and* 11 *in the encoded flow table and their role will be discussed latter.*

q \ C,D	00	01	11	10
1	(1),0	(1),0	2,0	(1),0
2	(2),1	(2),1	(2),1	1,1

Figure 13.29. Reduced flow table for D-latch.

y \ C,D	00	01	11	10
0	0	0	1	0
1	1	1	1	0

Figure 13.30. Encoded flow table for D-latch.

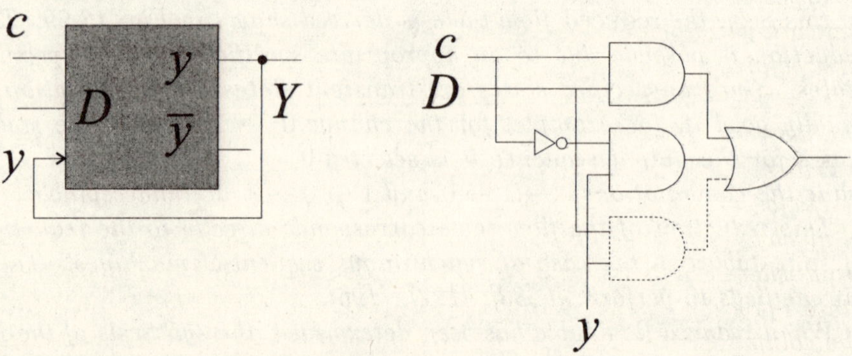

Figure 13.31. Model and circuit realization of D-latch.

7. Races and Hazards

In applications of asynchronous sequential networks two problems appears, the *hazard* and the *race*. Although being related to the combinatorial networks, since caused by the delay in circuits, these problems become even more important in asynchronous sequential networks where the delays are used in feedback connections to regulate normal functioning of networks.

7.1 Race

A *race* appear when a simultaneous change of two or more secondary variables is required. For instance, if the present state is $y_1y_2 = 00$, and the next state is $Y_1Y_2 = 11$, two secondary variables have to be changed. In may happen that y_1 changes first, and in this case, the transition would be $00 \rightarrow 10 \rightarrow 11$, in the other case, when y_2 changes before y_1, it would be $00 \rightarrow 01 \rightarrow 11$ and this is a race between y_1 and y_2 which may cause that the network enters the wrong state.

If the final state which the network has reached does not depend on the order in which the variables change, the race is called *non-critical* race, otherwise, it is a *critical race* and has to be avoided.

The races in sequential machines will be illustrated by the following example discussed in [83].

EXAMPLE 13.7 *(Race)*
Consider a sequential machine whose model and excitation table are shown in Fig. 13.32. For the input $x_1x_2 = 00$ *and the present state* $y_1y_2 = 00$, *the next state is* $Y_1Y_2 = 11$. *Therefore, both secondary variables* y_1 *and* y_2 *has to be changed, and this is a race, since it can hardly be expected that both delay circuits* Δ_1 *and* Δ_2 *will perform ideally. The network will change the secondary variables into* $y_1y_2 = 01$ *or* $y_1y_2 = 10$ *first before they become* $y_1y_2 = 11$. *Since in both cases, the next state is* $Y_1Y_2 = 11$, *as specified in the corresponding rows in the excitation table, the network will finally reach the required stable state. This race is not a critical race.*

If $x_1x_2 = 01$ *and* $y_1y_2 = 11$, *the required next stable state is* $Y_1Y_2 = 00$. *If* y_1 *changes faster than* y_2, *i.e., for* $y_1y_2 = 01$, *it would be* $Y_1Y_2 = 00$, *from where, after* y_2 *change,* $y_1y_2 = 00$, *it will be directed into the stable state* $Y_1Y_2 = 00$ *as shown in the entry at the crossing of the row* 00 *and the column* 01 *in the excitation table. However, if* y_2 *changes first, i.e.,* $y_1y_2 = 10$, *the network will go to the state* $Y_1Y_2 = 10$, *which is a stable state, and will therefore, remain there. Thus, this is a critical race and must be always avoided.*

Consider now the case when $x_1x_2 = 11$ *and* $Y_1y_2 = 01$. *Then, the transition into the stable state* $Y_1Y_2 = 10$ *is required. Simultaneous change of both secondary variables* y_1 *and* y_2 *is required and it may be that first unstable state* 11 *in the row* 01 *column* 11 *is entered, and the networks will be directed to the row* 11 *and through another unstable state* 01 *will finally reach the stable state* 10 *in the row* 10.

The unique sequence of unstable states which the network went through to perform the required state change is called a *cycle*. It has to be ensured that each cycle contain a stable state, otherwise the network will

y_1y_2 \ x_1x_2	00	01	11	10
00	11	00	10	01
01	11	00	11	01
11	11	00	10	11
10	11	10	10	11

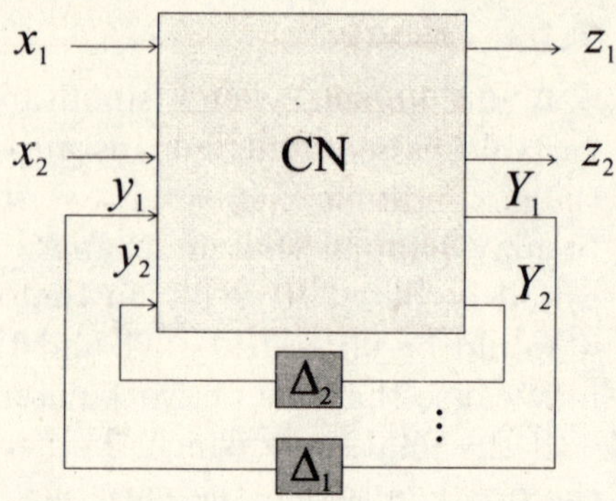

Figure 13.32. Model and excitation table for the sequential machine in Example 13.7.

y_1y_2 \ x_1x_2	00	01	11	10
00	10	00	10	01
01	10	00	11	01
10	10	00	11	10
11	10	11	11	10

Figure 13.33. A valid assignment of states for the sequential machine in Example 13.7.

go through unstable states until the input state has changed, and this has to be avoided.

The problem of races can be solved by a suitable selection of assignment of binary sequences in encoding the states. An assignment which does not contain critical races or cycles without stable states is a *valid* assignment. There are methods and algorithms to solve the problem of races in sequential networks [83], [122], [155], [196].

EXAMPLE 13.8 *Fig. 13.33 shows a valid assignment of states for the sequential machine in Example 13.7.*

7.2 Hazards

A *static hazard* appears when a single input variable change for which the output should remain constant, might cause a momentary incorrect output. For instance, the *static* 1-*hazard* appears when due to the change of an input combination which produces the output 1, to another input

x_3x_4 \ x_1x_2	00	01	11	10
00	0	0	1	1
01	0	0	Y 1	1
11	0	X 1	0	0
10	1	0	0	0

Figure 13.34. Function with 1-hazard.

combination for which the output is also 1, the appearance of a spurious output 0 occurs. The *static* 0-*hazard* is defined similarly.

The static hazard is often related to *adjacent* input states. Two input combinations are adjacent if they differ by the value of just a single input variable. For example, $\overline{x}_1x_2x_3$ and $x_1x_2x_3$ are adjacent input combinations. If for a transition between pairs of adjacent input combinations for which the output should remain the same, it is possible generation of a momentary spurious output, then this transition contains a static hazard. As it was shown in [195], such hazards may occur whenever there exists a pair of adjacent input states which produce the same output and there is not a subcube containing both combinations. In terms of Karnaugh maps, that means subcubes covering pairs of adjacent 1 or 0 values. Conversely, a combinatorial circuit is *hazard free* is every pair of adjacent 1 values and adjacent 0 values in the Karnaugh map is covered by a subcube.

EXAMPLE 13.9 *Fig. 13.34 shows a Karnaugh map for a function having the value* 1 *in the entries* X *and* Y *corresponding to the input signals* 0111, *and* 1101, *respectively. The transition from the input combination* X *to* Y *requires change at two coordinates* x_1 *and* x_3. *In real circuits, it can be hardly expected that this change performs simultaneously due to physical characteristics of circuits. Therefore, the transition form* X *to* Y *can be done over* $Q = (1111)$ *if* x_1 *changes first, or* $R = (0101)$ *when* x_3 *changes before* x_1. *In both input states* Q *and* R, *the output is* 0, *and it may momentary appear, as a wrong output during the change of input state* X *to* Y. *The product* Dy *is realized by the additional AND circuit in Fig. 13.31.*

EXAMPLE 13.10 *The excitation table for the* D*-input of the* D*-latch in Fig. 13.30 contains a static* 1*-hazard in the transition from the input state* (101) *to* 011), *since in both cases the output is* 1 *and it may happen that the transition goes over* (001), *in which case the output* 0 *may shortly appear. To eliminate this hazard, the adjacent values* 1 *should be covered* *by cubes, which implies to add another implicant Dy in the realization of D-latch, as shown by dotted lines in Fig.13.31. Therefore, for a hazard-free D-latch the excitation function is $Y = CD + \overline{C}y + Dy$.*

Besides the static hazards, the phenomenon called *essential hazard* occurs in fundamental mode networks whenever three consecutive input changes take the network into a different stable state than the first change alone [195]. The essential hazard described above is called the *steady state* essential hazard. There is may occur also the *transient essential hazard* consisting in appearance of a spurious output pulse between state transitions. Delays in feedback paths when properly determined can prevent both transient and steady state hazards [196].

When designed, asynchronous sequential machines should be analyzed to check for the existence of critical races or hazards. The analysis procedure consists basically in performing the synthesis procedure in reverse [196].

8. Exercises and Problems

EXERCISE 13.1 *Realize a sequential machine whose output Z takes the value 1 when the input sequence x consists of two consecutive values 1 followed by two values 0, or two values 0 followed by two values 1. In other cases, the output is $Z = 0$. For the realization use JK-flip-flops and (2×1) multiplexers.*

EXERCISE 13.2 *Realize a sequential machine whose input is an arbitrary binary sequence, and the output takes the value 1, when the total number of values 1 after the start of the machine is even. For the realization, use SR-flip-flops and $NAND$ circuits with two inputs.*

EXERCISE 13.3 *Determine the state diagram for the quaternary counter which counts as $0, 1, 2, 3, 0, 1, 2, 3, \cdots$ and $0, 1, 3, 2, 0, 1, 3, 2, 0, \cdots$ for the control input $x = 1$ and $x = 0$, respectively. Realize this sequential machine by different flip-flops and compare the complexities of the realizations in the number of required circuits.*

EXERCISE 13.4 *Draw the state diagram and the state transition table for a two-bit counter with two control inputs k_1, k_2 defined as follows*

If $k_1k_2 = 00$, stop counting,
If $k_1k_2 = 01$, count up by 1,
If $k_1k_2 = 10$, count down by 1,
If $k_1k_2 = 11$, count by two.

Implement the counter by T, D, and JK-flip-lops and compare the complexities of realizations in the number of circuits count. Available are two-input circuits.

EXERCISE 13.5 *[79]*
Consider a device with two control inputs k_1 and k_2 specified as follows

If $K_1 k_1 = 00$, it works as a Gray code up-counter,
If $k_1 k_2 = 01$, is works as a Gray code down-counter,
If $k_1 k_2 = 10$, it works as a Gray code counter by two,
If $k_1 k_2 = 11$, counter hold his present state.

Fig 13.35 shows the state diagram for this machine. Determine the state table and the minimized next state functions.

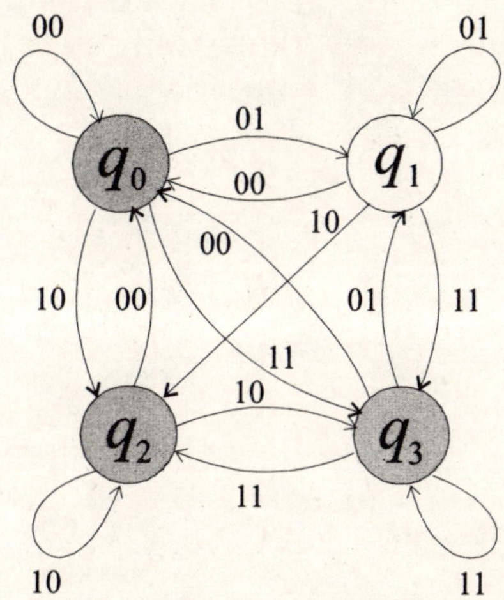

Figure 13.35. State diagram for the sequential machine in Exercise 13.5.

EXERCISE 13.6 *[79]*
Design the state diagram and the state transition table for the Moore machine with a single input x and and the output y specified as follows.

The output y takes the value 1 *and keeps this value thereafter when at least the sequence* 00 *or* 11 *occurs at the input, irrespectively of the order of occurrence. Show that this machine requires no more than 9 states.*

EXERCISE 13.7 *Realize the sequential machine in Exercise 12.6 by a clocked sequential machine with SR-flip-flops.*

EXERCISE 13.8 *Compare complexities of the realizations of the vending machine specified in the Exercise 12.10 by D-flip-flops and SR-flip-flops.*

References

[1] Abramovici, M.M., Breuer, A., Friedman, A., *Digital Systems Testing and Testable Design*, Wiley-IEEE Press, New York, USA, 1994.

[2] Agaian, S., Astola, J.T., Egiazarian, K., *Binary Polynomial Transforms and Nonlinear Digital Filtering*, Marcel Dekker, New York, USA, 1995.

[3] Ahmed, E., Rose, J., "The effect of LUT and cluster size on deep-submicron FPGA performance and density", *IEEE Trans. on Very Large Scale Integration (VLSI) Systems*, Vol. 12, No. 3, 2004, 288-298.

[4] Aizenberg, N.N., Trofimljuk, O.T., "Conjunctive transforms for discrete signals and their applications of tests and the detection of monotone functions", *Kibernetika*, No. 5, K, 1981, in Russian.

[5] Akers, S.B., "On a theory of Boolean functions", *J. Soc. Ind. Appl. Math.*, Vol. 7, No. 4, 1959, 487-498.

[6] Ashar, P., Devadas, S., Newton, A.R., "Optimum and heuristic algorithms for finite state machine decomposition and partitioning", *Proc. IEEE Int. Conf. Computer-Aided Design*, Santa Clara, CA, USA, November 5-9, 1989, 216-219.

[7] Ashar, P., Devadas, S., Newton, A.R., "A unified approach to the decomposition and redecomposition of sequential machines", *Proc. 27th ACM/IEEE Design Automation Conference*, Orlando, FL, USA, June 24-28, 1990, 601-606.

[8] Ashar, P., Devadas, S., Newton, A.R., "Optimum and heuristic algorithms for an approach to finite state machine decomposition", *IEEE Trans. Computer-Aided Design of Integrated Circuits and Systems*, Vol. 10, No. 3, 1991, 296-310.

[9] Ashar, P., Devadas, S., Newton, A.R., *Sequential Logic Synthesis*, Kluwer Academic Publishers, Boston, MA, USA, 1992.

[10] Bae, J., Prasanna, V.K., "Synthesis of area-efficient and high-throughout rate data format converters", *IEEE Trans. Very Large Scale Integrated (VLSI) Systems*, Vol. 6, No. 4, 1990, 697-706.

[11] Bae, J., Prasanna, V.K., "Synthesis of a class of data format converters with specific delays", *Proc. IEEE Int. Conf. on Application Specific Array Processor*, San Francisco, CA, USA, August 22-24, 1994, 283-294.

[12] Beauchamp, K.G., *Applications of Walsh and Related Functions with an Introduction to Sequency Theory*, Academic Press, Bristol, UK, 1984.

[13] Bollig, B., Wegener, I., "Improving the variable ordering of OBDDs is NP-complete," *IEEE Trans. Comput.*, Vol. C-45, No. 9, 1996, 993-1002.

[14] Bolton, M., *Digital System Design with Programmable Logic*, Addison-Wesley, Wokingham, England, 1990.

[15] Boole, G., *An Investigation of the Laws of Thought*, 1854. Reprinted by Dover Publications, Inc., New York, USA, 1954.

[16] Brayton, R.K., "The future of logic synthesis and verification", in Hassoun, S., Sasao, T., (eds.), *Logic Synthesis and Verification*, Kluwer Academic Publishers, Boston, MA, USA, 2002, 403-434.

[17] Brayton, R.K., Hachtel, G.D., McMullen, C.T., Sangiovanni-Vincentelli, A.L.M., *Logic Minimization Algorithms for VLSI Synthesis*, Kluwer Academic Publishers, Boston, MA, USA, 1984.

[18] Brown, S.D., Francis, R.J.,, Rose, J., Vranecis, Z.G., *Field Programmabel Gate Arrays*, Kluwer Academic Publishers, Boston, MA, USA, 1992.

[19] Bryant, R.E., "Graph-based algorithms for Boolean functions manipulation," *IEEE Trans. Comput.*, Vol. C-35, No. 8, 1986, 667-691.

[20] Bryant, R.E., Chen, Y.-A., "Verification of arithmetic functions with binary moment diagrams," May 31, 1994, Tech. Rept. CMU-CS-94-160.

[21] *BuildGates User Guide Release 2.0*, Ambit Design Systems, Santa Clara, CA, USA, Dec. 1997.

[22] Burgun, L., Dictus, N., Prado Lopes, E., Sarwary, C., "A unified approach for FSM synthesis on FPGA architectures", *Proc. 20th EUROMICRO Conference System Architecture and Integration*, Liverpool, England, September 5-8, 1994, 660-668.

[23] Butler, J.T., Sasao, T., Matsuura, M., "Average path length of binary decision diagrams", *IEEE Trans. Computers.*, Vol. 54, No. 9, 2005, 1041-1053.

[24] Chattopadhyay, S., Reddy, P.N., "Finite state machine state assignment targeting low power consumption", *IEE Proc. Computers and Digital Techniques*, Vol. 151, No. 1, 2004, 61-70.

[25] Chen, D., Cong, J., "Register binding and port assignment for multiplexer optimization", *Proc. Int. Conf. Asia and South Pacific Design Automation Conference*, Yokohama, Japan, January 27-30, 2004, 68-73.

[26] Chen, Y.A., Bryant, R.E., "An efficient graph representation for arithmetic circuit verification," *IEEE Trans. CAD*, Vol. 20, No, 12, 2001, 1443-1445.

[27] Clarke, E.M., McMillan, K.L., Zhao, X., Fujita, M., "Spectral transforms for extremely large Boolean functions," in: Kebschull, U., Schubert, E., Rosenstiel, W., Eds., *Proc. IFIP WG 10.5 Workshop on Applications of the Reed-Muller Expansion in Circuit Design*, 16-17.9.1993, Hamburg, Germany, 86-90.

[28] Cong, J., Wu, Ch., "Optimal FPGA mapping and retiming with efficient initial state computation", *Proc. Design Automation Conference*, San Francisco, CA, USA, June 15-19, 1998, 330-335.

[29] Cooley, J.W., Tukey, J.W., "An algorithm for the machine calculation of complex Fourier series," *Math. Computation*, Vol. 19, 297-301, 1965.

[30] Davio, M., Deschamps, J.-P., Thayse, A., *Digital Systems with Algorithm Implementation*, Wiley, New York, USA, 1983.

[31] Debnath, D., Sasao, T., "GRMIN: A heuristic minimization algorithm for generalized Reed-Muller expression", *IFIP WG 10.5 Workshop on Applications of the Reed-Muller Expansions in Circuit Design (Reed-Muller '95)*, Makuhari, Japan, Aug. 27-29, 1995.

[32] Debnath, D., Sasao, T., "GRMIN2 - A heuristic simplification algorithm for generalized Reed-Muller expressions", *IEE Proc. Computers and Digital Techniques*, Vol. 143. No.6, 1996, 376-384.

[33] De Micheli, G., *Synthesis and Optimization of Digital Circuits*, McGraw-Hill, New York, USA, 1994.

[34] De Micheli, G., Sangiovanni-Vincentelli, A., "Multiple constrained folding of Programmable Logic Arrays, Theory and Applications" *IEEE Trans. Computer-Aided Design of Integrated Circuits and Systems*, Vol. 2, No. 3, 1983, 151-167.

[35] *DesigWare Components Quick Reference Guide, Verson 1998.02*, Synopsys, Mountain View, CA, USA, Feb. 1998.

[36] Drechsler, R., Becker, B., *Binary Decision Diagrams, Theory and Implementation*, Kluwer Academic Publishers, Boston, MA, USA, 1998.

[37] Drechsler, R., Hengster, H., Schäfer, H., Hartmann, J., Becker, B., "Testability of 2-level AND/EXOR circuits", *Journal of Elecrtronic Testing*, Vol. 14, No. 3, 1999, 219-225.

[38] Dubrova, E.V., Muzio,J.C., "Testability of generalized multiple-valued Reed-Muller circuits", *Proc. 26th Int. Symp. on Multiple-Valued Logic*, Santiago de Compostela, Spain, January 19 - 31, 1996, 56-61.

[39] Dubrova, E.V., Muzio, J.C., "Easily testable multiple-valued logic circuits derived from Reed-Muller circuits", *IEEE Trans. Computers*, Vol. 49, No. 11, 2000, 1285-1289.

[40] Edwards, C.R., "The generalized dyadic differentiator and its application to 2-valued functions defined on an *n-space, IEE Proc. Comput. and Digit. Techn.*, Vol. 1, No. 4, 1978, 137-142.

[41] Edwards, C.R., "The Gibbs dyadic differentiator and its relationship to the Boolean difference," *Comput. and Elect. Engng.*, Vol. 5, 1978, 335-344.

[42] Egan, J.R., Liu, C.L., "Bipartite foldign and partitioning of a PLA", *IEEE Trans. Computer-Aided Design*, Vol. CAD-3, 1982, 1982, 191-199.

[43] Ercolani, S., De Micheli, G., "Technology mapping for electrically programmable gate arrays", *Proc. 28th Design Automation Conf.*, San Francisco, CA, USA, June 7-11, 1991, 234-239.

[44] Falkowski, B.J., "A note on the polynomial form of Boolean functions and related topics", *IEEE Trans. on Computers*, Vol. 48, No. 8, 1999, 860-864.

[45] Falkowski, B.J., Perkowski, M.A., "A family of all essential radix-2 addition/subtraction multi-polarity transforms: Algorithms and interpretations in Boolean domain", *Proc. Int. Symp. on Circuits and Systems, (23rd ISCAS)*, New Orelans, LA, USA, May 1990, 2913-2916.

[46] Francis, R.J., Rose, J., Vranesic, Z., "Chartle-crf - fast thecnologuy mapping for Look-up table based FPGAs", *Proc. 28th Design Automation Conference*, San Francisco, CA, USA, June 17-21, 1991, 227-233.

[47] Francis, R.J., Rose, J., Vranesic, Z., "Technology mapping of look-up table based FPGAs for performance", *Proc. Int. Conf. Computer Aided Design*, Santa Clara, CA, USA, March 11-14, 1991, 568-571.

[48] Fujiwara, H., *Logic Testing and Design for Testability*, MIT Press, Boston, MA, USA, 1985.

[49] Fujiwara, H., *Design and Test of Digital Systems*, Kogakutosho, Tokyo, 2004, (in Japanese).

[50] Geiger, M., Muller-Wipperfurth, T., "FSM decomposition revisited: algebraic structure theory applied to MCNC benchmark FSMs", *Proc. 28th ACM/IEEE Design Automation Conference*, San Francisco, CA, USA, June 17-21, 1991, 182-185.

[51] Gibbs, J.E., "Instant Fourier transform," *Electron. Lett.*, Vol. 13, No. 5, 122-123, 1977.

[52] Good, I.J., "The interaction algorithm and practical Fourier analysis," *J. Roy. Statist. Soc.*, ser. B, Vol. 20, 1958, 361-372, Addendum, Vol. 22, 1960, 372-375.

[53] Günther, W., Drechsler, R., "BDD minimization by linear transforms", *Proc. 5th Int. Conf. Advanced Computer Systems*, Szczecin, Poland, November 10-20, 1998, 525-532.

[54] Günther, W., Drechsler, R., "Efficient manipulation algorithms for linearly transformed BDDs," *Proc. 4th Int. Workshop on Applications of Reed-Muller Expansion in Circuit Design*, Victoria, Canada, May 20-21, 1999, 225-232.

[55] Gunther, W., Drechsler, R., "Action: combining logic synthesis and technology mapping for MUX based FPGAs", *Proc. of the 26th Euromicro Conf.*, Maastricht, Netherlands, Sept. 5-7, 2000, Vol. 1, 130-137.

[56] Gunther, W., Drechsler, R., "Performance driven optimization for MUX based FPGAs", *Proc. Fourteenth Int. Conf. on VLSI Design*, Bangalore, India, January 3-7, 2001, 311-316.

[57] Hachtel, G.D., Newton, A.R., Sangiovanni-Vincentelli, A.L., "Some results in optimal PLA folding", *Proc. Int. Circuits Comp. Conf.*, New York, 1980, 1023-1028.

[58] Hachtel, G.D., Newton, A.R., Sangiovanni-Vincentelli, A.L., "An algorithm for optimal PLA folding", *IEEE Trans. Computer-Aided Design*, Vol. CAD-1, 1982, 63-77.

[59] Hachtel, G.D., Somenzi, F., *Logic Synthesis and Verification*, Kluwer Academic Publishers, Boston, MA, USA, 2000.

[60] Hartmanis, J., "Symbolic analyses of a decomposition of information processing machines", *Inf. Contr.*, 8, 1960, 154-178.

[61] Hartmanis, J. "On the state assignment problem for sequential machines", *IRE Trans.*, Vol. EC-10, 1961, 157-65.

[62] Hartmanis, J., Stearns, R., *Algebraic Structure Theory of Sequential Machines*, Prentice-Hall, Englewood Cliffs, NJ, 1966.

[63] Heidtmann, K.D., "Arithmetic spectra applied to stuck-at-fault detection for combinatorial networks", *Proc. 2nd Technical Workshop New Directions in IC Testing*, 4.1-4.13, Winnipeg, Canada, April 1987.

[64] Heidtmann, K.D., "Arithmetic spectrum applied to fault detection for combinatorial networks", *IEEE Trans. Computers,* Vol.40, No. 3, March 1991, 320-324.

[65] Hewitt, E., Ross, K.A., *Abstract Harmonic Analysis*, Vol. I, Springer, Berlin, 1963, Vol. II Springer, Berlin, 1970.

[66] Huffman, D.A., "The synthesis of sequential switching circuits", *J. Franklin Inst.*, Vol. 257, March-April 1954, 275-303.

[67] Huffman, D.A., "Study of the memory requirements of sequential switching circuits", M.I.T. Res. Lab. Electron. Tech. Rept., 293, April 1955.

[68] Hung, D.L., Wang, J., "A FPGA-based custom computing system for solving the assignment problem", *Proc. IEEE Symp. FPGAs for Custom Computing Machines*, Napa Villey, CA, USA, April 15-17, 1998, 298-299.

[69] Hurst, S.L., *Logical Processing of Digital Signals*, Crane Russak and Edward Arnold, London and Basel, UK and Switzerland, 1978.

[70] Hurst, S.L., "The Haar transform in digital network synthesis," *Proc. 11th Int. Symp. on Multiple-Valued Logic*, Oklahoma City, OK, USA, 1981, 10-18.

[71] Hurst, S.L., Miller, D.M., Muzio, J.C., *Spectral Techniques in Digital Logic*, Academic Press, Bristol, 1985.

[72] Iranli, A., Rezvani, P., Pedram, M., "Low power synthesis of finite state machines with mixed D and T flip-flops", *Proc. Asia and South Pacific Design Automation Conference*, Kitakyshu, Japan, January 21-24, 2003, 803-808.

[73] Jacobi, R.P., "LogosPGA - Synthesis system for LUT devices", *Proc. XI Brazilian Symp. on Integrated Circuit Design*, Rio de Janeiro, Brazil, September 30 - October 3, 1998, 217-220.

[74] Jennings, P.I., Hurst, S.L., Mcdonald, A., "A higly routable ULM gate array and its automated customization", *IEEE Trans. Computer-Aided Design*, Vol. CAD-3, No. 1, 1984, 27-40.

[75] Jozwiak, L., Slusarczyk, A., "A new state assignment method targeting FPGA implementations", *Proc. 26th Euromicro Conf.*, Maastricht, Nitherlands, September 5-7, 2000, Vol. 1, 50-59.

[76] Karnaugh, M., "The map method for synthesis of combinational logic circuits", *AIEE Trans. Comm. and Electronics*, Vol. 9, 1953, 593-599.

[77] Karpovsky, M.G., *Finite Orthogonal Series in the Design of Digital Devices*, Wiley and JUP, New York and Jerusalem, USA and Israel, 1976.

[78] Karpovsky, M.G., Stanković, R.S., Astola, J.T., "Reduction of sizes of decision diagrams by autocorrelation functions", *IEEE Trans. Computers*, Vol. 52, No. 5, 2003, 592-606.

[79] Katz, R.H., *Contemporary Logic Design*, The Benjamin/Cummings Publishing Company, Inc., Redwood City, CA, USA, 1995.

[80] Kebschull, U., Schubert, E., Rosenstiel, W., "Multilevel logic synthesis based on functional decision diagrams," *Proc. 3rd European Design Automation Conference*, Brussels, Belgium, March 16-19, 1992, 43-47.

[81] Koda, N., Sasao, T., "An upper bound on the number of products in minimum ESOPs", *IFIP WG 10.5 Workshop on Applications of the Reed-Muller Expansions in Circuit Design (Reed-Muller '95)*, Makuhari, Japan, August 1995, 27-29.

[82] Koda, N., Sasao, T., "A method to simplify multiple-output AND-EXOR expressions",(in Japanese), *Trans. IEICE*, Vol. J79-D-1, No. 2, February 1996, 43-52.

[83] Kohavi, Z., *Swithcing and Finite Automata Theory*, Tata McGraw-Hill Publishing Co. Ltd., New Delhi, India, 1978, third reprint 1982.

[84] Komamiya, Y., "Theory of relay networks for the transformation between the decimal and binary system", *Bull. of E.T.L.*, Vol. 15, No. 8, August 1951, 188-197.

[85] Komamiya, Y., "Theory of computing networks", *Researches of E.T.L.*, No. 526, November 1951, *Proc. of the First National Congress for Applied Mathematics*, Tokyo, Japan, May 1952, 527-532.

[86] Komamiya, Y., "Application of Logical Mathematics to Information Theory (Application of Theory of Group to Logical Mathematics)", *The Bulletin of the Electrotechnical Laboratory in Japanese Government*, Tokyo, Japan, April 1953.

[87] Komamiya, Y., *Theory of Computing Networks, Researches of the Applied Mathematics Section of Electrotechnical Laboratory in Japanese Government*, 2 Chome, Nagata-Cho, Chiyodaku, Tokyo, Japan, July 10, 1959, pages 40.

[88] Kondrfajev, V.N., Shalyto, A.A., "Realizations of a system of the Boolean functions by using arithmetic polynomials", *Automatika and Telemekhanika*, No.3, 1993.

[89] Kouloheris, J.L, Gamal, A., "FPGA performance versus cell granularity", *Proc. IEEE Custom Integrated Circuits Conf.*, San Diego, CA, USA, May 12-15, 1991, 6.2/1 - 6.2/4.

[90] Krueger, R., Przybus, B., "Xilinx Virtex Devices - Variable Input LUT Architecture", *The Syndicated, A Technical Newsletter for ASIC and FPGA Designers*, 2004, (www.synplicity.com).

[91] Kukharev, G.A., Shmerko, V.P., Yanushkevich, S.N., *Technique of Binary Data Parallel Processing for VLSI*, Vysheyshaja shcola, Minsk, Belarus, 1991.

[92] Lai, Y.F., Pedram, M., Vrudhula, S.B.K., "EVBDD-based algorithms for integer linear programming, spectral transformation, and functional decomposition," *IEEE Trans. Computer-Aided Design of Integrated Circuits and Systems*, Vol.13, No.8, 1994, 959-975.

[93] Lai Y.-T., Sastry, S., "Edge-valued binary decision diagrams for multi-level hierarchical verification," *29th ACM/IEEE Design Automation Conference*, Anahweim, CA, USA, June 1992, 668-613.

[94] Lazić, B., Ž., *Logic Design of Computers*, Nauka i Elektrotehnički fakultet, Belgrade, Serbia, 1994, (in Serbian).

[95] Lechner, R.J., Moezzi, A., "Synthesis of encoded PLAs", *Proc. of Int. Conf. Fault Detection Spectral Techniques*, Boston, MA, USA, 1983, 1.3-1.11.

[96] Lee, S.C., *Modern Switching Theory in Digital Design*, Prentice Hall, Englewood Cliffs, NJ, USA, 1978.

[97] Lin, C.C., Marek-Sadowska, M., "Universal logic gate for FPGA design", *Proc. ICCAD*, San Jose, CA, USA, October 1994, 164-168.

[98] Macchiarulo, L., Shu, S-M., Marek-Sadowska, M., "Pipelining sequential circuits with wave steering", *IEEE Trans. Computers*, Vol. 53, No. 9, 2004, 1205-1210.

[99] Malyugin, V.D., "On a polynomial realization of a cortege of Boolean functions", *Repts. of the USSR Academy of Sciences*, Vol. 265, No. 6, 1982.

[100] Malyugin, V.D., *Elaboration of theoretical basis and methods for realization of parallel logical calculations through arithmetic polynomials*, Ph.D. Thesis, Inst. of Control, Russian Academy of Science, Moscow, Russia, 1988.

[101] Malyugin, V.D., *Paralleled Calculations by Means of Arithmetic Polynomials*, Physical and Mathematical Publishing Company, Russian Academy of Sciences, Moscow, Russia, 1997, (in Russian).

[102] Malyugin, V.D., Sokolov, V.V., "Intensive logical calculations", *Automatika and Telemekhanika*, No. 4, 1993, 160-167.

[103] Malyugin, V.D., Veits, V.A., "Intensive calculations in parallel logic", *Proc. 5th Int. Workshop on Spectral Techniques*, 15.-17.3.1994, Beijing, China, 63-64.

[104] Mariok, M., Pal, A., "Energy-aware logic synthesis and technology mapping for MUX-based FPGAs", *Proc. 17th Int. Conf. on VLSI Design*, Mumbai, India, January 5-9, 2004, 73-78.

[105] Marple, D., Cooke, L., "Programming antifuses in Crosspoint's FPGAs", *Proc. IEEE Custom Integrated Circuits Conf.*, San Diego, CA, USA, 1994, 185-188.

[106] Maxfield, C., *The Design Warrior's Guide to FPGAs*, Elsevier, Amsterdam, Netherlands, 2004.

[107] McCluskey, E.J., "Fundamental mode and pulse mode sequential circuits", *Proc. IFIP Congress 1962*, North Holland, Amsterdam, Netherlands, 1963.

[108] McCluskey, E.J., *Logic Design Principles with Emphasis on Testable Semicustom Circuits*, Prentice Hall, Englewood Cliffs, N.J., 1986.

[109] Meinel, Ch., Theobald, T., *Algorithms and Data Structures in VLSI Design, OBDD - Foundations and Applications*, Springer, Berlin, Germany, 1998.

[110] Meinel, Ch., Somenzi, F., Tehobald, T., "Linear sifting of decision diagrams and its application in synthesis," *IEEE Trans. CAD*, Vol. 19, No. 5, 2000, 521-533.

[111] Miller, D.M., "Multiple-valued logic design tools", *Proc. 23rd Int. Symp. on Multiple-Valued Logic*, Sacramento, California, USA, May 24-27, 1993, 2 - 11.

[112] Minato, S., "Zero-suppressed BDDs for set manipulation in combinatorial problems," *Proc. 30th ACM/IEEE Design Automation Conference*, Dallas, TX, USA, June 14-18, 1993, 272-277.

[113] Minato, S., *Binary Decission Diagrams and Applictions for VLSI Synthesis*, Kluwer Academic Publishers, Boston, MA, USA, 1996.

[114] Minato, S., Ishiura, N., Yajima, S., "Shared binary decision diagrams with attributed edges for efficient Boolean function manipulation", *Proc. 27th IEEE/ACM Design Automation Conference*, Orlando, FL, USA, June 24-28, 1990, 52-57.

[115] Mitra, S., Avra, L.J., McCluskey, E.J., "Efficient multiplexer synthesis techniques", *IEEE Design and Test of Computers*, October-December 2000, 2-9.

[116] Mohammedali, R., "New Stratix II Devices Now Supported by Synplify Software", *The Syndicated, A Technical Newsletter for ASIC and FPGA Designers*, 2004, (www.synplicity.com).

[117] Monteiro, J.C., Oliveria, A.L., "Finite state machine decomposition for low power", *Proc. 35th ACM/IEEE Design Automation Conference*, San Francisco, CA, USA, June 15-19, 1998, 758-763.

[118] Monteiro, J.C., Oliveira, A.L., "Implicit FSM decomposition applied to low-power design", *IEEE Trans. Very Large Scale Integration (VLSI) Systems*, Vol. 10, No. 5, 2002, 560-565.

[119] Muller, D.E., "Application of Boolean algebra to switching circuits design and to error detection," *IRE Trans. Electron. Comp.*, Vol.EC-3, 1954, 6-12.

[120] Muller-Wipperfurth, T., Geiger, M., "Algebraic decomposition of MCNC benchmark FSMs for logic synthesis", *Proc. Euro ASIC'91*, Paris, France, May 27-31, 1991, 146-151.

[121] Muorga, S., *Logic Design and Switchign Theory*, Jon Wiley and Sons, 1979, Reprinted edition Krieger Publishing Company, Malaber, FL, USA, 1990.

[122] Murgai, R., Brayton, R.K., Sangiovanni-Vincentelli, A.L., *Logic Synthesis for Field-Programmable Gate Arrays*, Kluwer Academic Publishers, Boston, MA, USA, 1995.

[123] Muzio, J.C., "Stuck fault sensitivity of Reed-Muller and Arithmetic coefficients", C. Moraga, Ed., *Theory and Applications of Spectral Techniques*, Dortmund, 1989, 36-45.

[124] Muzio, J.C., Wesselkamper, T.C., *Multiple-Valued Switching Theory*, Adam Hilger, Bristol, UK, 1986.

[125] Nakashima, A., "A realization theory for relay circuits", *Preprint. J. Inst. Electrical Communication Engineers of Japan*, Sept. 1935, (in Japanese).

[126] Nakashima, A., Hanzawa, M., "The theory of equivalent transformation of simple partial paths in the relay circuit", *J. Inst. Electrical Communication Engineers of Japan*, No. 165, 167, Dec. 1936, Feb. 1937, (in Japanese).

[127] Nakashima, A., Hanzawa, M., "Algebraic expressions relative to simple partial paths in the relay circuits", *J. Inst. Electrical Communication Engineers of Japan*, No. 173, Aug. 1937, (in Japanese), (Condensed English translation : Nippon Electrical Comm. Engineering, No. 12, Sept. 1938, 310-314) Section V, "Solutions of acting impedance equations of simple partial paths".

[128] Pal, A., "An algorithm fro optimal logic design usign mumtiplexers", *IEEE Trans. on Computers*, Vol. C-35, No. 8, 1986, 755-757.

[129] Pal, A., Gorai, R.K., Raju, V.V., "Synthesis of multiplexer network using ratio parameters and mapping onto FPGAs", *Proc. 8th Int. Conf. on VLSI Design*, New Delhi, India, January 1995, 63-68.

[130] Perkowski, M.A., Csanky, L., Sarabi, A., Schäfer, I., "Fast minimization of mixed-polarity AND-XOR canonical networks", *Proc. Int. Conf on Computer Design*, Cambridge, MA, USA, October 11-14, 1992, 33-36.

[131] Pichler, F., Prähofer, H., "CAST-FSM computer aided system theory, Finite state machines", in R. Trappl (ed.), *Cybernetics and Systems*, Kluwer Academic Publishers, Dordrecht, Netherlands, 1988.

[132] Pichler, F., Schwartzel, H., *CAST Computerunterstützte Systemtheorie*, Springer-Verlag, Berlin, Germany, 1990.

[133] Piesch, H., "Begriff der Allgemeinen Schaltungstechnik", *Arch f. F. Elektrotech*, Vol. 33, 1939, 672-686, (in German).

[134] Pradhan, D.K., "Universal test sets for multiple fault detection in AND-EXOR arrays", *IEEE Trans. Computers*, Vol. 27, No. 2, 1978, 181-187.

[135] Rademacher, H., "Einige Sätze von allgemeinen Orthogonalfunktionen", *Math. Annalen*, 87, 1922, 122-138.

[136] Rahardja, S., Falkowski, B.J., "Application of linearly independent arithmetic transform in testing of digital circuits", *Electronic Letters*, Vol. 35, No. 5, 1999, 363-364.

[137] Rama Mohan, C., Chakrabarti, P.P., "A new approach to synthesis of PLA-based FSMs", *Proc. the Seventh Int. Conf. VLSI Design*, Calcuta, India, January 5-8, 1994, 373-378.

[138] Rawski, M., Selvaraj, H., Luba, T., "An application of functional decomposition in ROM-based FSM implementation in FPGA devices", *Proc. 29th Euromicro Symp. Digital System Design*, Belek-Antalya, Turkey, September 1-6, 2003, 104-110.

[139] Reddy, S.M., "Easily Testable Realization for Logic Functions," Technical Report No. 54, Univ. of Iowa, IA, USA, May 1972.

[140] Reddy, S.M., "Easily Testable Realizations for Logic Functions", *IEEE Trans. Computers*, Vol. 21, No. 11, 1972, 1183-1188.

[141] Reed, S.M., "A class of multiple error correcting codes and their decoding scheme," *IRE Trans. Inf. Th.*, Vol. PGIT-4, 1954, 38-49.

[142] Rose, J., Francis, R.J., Lewis, D., Chow, P., "Architecture of Field Proframmable Gate Arrays, the effect of logic block fucntionality on arrea efficiency", *IEEE Journal on Solid-State Circuits*, Vol. 25, No. 5, 1990, 1217-1225.

[143] Rose, J., Gamal, A., Sangiovanni-Vincentelli, A., "Architecture of Field Programmable Gate Arrays", *Proc. IEEE*, Vol. 81, No. 7, 1993, 1013-1029.

[144] Rudell, R., "Dynamic variable ordering for ordered binary decision diagrams," *Proc. IEEE Conf. Computer Aided Design*, Santa Clara, CA, 1993, 42-47.

[145] Rudell, R.L., Sangiovanni-Vincentelli, A.L., "Multiple-valued minimization for PLA optimization", *IEEE Trans. on CAD*, Vol. CAD-6, No. 5, 1987, 727-750.

[146] Salomaa, A., *Theory of Automata*, Pergamon Press, Oxford, UK, 1969.

[147] Saluja, K.K., Reddy, S.M., "Fault detecting test sets for Reed- Muller canonic networks", *IEEE Trans. Computers*, Vol. 24, No. 1, 1975, 995-998.

[148] Sarabi, A., Perkowski, M.A.. "Fast exact and quasi-minimal minimization of highly testable fixed polarity AND/XOR canonical networks", *Proc. 29th ACM/IEEE Design Automation Conf.*, Anaheim, CA, USA, June 8-12, 1992, 20-35.

[149] Sasao, T., "Input-variable assignment and output phase optimization of programmable logic arrays", *IEEE Trans. on Compters*, Vol. C-33, 1984, 879-894.

[150] Sasao, T., "Easily testable realization for generalized Reed-Muller expressions", *IEEE The 3rd Asian Test Symposium*, November 15-17, 1994, Nara, Japan, 157-162.

[151] Sasao, T., *Logic Design: Switching Circuit Theory*, Kindai, Kaga-ku, Tokyo, Japan, 1995.

[152] Sasao, T., Debnath, D., "Generalized Reed-Muller expressions - Complexity and an exact minimization algorithm", *IEICE Transactions*, Vol. E79-A, No. 12, 1996, 2123-2130.

[153] Sasao, T., "Representations of logic functions by using EXOR operators," in Sasao, T., Fujita, M., (ed.), *Representations of Discrete Functions*, Kluwer Academic Publishers, Boston, MA, USA, 1996, 29-54.

[154] Sasao, T., "Easily testable realizations for generalized Reed-Muller expressions", *IEEE Trans. Computers*, Vol. 46, No. 6, 1997, 709-716.

[155] Sasao, T., *Switching Theory for Logic Synthesis*, Kluwer Academic Publishers, Boston, MA, USA, 1999.

[156] Sasao, T., Besslich, Ph.W., "On the complexity of mod 2 PLA's", *IEEE Trans. Comput.*, Vol. C-39, No. 2, 1991, 262-266.

[157] Sasao, T., "Logic design of ULSI systems", *Post Binary Logic Workshop*, Sendai, Japan, May 1992.

[158] Sasao, T., Butler, J.T., "A design method for look-up table type FPGA by pseudo-Kronecker expansions," *Proc. 24th Int. Symp. on Multiple-Valued Logic*, Boston, MA, USA, May 25-27, 1994, 97-104.

[159] Sasao, T., Fujita, M., (ed.), *Representations of Discrete Functions*, Kluwer Academic Publishers, Boston, MA, USA, 1996.

[160] Sasao, T., Fujiwara, H., "A design method of AND-EXOR PLAs with universal tests", (in Japanese), Technical Report IECE Japan FTS86-25, February 1987.

[161] Schafer, I., Perkowski, M.A., "Synthesis of multilevel multiplexer circuits for incompletely specified multioutput Boolean functions with mapping to multiplexer based FPGA's", *IEEE Trans. Comput.-Aided Design of Integrated Circuits and Systems*, Vol. 12, No. 11, 1993, 1655-1664.

[162] Schafer, I., Perkowski, M.A., "Extended spectral techniques for logic synthesis", in Stanković, R.S., Stojić, M.R., Stanković, M.S., *Recent Development in Abstract Harmonic Analysis with Applications in Signal Processing*, Nauka i Elektronski fakultet, Belgrade and Niš, Serbia, 1996, 217-259.

[163] Shannon, C.E., "A symbolic analysis of relay and switching circuits", *Trans. AIEE*, Vol. 57, 1938, 713-723.

[164] Shannon, C.E., "The synthesis of two-level switching circuits", *Bell Sys. Tech. J.*, Vol. 28, No. 1, 1949, 59-98.

[165] Shelar, R.S., Desai, M.P., Narayanan, H., "Decomposition of finite state machines for area, delay minimization", *Proc. Int. Conf. Computer Design*, Ostin, TX, USA, October 10-13, 1999, 620-625.

[166] Shestakov, V.I., "Some mathematical methods for construction and simplification of two-terminal electrical networks of class A", Dissertation, Lomonosov State University, Moscow, Russia, 1938, (in Russian).

[167] Sieling, D., "On the existence of polynomial time approximation schemes for OBDD minimization", *Proc. STACS'98*, Lecture Notes in Computer Sci., Vol. 1373, Springer, Berlin, Germany, 1998, 205-215.

[168] Smith. C.K., Gulak, P.G., "Prospects for multiple-valued integrated circuits"; *IEICE Trans. Electron.*, Vol. E.76-C, No. 3, 1993, 372-382.

[169] Somenzi, F., "CUDD Decision Diagram Package", http://bessie.colorado.edu /~fabio/CUDD

[170] Somenzi, F., "Efficient manipulation of decision diagrams", *Int. Journal on Software Tools for Technology Transfer*, 3, 2001, 171-181.

[171] Stanković, R.S., "Some remarks on the canonical forms for pseudo-Boolean functions", *Publ. Inst. Math. Beograd*, (N.S.), 37, 51, 1985, 3-6.

[172] Stanković, R.S., "Walsh and Reed-Muller transforms in logic design", *Avtomatika i Telemekhanika*, No.4, 1996, 130-147, (in Russian).

[173] Stanković, R.S., "Some remarks about spectral transform interpretation of MTBDDs and EVBDDs," *Proc. Asia and South Pacific Design Automation Conf., ASP-DAC'95*, Chiba, Tokyo, Japan, August 29 - September 1, 1995, 385-390.

[174] Stanković, R.S., Astola, J.T., "Relationships between logic derivatives and ternary decision daigrams", *Proc. 5th Int. Workshop on Boolean Problems*, Freiburg, Germany, September 19-20, 2002.

[175] Stanković, R.S., Astola, J.T., *Spectral Interpretation of Decision Diagrams*, Springer, New York, USA, 2003.

[176] Stanković, R.S., Falkowski, B.J., "Haar functions and transforms and their generalizations", *Proc. Int. Conf. on Information, Communications and Signal Processing, (1st ICICS)*, Singapore, September 1997, Vol. 4, 1-5.

[177] Stanković, R.S., Moraga, C., Astola, J.T., "From Fourier expansions to arithmetic-Haar expressions on quaternion groups", *Applicable Algebra in Engineering, Communications and Computing*, Vol. AAECC 12, 2001, 227-253.

[178] Stanković, R.S., Moraga, C., Astola, J.T., "Derivatives for multiple-valued functions induced by Galois field and Reed-Muller-Fourier expressions", *Proc. 34th*

Int. Symp. on Multiple-Valued Logic, Toronto, Canada, May 19-22, 2004, 184-189.

[179] Stanković, R.S., Sasao, T., "A discussion on the history of research in arithmetic and Reed-Muller expressions", *IEEE Trans. CAD*, Vol. 20, No. 9, 2001, 1177-1179.

[180] Stanković, R.S., Stojić, M.R., Stanković, M.S., (eds.), *Recent Developments in Abstract Harmonic Analysis with Applications in Signal Processing*, Nauka and Elektronski fakultet, Belgrade and Niš, Serbia, 1995.

[181] Stojić, M.R., Stanković, M.S., Stanković, R.S., *Discrete Transforms in Applications*, Nauka, Belgrade, Serbia, 1993, (in Serbian).

[182] Stone, H.S., "Paralel processing with the perfect shuffle", *IEEE Trans. on Computers*, Vol. C-20, 1971, 153-161.

[183] Thakur, S., Wong, D.F., Krishnamurthy, S., "Delay minimal decomposition of multiplexers in technlogy mapping", *Proc. ACM/IEEE Design Automation Conf.*, New York, USA, June 3-7, 1996, 254-257.

[184] Thakur, S., Wong, D.F., "On designing ULM-based FPGA modules", *Proc. 3rd Int. Symp. FPGAs*, Monterey, CA, USA, February 1995, 3-9.

[185] Thayse, A., *Boolean Differential Calculus*, Springer-Verlag, Heidelberg, Germany, 1980.

[186] *The Annals of the Computation Labaratory of Harvard University*, Volume XXVII, *Synthesis of Electronic Computing and Control Circuits*, Cambridge, MA, USA, 1951.

[187] Thomas, L.H., "Using a computer to solve problems in physics", in *Application of Digital Computers*, Ginn, Boston, MA, USA, 1963.

[188] Touai, N., Savoy, H., Lin, B., Brayton, R., Sangiovanni-Vincentelli, A., "Imlicit state enumeration of finite staste machines using BDDs", *Proc. Int. Conf. Computer Aided Design*, Santa Clara, CA, USA, November 11-15, 1990, 130-133.

[189] Trachtenberg, E.A., "SVD of Frobenius Groups and their use in signal processing", in Deprettere, E.F., (ed.), *SVD and Signal Processing*, North-Holland: Elsevier, Amsterdam, Netherlands, 1988.

[190] Trachtenberg, E.A., "Application of Fourier analysis on groups in engineering practice", in Stanković, R.S., Stojić, M.R., Stanković, M.S., (eds.), *Recent Developments in Abstract Harmonic Analysis with Applications in Signal Processing*, Nauka and Elektronski fakultet, Belgrade and Niš, 1995, 331-403.

[191] Trakhtman, A.M., Trakhthman, V.A., *Basis of the Theory of Discrete Signals on Finite Intervals*, Sovetskoe radio, Moscow, Russia, 1975, (in Russian).

[192] Trimberger, S., (ed.) *Field-Programmable Gate Arrays*, Kluwer Academic Publishers, Boston, MA, USA, 1994.

[193] Trimberger, S., "Effect of FPGA architecture to FPGA routing", *Proc. 32nd Design Automation Conf.*, San Francisco, CA, USA, June 12-16, 1995, 574-578.

[194] Tsuchiya, K., Tekefuji, Y., "A neural network approach to PLA foldign problems", *IEEE Trans. Computer-Aided Design of Integrated Circuits*, Vol. CAD-15, No. 10, 1996, 1299-1305.

[195] Unger, S.H., *Asynchronous Sequential Switching Circuits*, John Wiley & Sons, Inc., New York, USA, 1969.

[196] Unger, S.H., *The Essence of Logic Circuits*, IEEE Press and John Wiely and Sons, New York, USA, 1997.

[197] Villa, T., Sangiovanni-Vincentelli, A., "NOVA - State assignment for finite state machines for optimal two-level logic implementation", *IEEE Trans. CAD/ICAS*, Vol. CAD-8, No. 9, 1990, 905-924.

[198] Vrudhula, S.B.K., Pedram, M., Lai, Y.-T., "Edge valued binary decision diagrams", in Sasao, T., Fujita, M., (ed.), *Representations of Discrete Functions*, Kluwer Academic Publishers, 1996, 109-132.

[199] Walsh, J.L., "A closed set of orthogonal functions", *Amer. J. Math.*, 55, 1923, 5-24.

[200] Wod, R.A., "A high density programable logic array chip", *IEEE Trans. on Computers*, Vol. C-28, 1979, 602-608.

[201] Wolf, W., *FPGA-Based System Design*, Prentice-Hall, Englewood Cliffs, NJ, USA, 2004.

[202] Yanushkevich, S.N., *Logic Differential Calculus in Multi-Valued Logic Design*, Techn. University of Szczecin Academic Publishers, Poland, 1998.

[203] Yamada, T., "Easily testable AND-XOR combinational logic circuits", *Trans. IECE*, Vol. J.66-D, No. 1, 1983, 105-110.

[204] Yang, W.L., Owen, R.M., Irwin, M.J., "FPGA-based synthesis of FSMs through decomposition", *Proc. Fourth Great Lakes Symp. Design Automation of High Performance VLSI Systems*, Notre Dame, IN, USA, March 4-5, 1994, 97-100.

[205] Zeidman, B., *Design with FPGAs and CPLDs*, CMP Books, Manhaset, NY, USA, 2002.

[206] Zhegalkin, I.I., "O tekhnyke vychyslenyi predlozhenyi v symbolytscheskoi logykye", *Math. Sb.*, Vol. 34, 1927, 9-28, (in Russian).

[207] Zhegalkin, I.I., "Arifmetizatiya symbolytscheskoi logyky", *Math. Sb.*, Vol.35, 1928, 311-377, (in Russian).

[208] Zilic, Z., Vranesic, Z.G., "Using decision diagrams to design ULMs for FPGAs", *IEEE Trans. Computers*, Vol. 47, No. 9, 1998, 971-982.

Index